Old Southgate an Palmers Green

Bernard Byrom

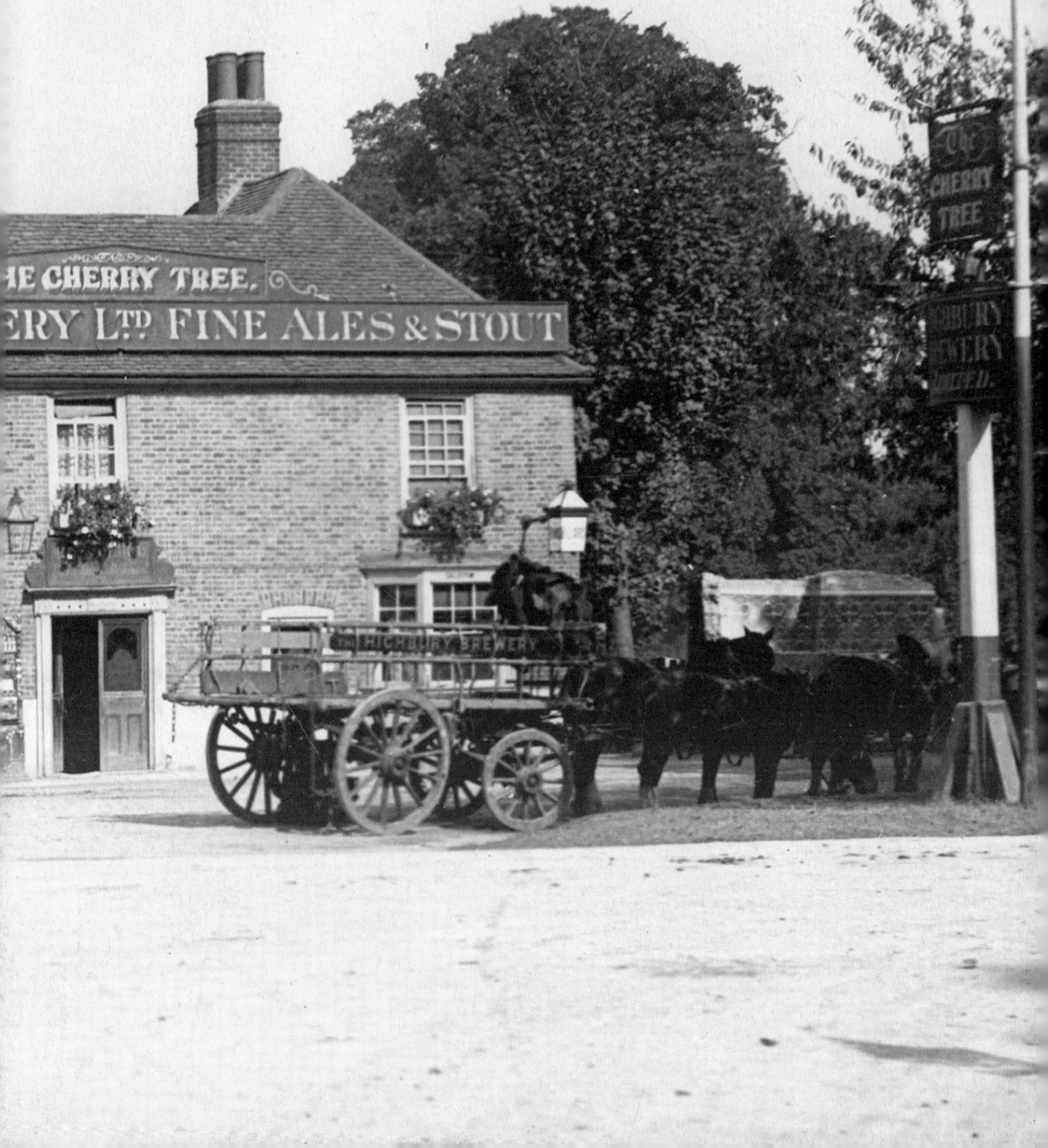

First published in the United Kingdom, 2008,
by Stenlake Publishing Ltd.
Telephone: 01290 551122
www.stenlake.co.uk
Printed in the UK by St Edmundsbury Press
ISBN 9781840334241

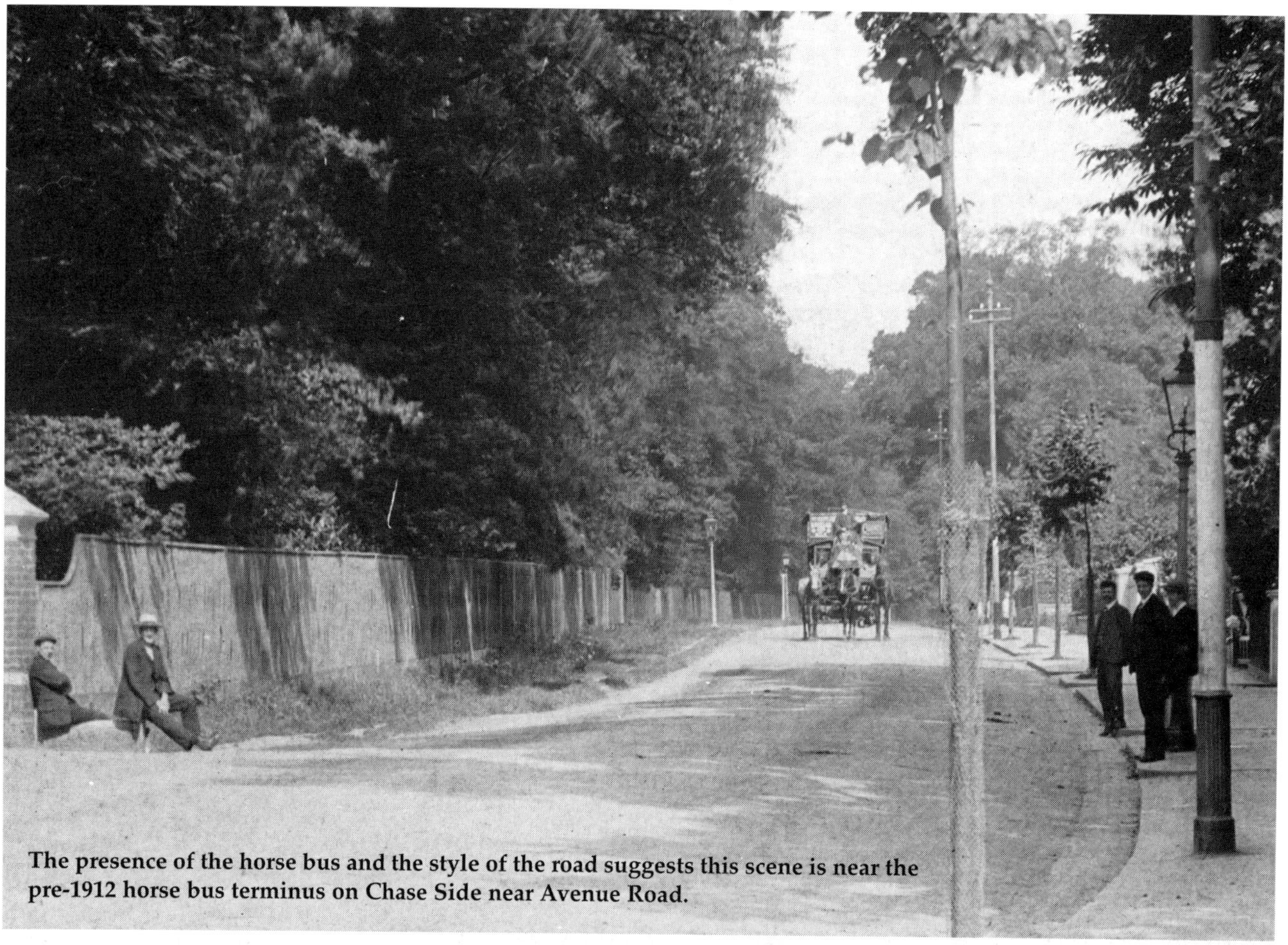

The presence of the horse bus and the style of the road suggests this scene is near the pre-1912 horse bus terminus on Chase Side near Avenue Road.

ACKNOWLEDGEMENTS

The author's thanks are due to Melanie Mordsley, from whose personal collection these pictures are taken, and to Graham Dalling, Local History Librarian of the Borough of Enfield, who gladly shares his detailed knowledge of the area, past and present, with interested visitors. Mark Leaver at The Woodman on Bourne Hill was very helpful with the history of that ancient hostelry. The author also gratefully acknowledges the contributions made by his wife Rosemary and eldest son Andrew who joined him in walking for miles around the area carrying out detailed field research and wearing out their shoes in the process!

FURTHER READING

The books listed below were used by the author during his research. None of them is available from Stenlake Publishing. Those interested in finding out more are advised to contact their local bookshop or reference library.

Henrietta Cresswell, *Winchmore Hill, Memories of a Lost Village*, 1912, reprinted 1982.
Graham Dalling, *Southgate and Edmonton Street Names*, Edmonton Hundred Historical Society, 1990.
Graham Dalling, *Southgate and Edmonton Past*, Historical Publications Ltd, 1996.
Alan Dumayne, *Southgate: A Glimpse into the Past*, 1987.
Alan Dumayne, *The Old Borough of Southgate*, 1998.
Alan Dumayne, *Once Upon a Time in Palmers Green*, 1998.
Alan Dumayne, *Fond Memories of Winchmore Hill*, 1990.
Matthew Eccleston, *Enfield, Portrait of a London Borough*, 1996.
Tom Mason, *The Story of Southgate*, 1948.
Herbert W. Newby, *'Old' Southgate*, 1949.
The Palmers Green, Winchmore Hill & Southgate Recorder
Kelly's Directories, 1882 onwards.
Who's Who of Cricketers.
1801/02 Enclosure Award map.
Ordnance Survey maps, 1896 onwards.

INTRODUCTION

The historic area covered by this book corresponds roughly to today's postal districts of N14 Southgate and N13 Palmers Green, with a brief foray into N21 Winchmore Hill.

In medieval times the hamlet of Southgate lay literally at the south gate of Enfield Chase. The location of the gate was roughly in today's Southgate Circus where Chase Side joins Winchmore Hill Road. A little further to the south was another small settlement called South Street which grew up around a village green; by 1829 the two settlements had merged into one and the village green became today's Southgate Green.

Enfield Chase used to be a royal hunting ground but an Act of Parliament in 1777 resulted in its enclosure. Most of the Chase remained as part of Enfield; the rest was allocated to the parishes of Edmonton, South Mimms and Monken Hadley as compensation for their lost grazing rights. At this time the area was thinly populated, communications were poor and so the land was underdeveloped.

A little further to the south, Palmers Green appears on maps even as relatively late as 1867 as a tiny hamlet consisting of the Fox public house and a few surrounding cottages clustered around it where Fox Lane and Hazelwood Lane join Green Lanes.

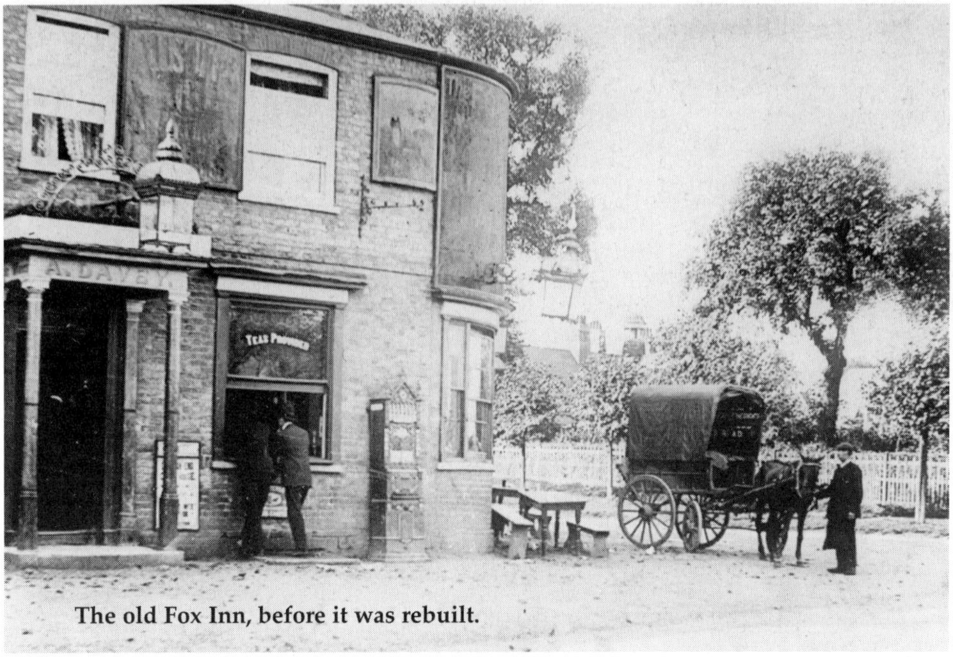

The old Fox Inn, before it was rebuilt.

To the north of Southgate and Palmers Green lay the remote woodland hamlet of Winchmore Hill where there was, from the early middle ages, an established coppicing industry. In the fourteenth century Winchmore Hill had been known as 'Wynsemerhull' and was populated largely by woodcutters, charcoal burners and bark peelers; the area had not been cleared of trees as the heavy clay soil was highly unworkable and therefore no good for arable farming.

In the coppicing industry trees were allowed to grow and were then cut in rotation every ten years. A good deal of this wood was sold as logwood in four feet lengths as fuel for the broad hearths of large houses whilst the shreddings were bundled into faggots, many of them being sold to bakers for use in heating their large ovens. Some of the wood was also used by the charcoal burners of Winchmore Hill; at one time this was a valuable fuel used extensively on blast furnaces for iron smelting but its importance declined with the introduction of coke. Nothing was wasted: even the bark was peeled and sold to the tanneries in Enfield and Edmonton. However, the coppicing industry in Winchmore Hill gradually died out as farming techniques improved, allowing the soil to be worked, and the village grew into an agricultural community. Eventually, around 1801, the old open fields and common land were finally enclosed and the local landscape changed to become a pleasant combination of fields, farms and country lanes. Very significantly, many wealthy gentry and city merchants – particularly those connected with the brewing industry – chose to make their homes here and at Southgate. It was a reasonable carriage ride from London and possessed both rural charm and scenic beauty.

The two most significant influences on the development of the area were the railways and the great landowners who had moved into the area in the early nineteenth century. By far the greatest of the landed estates was Grovelands, which had once been owned by Lord Burghley and was known as Lord's Grove. In the eighteenth century Mr Walker Gray, a brewer and brandy merchant from Tottenham, bought the estate from the Duke of Chandos's son-in-law; Gray had the house built in 1797/98 and changed the name to Southgate Grove. After his death the house and estate, which amounted to around 230 acres, was bought by his nephew, John Donnithorne Taylor, who initially changed its name to Woodlands but soon renamed it Grovelands. By the time he died there on 13 December 1885, aged 87, he had increased the size of the estate to 600 acres.

John Donnithorne Taylor was a member of the brewing family of Taylor Walker, the well-known brewers of Limehouse. The firm of Harford & Taylor was founded in 1730 but when Isaac Walker joined in 1816 the name was changed to Taylor Walker. In 1827 John Donnithorne Taylor became a partner in the firm, but in 1843 the Taylor family sold out to Isaac and Edwin Walker. From then on the Walkers were in sole control of the brewery, the company passing down through the family until well into the twentieth century.

The Walker family lived at the mansion at Southgate Green known as Arnos Grove and had a great affinity with the Taylors, being related by marriage and united by business. But most important of all was their alliance in policy as landowners. Because of the large-scale demolition of working class houses in 1874 necessitated by the Great Eastern Railway's extension of its line from its temporary terminus at Bishopsgate into London's Liverpool Street Station, Parliament inserted a clause into the Act requiring the GER to run workmen's trains into London at the cheap return fare of 2*d*. The result was a working class surge up both sides of the Lee Valley. On the Essex side Walthamstow bore the brunt of the exodus from the East End whilst on the Middlesex side the immigration concentrated on Tottenham and Edmonton. This had a dramatic effect on these last two areas, which had hitherto been quite rural and select; now they suddenly found themselves swamped by new, cheap, working class housing. This was particularly apparent in Edmonton and its big red brick Georgian houses began to disappear as the gentry moved further out towards Southgate, Palmers Green and Winchmore Hill.

The development of these neighbouring areas was viewed with alarm by the Taylors and the Walkers, who set about operating their own private Green Belt policy. They both bought up land as it became available to gradually increase the size of their estates and by these methods they retained control of local development. John Donnithorne Taylor was convinced that the Great Northern Railway Company's proposed branch line to Enfield, which was to cut through Winchmore Hill, would pose a serious threat to the seclusion and pleasantness of his surroundings. Throughout the 1860s he fought tirelessly to prevent a railway being built through the village and a station being opened there, but in the end he was unsuccessful; by 1871 the railway had become a reality. The Great Northern Railway's extension to Enfield arrived at Palmers Green and Winchmore Hill in 1871, but its effect on the area was far less dramatic than the Great Eastern's further to the east. Here, the western half of the parish (Southgate, Palmers Green and Winchmore Hill) remained a rural backwater of big estates, farms and middle class villas, thanks to the Green Belt policies of its landowners. Even five years after the railway arrived at Winchmore Hill, James Thorne was able to write of it in his 1876 *Handbook to the Environs of London* that, 'The country hereabouts is undulating, abundantly wooded, and agreeable, and it has long been a favourite residence with City men, whose comfortable homes are seen on every hand.'

The local gentry understandably wanted to keep it that way. But it couldn't last forever. Following John Donnithorne Taylor 's death in 1885, his son, Robert Kirkpatrick Taylor, took control of the estates until his own death in 1901 when his son, Capt. John Vickris Taylor of the Welsh Guards, took over. He planned to marry and move out to Oxfordshire and on 9 June 1902 the Taylor estates in their entirety were put on the market in 13 separate lots covering Southgate, Palmers Green and Winchmore Hill.

Down the road at Arnos Grove there had been seven Walker brothers, none of whom married, but by the time the Taylor estates went up for sale in 1902 there were only two left alive: Vyell Edward Walker, the head of the Arnos Grove household, who was 65, and his 60-year-old brother, Russell. The sale of the Taylor estates in 1902 was a major landmark and the Walker estates followed in 1918 after the death of the last surviving brothers.

The next fifteen years or so saw the break-up of all the big estates and farmsteads, the disappearance of many of the large houses and their grounds, the development of roads, shops and housing over a wide area, and the change from village life to suburbia. Planning applications in 1905, for example, included Hazelwood Park Estate, Old Park Estate and Broomfield Park Estate. The three biggest builders were Edmondson, H.G. Stacey and W.J. Hardy. The Old Park Grange estate at Winchmore Hill was built by Richard Metherell & Son in 1907 with semi-detached houses on sale from £500 leasehold or for rent from £48 per annum.

Most immigrants to Southgate at this time were from the old middle class suburbs of inner north London, especially Stoke Newington and Islington, and included a significant number of Jewish families. The statistics for 1900 show that Southgate was one of the healthiest places to live in outer London, with both birth rates and mortality rates far lower than its neighbours in Tottenham and Edmonton. In the sixty years between 1891 and 1951 its population grew from 10,970 to 73,377.

The major extension of the tramway northwards from Manor House along the Green Lanes as far as Winchmore Hill was completed by the autumn of 1907. Initially the trams only went as far as the Green Dragon public house, but by 1909 the service had been extended to Enfield. This established Green Lanes as a major route into and out of London and led to development along its road frontages.

Until 1912 the only bus operating in Southgate was a horse-drawn vehicle which ran between Avenue Road and Palmers

Broomfield Avenue, 1910.

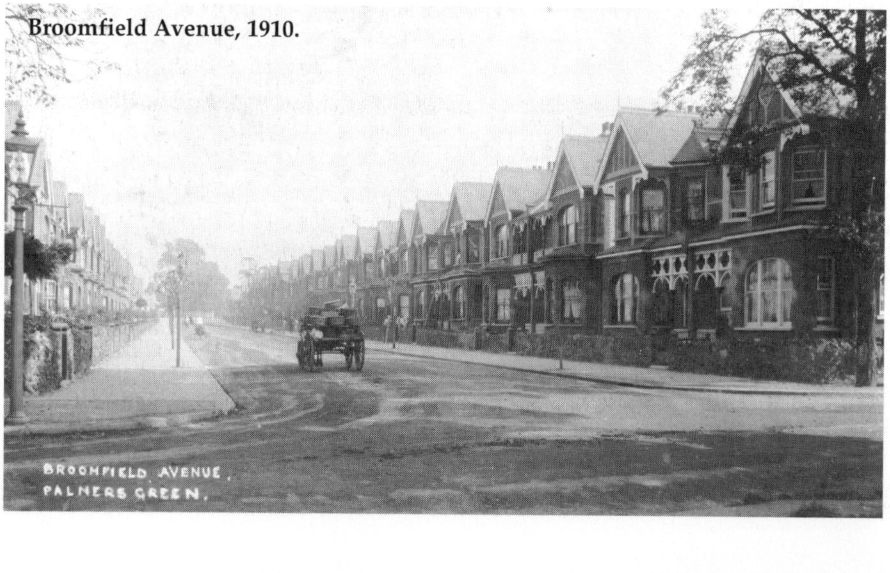

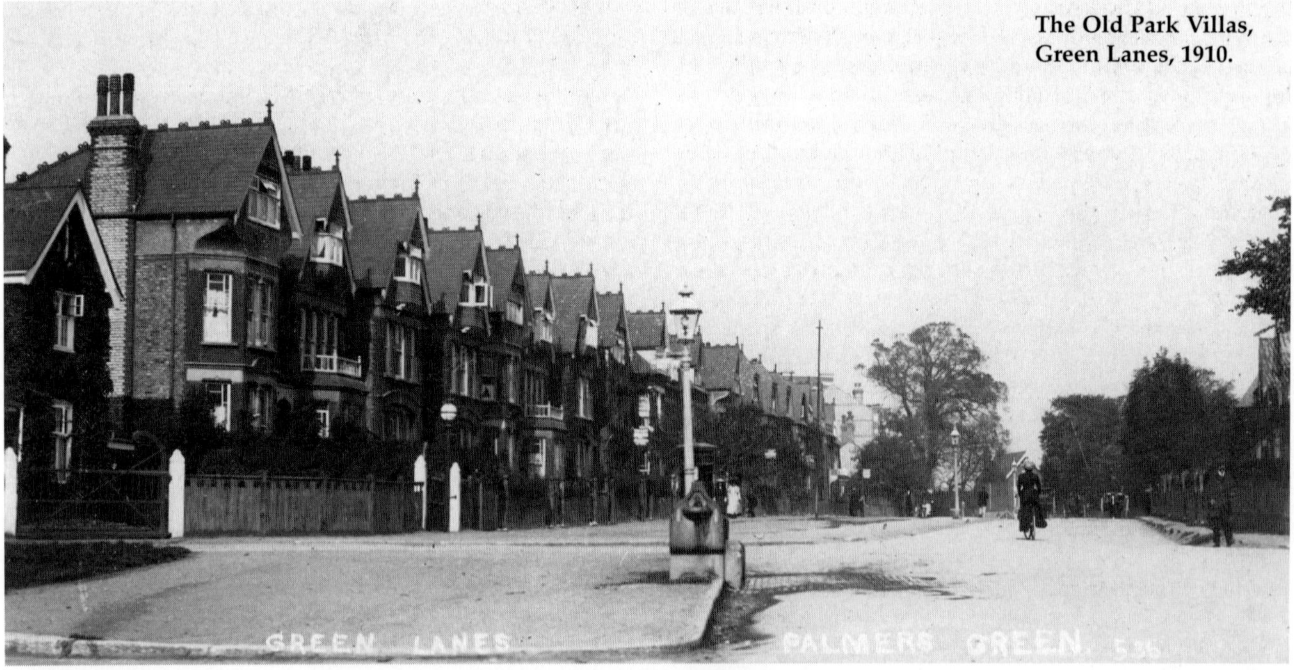

The Old Park Villas, Green Lanes, 1910.

Green Station. In February of that year the London General Omnibus Company bought up the derelict Rosalie roller skating rink in Regents Avenue and in June the No. 29 bus route was extended from Wood Green to the Cherry Tree in Southgate Green; in August the Sunday service was extended further north to Cockfosters. 1938 saw the end of trams in the area and the introduction of trolleybuses, which were themselves replaced by conventional diesel buses in 1961.

The extension of the Piccadilly Line from Wood Green out to Cockfosters in 1933 had an immediate effect on house building in neighbouring areas such as Oakwood, Southgate and Arnos Grove. Gradually the joining up process continued as suburb linked to suburb and the open spaces became fewer and fewer.

Having been under the control of Edmonton for more than 500 years, by the 1870s Southgate, Palmers Green and Winchmore Hill had little in common with their eastern neighbour and wished to become a separately governed council. Sir Ralph Littler QC, the last tenant of Broomfield House, set up the separatist movement and it was largely due to his efforts that Southgate Local Board came into existence in 1881 after much opposition. It became an Urban District in 1894 and subsequently a Municipal Borough in 1933, totalling 3,765 acres. Southgate positively benefited from the separation, but in Edmonton the loss of the high rateable value of the western district was to cause severe problems (for example, cuts in social services due to the loss of income from rates) for many years to come.

In 1881 Southgate's population had been 8,289 persons living in 1,694 houses; by 1931 this had climbed to 55,570 persons living in 14,750 houses. In 1965, under the London Government Act of 1963, Southgate Borough came under the control of the London Borough of Enfield.

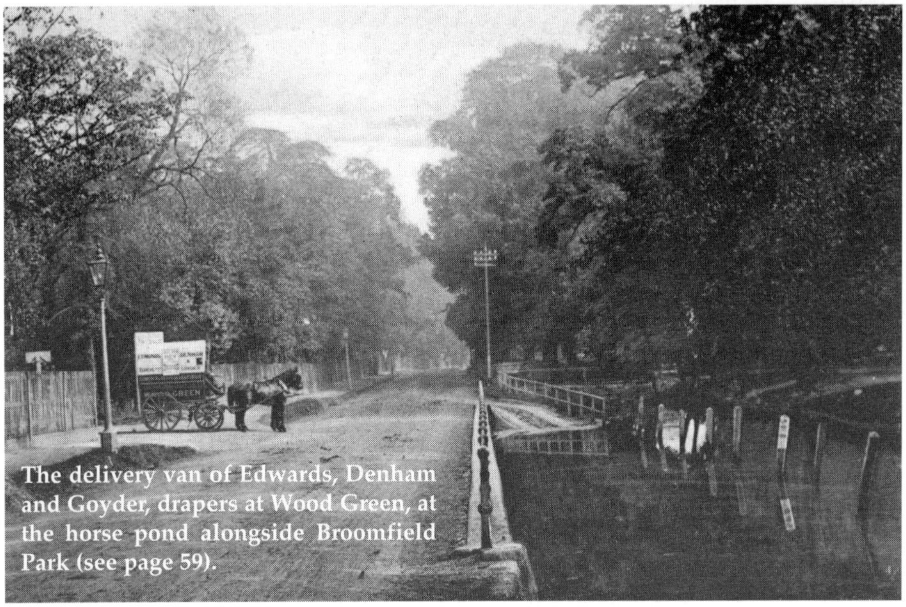

The delivery van of Edwards, Denham and Goyder, drapers at Wood Green, at the horse pond alongside Broomfield Park (see page 59).

When the Taylor estates had been put up for sale in 1902, Lot No. 1 was the Old Park estate of about 130 acres between Aldermans Hill and Fox Lane, with frontages to Aldermans Hill, Fox Lane, Cannon Hill and High Street. The British Land Company's bid of £45,000 for the whole 130 acres, plus a timber valuation not to exceed £1,500, was successful and they disposed of the land in parcels to various builders. Housing development began immediately and Old Park Road was one of the first roads to be laid out; the others soon followed.

Lot 9 had comprised the Grovelands estate itself, extending to 314 acres, and didn't reach its reserve price. A consortium was then formed by Milner, Son & White, the famous landscape gardeners who had laid out Kaiser Wilhelm's gardens at Potsdam. Their plans for the estate featured building a 'Woodlands City' that would be a showpiece for the rest of the world. A central drive, named Broad Walk, would replace the old footpath and there would be a series of winding roads running through the woodland; on the central drive there would be wide boulevards and luxury homes slotted amongst the trees. A shopping complex and a railway station in Hoppers Road opposite Fernleigh Road would provide essential facilities for the new estate, whilst Grovelands House itself would be used as a private clubhouse and meeting point for residents. The carriageway would be 30 feet wide; the lake would be stocked with fish and would provide excellent boating, fishing, skating and swimming facilities for residents who would be given keys by which they could enter and use the park for their own recreation. By February 1910 the *Palmers Green, Winchmore Hill & Southgate Recorder* was reporting that, 'A good number of shops have been booked, and it is expected that something novel in the way of suburban shopping will be introduced. In the shopping centre scheme it is proposed to have large ladies' outfitters stores, fitted and stocked in West End style by a leading West End firm. It is intended to have shops of a class which will not only attract the new residents, but will draw ladies from Enfield, Palmers Green, Bowes Park, and the best parts of Wood Green.'

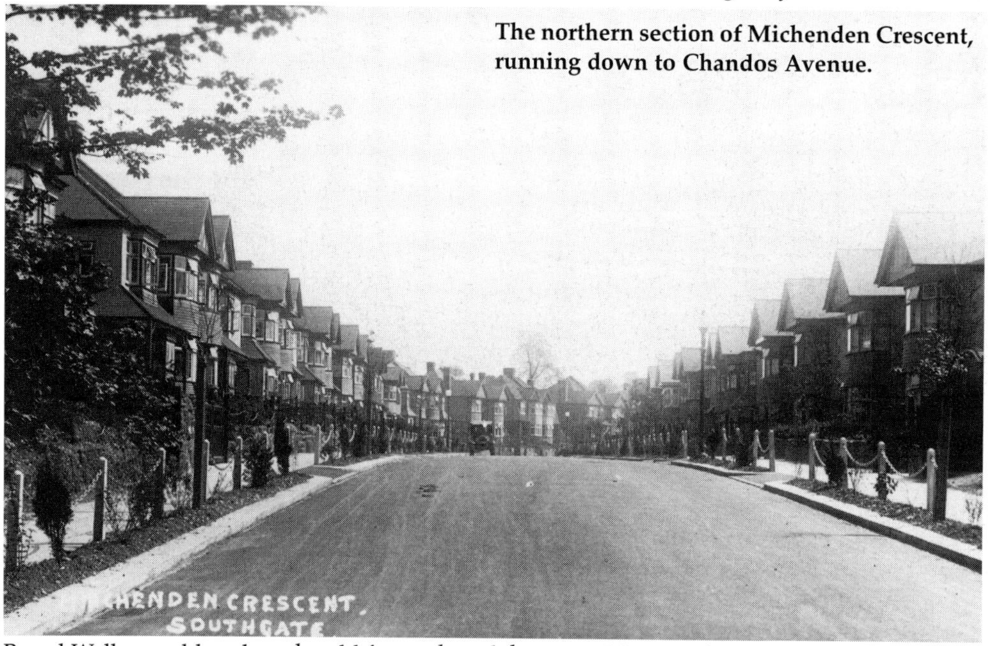

The northern section of Michenden Crescent, running down to Chandos Avenue.

Eventually this grandiose scheme fell through but there were still plans to make Broad Walk into a boulevard of two carriageways with a 54-feet-wide belt of existing mature oak trees standing in the middle. This also proved to be too ambitious and the present plan – a single carriageway, without trees in the middle – was started in 1913 although progress was slow and was delayed by the First World War. Its development continued through the 1920s and into the 1930s. Meanwhile, in 1911 Southgate UDC purchased 64 acres of the parkland and Grovelands Park was officially opened to the public on 12 April 1913.

There have been many changes during the past century but the photographs in this book show how Southgate and Palmers Green used to look around the late nineteenth and early twentieth centuries, when the Tube was generally confined to the London area and the normal means of public transport was a horse bus or early motor bus; a time when traffic on the roads was so sparse that pedestrians could stroll along the middle of what is now the North Circular Road without any fear of being run down. The book begins its street-by-street exploration of the area at the north-west corner of Southgate and finishes at the south-east side of Palmers Green.

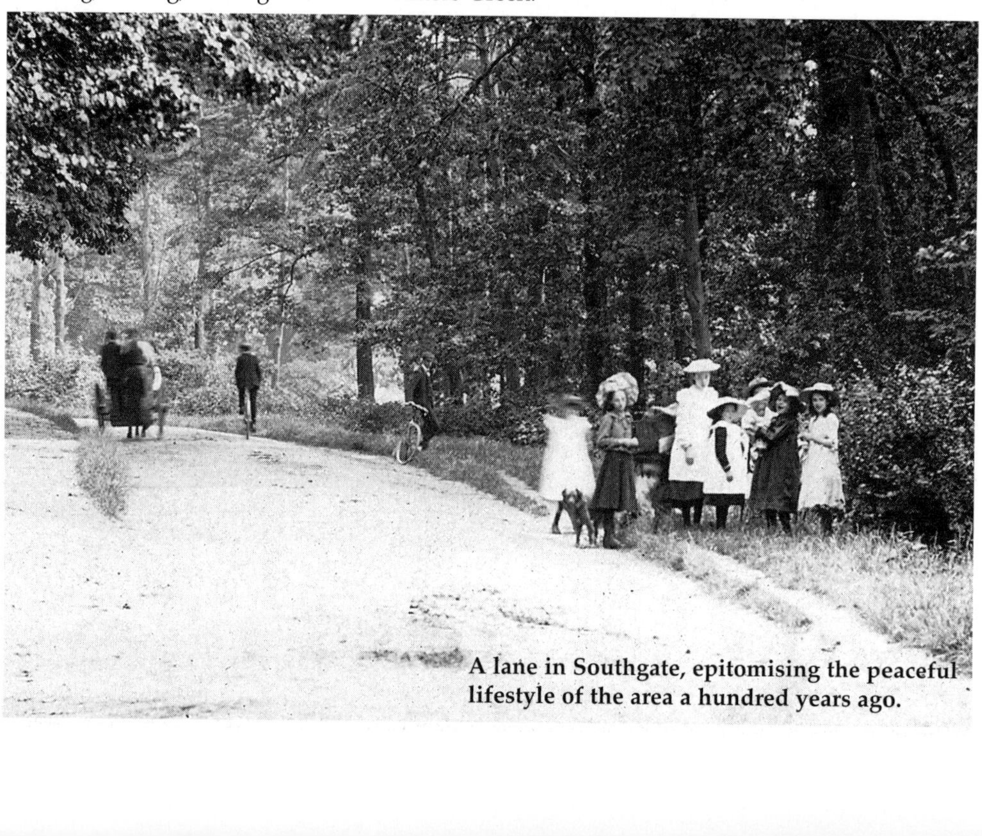

A lane in Southgate, epitomising the peaceful lifestyle of the area a hundred years ago.

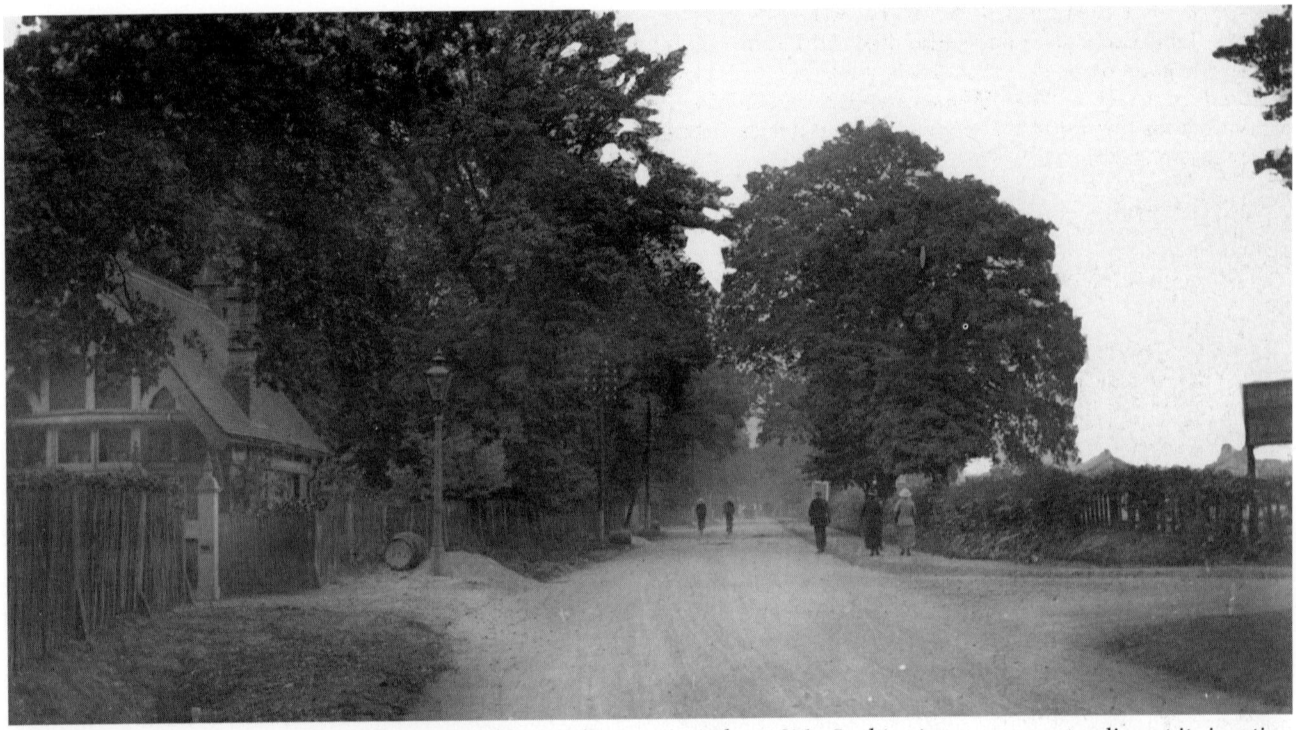

We'll begin our exploration of old Southgate at the northern end of Chase Side. In this picture we are standing at its junction with Bramley Road which enters from the east and makes a 'T' junction with the main road to the north. The view is looking northwards down Cockfosters Road towards the little village of Cockfosters itself.

The building on the left is the entrance to Bohun Lodge, which was owned by Baring Young; after his death in 1928 it was opened as a theological college for younger students. Older theological students were trained at nearby Oakhill, which had been his principal home. After 1937 all training was carried out at Oakhill, which is nowadays part of Middlesex University. Bohun Lodge was closed and subsequently demolished; its site is now incorporated into the university precincts.

Nowadays the 'T' junction is still there but the main road from Enfield doesn't use it. Instead, a cut-off has been constructed which branches to the right off Bramley Road just short of the junction, crosses the top end of Chase Side and continues west along Cat Hill towards Barnet.

Coming down Chase Side, and looking towards Avenue Road, this little shop with the lady proprietors standing outside used to sell a variety of goods including confectionery, tobacco products and stationery.

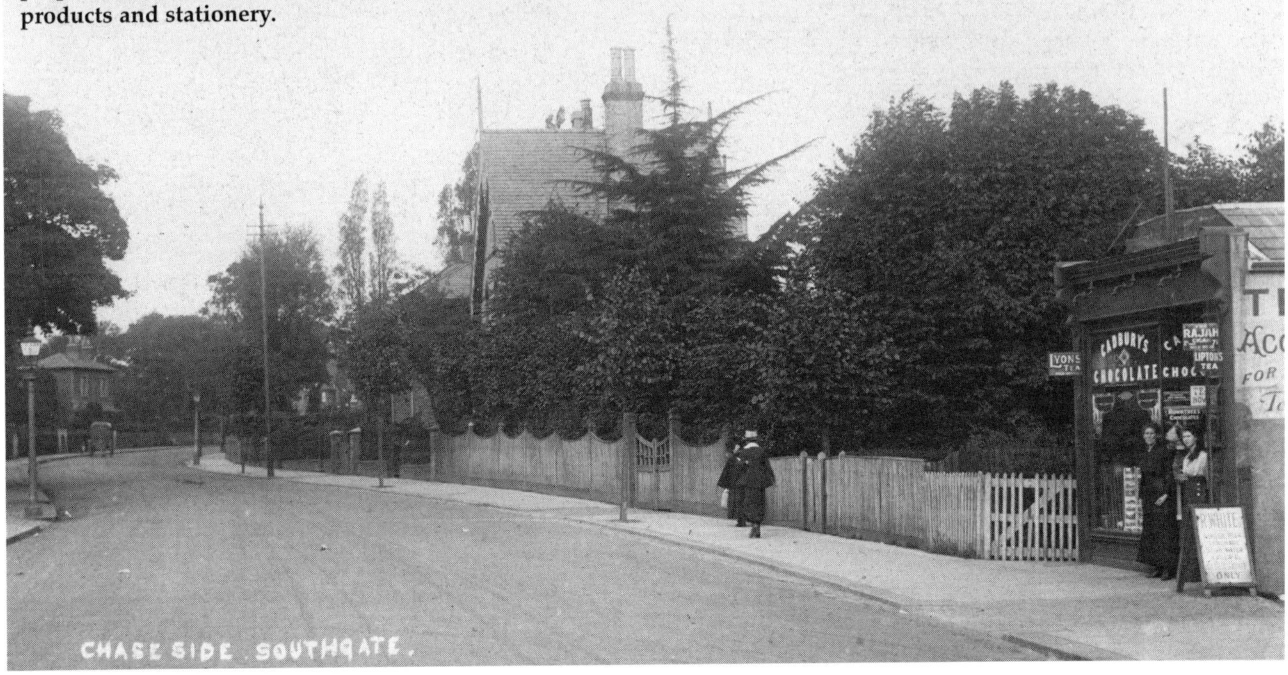

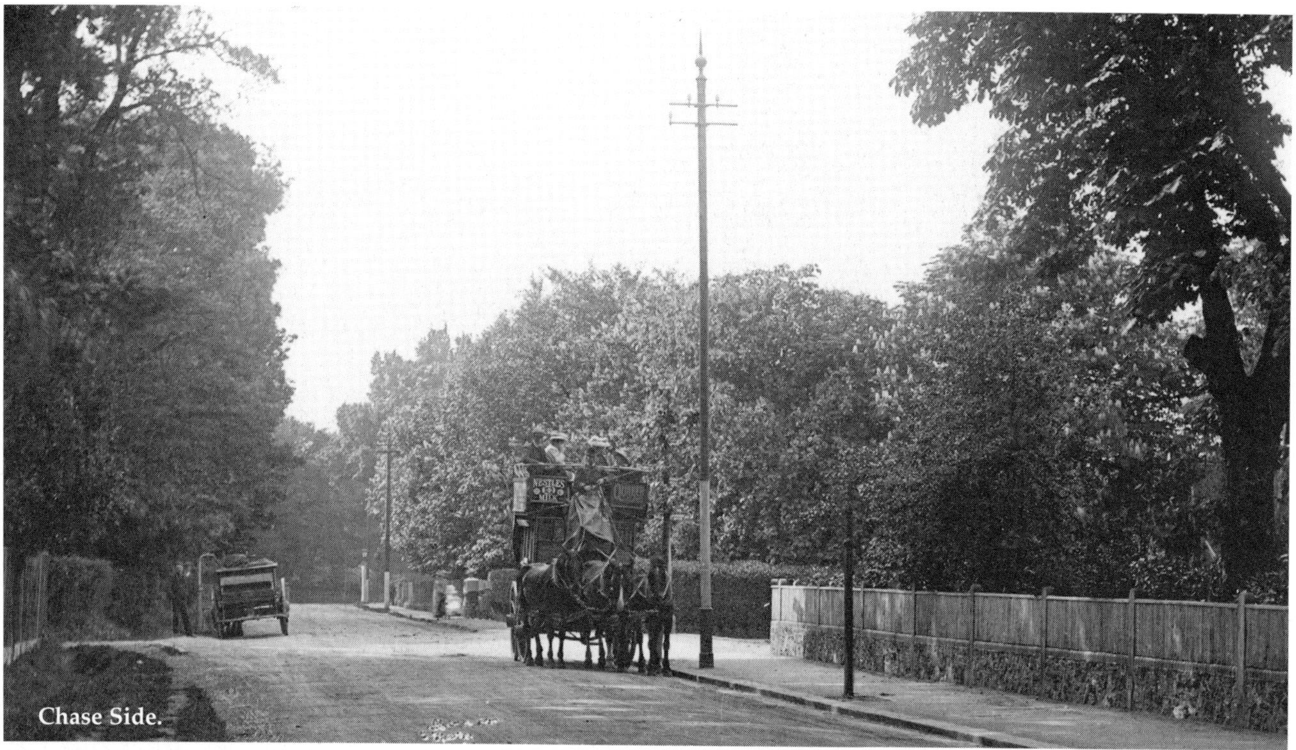

Chase Side.

When the Great Northern Railway extended its suburban network to Enfield in 1871 and built a station at Palmers Green, this two-horse bus service was instituted to run from near Avenue Road to Palmers Green Station. It ran from 1871 to 1912 when it was superseded by a motor bus service.

Note the driver's completely exposed position, sitting on the front of the bus above the horses. The heavy cape, here wrapped around his legs, was his only protection against the weather.

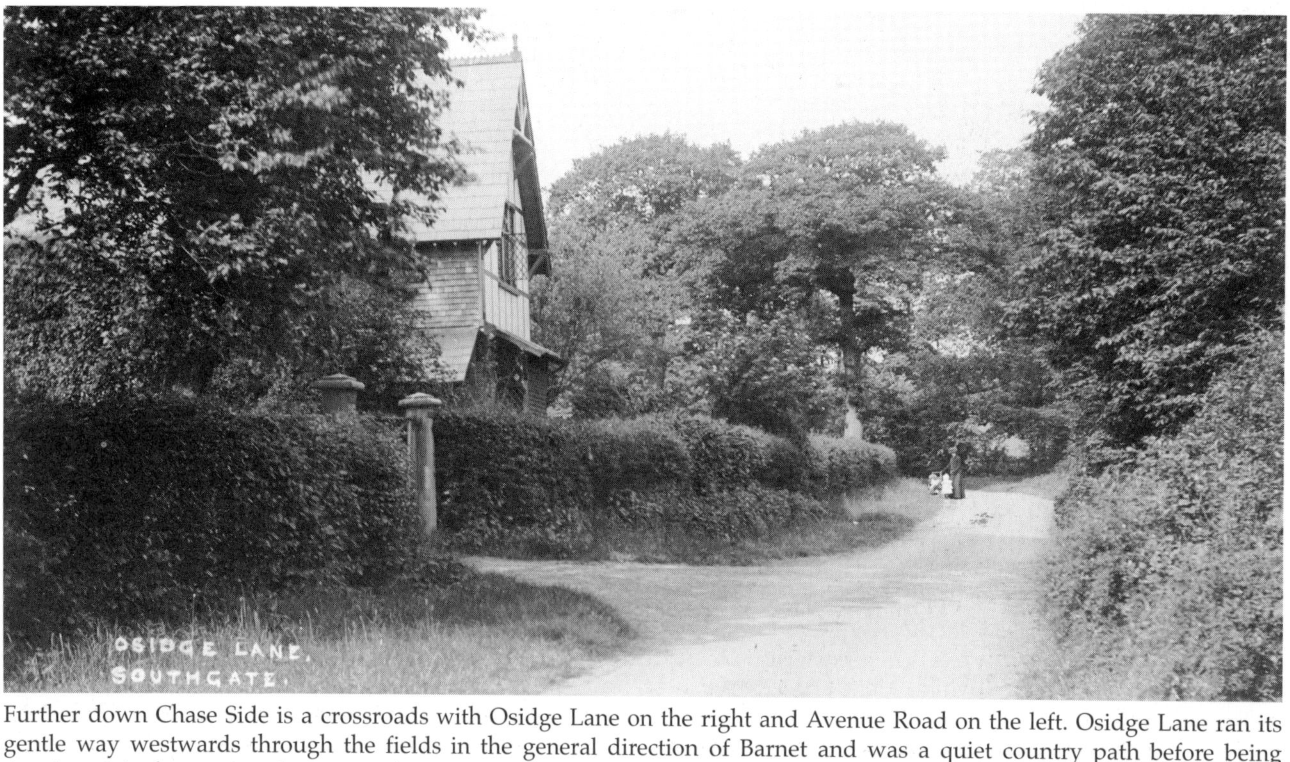

OSIDGE LANE, SOUTHGATE.

Further down Chase Side is a crossroads with Osidge Lane on the right and Avenue Road on the left. Osidge Lane ran its gentle way westwards through the fields in the general direction of Barnet and was a quiet country path before being developed for housing in the 1930s. The building in this picture is the Lodge which stood at the end of the driveway up to Ferney House. It was demolished in 1932 and was replaced by a fried fish shop, which later became a pizza shop. The view is looking east up to what is now Hampden Square. The little footpath that ran from Chase Side and skirted the gardens of Osidge House joined Osidge Lane at the bend in the road.

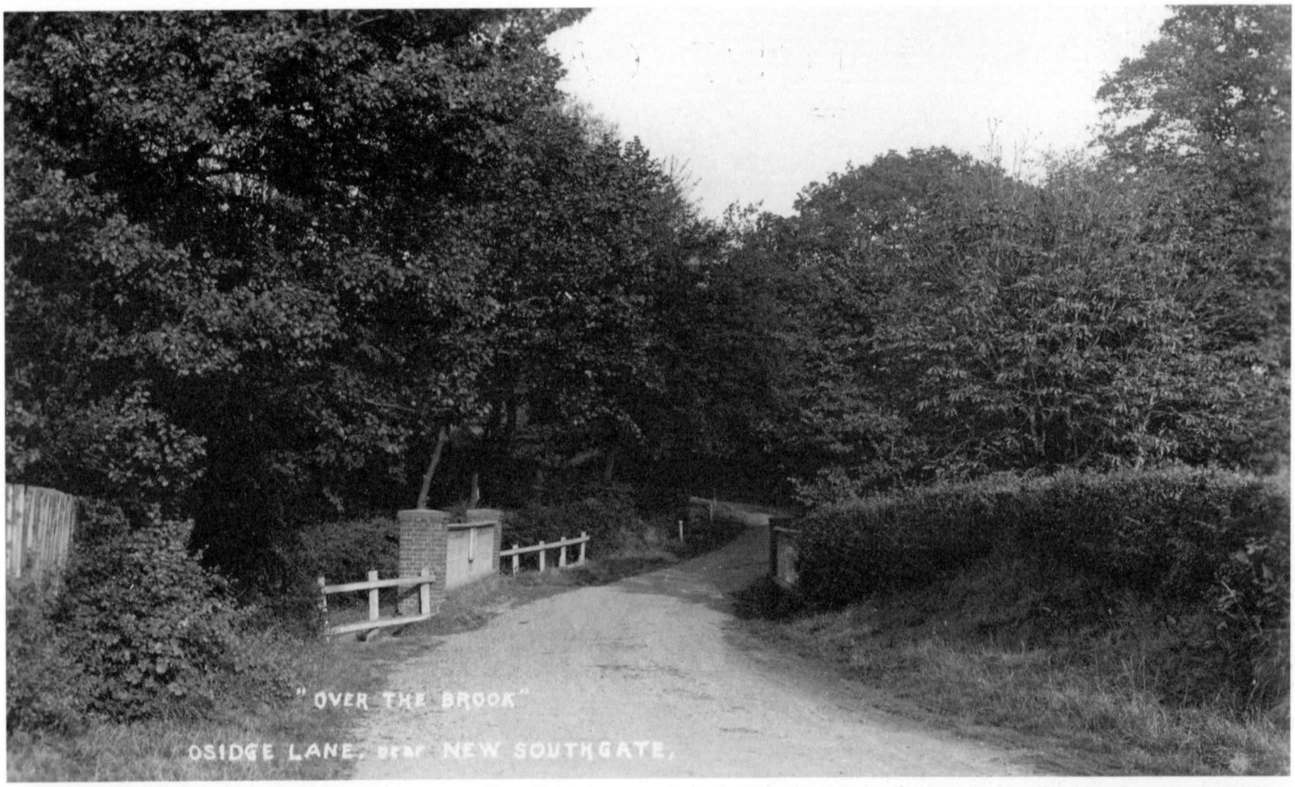

A little further along Osidge Lane the road crossed the Pymmes Brook on this bridge. The brook was first bridged in 1887, but the bridge in this 1923 picture looks to be a newer one. This view is looking east towards the location of the last picture but can't be easily recognised nowadays because the road was straightened when houses were built on it in the 1930s.

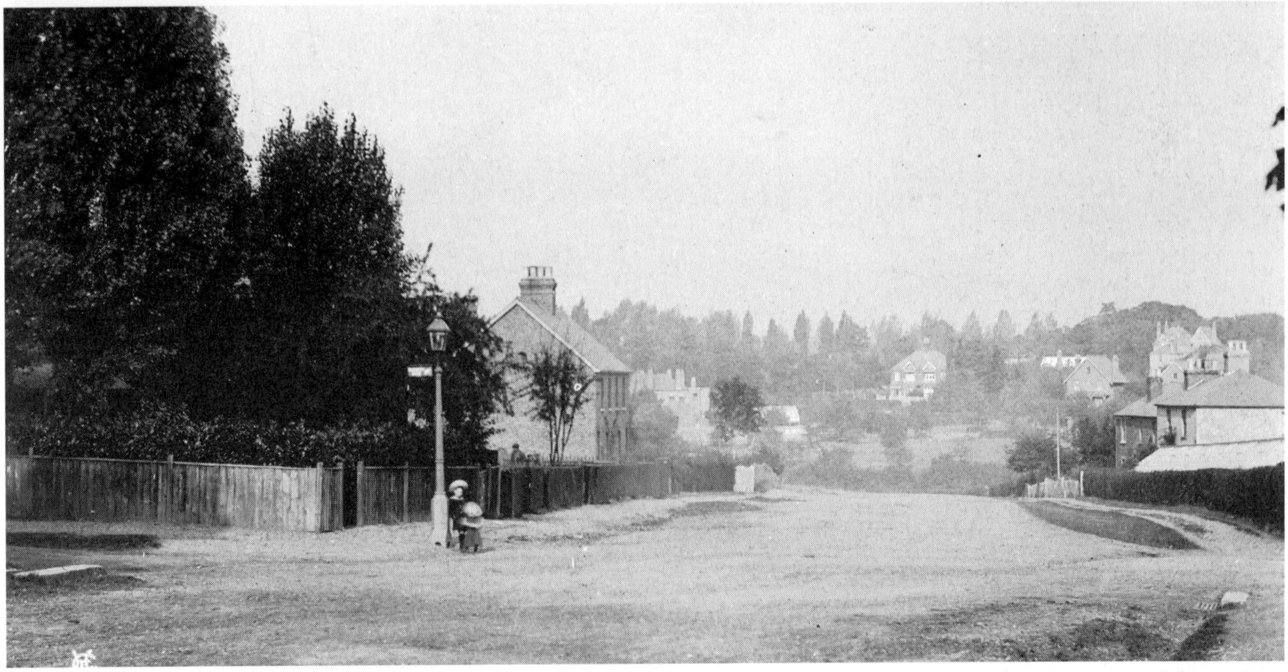

Avenue Road was part of the Southgate estate which was sold for building in 1853 and was therefore one of the earliest housing developments in Southgate. This portion of the estate was purchased by the Lambeth & Provincial Street Borough and consisted of most of the land between Bramley Road and Southgate Circus. It was bounded on the west by Chase Side and on the east by Chase Road. By 1867 there had been some development near the junction with Chase Side but not much else.

This view is looking east along the road from near its junction with Chase Side and onwards towards its junction with Chase Road, which can be seen in the distant background. The road joining from the left was Nursery Road, which was subsequently extended and is nowadays named Trent Gardens.

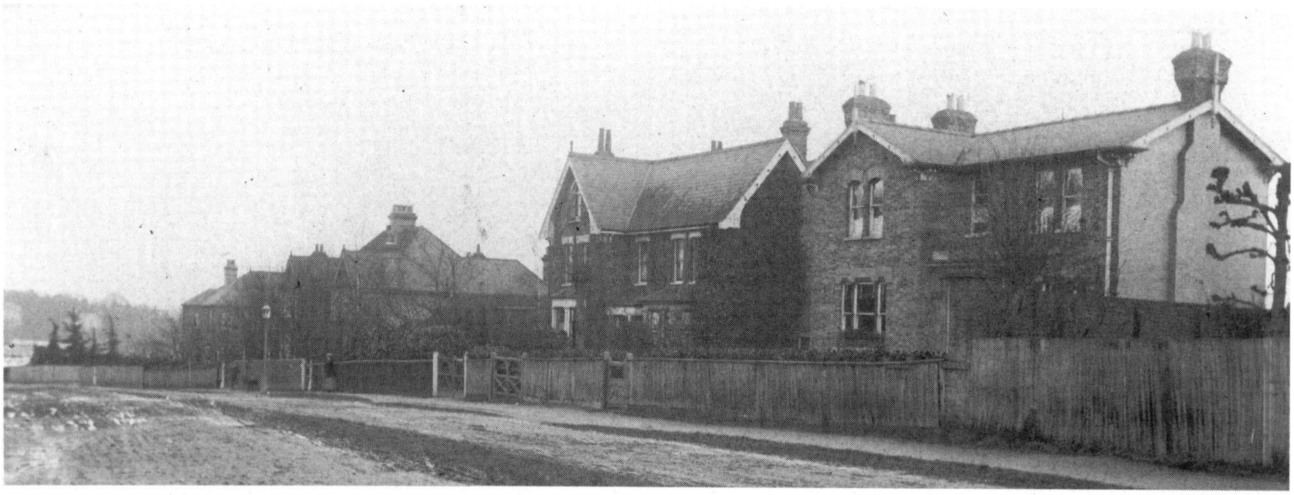

Looking west, solid Victorian villas are in evidence in this view of Avenue Road near its junction with Chase Side, but look at the state of the road! It wasn't until the early 1890s that the Southgate Local Authority took over responsibility for Avenue, Nursery and Chelmsford Roads, which were then made up, kerbed and channelled.

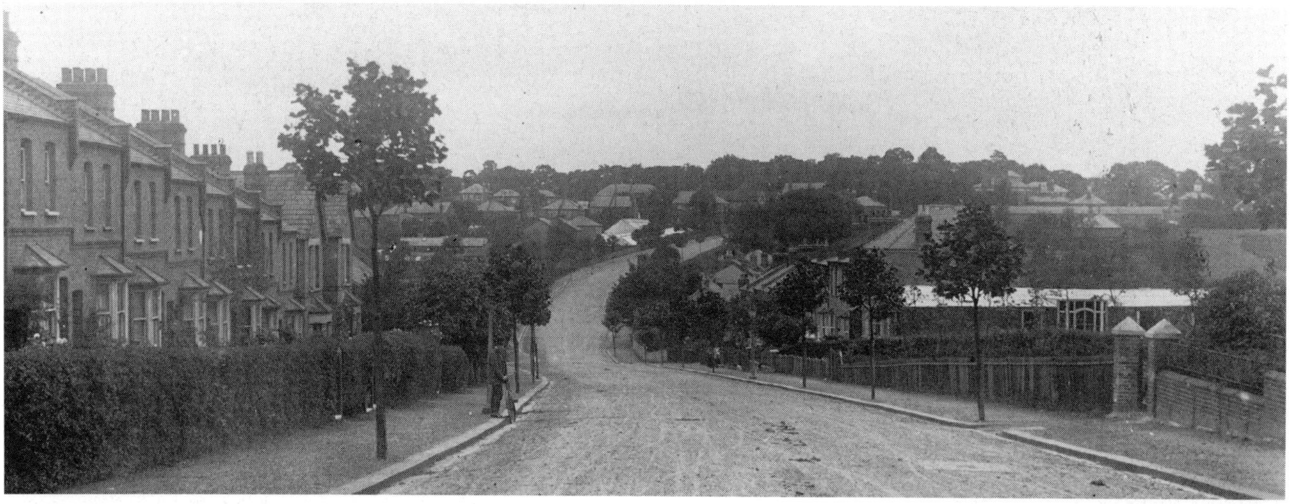

Above: This view is further down Avenue Road heading east towards Chase Road. The houses on the left are still there; the horticultural nurseries, on the right, which gave their name to Nursery Road are long gone.

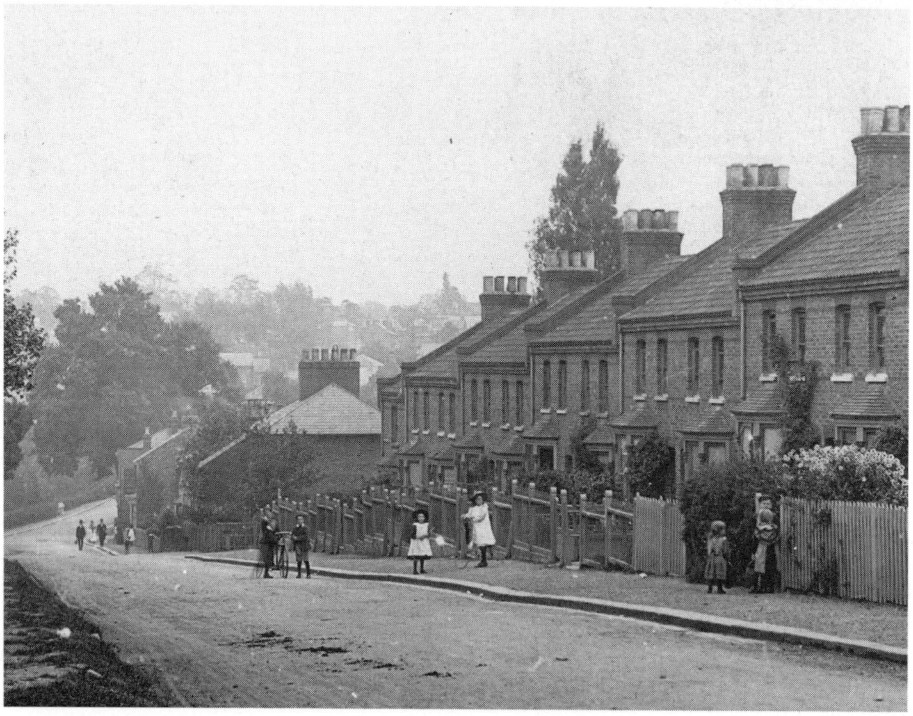

Right: At the eastern end of Avenue Road we turn right into Chase Road, which was one of the roads built after the enclosure of Enfield Chase in 1777. On the 1801 Enclosure map it was shown as a private road. This view is looking south towards Southgate Circus and the sturdy terraced houses are still there today but unfortunately without their stylish wooden garden fences. Similarly the girl in the all-white dress playing with a metal hoop has probably been replaced with a girl in jeans on a skateboard.

Further southwards down Chase Road, this is a view looking north. The cottages in the previous picture are hidden behind the large tree in the left distance. The wooden house on the left was demolished in the 1950s to make way for an extension to St Andrew's school.

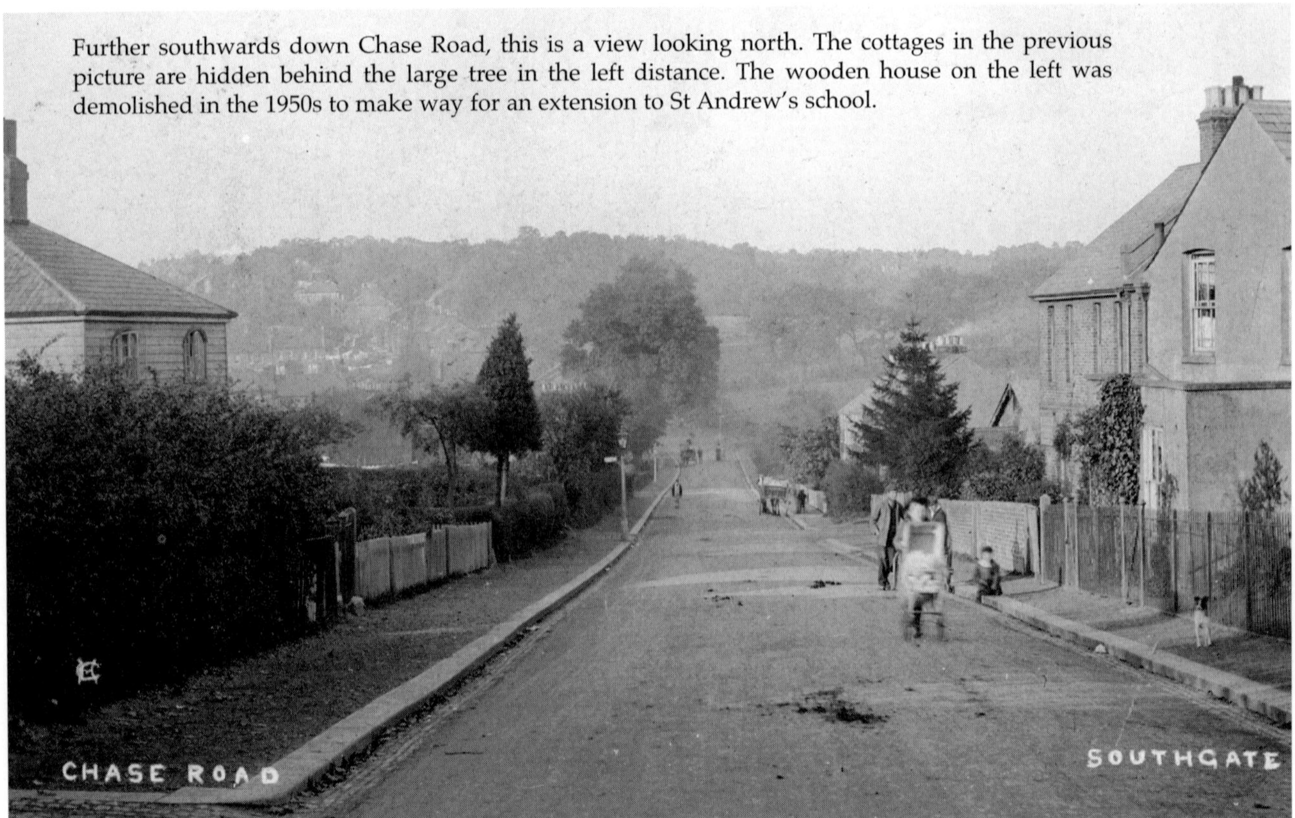

The photograph below was taken from the Southgate Circus end, looking north up Chase Road. The premises of Ephraim Kerry & Son, builders and decorators, are on the left and the White Hart pub is on the right. Albert Tom Passmore was licensee in 1892/93, which is around the time this picture was taken. Myrtle Cottage is just beyond the pub, hidden by the trees on the right.

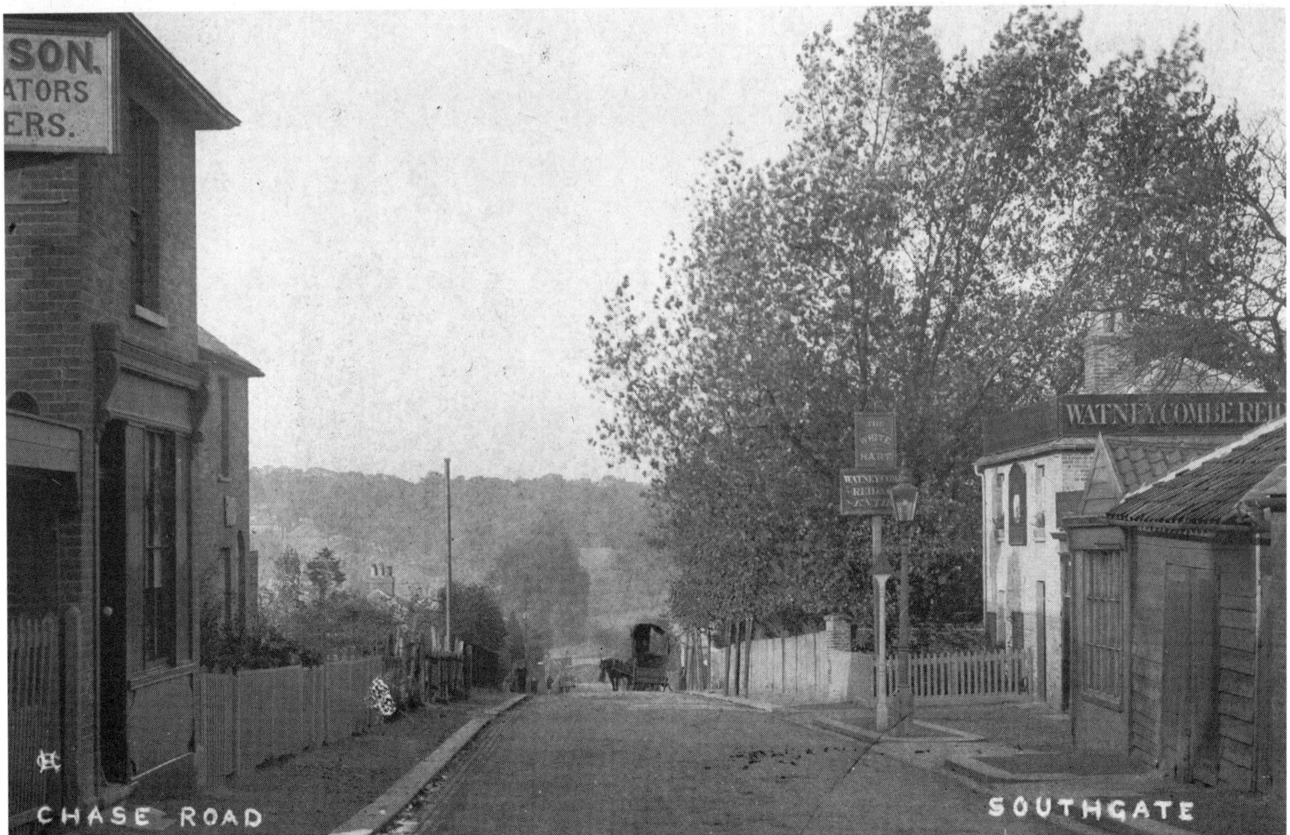

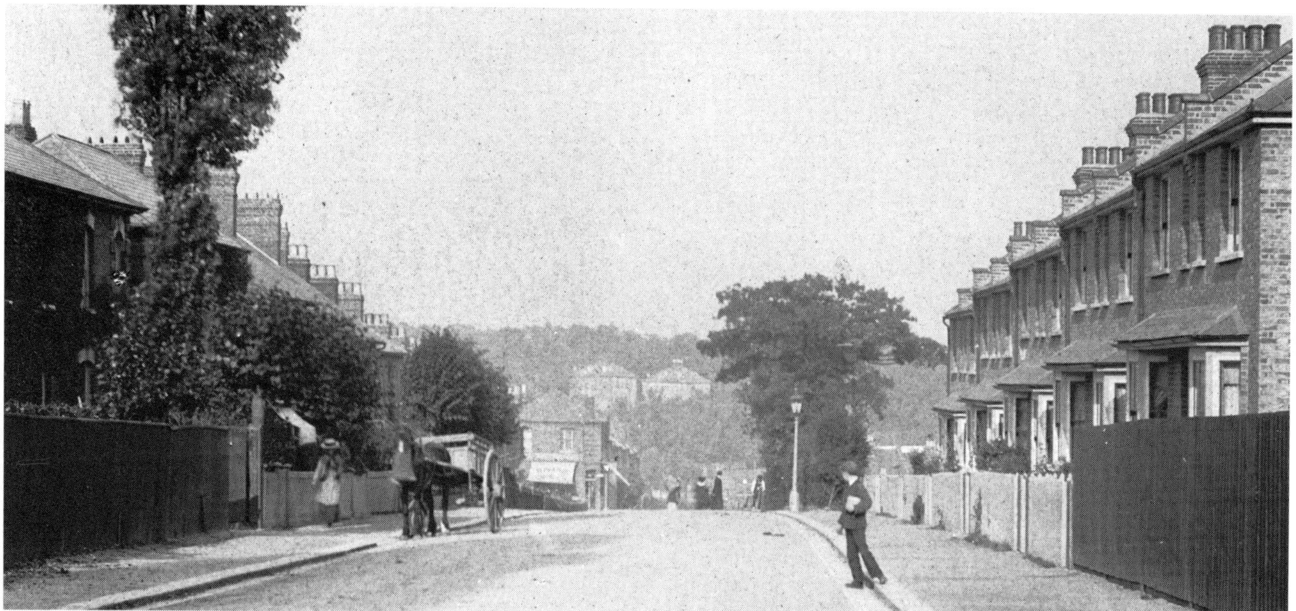

Retracing our steps back along Chase Road for a short distance we now turn left into Chelmsford Road which, like Avenue Road, was part of the Southgate estate broken up as early as 1853 for building development. At that time the price for a plot of just over an acre was £100.

The 1867 Ordnance Survey map shows that only two houses had been built by that date but it wasn't long before the whole road was filled with what were described as 'respectable working class houses'. One wonders what their first occupants would have thought of the price of them today! Originally a road without a name, by 1881 it had been named after Frederick Thesiger, the 2nd Lord Chelmsford, who had commanded the British forces in the Zulu War of 1879.

The shop halfway down the road on the left with the blind is an off-licence on the corner of Nursery Road. The shop was named Chelmsford House and was owned by Mrs Mary Bivand. The groups of nearer houses on the left are named respectively Elizabeth, Zulu and Madras Cottages, then come Ada Villas which are just out of the view.

The French Cleaning and Dyeing Company established an extensive works in Chelmsford Road in the 1880s. It had a reputation for high-class work and included several members of the Royal Family amongst its clientele. At one time the business had several branches in the City and the West End.

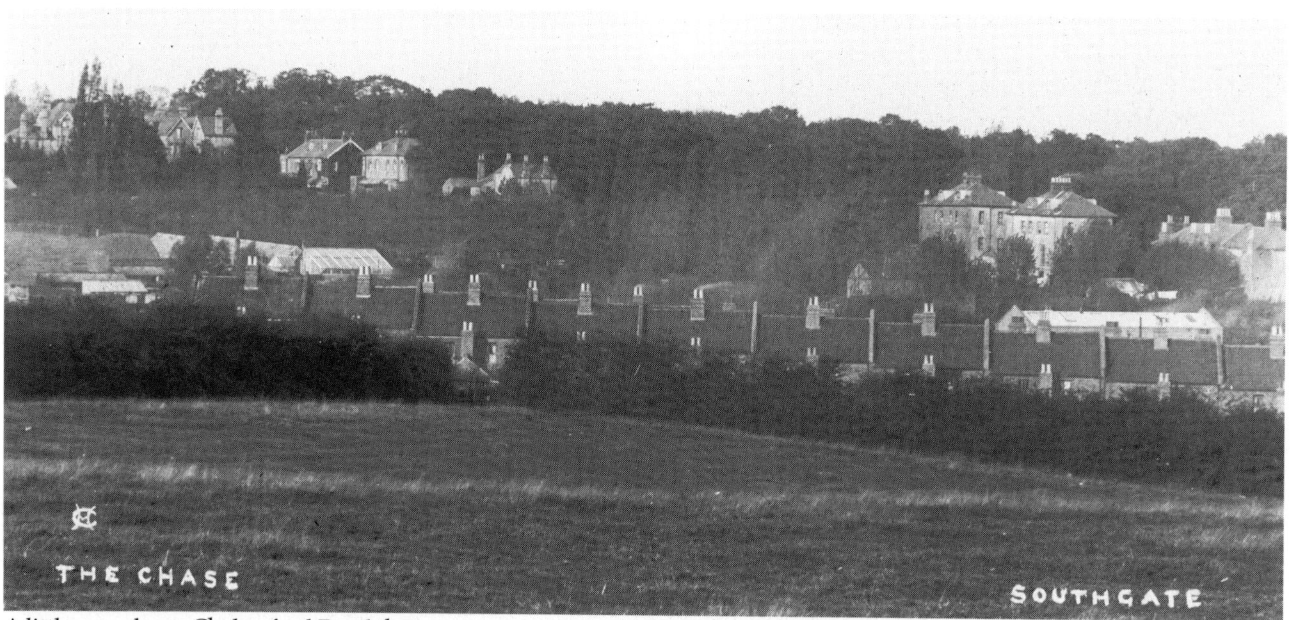

A little way down Chelmsford Road there was once a road which ran off to the left and used to join Chase Road. Built by 1881 and called Travers Road, it was later renamed Ivy Road. It acquired its present name of Ivy Close in the 1970s after extensive redevelopment closed off its exit to Chase Road and left it as a cul-de-sac from Chelmsford Road. The terraced houses in the foreground are on Ivy Road/Close, running down from Chelmsford Road on the left. Chase Road can be seen in the background.

Nursery Road leads off northwards from halfway along Chelmsford Road and connects it with the Avenue. The 1896 Ordnance Survey map shows an impressive collection of greenhouses, which prompted the road's name.

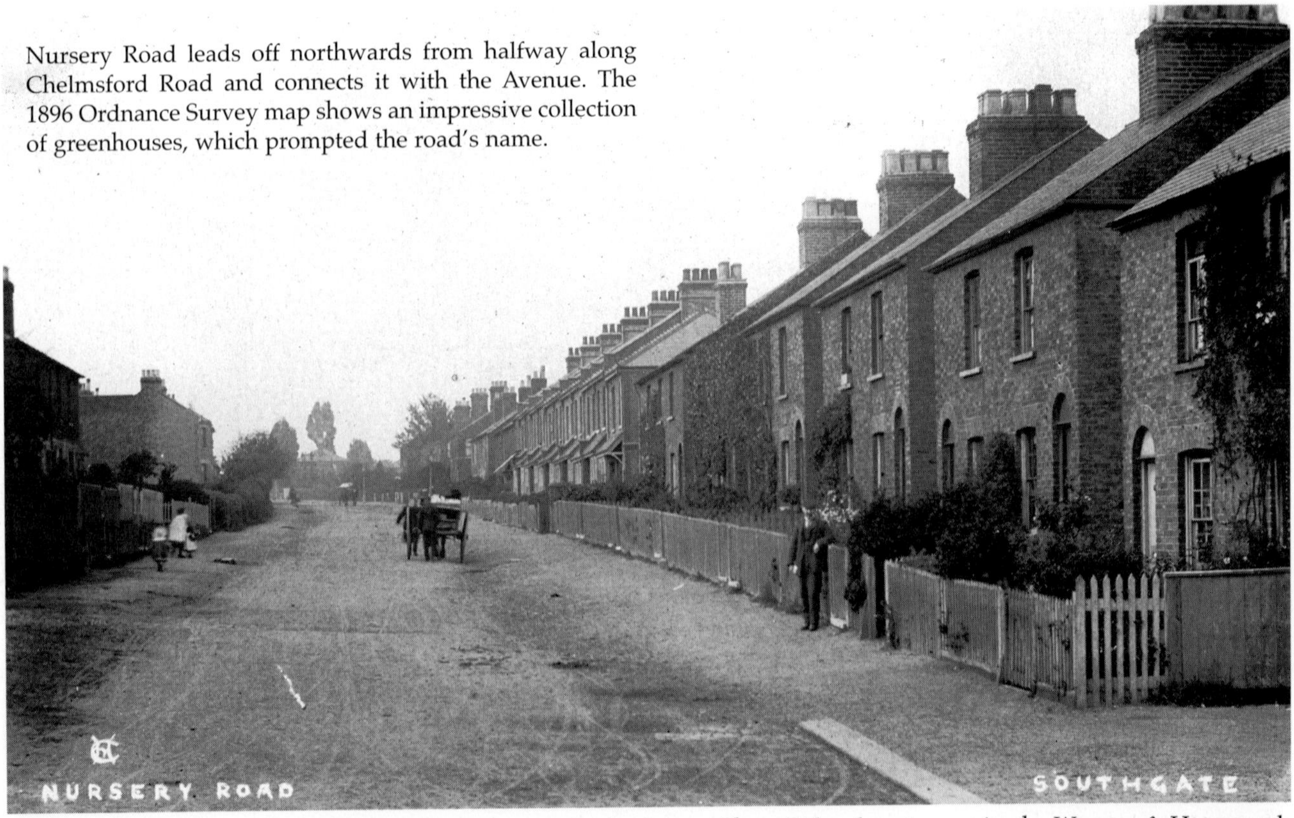

Below: At the western end of Chelmsford Road we arrive back onto Chase Side, almost opposite the Waggon & Horses pub which stands on the left-hand side of the road in this photograph. This Victorian hostelry was rebuilt in 1900 and again in 1930; this picture shows it after its 1900 rebuilding.

The horse trough in front of the pub was particularly appreciated by animals on the horse-drawn bus as they plodded along the road to their terminus near Avenue Road. By the time of this picture the horse-drawn buses had been replaced by motor buses and the trough, whilst being retained in its original position, appears to have been slanted at an angle to prevent motor vehicles from driving through the forecourt.

In recent times the pub has been converted into a Latin-themed salsa bar, Bar Latina.

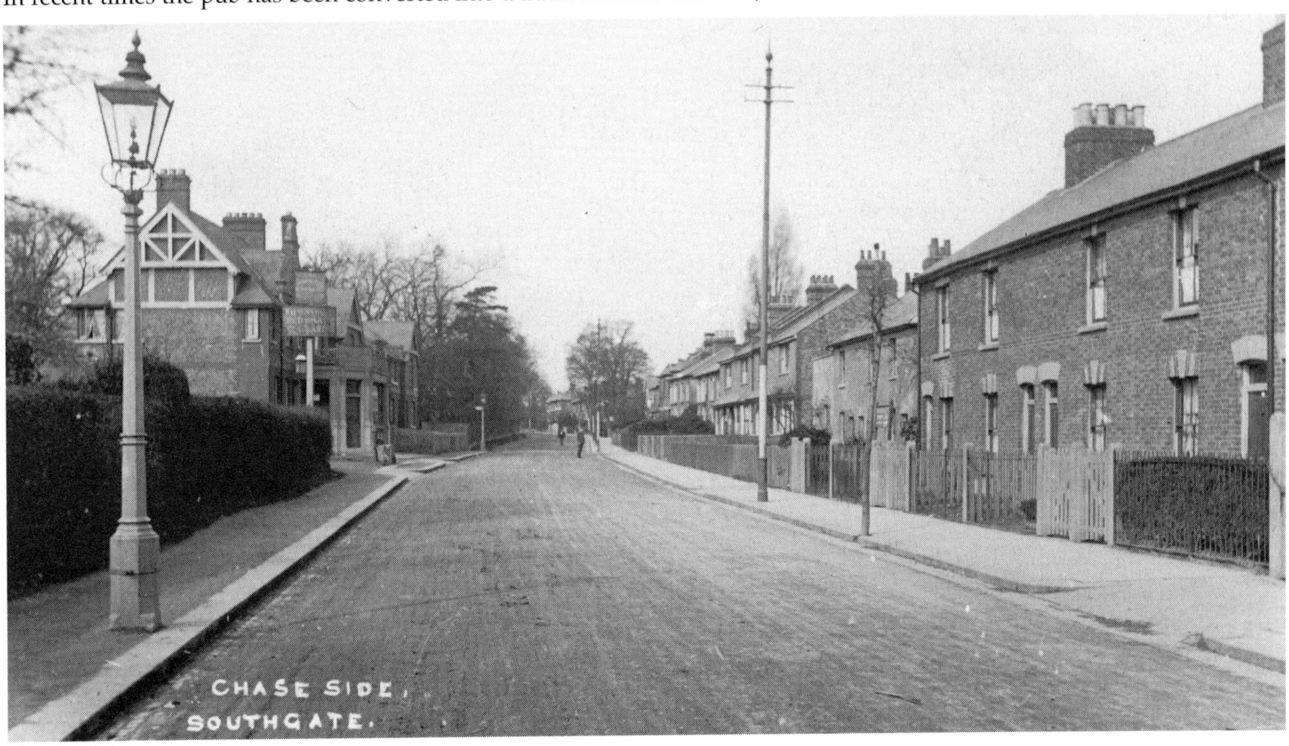

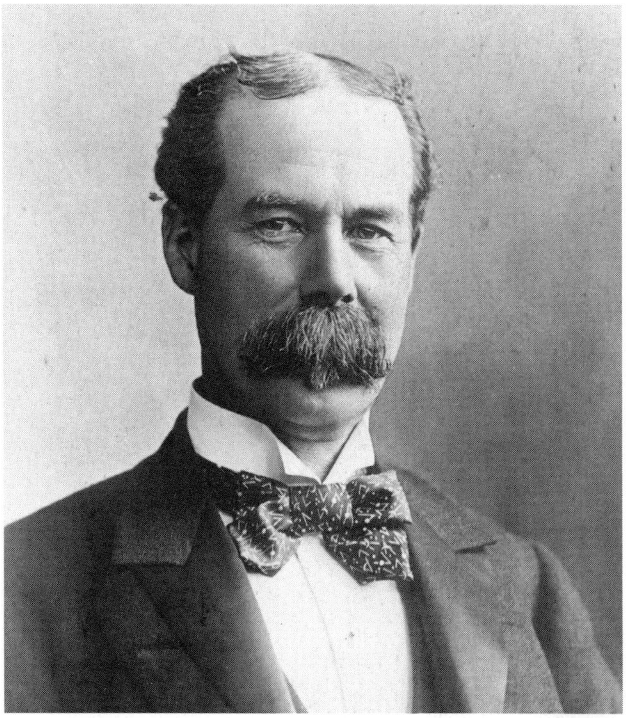

We cannot leave Chase Side without turning right for a few yards and crossing the road to view Osidge, the former residence of Sir Thomas Johnstone Lipton.

Born the son of a poor Glasgow family on 10 May 1850, Lipton decided to go into the grocery business and managed to open a small shop in that city. His business prospered and so began the Lipton grocery empire, which eventually extended throughout Britain. Amongst its best-known products was Ceylonese tea and in Edwardian Britain there were very few towns and villages that did not have at least one shop displaying a 'Lipton's Tea' advertisement.

Lipton became a friend of the future King Edward VII and was also famous for his persistent attempts to win the Americas Cup in a series of yachts. Unfortunately, he never succeeded in this ambition but his sportsmanship made him many friends on both sides of the Atlantic, and his sailing endeavours and his philanthropy brought him a well-deserved knighthood.

After moving from Scotland when the size of his business empire made it necessary to relocate his headquarters to London, Lipton made his home in Southgate. He died there on 2 October 1931, aged 81. He was buried in his native Glasgow and left his large fortune to various charities to be used for the benefit of poor citizens of that city.

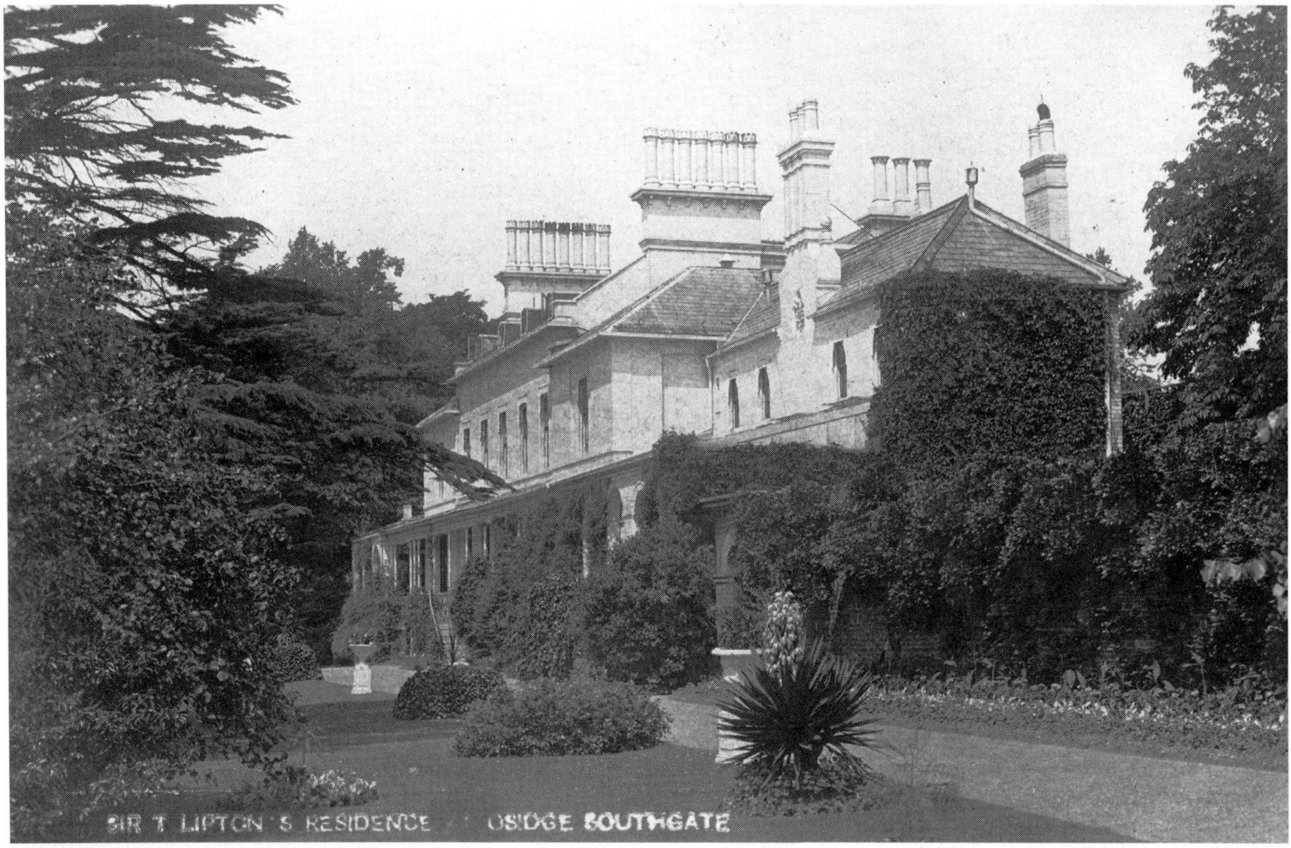

Sir Thomas Lipton came to live in Southgate in 1892 in the mansion known as Osidge. From here he had a direct telephone line to his City Road office: this was the first private telephone in the village.

Before moving in, Lipton spent a lot of money on improving it. He employed architect Mr A.R. Barker to build a new billiards room, greatly enlarged the stables and rerouted the path which ran across the estate from Crown Lane to Osidge Lane so that it was as far away from the house as possible. He entirely redecorated the house and renewed most of the fencing. Before motor cars became the usual method of transport, Sir Thomas always kept at least three pairs of fast carriage horses in his stables and was driven to his office in City Road about 9 a.m. every working day.

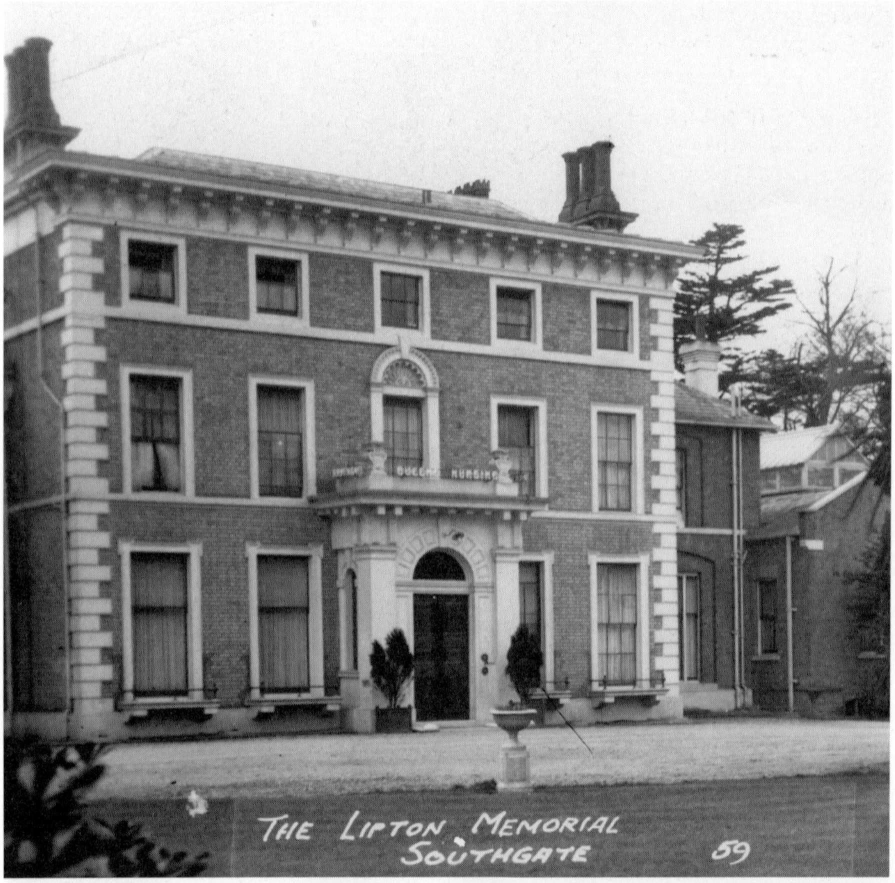

Left: The front entrance to Osidge House. In his will Sir Thomas Lipton left the mansion to be a home for retired nurses, a philanthropic purpose it fulfils to this day.

Below: To its rear Osidge had extensive gardens where Sir Thomas Lipton used to hold parties and entertain his guests. Because he owned tea plantations in Ceylon he always used to employ a number of Sinhalese servants. The tree house was one of the features of the grounds; the man with the moustache standing looks to be Sir Thomas himself.

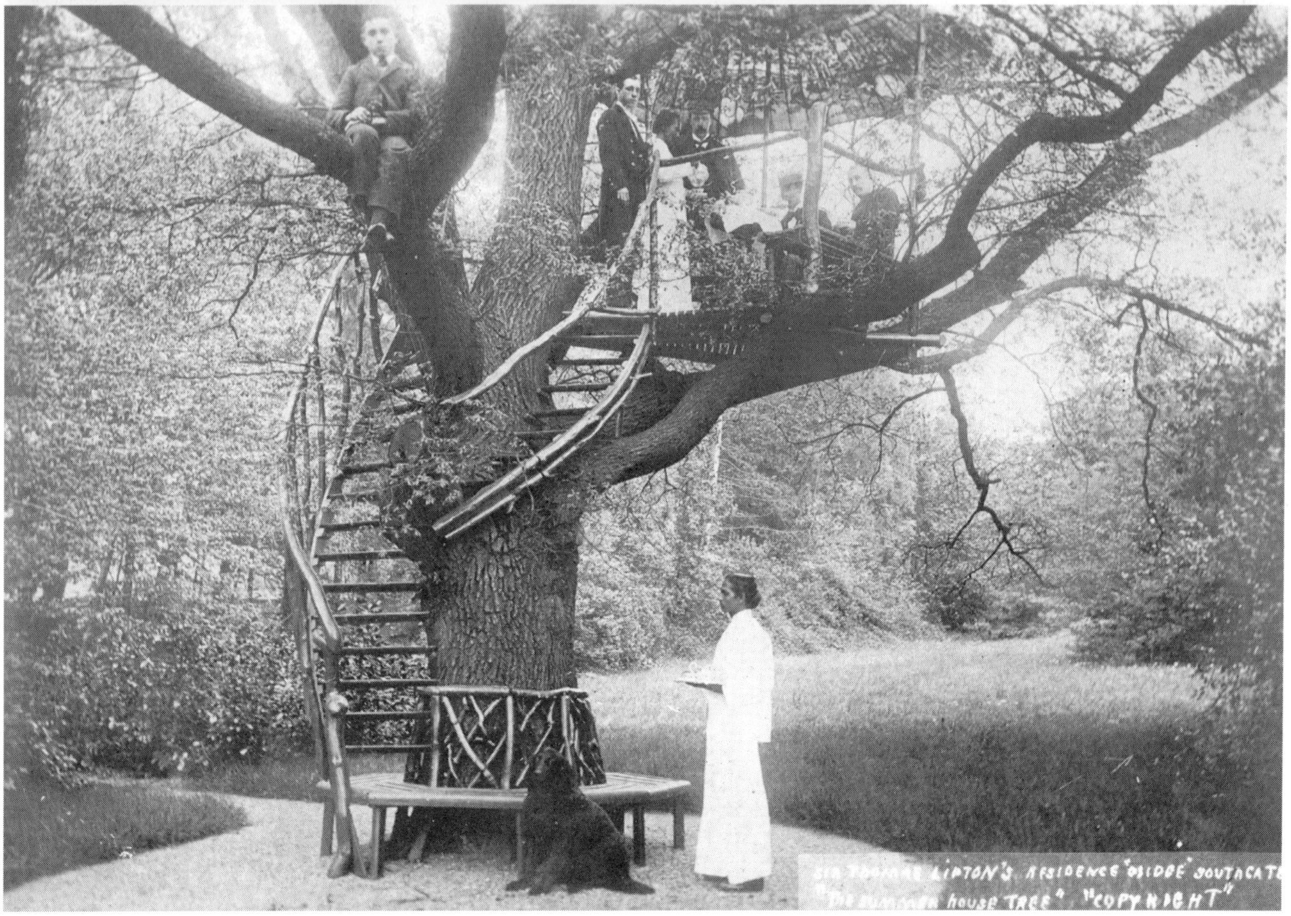

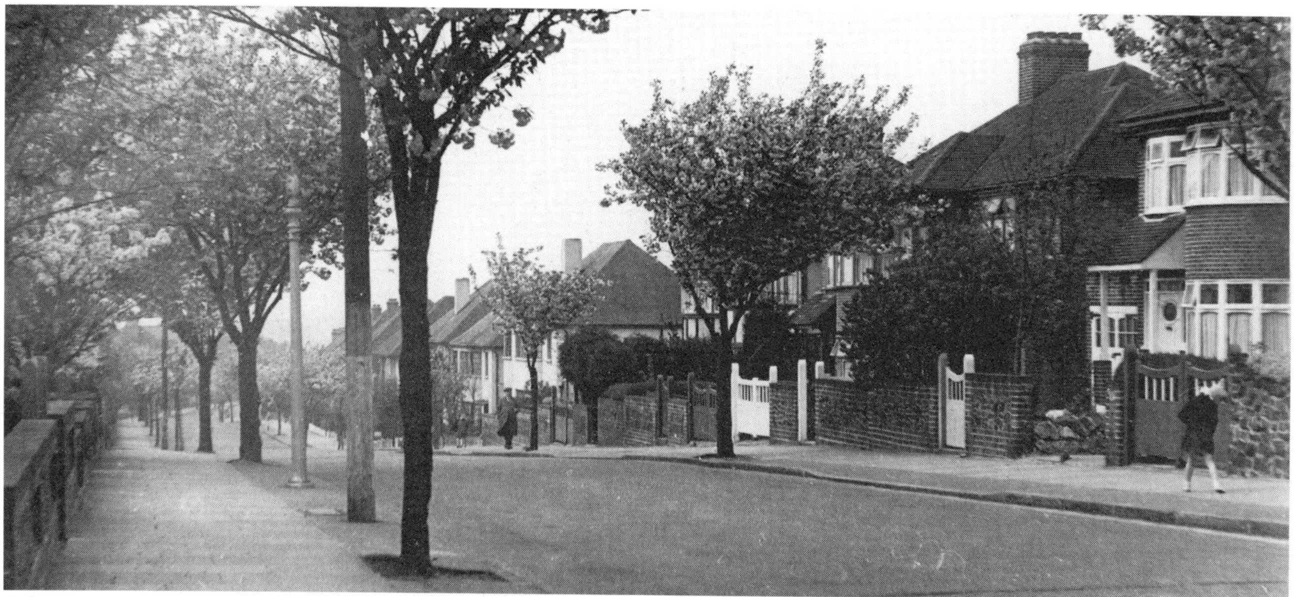

Retracing our route back down Chase Side as far as the Waggon & Horses, we come to Chase Way, which runs off to the right and joins Hampden Way at the bottom of the hill. On the 1897 Ordnance Survey map it is shown as merely a lane, which becomes a footpath and joins Osidge Lane near the lodge to Ferney House. This was the lane that was diverted away from Osidge mansion when Sir Thomas Lipton took up residence there. Compared with much of Southgate, Chase Way is a relatively modern development of the inter-war years; even so, the houses were built before garages became an essential part of the home. As a result most of the trees and garden gates in the picture have disappeared and have been replaced by paved drives but the road and houses still look as spick and span as they do here.

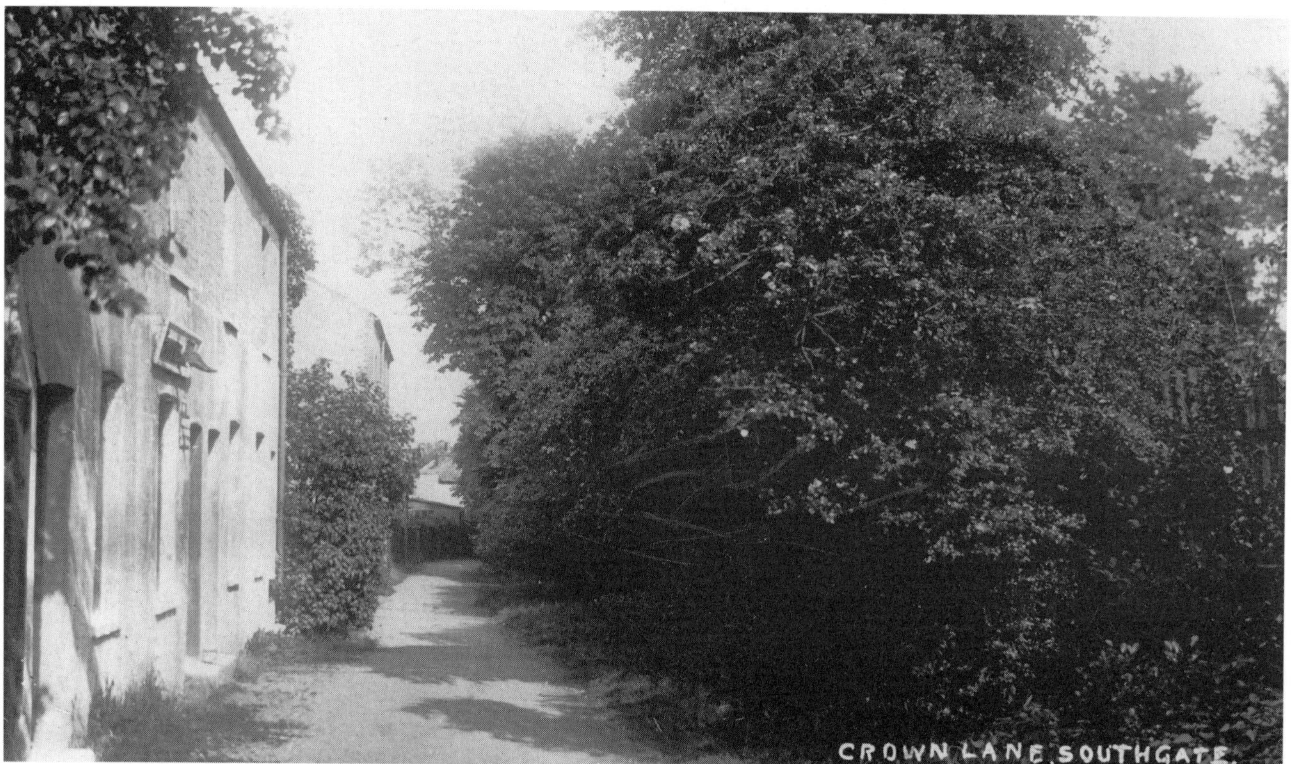

Only a few yards down Chase Way we come to the ancient Crown Lane. In 1841 it was recorded on maps as Crown Alley, but it had acquired its present name by 1861. It was originally a track that led from Chase Side to the Crown Hotel, which at that time faced onto the lane. On the right were the gardens of a large house named The Lawns. Until 1965 the lane formed part of the boundary between Middlesex and Hertfordshire.

Nowadays the lane is much wider but the old houses still stand. The nearest one in the picture is Gloucester Terrace; then comes Crown Terrace, which is hidden by the bush, and finally the taller building beyond has nowadays been converted into a loading bay for MacDonald's restaurant on Chase Side.

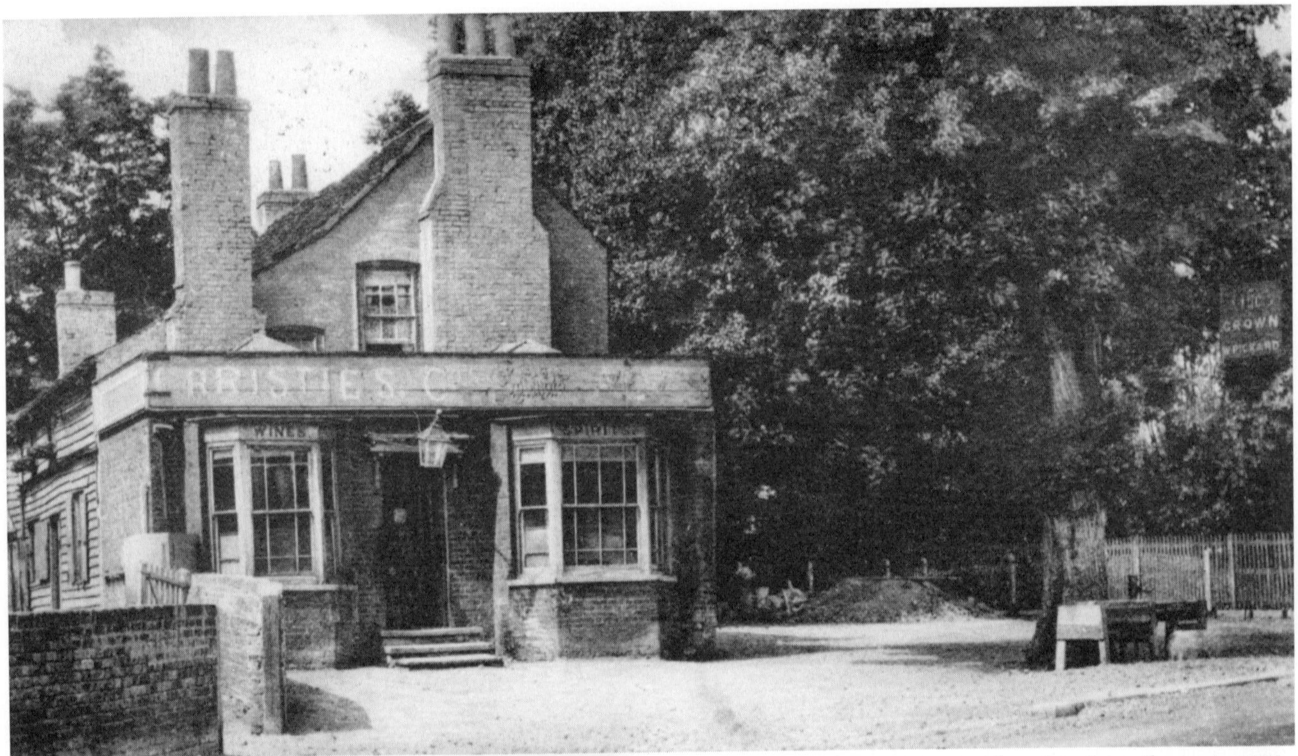

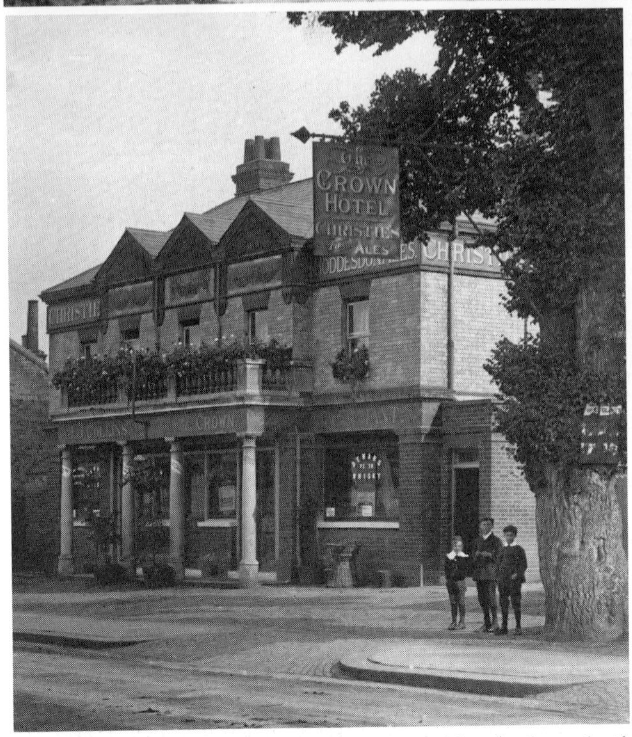

The original Crown Hotel was said to date from the early 1500s and was a small wooden-framed cottage that faced onto Crown Lane. It was later enlarged into a wooden two-storey building with its front built almost at a right angle to Chase Side. It had a brick gable end facing Chase Side and a single-storey extension was later added to it, forming a new entrance to the hotel. That is the view in the picture above, with the bay window of the bar on the right. Christie's brewery was at Hoddesdon and was subsequently taken over by Taylor Walker.

William Pickard was the landlord for many years (and the last before the hotel was rebuilt in 1895) and he ran a horse-bus service each weekday from the Crown to the Bank of England, leaving the hotel at 8.50 a.m. and returning from the New Inn at 4 p.m. The fare was 1/- each way. Although the railway station at Palmers Green was opened in 1871, this bus service to the City continued until 1879 and was believed to have been subsidised by John Donnithorne Taylor of Grovelands, who had fought against the railway coming to Palmers Green.

The hotel's sign was made of copper and swung from a branch on the tree. Below the sign can be seen the horse trough, pump and well. There was ample room for the horse-bus to pull off the road and for the horse to take refreshment. The bus and horses were stabled across the yard.

In 1895 the old Crown Hotel was replaced by the large building in the lower picture. The new premises were constructed in the old stable yard in front of the stable building, then the old hotel was demolished and the stables rebuilt on its site.

The main entrance of the new hotel now faced onto Chase Side but was set well back from the road. This picture shows it soon after opening, by which time it was under John Joshua Collins's management but still sold Christie's Hoddesdon Ales. Traffic along the main road was still very light at that time; it was reported that ducks frequently used to waddle across the road and chickens that were kept in the stable yard could often be seen pecking around Chase Side in search of food dropped from the nosebags of horses standing outside the hotel.

Even stylish pub buildings could not escape the developers in the dark days of the 1960s and the Crown duly fell victim to their 'improvements' in 1963, being demolished and replaced by a shopping complex. Subsequently, a new pub was built on the other side of the road, a little to the north of where the Crown had stood, and was duly named The New Crown.

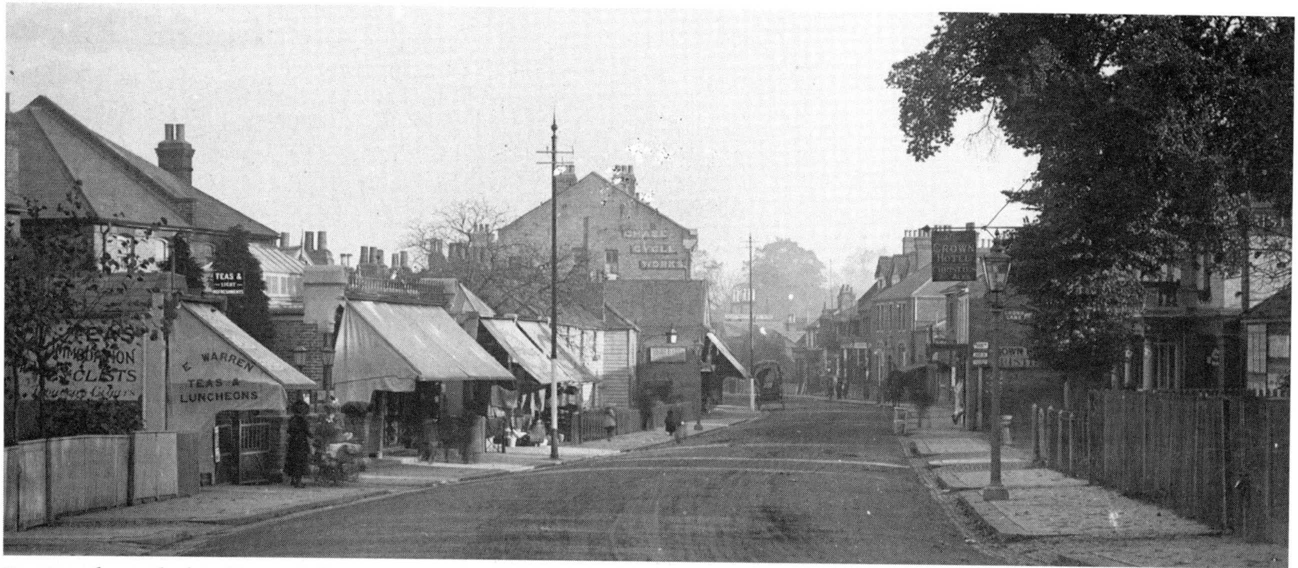

Passing through the alleyway that ran from Crown Lane alongside the Crown Hotel and emerged onto Chase Side, we enter the main highway from Southgate to the north. It is now time to walk down Chase Side and look at the Victorian (and earlier) buildings on either side of that historic road.

Both of these photographs date from around 1906 and are taken from almost the same position looking down Chase Side towards what is now Southgate Circus. In the picture above, taken from just above the Crown Hotel, the first shop on the right is Collins the Butchers. The next large building on the same side of the road housed the Southgate Reading Rooms and Library. On the left-hand side is the Teas and Luncheons shop owned by E. Warren. His advertisement on the wall to the left of the shop blind tempts cyclists with the odd combination of accommodation, teas and cigars! Next to it are the shops belonging to A.J. Frost & Co., house furnishers and estate agents. Two short blocks of old clapboard houses come next, followed by the brick-built premises of John Eaton who was the village jobmaster (i.e. someone who hired out coaches and horses) and coachmaster. The sign attached to his wall advertises his livery stables; at that time he used to hire out every type of horse-traffic conveyance imaginable.

A heavily laden cart is toiling up the hill in the afternoon sunshine in the picture below, which shows the buildings on the right-hand side more clearly. The Collins Brothers' butchers is followed by W. Spendlove & Son, greengrocer, William Booker, tobacconist, and then Charles Davies, baker and corn dealer. The premises of Newby & Brothers, builders, comes next, then the larger building of the Metropolitan Police station, followed, behind the lamppost, by the Southgate Reading Rooms and Library. Further down the road the taller building with the dormer windows is the Rising Sun public house. On the left, the Chase Cycle Works was owned by William Watkin & Son, ironmongers.

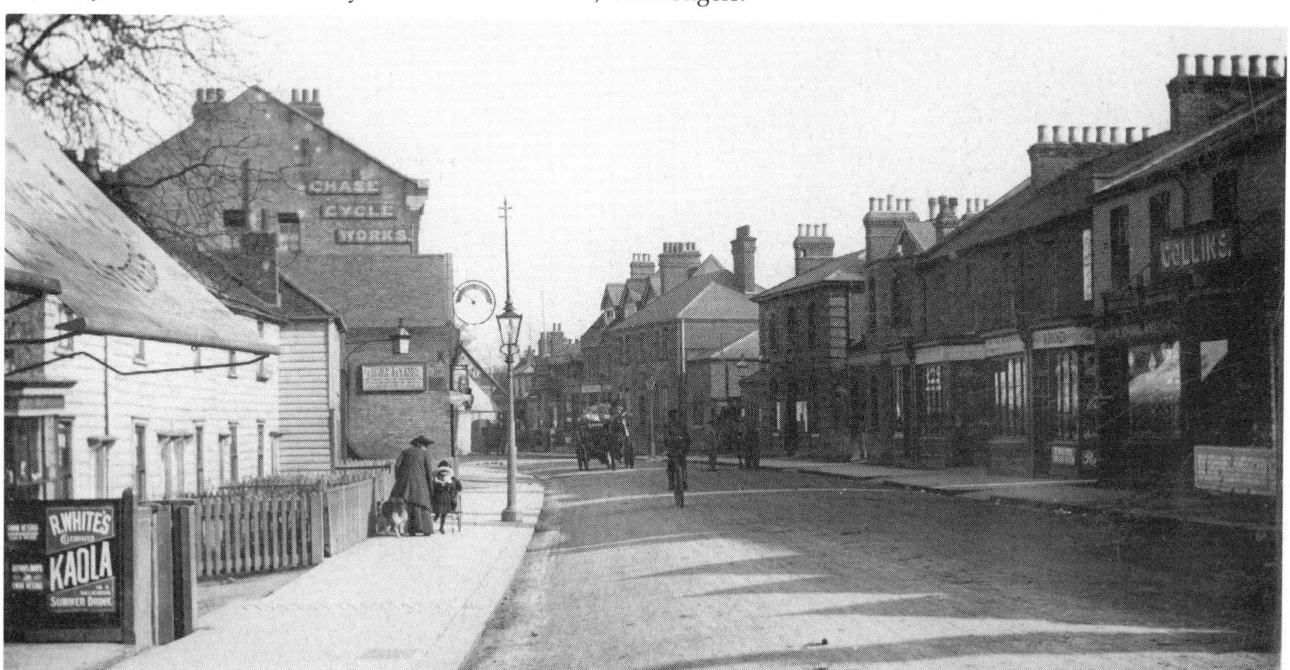

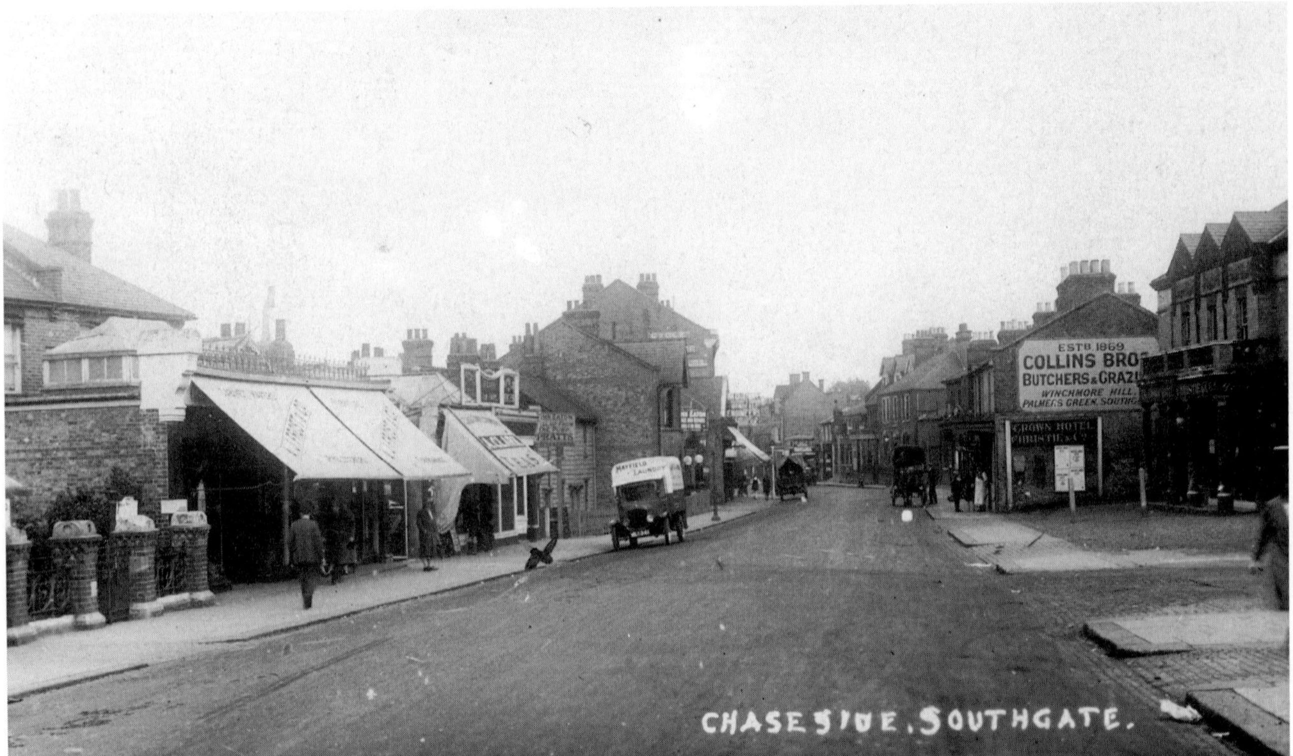

These two pictures show the same views as the last two, but they were taken a few years later and what a difference! The internal combustion engine has now made an appearance with the Mayfield Laundry delivery vehicle, and in the distance, a motor bus is making its way up the road towards its terminus at the Avenue. A.J. Frost & Co. still occupy the left-hand shop but next door is now a teashop. The further block of clapboarded houses in the earlier pictures has been demolished, as has half of the nearer block; in their place is a large brick-built house and workshop. John Eaton's sign advertises his services as a motor engineer; the livery stables have gone and he now hires out Daimlers to his prosperous customers. His entry in the 1929 local directory offers 'First Class cars for weddings, theatre and seaside runs'.

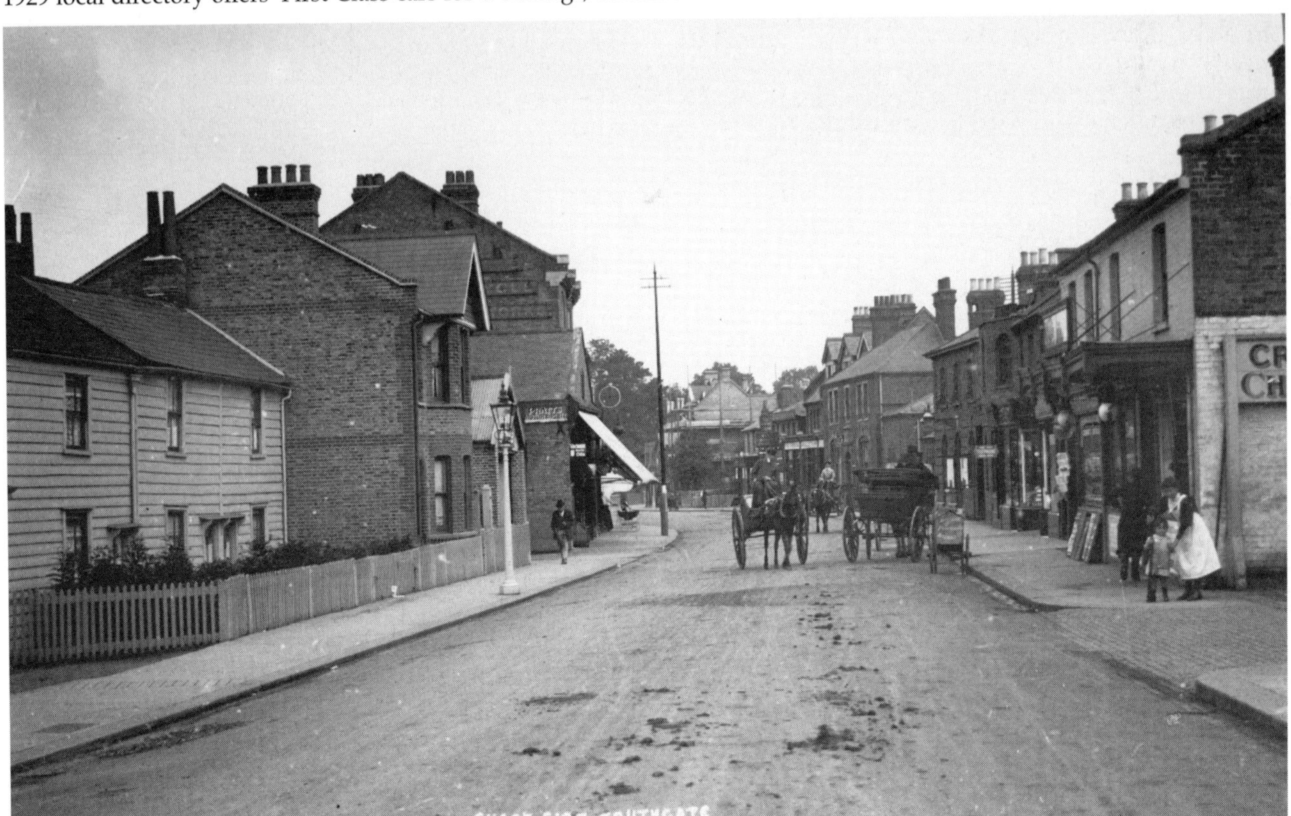

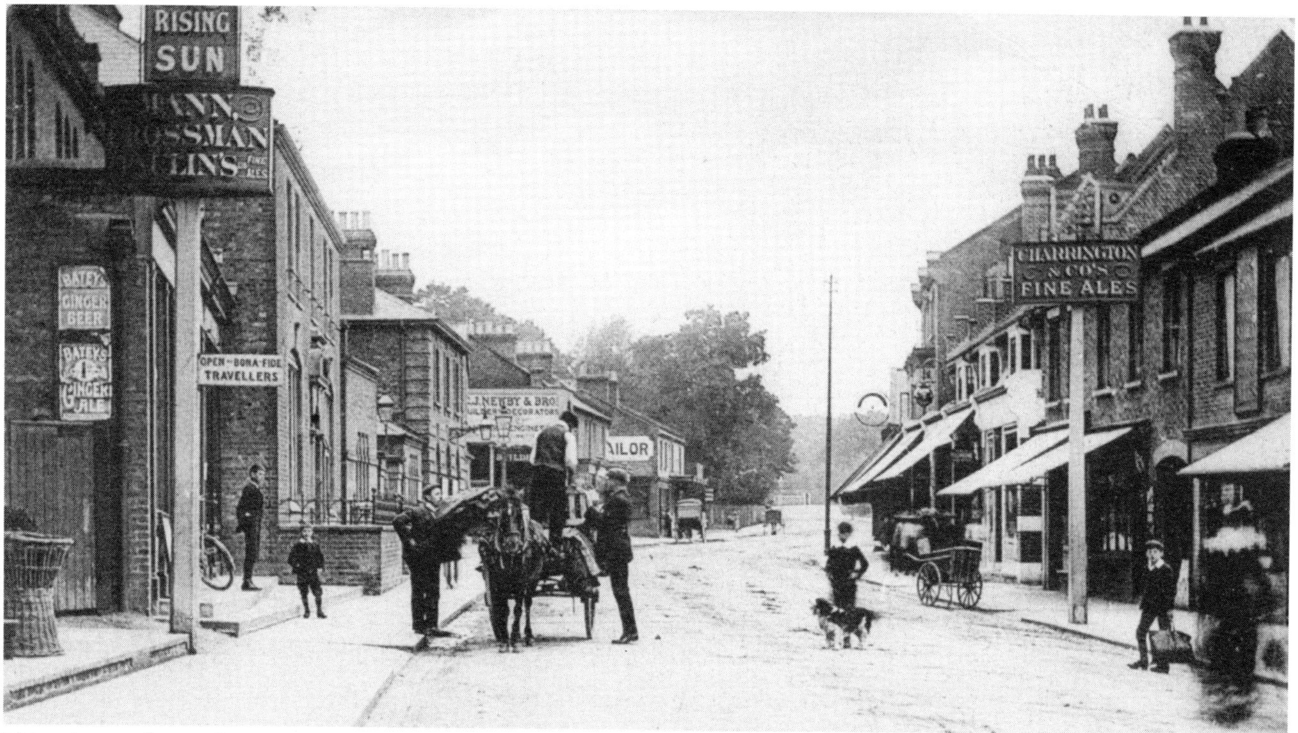

This picture shows the view up Chase Side back towards the Crown around 1900. The Rising Sun public house on the left foreground must have tried to discourage local drinkers because its sign advertises that it was open for *bona-fide* travellers. Above the sign is the name of the brewery whose beers it sold – the old-established firm of Mann, Crossman & Paulin. They survived as an independent firm until the brewing industry's rationalisation programme in the 1950s when they merged with Watney, Combe, Reid & Co. in 1958 to become Watney Mann Ltd. The combined firm continued to brew their beers mainly at Mann's Albion Brewery in Whitechapel, but in 1972 they merged with Grand Metropolitan Hotels Ltd and the Albion brewery was shut down in 1979. The Rising Sun itself was rebuilt in 1932.

Across the road was another pub, the Chase Gate Tavern, whose sign depicting a gate can just about be made out above the Charrington & Co.'s Fine Ales sign. This pub closed down in 1909 and the landlord removed to the Fishmongers Arms, taking the sign with him and re-erecting it outside his new premises.

The building next to the Rising Sun is the Southgate Reading Rooms and Library which was opened in 1889 but whose antecedents reached back to the Southgate Club formed in the 1840s. Beyond it are the premises of Thomas Gregory and then the police station, which was opened around 1861. Its occupants were 'Y' Division of the Metropolitan Police but it was not until the early 1890s that they had telegraphic communication with London. Until then their fastest means of communication was on horseback. In fact, Southgate still had two horse patrols until the late 1920s.

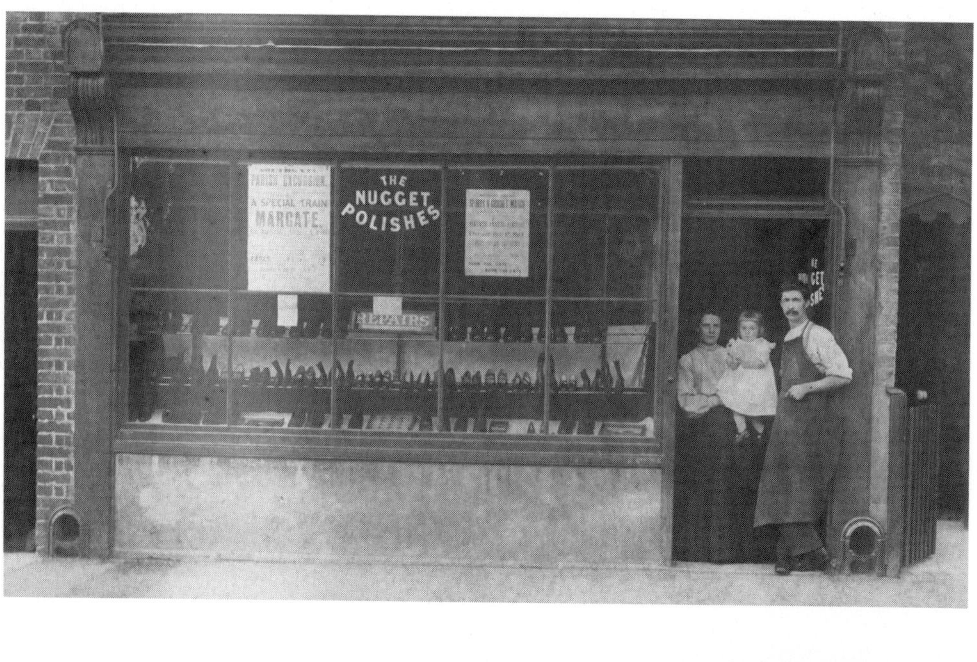

Right: An unidentified boot and shoe manufacturer in Southgate, probably in the Chase Side area. The left-hand poster is advertising a Southgate Parish Excursion by special train to Margate to be run on Tuesday, 1 August 1905. Tickets were 4/1*d*. for adults and 2/- for children, with lunch available at 1/6*d*. The poster on the right advertises the Southgate Village Sports & Cricket Match to be held on 10 August at the Chapel Fields.

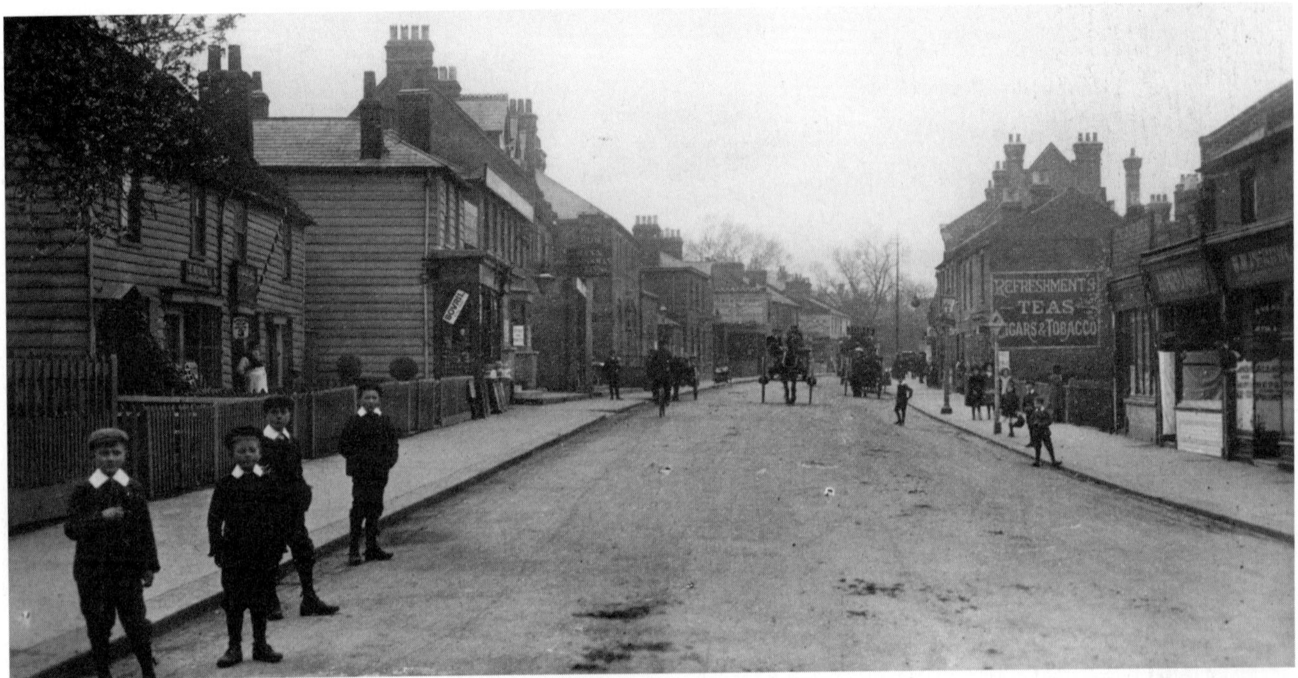

Four more pictures of much the same location and dating from around the same period. The first, above, shows the view up Chase Side from below the Rising Sun with Wadkin's barbers shop easily recognisable by the striped pole on the wall outside. His half-brother's greengrocer shop is out of sight behind the garden fence, but we shall come to it shortly.

In the second (below) and third pictures (overleaf top) the photographer is standing at the bottom of Chase Side in what is now Southgate Circus. The shop on the extreme left is that of A.A. Piper, fancy draper and milliner. Next to it is the Stag Hill Cycle Works owned by Mr Charles Dear, ironmonger. Judging from the brushes and shovels leaning against the wheels of the cart parked outside Mr Piper's shop, the street sweepers are about to begin clearing up the horse droppings that are littering the roadway.

The Rising Sun can be seen in all three pictures. It was from here, prior to 1871, that the licensee, Frank Lowe, ran a local horse-bus service to Colney Hatch's railway station (nowadays New Southgate) that provided a useful link for the villagers into Kings Cross. First class fares on the run to Colney Hatch and on to Kings Cross were 1/3*d*. single and 2/- return travelling inside the bus. Second class on the train and outside on the bus were 1/- and 1/6*d*. respectively. However, after the extension of the Great Northern Railway to Enfield and the opening of Palmers Green Station in 1871, the bus service switched to serve the new station.

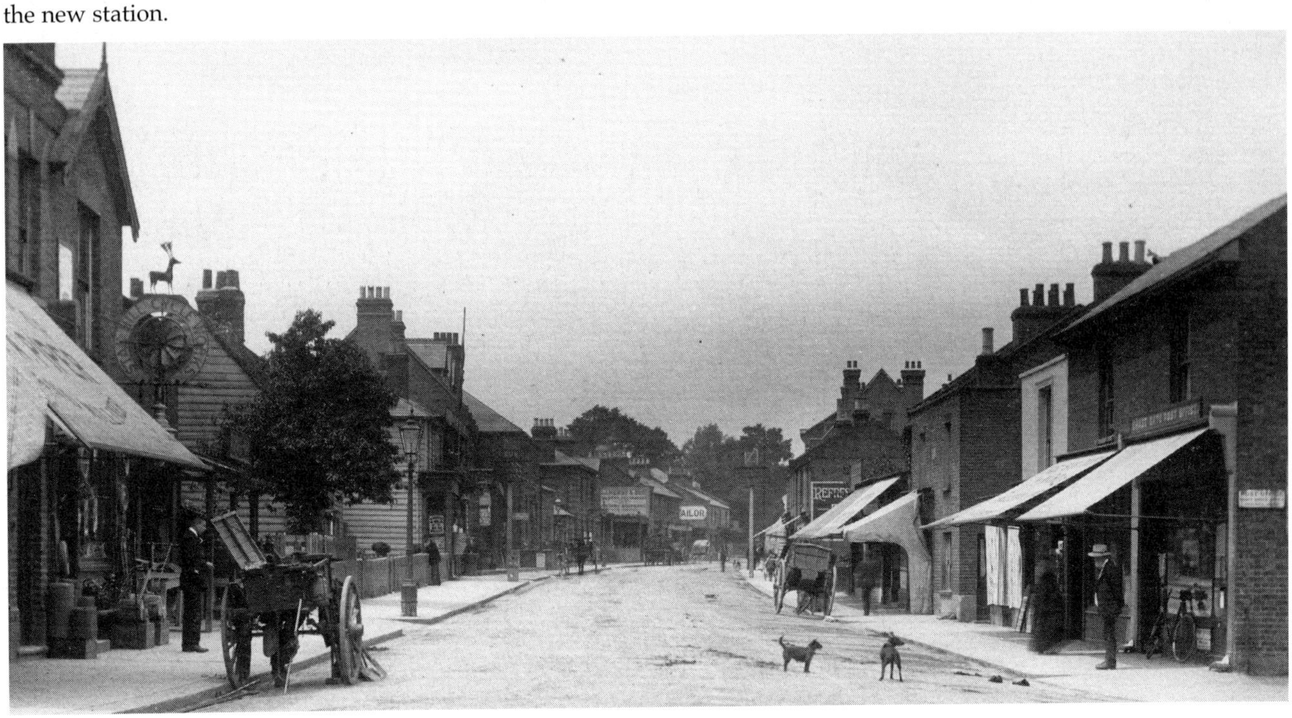

The third and fourth photographs were also taken from the bottom of Chase Side but at a slightly later date, probably in the 1920s, because a motor car has appeared in one of them. Nevertheless horse power still predominates and the street sweepers are in evidence with their brushes in the middle of the road in the third picture.

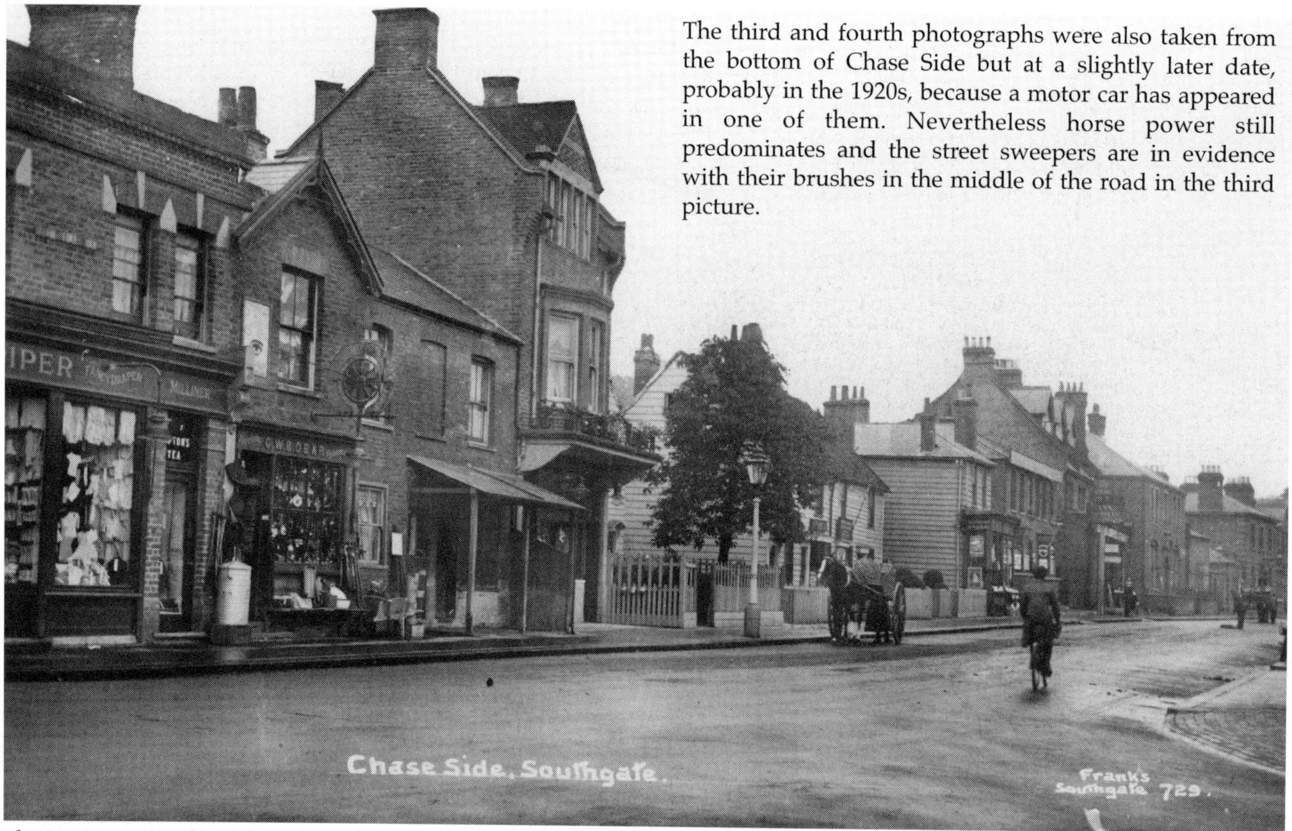

The buildings on the right side of the road in the fourth picture begin with Frederick Lees's grocery shop, which was also the village post office. Next comes the stationers formerly run by Miss Emma Franks, John Cocking the draper's old shop, now Martins, and then John Conisbee's bakery, founded in 1830, with the Hovis sign on the front.

Burgoyne's large sign on the side of the post office is very interesting. It is advertising Australian wine, a product that we generally associate with present times, yet here it is being advertised around 80 years ago.

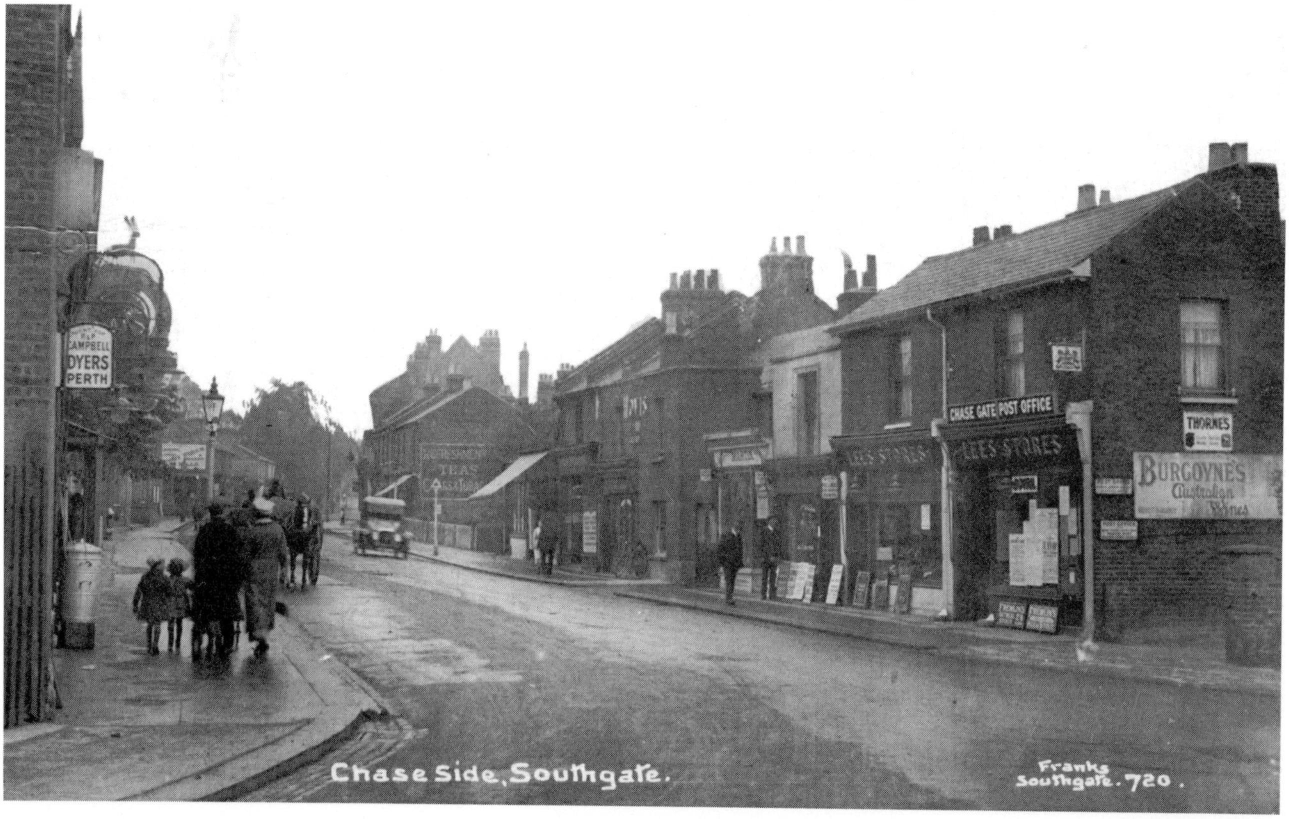

This picture is dated 1882, a time when clapboard buildings were a prominent feature of the lower end of Chase Side. Samuel Thomas Wadkins, pictured here, ran a fruiterer and greengrocer business from the little shop on the left. The next door premises housed a saddler (Charles Bishop), a laundress (Mrs Sarah Baldry) and a tailoress (Mrs Emma Wyblin), then came William Wadkin's barbers shop. In those days a boy's haircut cost 2*d*., while a man's was 4*d*. The barber was also the village pig slaughterer, his tally over the 20 years from 1878 to 1897 being 3,891 pigs. In 1885 alone he dispatched 365. This versatile man was also said to have been an undertaker's assistant, umbrella maker, musician and philosopher. Born in 1846 and known in the village as 'Old Dock', his shop was on the site taken by Bairstow Eves's estate agent today. Wadkins died in December 1922.

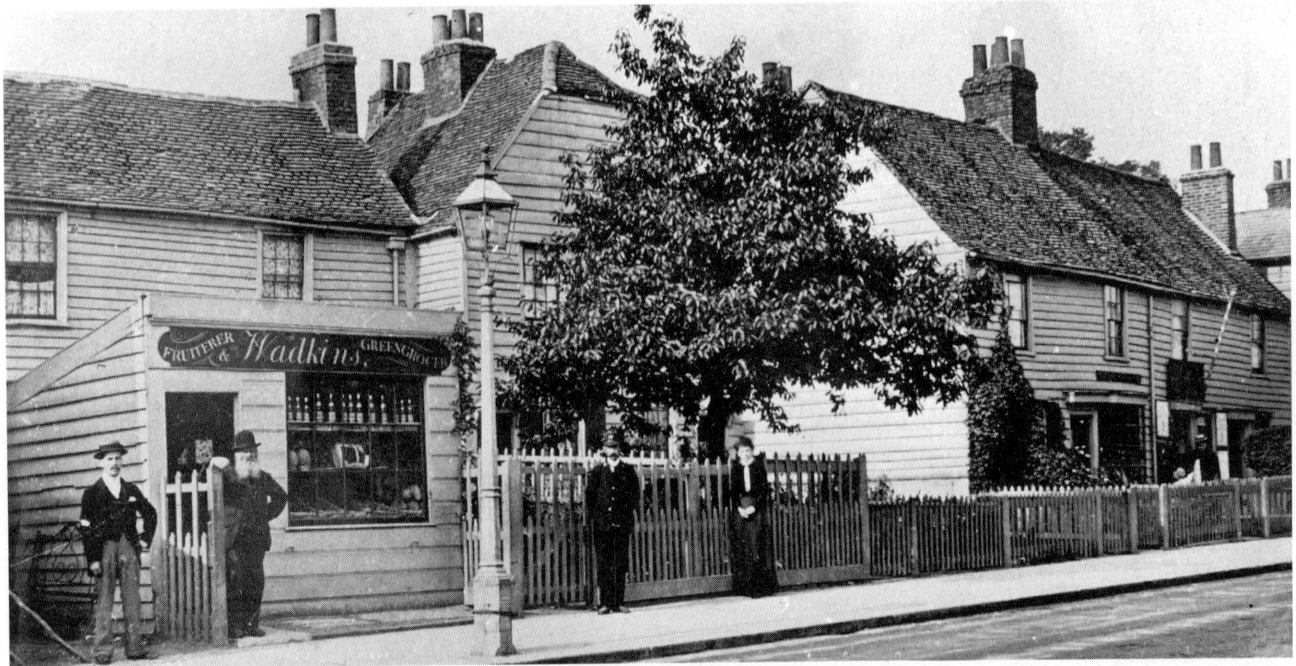

Just across the road from Wadkin's shops was Emma Frank's stationers and tobacconists shop at No. 10, next door to Lee's Stores. It was an old-established business, dating from around 1880. Her window display is very elaborate, ranging from dolls to doyleys, and there is an impressive selection of newspapers and periodicals hanging outside the shop door. Titles include *Harrison's Dressmaker, Home Circle, London Opinion, the Christian, the Countryside, Cycling and Amateur Gardening*, and there are many others on display whose titles are obscured. Note what appears to be a hole to the right of the door – this is actually the top of a boot scraper, which had been installed before the pavements were laid as the roads could be extremely muddy. When the pavements were put down the lower part of the scraper was covered over. A complete scraper can be seen on page 20.

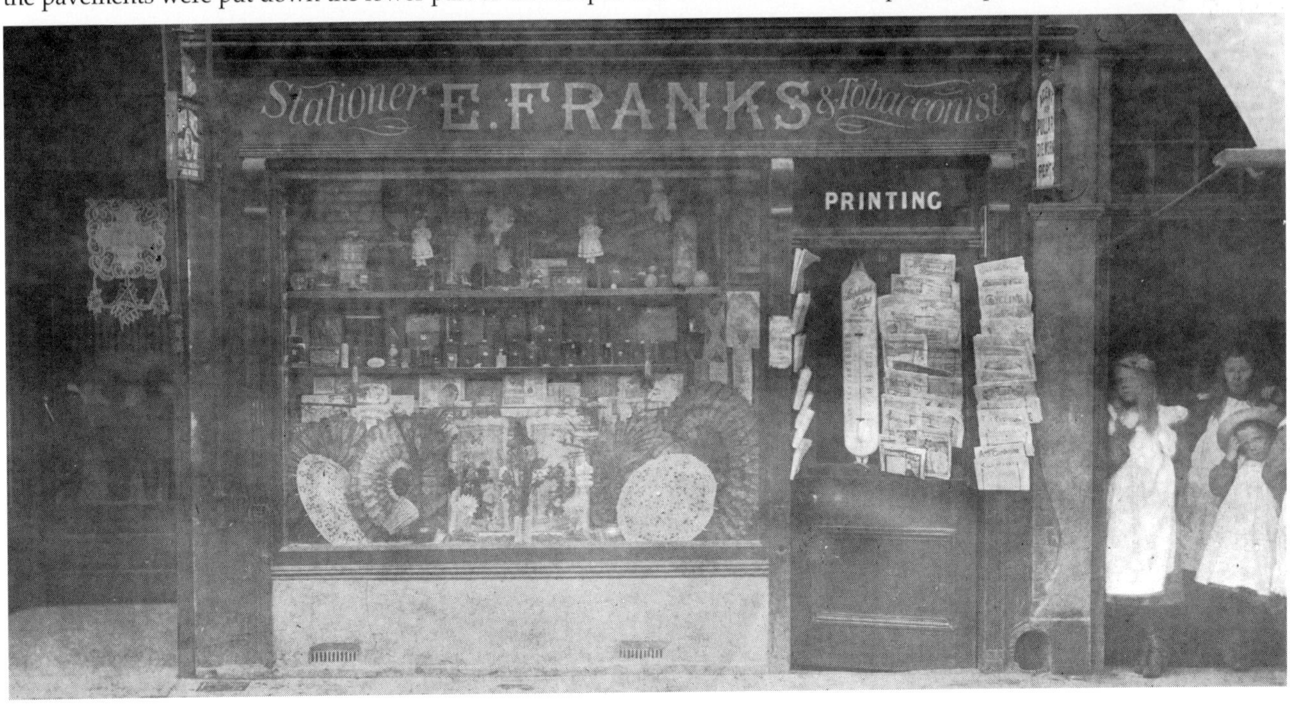

Before the turn of the nineteenth century Southgate Circus was often known as Bunkers Corner after George Bunker who set up in business as a wheelwright and ironworker in 1804 in a large, rambling clapboard building. The premises were demolished in 1897 and were replaced by some shops; the shops later made way for the tube station which stands exactly on the site of Bunker's shop.

The pub in the picture on the right is the Bell, one of Southgate's oldest inns. In 1882 it was recorded as selling beer at 4*d*. a quart and porter (strong beer) at 3*d*. a quart. (For the benefit of those readers brought up in the metric age, 1 quart = 2 pints).

Long before Southgate Circus came into being this junction was also known as Fiveways Corner, the five ways being Chase Side which runs off to the left in this picture, Chase Road which runs between the lampposts down the right-hand side of the Bell, Winchmore Hill Road which exits to the right, Bourneside (nowadays The Bourne) which is behind the photographer's right shoulder, and High Street in which he was standing.

The block of shops on the left were demolished in 1933 to make way for Southgate Circus. The Bell itself survived until 1963 when it was demolished as part of the area's redevelopment and was replaced by a Wimpy Bar, and a shop and office complex.

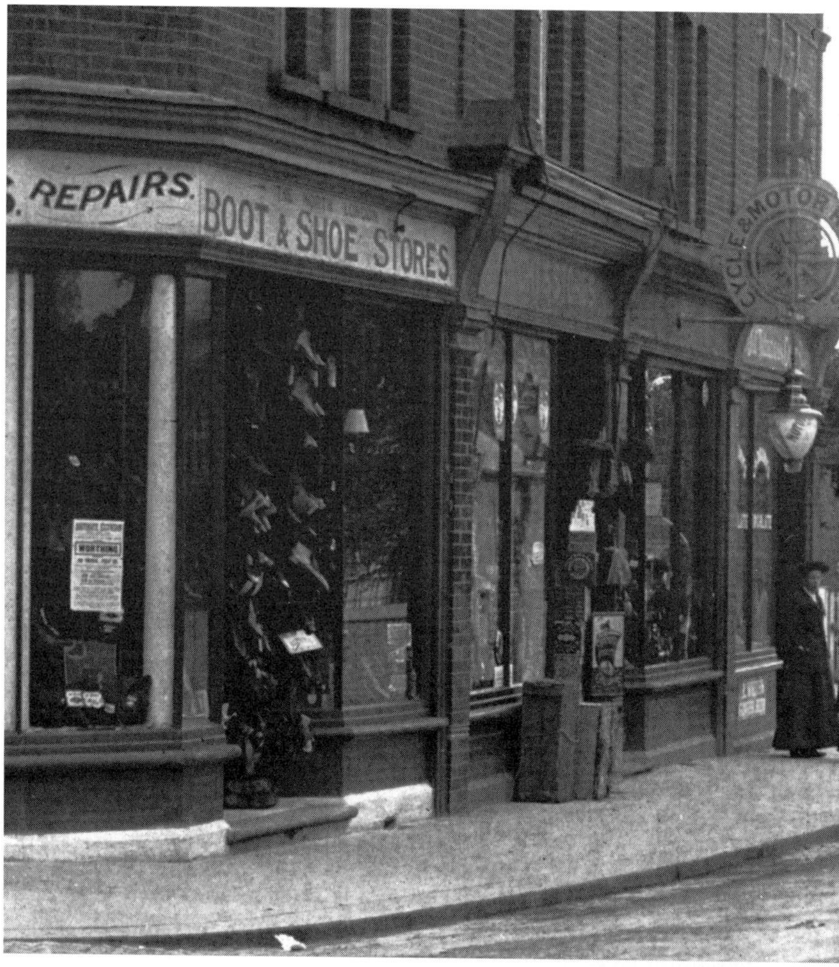

The Princess Royal arriving at Southgate in April 1913 to open the Queen Elizabeth Lodge. This was a Reformatory School for girls, initially licensed for 25 girls, and was run by the Church Army. The lodge was demolished sometime in the 1930s.

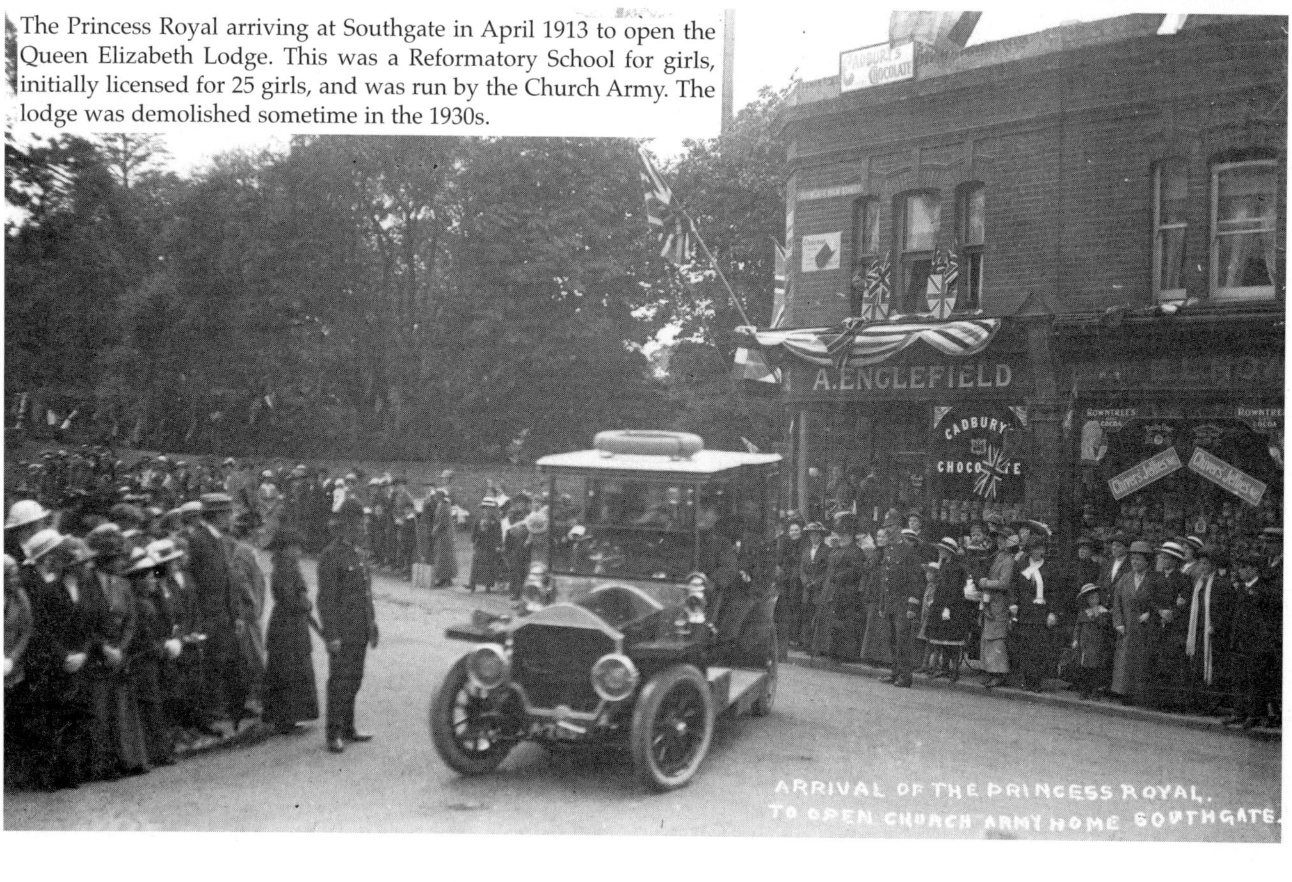

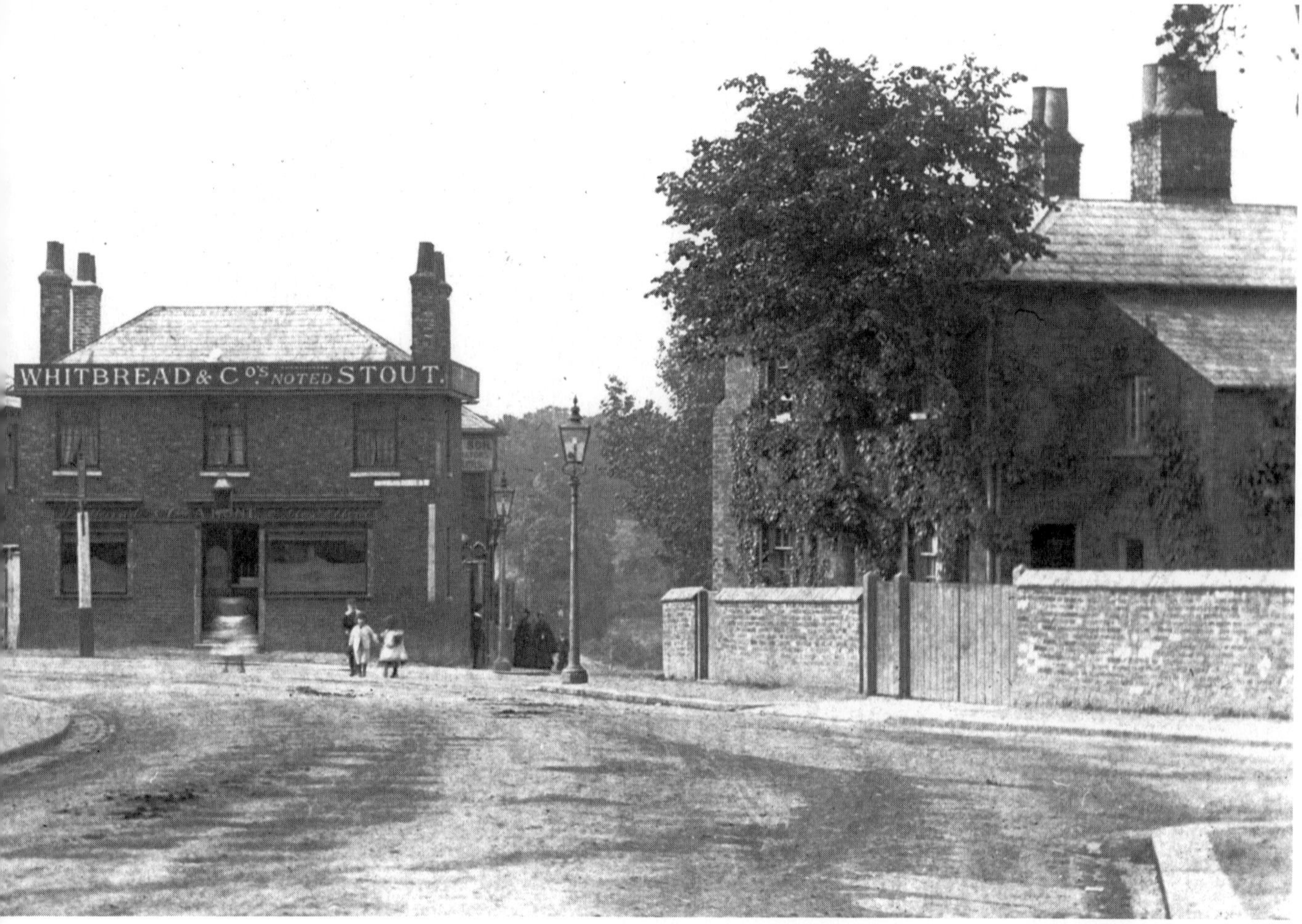

A last look back up old Chase Side. The Piccadilly Line Underground arrived in 1933 and all the old shops at Fiveways Corner and up the western side of Chase Side were demolished to make room for it. Soon afterwards the buildings on the east side between Conisbee's bakers shop (with the Hovis sign on the wall) and the tallest buildings further down the road were demolished and replaced by a new shopping parade. The remaining old shops, from Brigg's onwards, did not long survive them. Tube station signs were designed by Charles Holden; the one on the left belongs to Southgate Station, now a Grade 2 listed building.

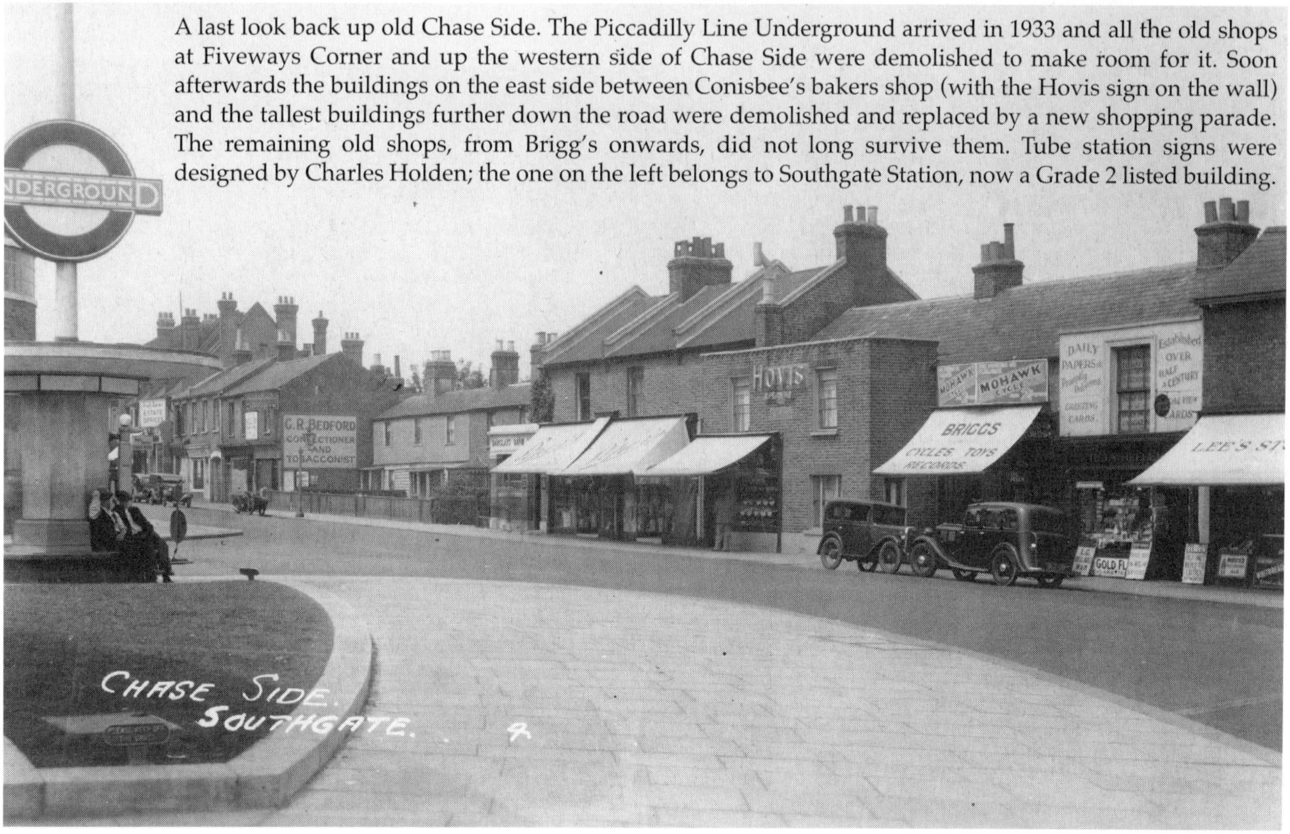

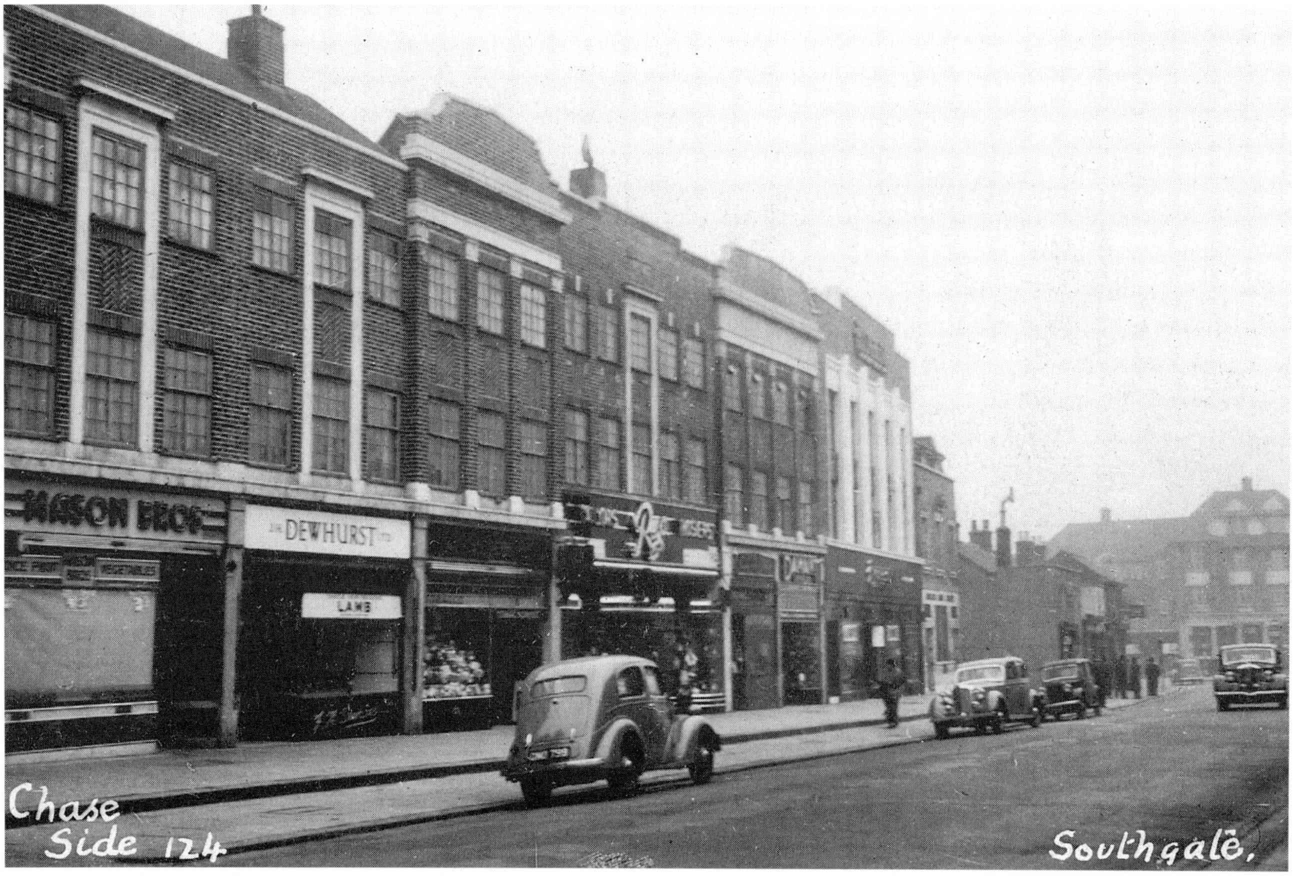

Above: This photograph, probably taken in the 1940s, shows the shopping parade built in 1933 that replaced the old shops on the east side of Chase Side leading down to Southgate Circus. A few older buildings further down the road did not survive for much longer beyond the time of this photograph.

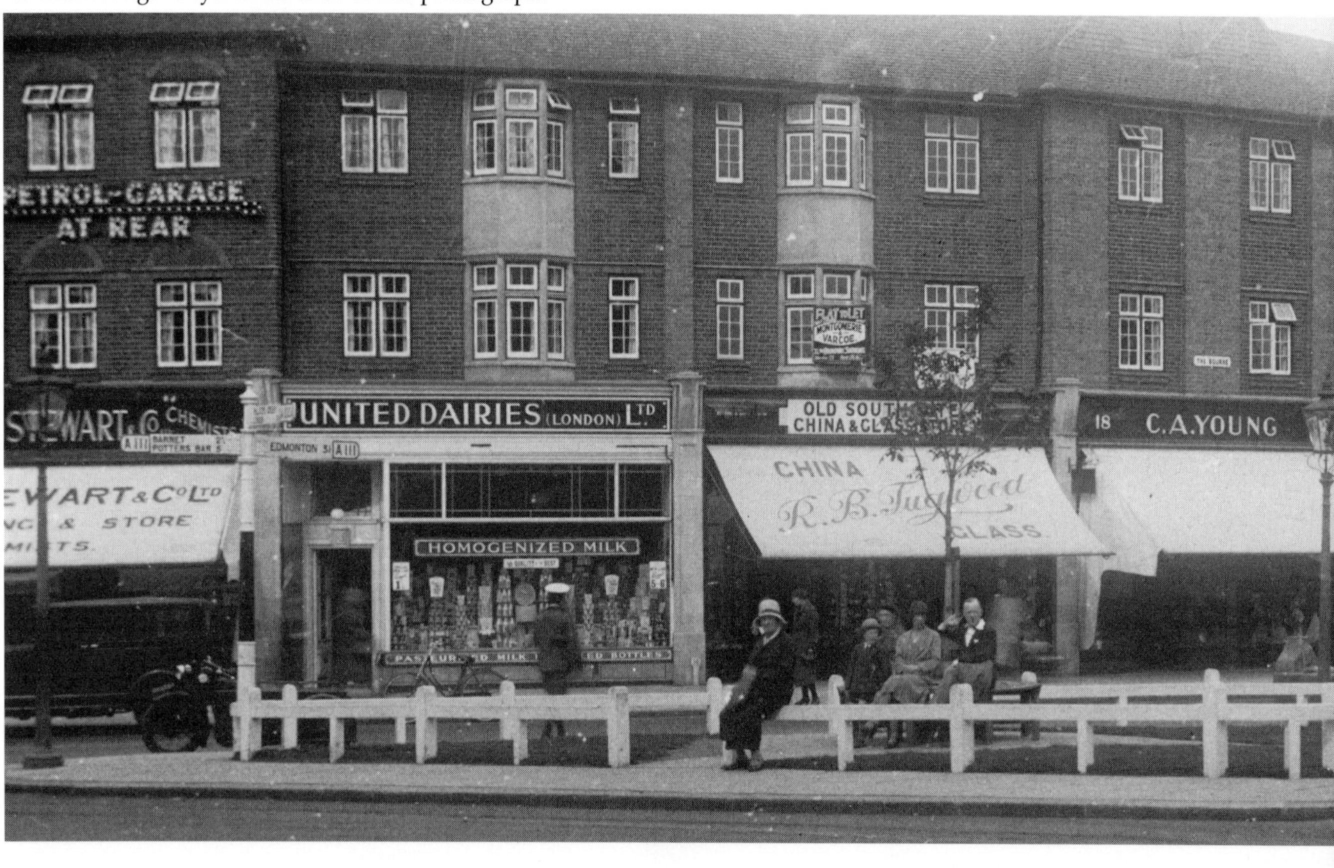

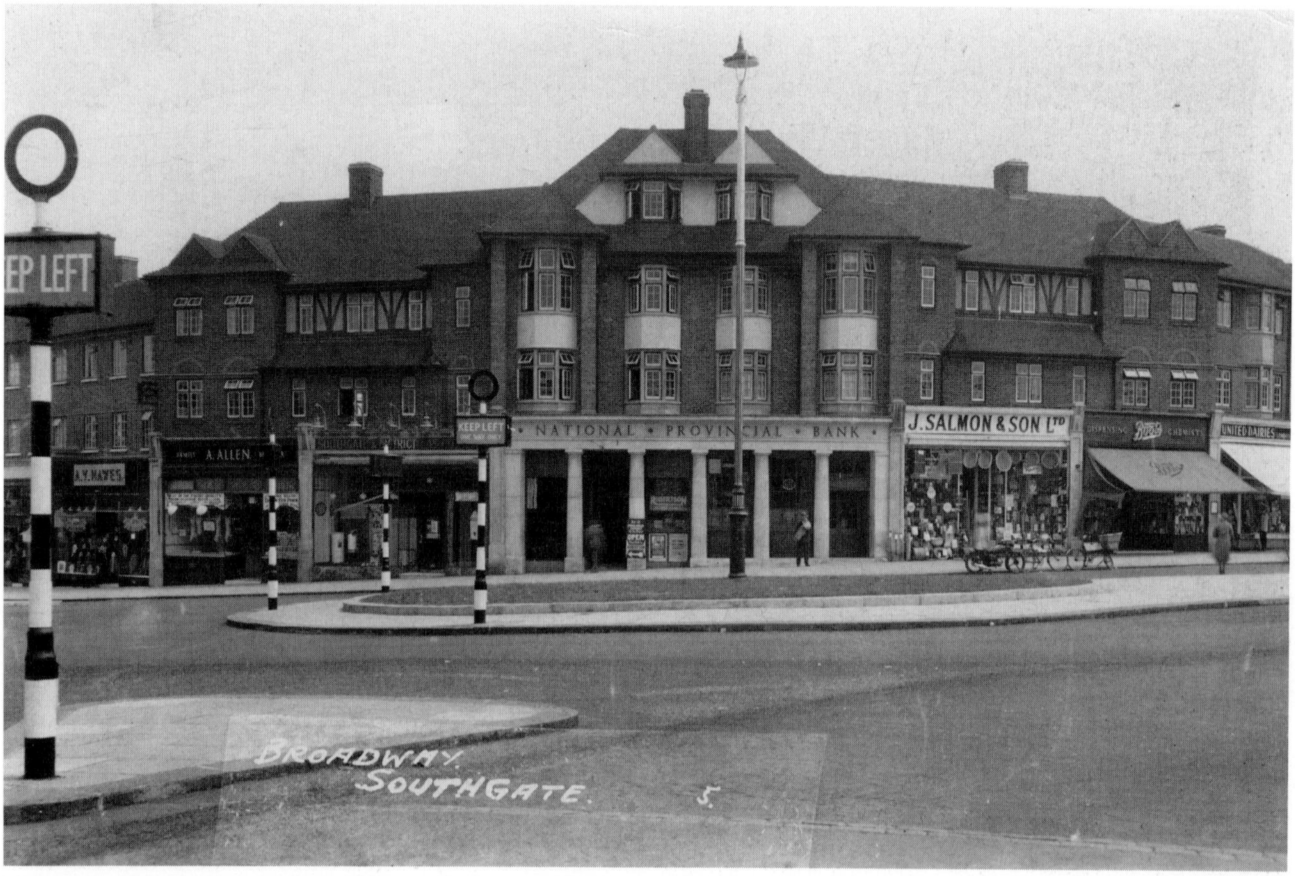

This is the vista that greeted travellers at the bottom of Chase Side at the former Fiveways Corner after the redevelopments of the 1930s. The parade was named Broadway; Winchmore Hill Road runs off to its left, the Bourne passes close to its right, and Southgate High Street comes in from the bottom right.

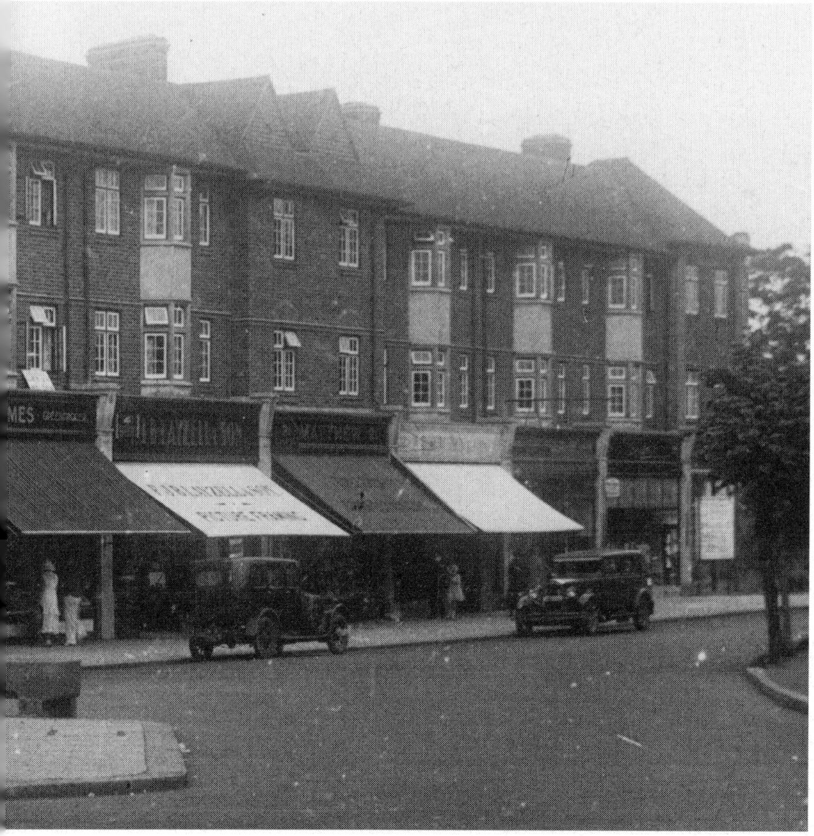

The picture on the left shows the Broadway soon after opening, when street lamps were still lit by gas and the central island looked more like a miniature village green. By this time the amount of horse-drawn traffic would be relatively small in comparison to motor traffic, yet a horse trough has been retained in the middle of a modern major junction.

By the time the photograph above was taken in 1938, the junction had acquired a one-way system round the traffic island and a tall electric lamp standard had replaced the smaller gas lamps. The fencing and seating on the island in the earlier picture had gone and the island itself had been reshaped.

The two pictures can be linked by the United Dairies shop whose sign is clearly visible in both. Note that R. Stewart & Co.'s shop, which in the earlier picture is advertising a petrol garage at the rear, had become a branch of Boots the chemists by the time of the later picture.

Today, the National Provincial Bank has been absorbed into the NatWest Bank and is adjoined on both sides by restaurants. Stewart's/Boots is now the Casa Cuchina restaurant whilst the United Dairies shop is now a branch of the HSBC bank.

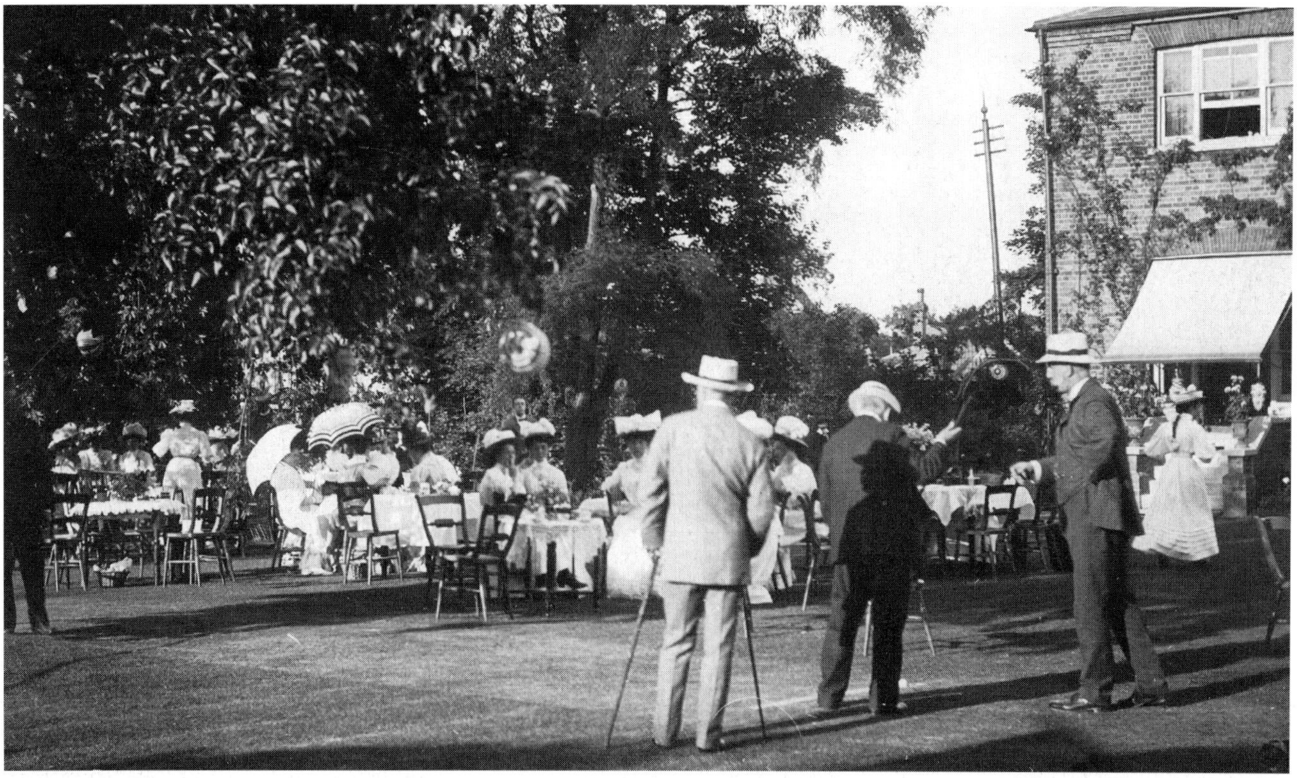

Our route from Southgate Circus now takes us south-westwards along the High Street. This used to be called South Street but had gained its present name by the mid 1860s. Almost immediately on our right are the gardens of a large house called the Lawns. Known to have existed in 1777, it was home for many years to Colonel Henry Francis Church and his wife Margaret. He died in 1899 at the age of 75.

In the 1903 Directory, the house was occupied by Messrs Vivian, Ransome & Bawtree, physicians and surgeons. It was also the home of Andrew Sidney Ransome, surgeon and medical officer of health to Southgate UDC, who lived here until 1927. The house was demolished in 1933 to make way for the tube.

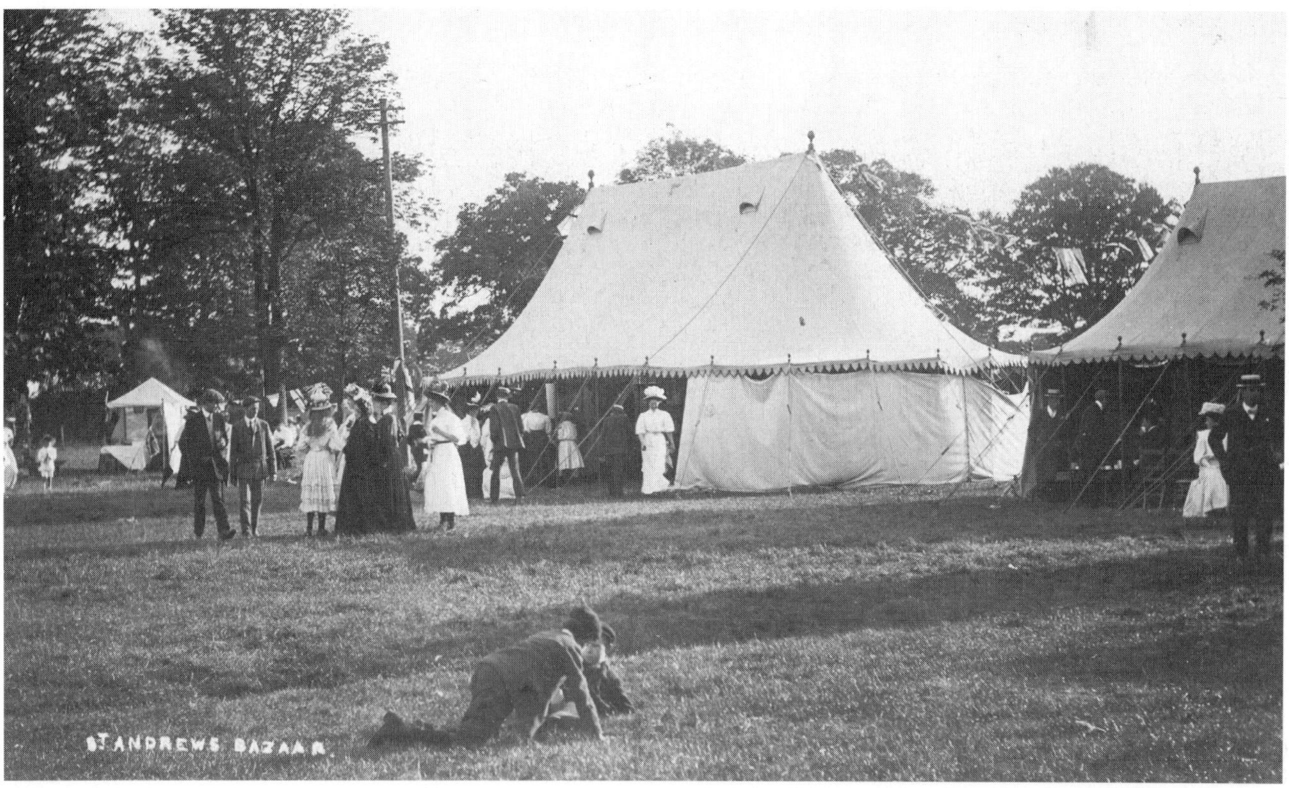

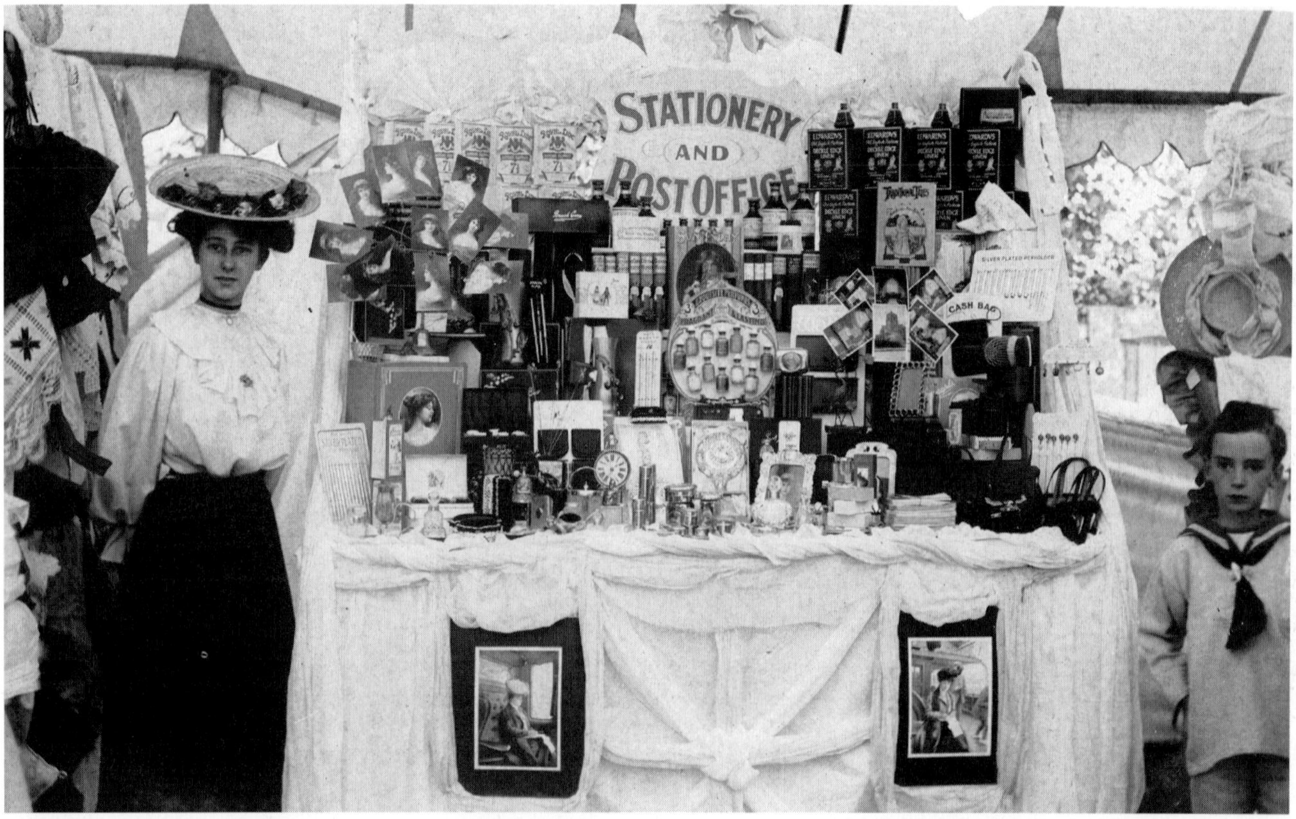

St Andrews Bazaar was held every summer in the Lawns' extensive grounds until about 1914. Marquees were erected, stalls were set up and everyone dressed up in their best finery. In the picture below the shield bearing the letters 'ER' indicate that these photographs were taken in Edwardian times. It's interesting to see that the stall with the shield is named 'Ye Olde Village Shoppe' which shows that the fashion for adding an 'e' to the end of a word to make it appear old and quaint is nothing new.

The attractive young lady on the stationery and post office stall above is selling a varied range of perfumes, trinkets, linen and photographs which may have been of beauties of the day, whilst the two pictures on the front of the stall show an elegant lady sitting in a very plush first class railway carriage.

The large white marquee on the lawn opposite left is probably serving refreshments, whilst the preponderance of men around the darker one suggests that it was the beer tent. Glorious days!

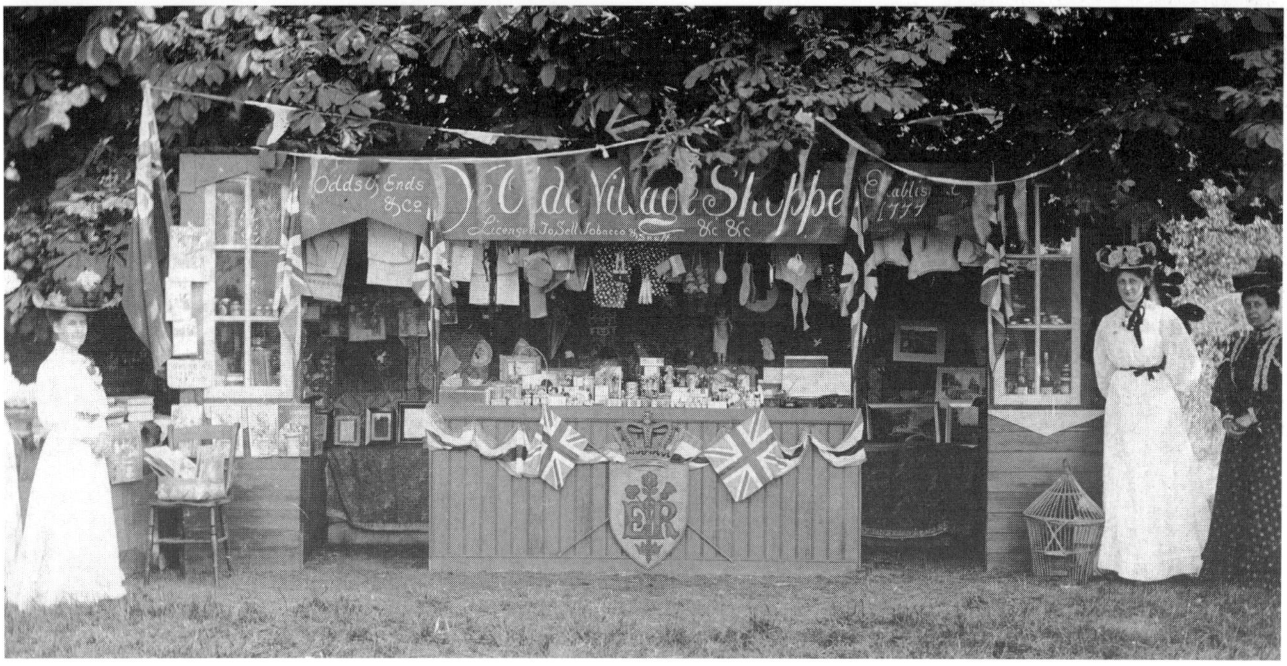

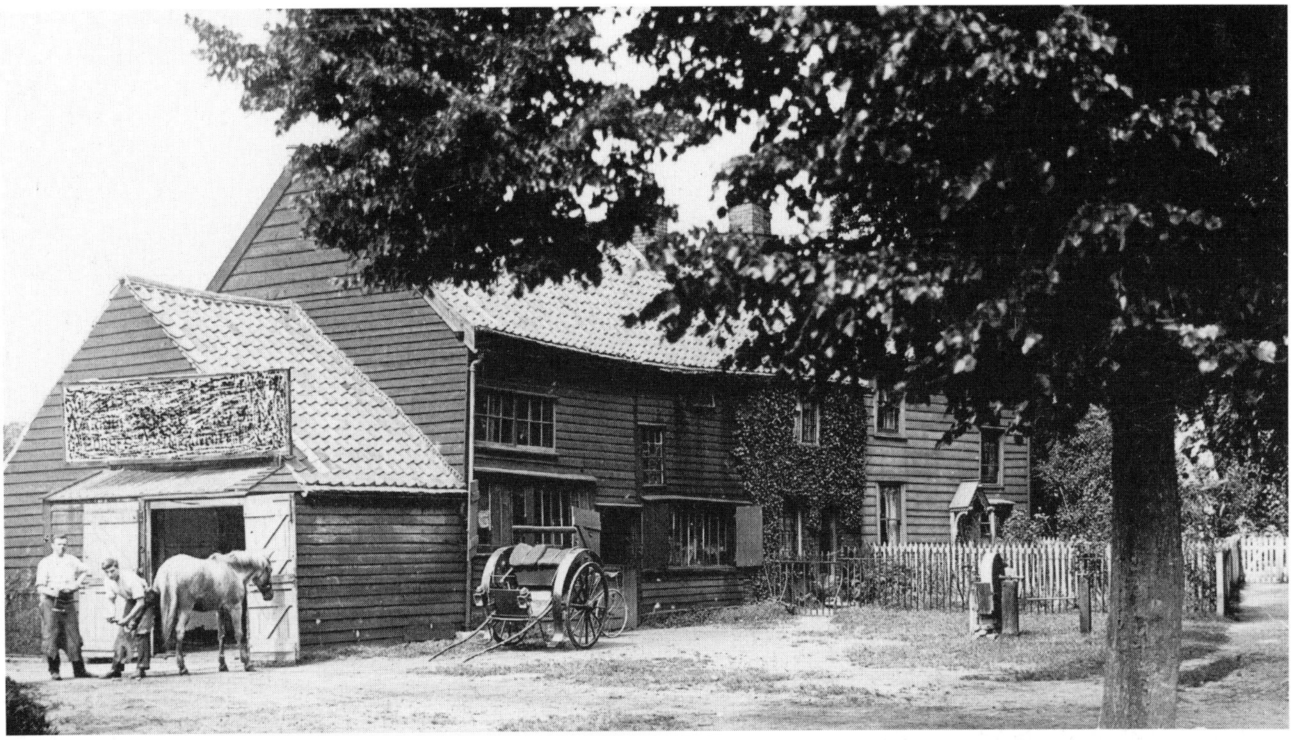

Back on the High Street and only a few yards beyond the Lawns' gardens was the village smithy. The building was about 300 years old and for generations the blacksmith had been a member of the Gladwin family, although by the early years of the twentieth century it was a man named Kettle. The last blacksmith was Ralph Brown who was there from 1911 until the smithy was closed and demolished in 1932 when the area was redeveloped. Ashfield Parade now stands on the site.

It is a mystery why the wording on the signboard has been scratched out in the photograph. A postcard, similar in detail to the photograph, shows the name of William J. Cain, gas and hot water engineer, locksmith, bellhanger and farrier, and who advertised 'horses shod on the improved principle'.

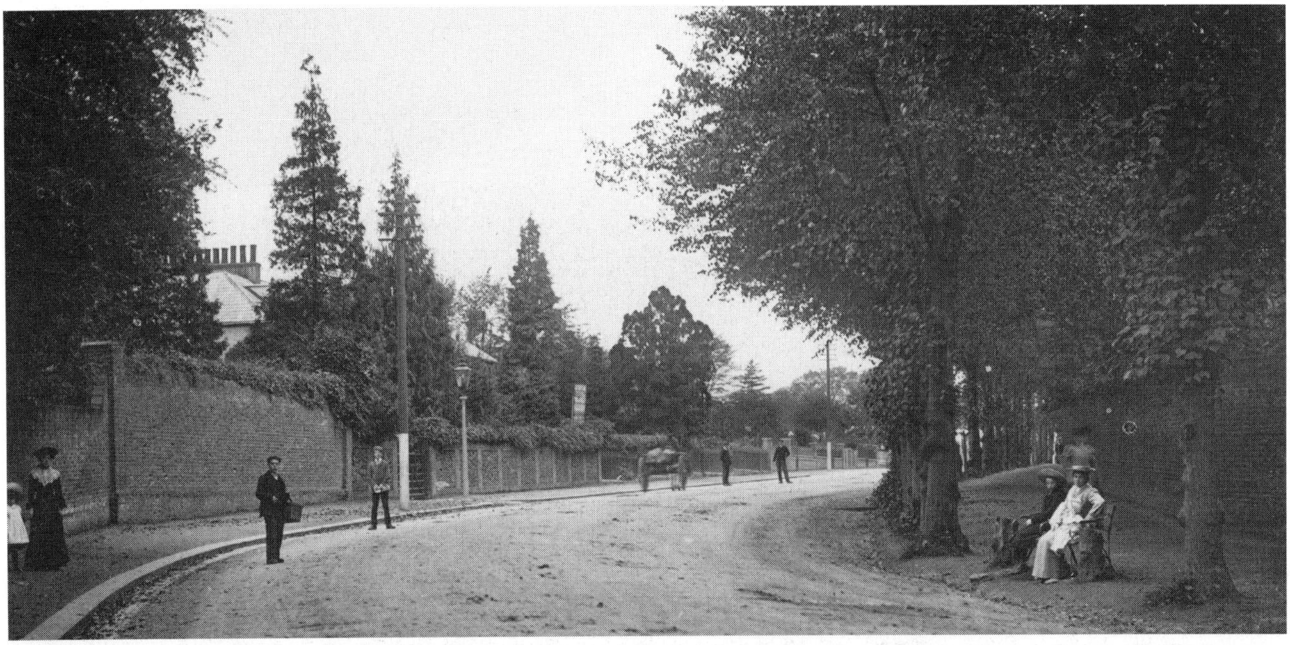

Continuing down High Street, this picture and the one top right are looking back towards Southgate Circus. Notice the trees lining the road and the absence of a paved footpath on the side where the ladies are sitting.

Joining on the left in the top right picture is Blagdens Lane, an ancient road that was marked on the 1801 Enclosure map and which was named after Robert Blagden who, in the mid-nineteenth century, ran a boys' boarding school in a house in Southgate High Street. Once upon a time it was called Zion Lane because Mr Blagden ran Zion House Academy on the corner of High Street.

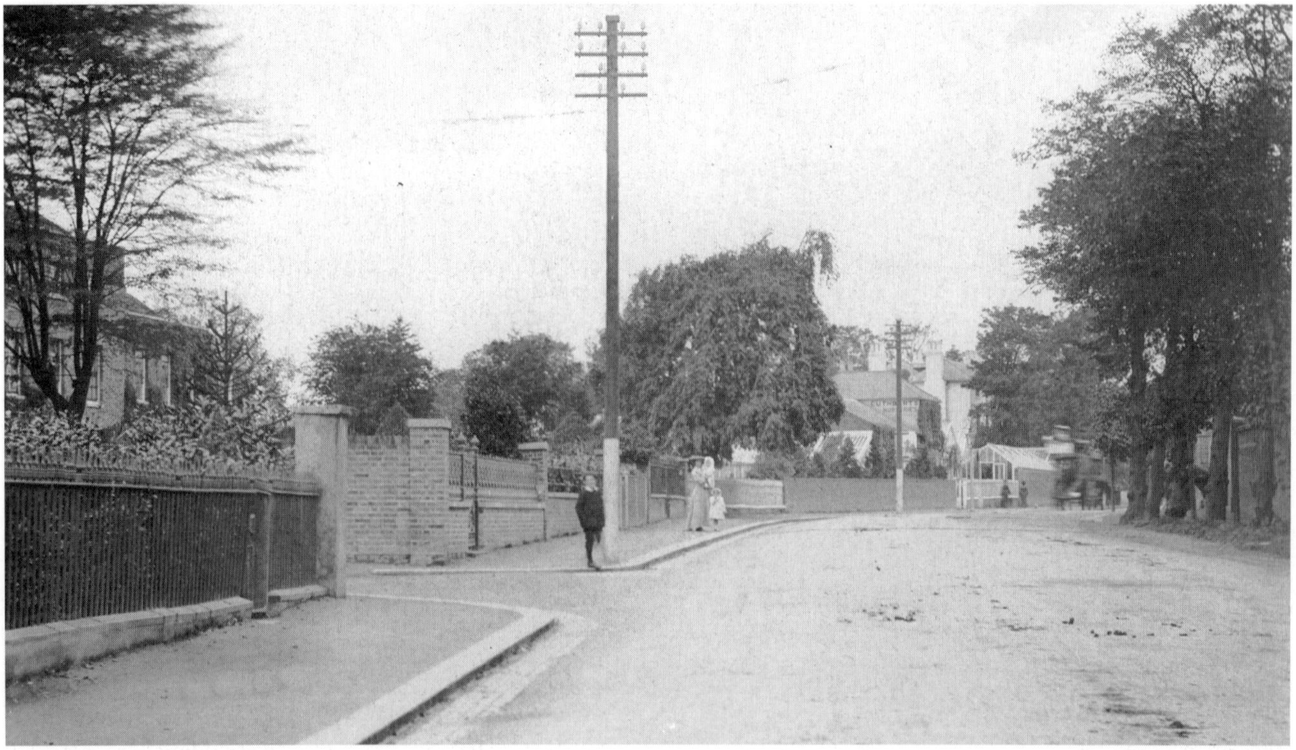

The attractive houses on the left beyond Blagdens Lane were once occupied by a poultry dealer, music teachers and surgeons, then came Cuthbert's nurseries whose sign can be seen on the side of the large building. The firm was founded in the 1790s by James Cuthbert, a Scotsman from Cupar in Fife, and by mid-Victorian times there were extensive glasshouses behind the building. They were regular exhibitors and prizewinners at the Royal Horticultural Society shows. Unfortunately trade began to decline after the First World War; the family sold the business in the early 1930s but the name was kept and continued to be famous for flowers, especially roses. The sites of the building and nurseries are now part of Southgate College.

The 1930s view below was taken from a similar position as the last two. The large house on the left is Wyphurst, which was destroyed by a bomb during the Second World War. Two women, aunts of the well-known novelist Paul Scott, were killed in the blast.

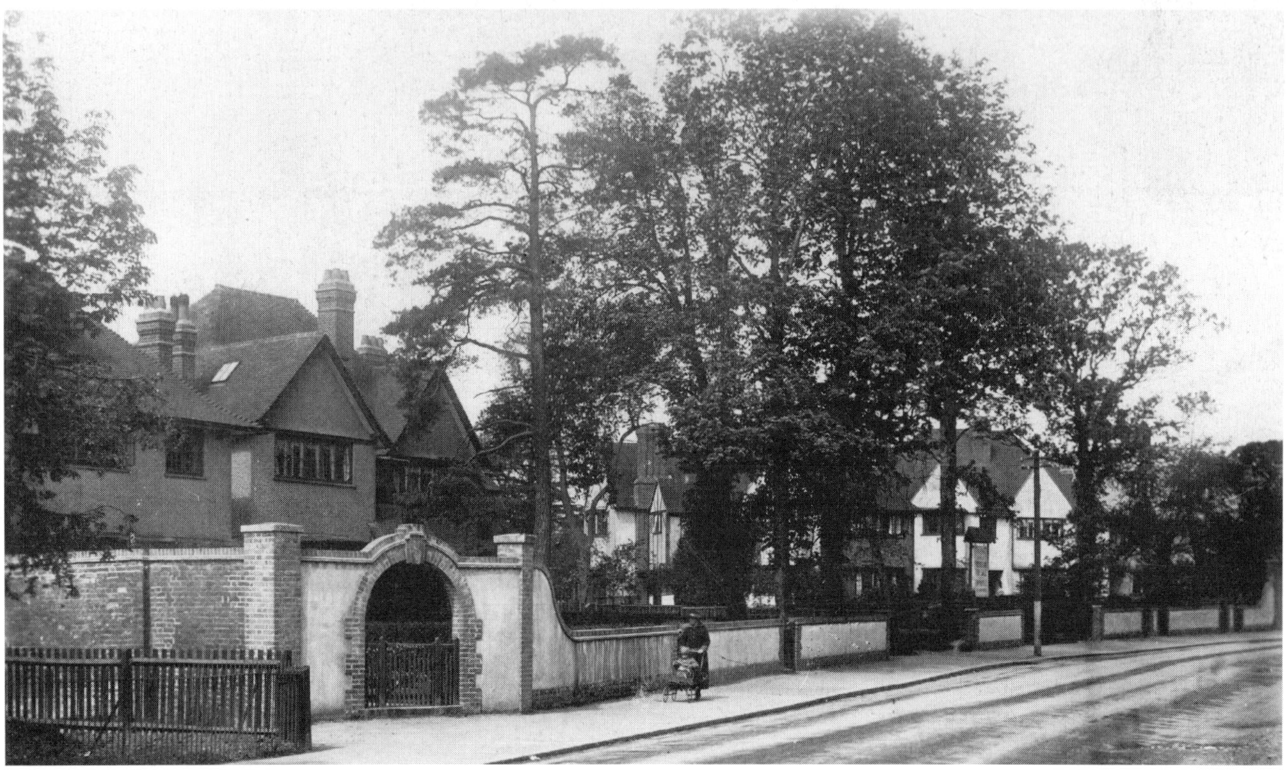

Resuming our journey down the right-hand side of High Street, a little way past Blagdens Lane we would have come to a large house set back from the road. This was Mayfield House and in the 1903 Directory it was listed as Miss Ellen Bowyer-Brown's Girls' School. This school was a very select and exclusive establishment but was also a successful one in its time. Unfortunately its time ran out; the school was closed and the house was demolished around 1914. Its name is commemorated by Mayfield Avenue.

In 1904 Miss Bowyer-Brown had also purchased a large Georgian house at Fiveways Corner between the Bourne and the foot of Winchmore Hill Road, which she named Queen Elizabeth Lodge and used as a preparatory school for Mayfield. It was demolished in 1930 and Tudor Way now stands more or less on its site.

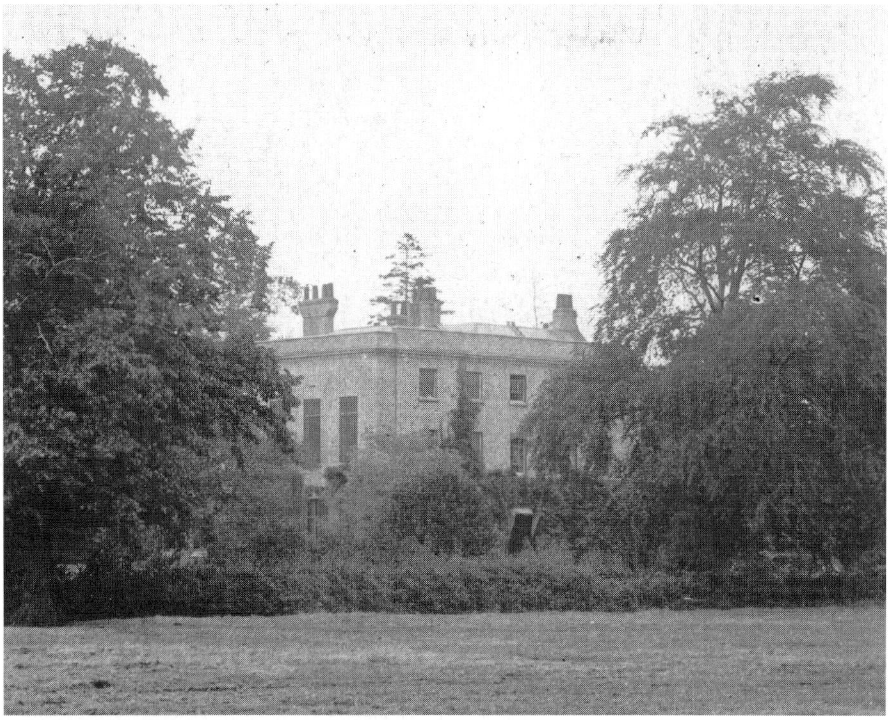

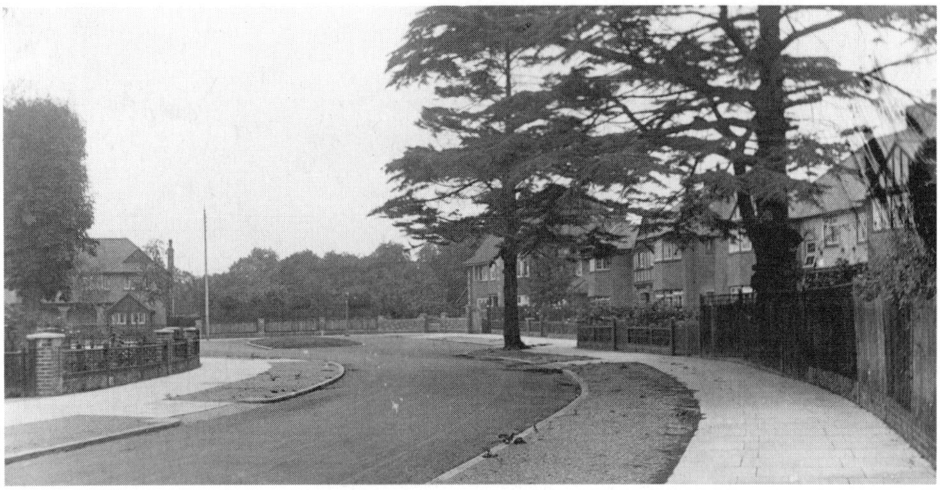

Just beyond Mayfield House a small unnamed lane ran off to the right, then turned left and joined Balaams Lane. It remained undeveloped for a long time but in the inter-war years a small estate of high-class houses was built on both sides of the lane, which was then renamed the Close.

Balaams Lane, which turns off High Street just after the Close and joins the latter at the beginning of Mayfield Avenue, is an old lane that appears to have been named after George Balaam, a blacksmith and farmer, who is listed in Kelly's Directory of 1845. This picture shows the old clapboard cottages which used to stand on Blewe Row adjoining the lane.

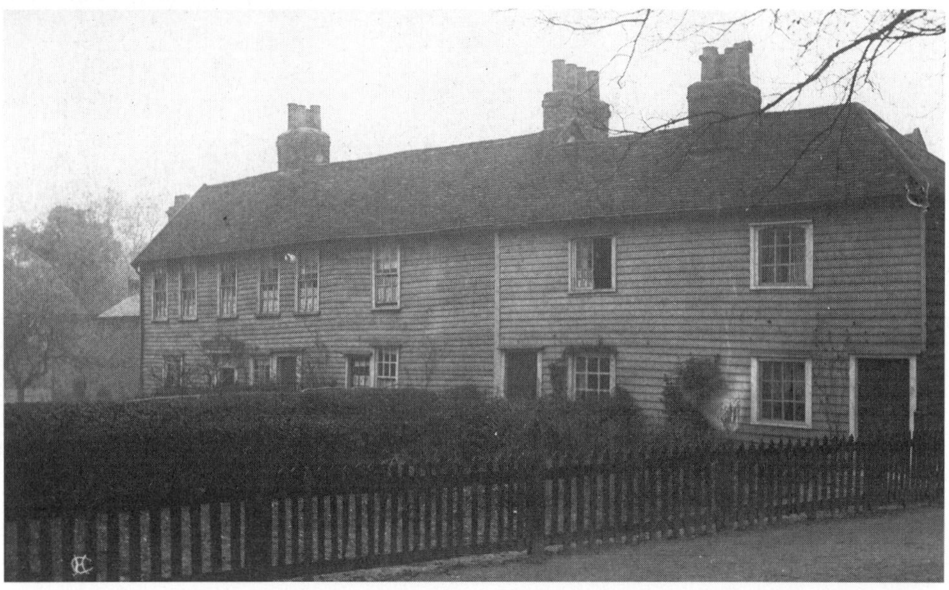

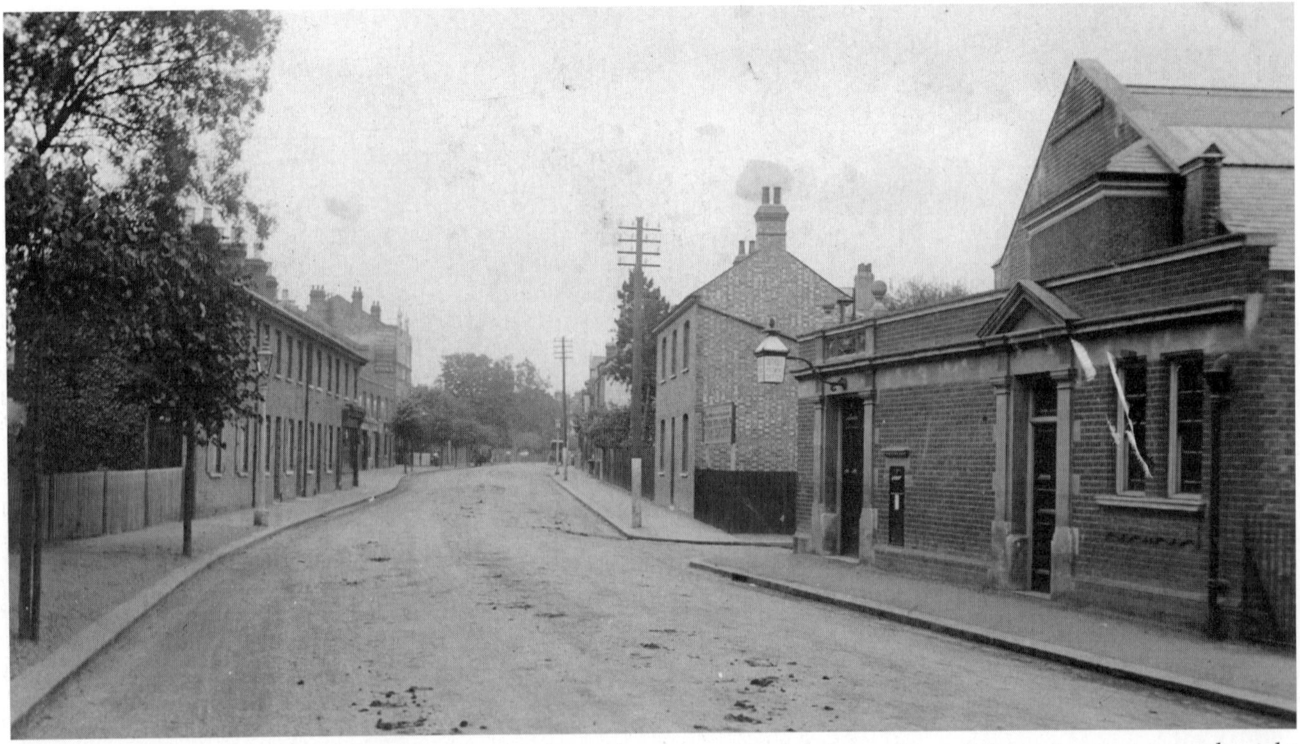

Now we are back on the High Street, looking towards Southgate Green in the picture above. Balaams Lane enters on the right and the building before it is the former post office and sorting office. The sorting office was moved many years ago; the building was enlarged and is nowadays Cherry Tree Flooring Services (on the right) and La Bottaga Italian restaurant on the left. Beyond Balaams Lane the building with three upstairs windows can still be recognised today as the Buffer Zone beauty treatment salon. On the other side of the road, the row of small shops beyond the terrace of houses is still there, occupied respectively by Antiques Fireplaces, R.F. Brenon building and decorating contractors and Crown Cars taxis. At the end of the row is the Woolpack Hotel which, before it was rebuilt around 1900, was simply the end two houses of the terrace. It was known to have been there in 1743.

The picture below shows much the same scene from the opposite direction, now looking back towards Southgate Circus with the Woolpack Hotel on the right behind the man on horseback. All the buildings on the other side of the road are still there today. The firm of Wilfred Lewis Best, plumbers and decorators, whose large sign adorns the side of their house, is nowadays H. Miller & Sons who ply the same trade. The house on the left with a signboard above the window belonged to Arthur Campion who was a tailor and was also clerk to the Burial Board Office; it is nowadays a private house.

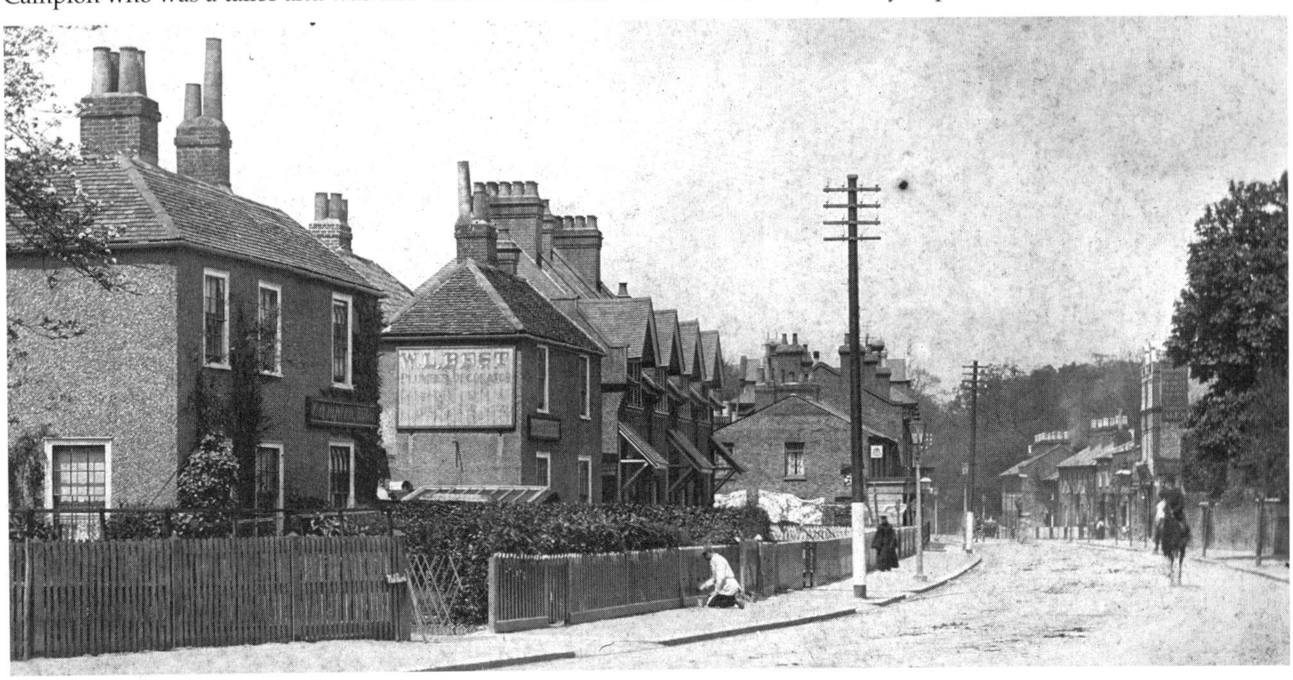

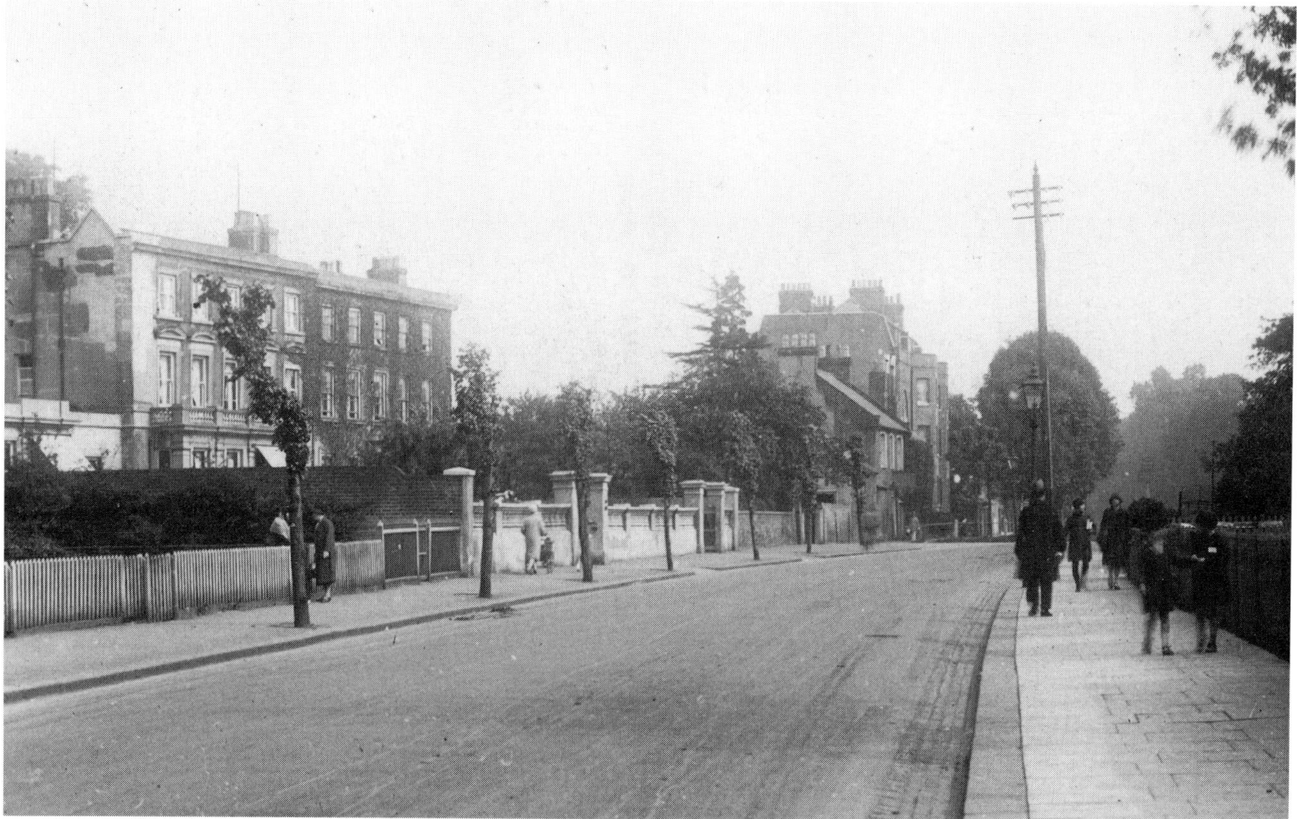

In this picture we are approaching Southgate Green, but how it has since changed! The left-hand side of the road used to be graced by the two dignified houses in this picture, Ashcroft and the White House. Sad to say, they were demolished some years ago and replaced by two blocks of modern apartments, which have been given the same names as their predecessors on the site. Happily, the taller buildings further along the road, Norbury House and Sandford House, have survived.

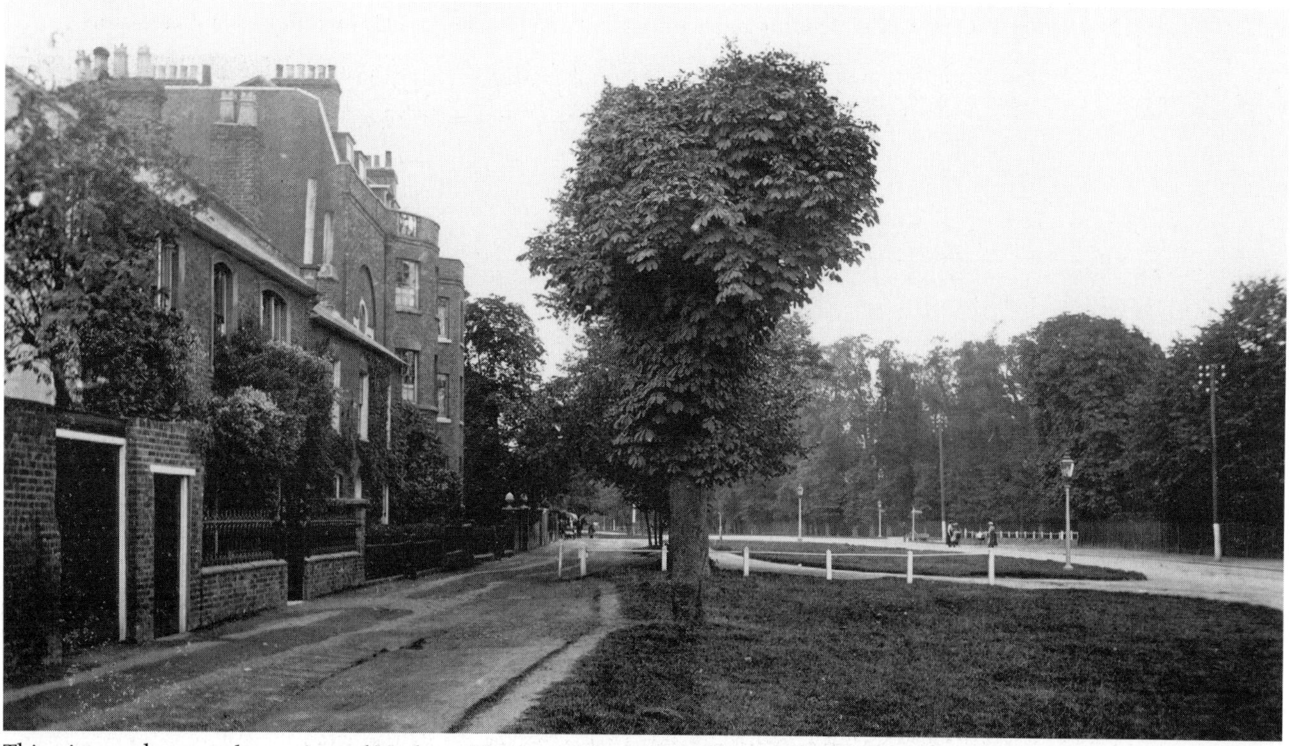

This picture shows a closer view of Norbury House and Sandford House with Ash Lodge in the foreground. A blue plaque since attached to the wall of Ash Lodge tells us that in 1881 it became the first seat of local government in Southgate, following the district's successful campaign to become independent of Edmonton.

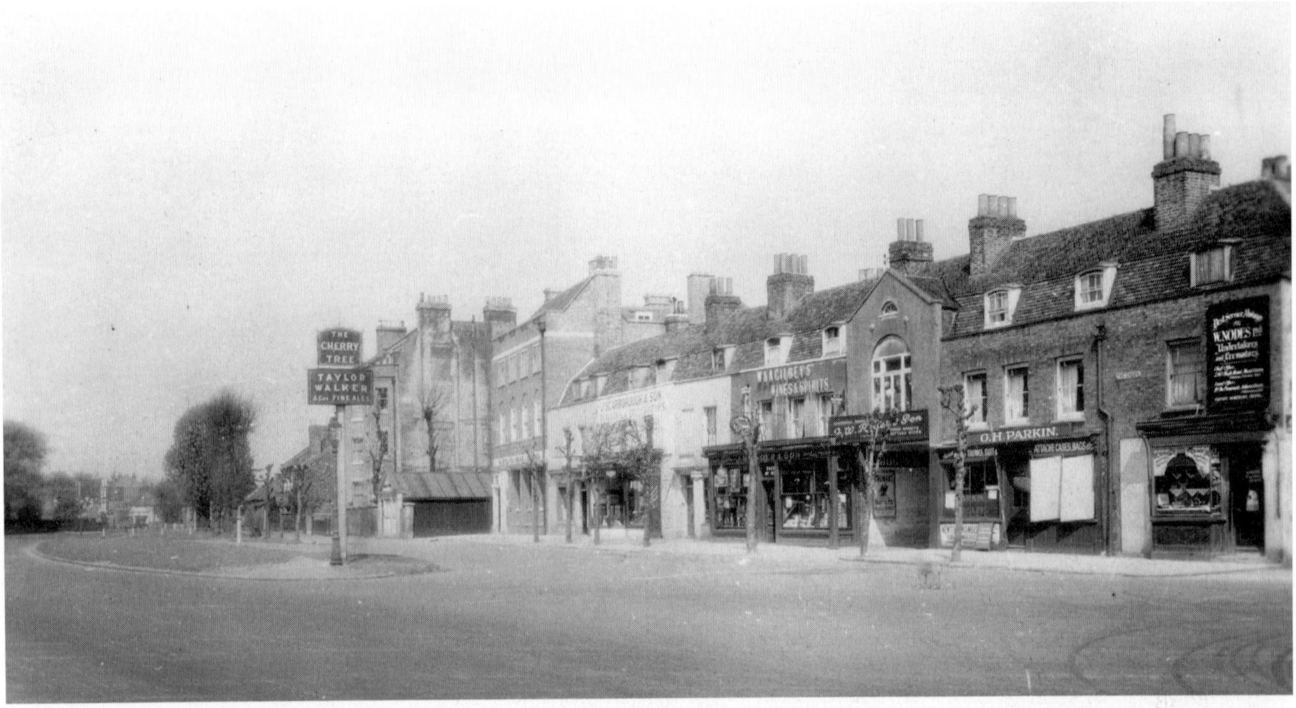

At last we arrive at Southgate Green. The area around the Cherry Tree and the Green was originally a separate hamlet called South Street, but by the middle of the nineteenth century it had merged with Southgate.

The Georgian cottages in the pictures were built in 1780 by the Valentine Poole Trust for the poor of Barnet. They were subsequently converted into shops, fell upon hard times and were only saved from demolition by the efforts of the Southgate Civic Trust. In 1981 they were reconstructed by Peake Estates Ltd and are now once again private houses.

The modern building at the end of the row is Barclays Bank, formerly the premises of the London & Provincial Bank, which was rebuilt in 1927 on the site of a house belonging to Revd Benjamin Waugh who in 1884 founded the NSPCC. It is now the Salcombe Day Nursery. The other businesses in the pictures belong to Joseph Scarborough & Sons, builder's stores, J.W. Ryder & Son, grocer and post office, G.H. Parkin, saddler and leather goods, and W. Nodes Ltd, undertakers and cremators.

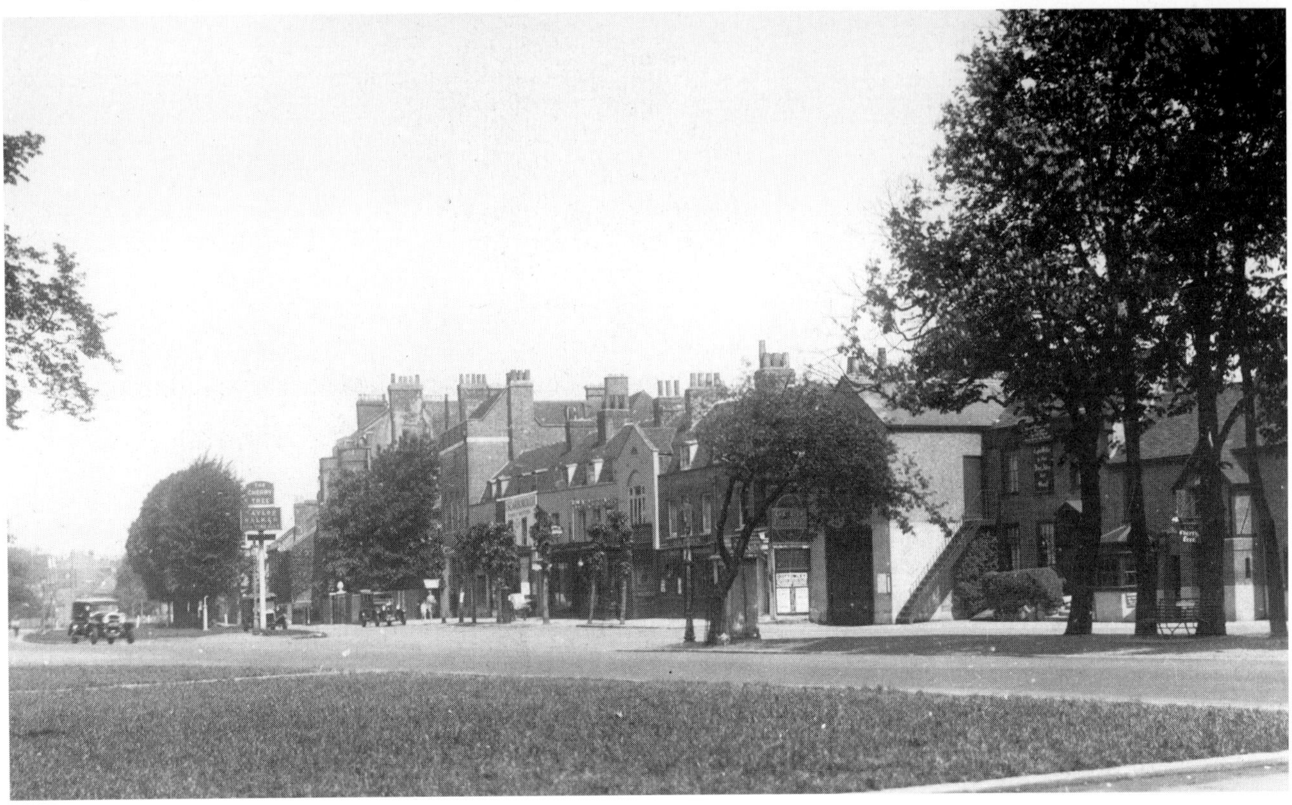

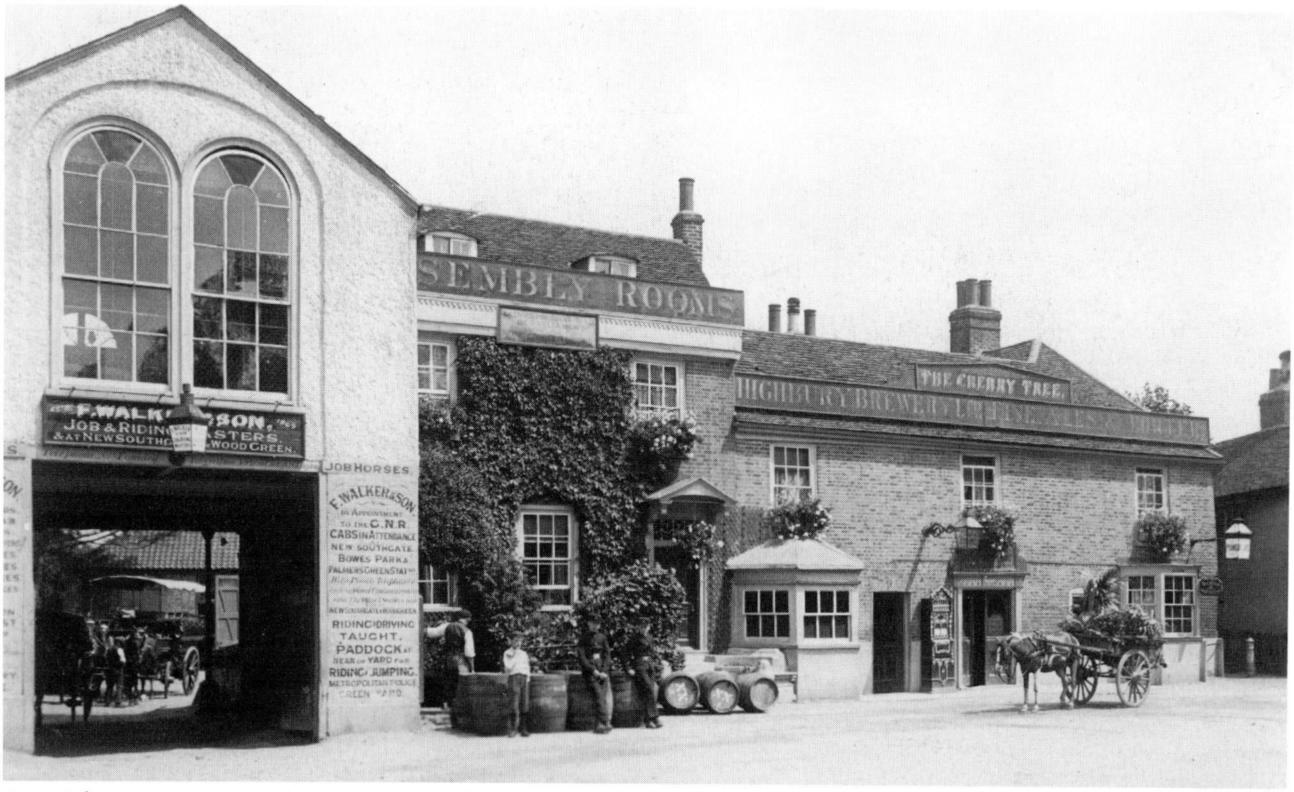

One of the most prominent buildings on Southgate Green is the Cherry Tree Inn, its name nowadays artificially antiquated to Ye Olde Cherry Tree. It is, however, genuinely one of the oldest inns in the area and is thought to date from the late sixteenth century. It is known to have been in business in 1695 and once was noted for its skittles alley. Several Friendly Societies used to meet here, the first being the Loyal Britain Society which met there from 1800 to 1833. It was (and still is) the centrepiece of Southgate Green, around which a tiny hamlet called South Street became established. In Georgian times the Cherry Tree became a posting inn; the coaches would drive through the entrance on the left into the courtyard for their passengers to disembark and enjoy refreshment and overnight accommodation whilst the horses would be stabled ready for the coachmen to resume their journey north the next morning. The entrance and the courtyard are still there but the stables have long gone.

The Cherry Tree was more than just a hostelry. The signs by the entrance advertise the proprietors to be 'Job and Riding Masters' who taught riding, driving and jumping to the Metropolitan Police and the public in their paddock at the rear of the hotel. Moreover, by appointment to the Great Northern Railway Company, they had cabs in attendance at New Southgate, Bowes Park and Palmers Green Stations.

The Assembly Rooms at the inn were at one time the only public rooms in the village that could be hired for social functions and meetings of local societies. Alcoholic beverages were supplied by Taylor Walker's Highbury brewery; this firm, which had so many connections with Southgate, was taken over in 1959 by Ind Coope.

In 1923 a bulge was discovered in the inn's façade. The resulting structural alterations included the additions of the porch and bays and the subsequent relocation of the entrance into the Mall which runs alongside the inn. The black weatherboarded sheds running alongside the Mall are now the inn's restaurant.

Returning to the Green, these are the village stocks which stood there for many years as an instrument of punishment for wrongdoers. The original stocks went missing during the Second World War and were replaced in 1953 as a coronation gift to the village. Although made of oak, this replacement eventually fell into disrepair but was restored in 2002 by the Southgate Green Association and is now back in its historic place.

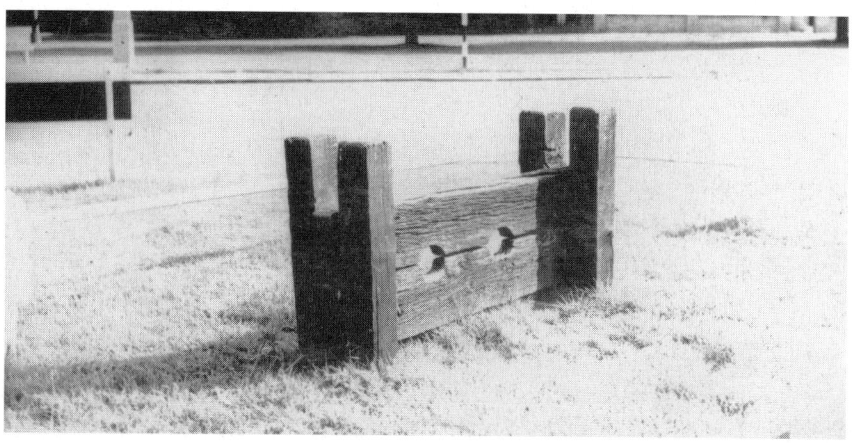

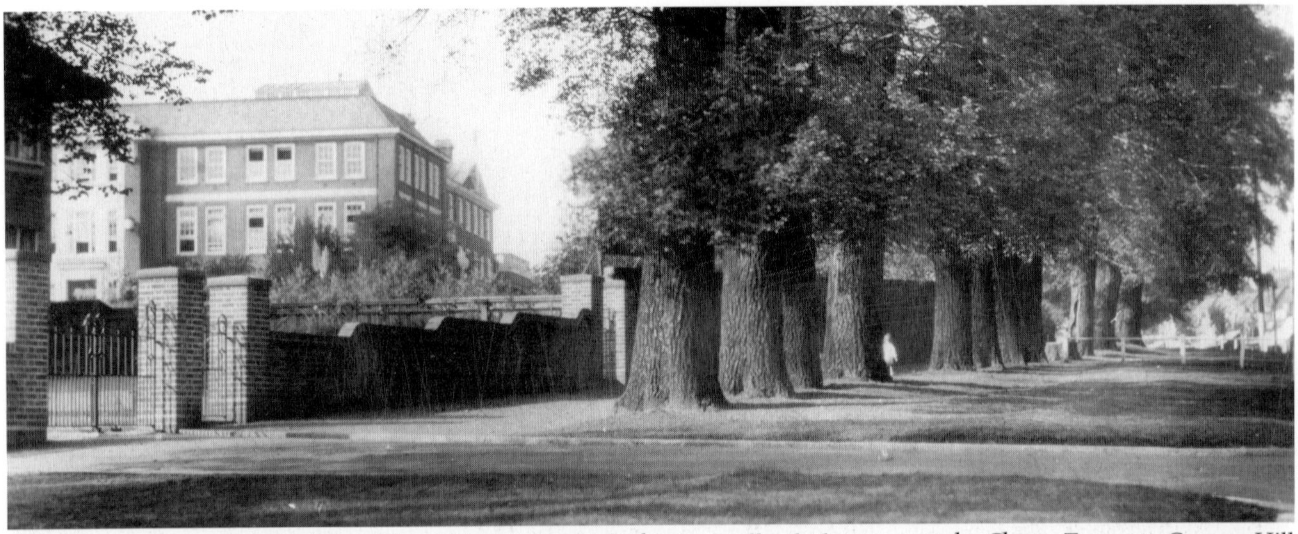

Before we further explore the Green, local history demands that we walk a little way past the Cherry Tree onto Cannon Hill and cross the road to the big house that used to be known as Arnos Grove.

It was built in the early 1720s as the successor to the home once owned by the Weld family and was the home of four generations of the Walker family from 1777 to 1918. The last of these comprised five daughters and seven sons; the five daughters all married but the seven sons remained unmarried to the end of their lives.

All seven sons were very good cricketers who played for Middlesex, but one of them - Vyell Edward Walker - excelled at the game. Born in 1837, he was a fine middle-order right-hand batsman and right-hand slow under-arm bowler, as well as being a good fielder. He played 52 matches for Middlesex between 1859 and 1877 and his first-class debut was for Gentlemen versus Players at Lords in 1856. He was, around 1860, the best all-round amateur cricketer in England. He captained Middlesex from 1864 to 1872 and also played for Bedfordshire. He died at Arnos Grove on 3 January 1906.

The family was very wealthy, being the Walker half of the prosperous Taylor Walker brewery firm, and were very generous in their gifts to the village over the years. We'll come across a number of these benefactions later in the book; the family name crops up time and time again.

After the last brother died the estate was purchased by Lord Inverforth, the wealthy shipowner, who stayed for 10 years until 1928 when the estate was developed and Arnos Park was created. The house and grounds were sold to the North Metropolitan Power Supply Company (Northmet) who built a large office block extension on the southern end in 1929 and another on the northern end in 1935, causing the destruction of the great portico which faced Southgate Green. The rest of the estate in 1928 was sold to developers who built the Minchenden estate and other nearby housing developments on it.

In 1975 the Legal & General Insurance Company bought the house and renamed it Southgate House. It later became a nursing home and nowadays it is divided into two parts. The main section of the house and the northern extension (of 1935) are now the Beaumont Retirement Home, operated by Barchester Care Homes, whilst the southern section, nearest the camera in this picture, is now a development of luxury apartments named Lulworth Court.

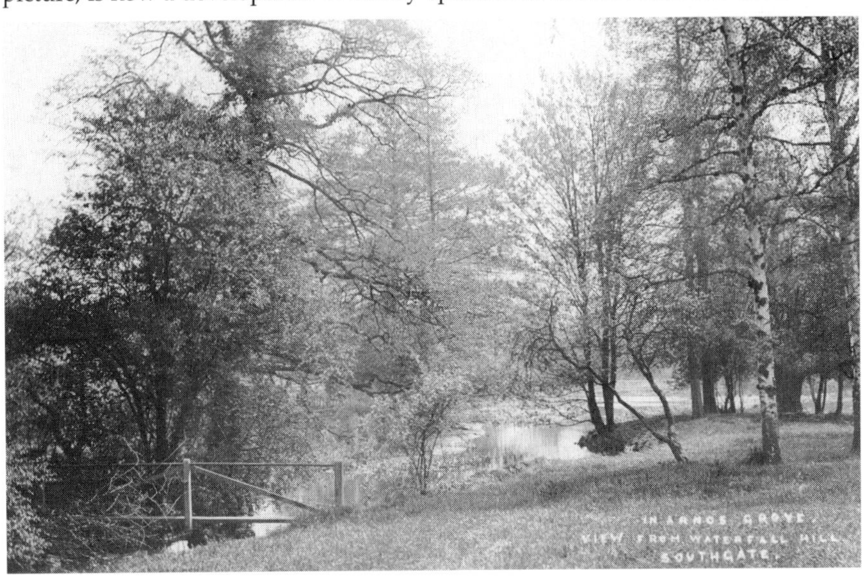

This photograph shows part of the beautiful gardens that once belonged to the Walker family at Arnos Grove, with Pymme's Brook flowing gently through a sylvan landscape. At the time the estate was put up for sale in 1918 by Russell, the last survivor of the seven Walker brothers, its boundaries ran from Cannon Hill down Powys Lane to Bowes road, then along to Landers Corner and back along Waterfall Road. This amounted to an area of around 100 acres and was purchased by Lord Inverforth, a well-known shipping magnate. He in turn sold it in 1928 and the estate began to be split up for development. Luckily, the council was able to purchase 44 acres of the estate and these now form today's Arnos Park.

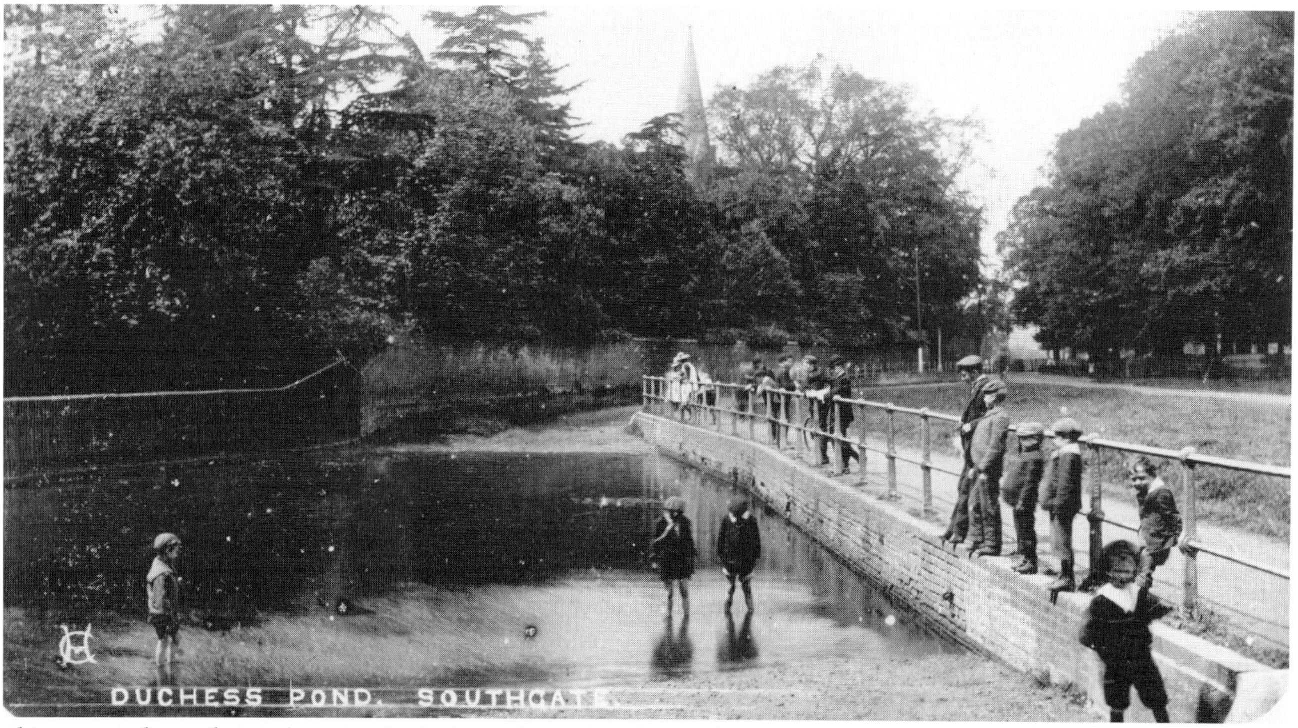

This picture shows the Duchess Pond, which was located on the south side of the Green. The gardens of Arnos Grove are on the left and Waterfall Road runs through the picture from the right towards Christ Church whose steeple can be seen above the trees. The pond was named in memory of the Duchess of Chandos who lived at the big house nearby called Minchenden. It was very popular with the young people of the village, especially on a hot summer's day, but redevelopment of the locality in the 1920s and the building of large houses along that side of the Green resulted in the pond being filled in during 1928.

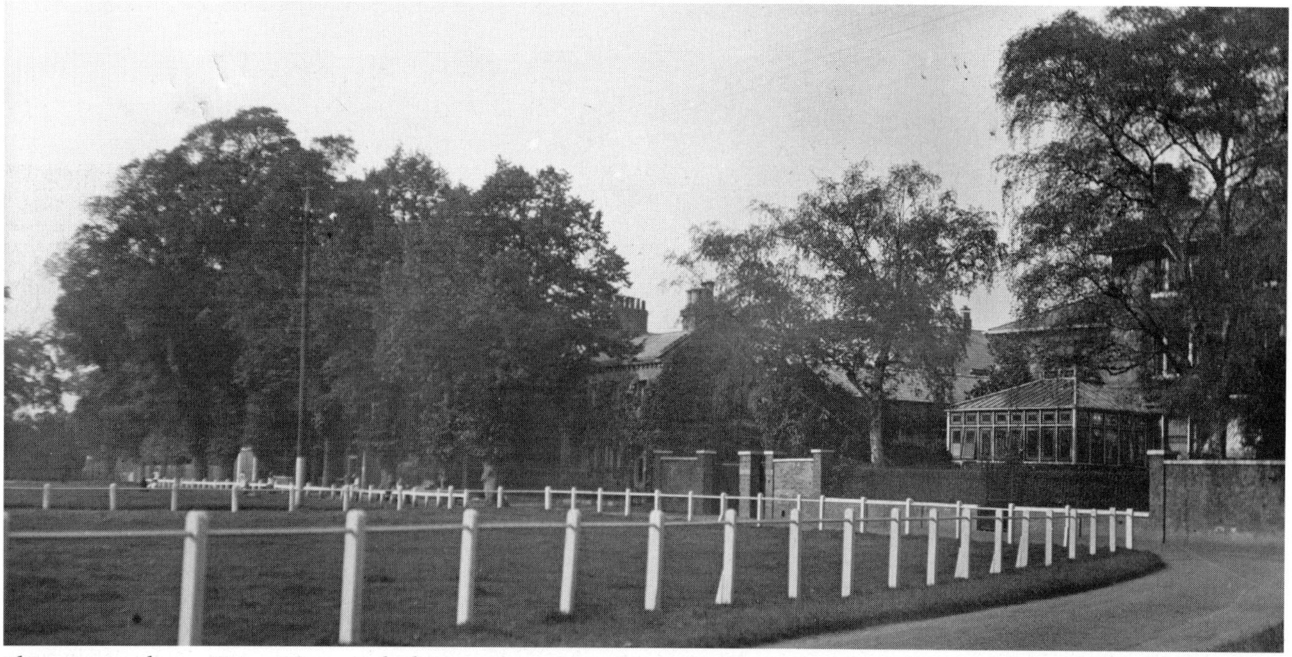

This picture shows Grove House, which was situated on the north side of the Green, facing south. It was a three-storied Georgian house, elegantly proportioned, with steps leading up to a porticoed entrance and a conservatory on the side.

For many years it was the home of the Barker family. Arthur Rowland Barker was an architect who designed many local buildings including the village hall (built in 1883 with accommodation for 400 people), the town hall in Palmers Green and the reading room (now the Southgate Club) in Chase Side. He came to Southgate from Matlock Bath in 1866 and married Miss Ada Turner of Grove House in 1869. He became a JP and held several public offices and was also a churchwarden at Christ Church for 25 years. He died in 1915.

The house was demolished in 1932 and replaced by Chandos Court flats.

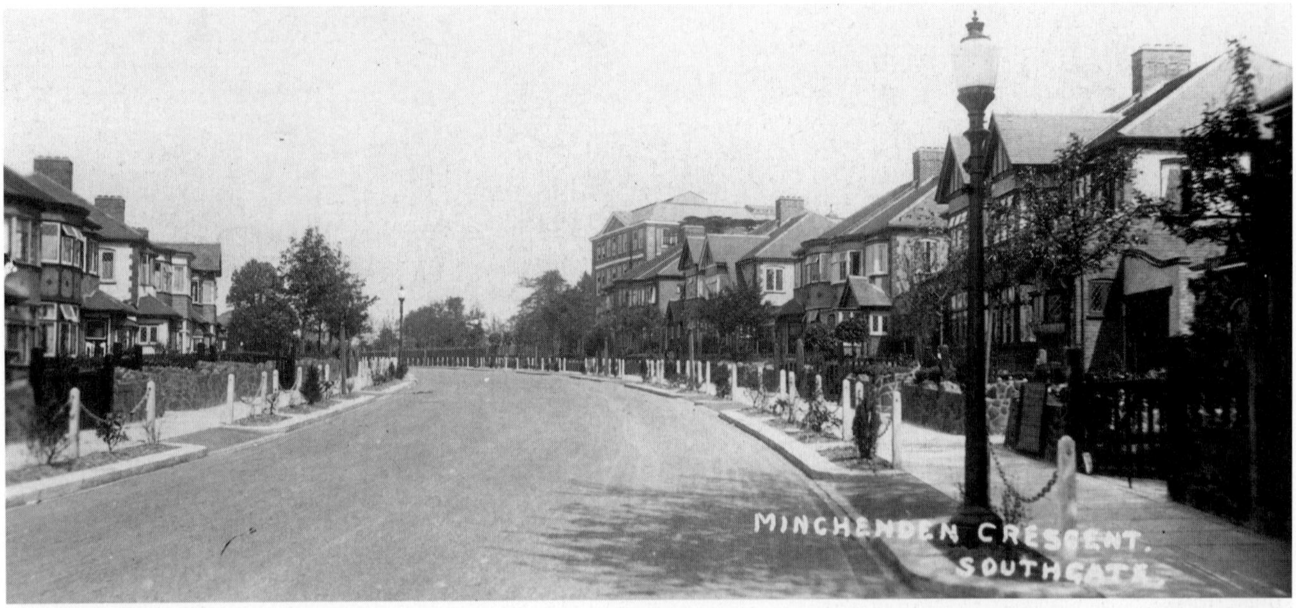

At this point we will cross the Green and head for Minchenden Crescent, which is situated just south of the Green and was one of the developments laid out after the sale of the Arnos Grove estate in 1928. It took its name from the large house named Minchenden, which also lay on the south side of Southgate Green. John Nichol, a wealthy London merchant, built this house in 1747 but he died a few months later and left the house and his fortune to his only daughter, Margaret. In 1753 she married the impecunious James Brydges, third Duke of Chandos, who was looking to restore his family fortunes, which had been dissipated by his father and grandfather. Minchenden House was demolished in 1853 when it was acquired by the Walkers, who incorporated its grounds into their Arnos Grove estate.

The crescent is in two halves, bisected by the road that runs from the Green down to Arnos Park. The picture above shows the southern part that was built first and the houses have good gardens with drives which has enabled many of them to add garages without sacrificing their gardens. The large building in the background is the rear of the former mansion of Arnos Grove as enlarged by Northmet.

The northern section (see page 6), which runs down to Chandos Avenue and then onto Waterfall Road, was built at a slightly later date than those in the southern section. The whole crescent had been completed by 1933 and overall it presents a very pleasing appearance today.

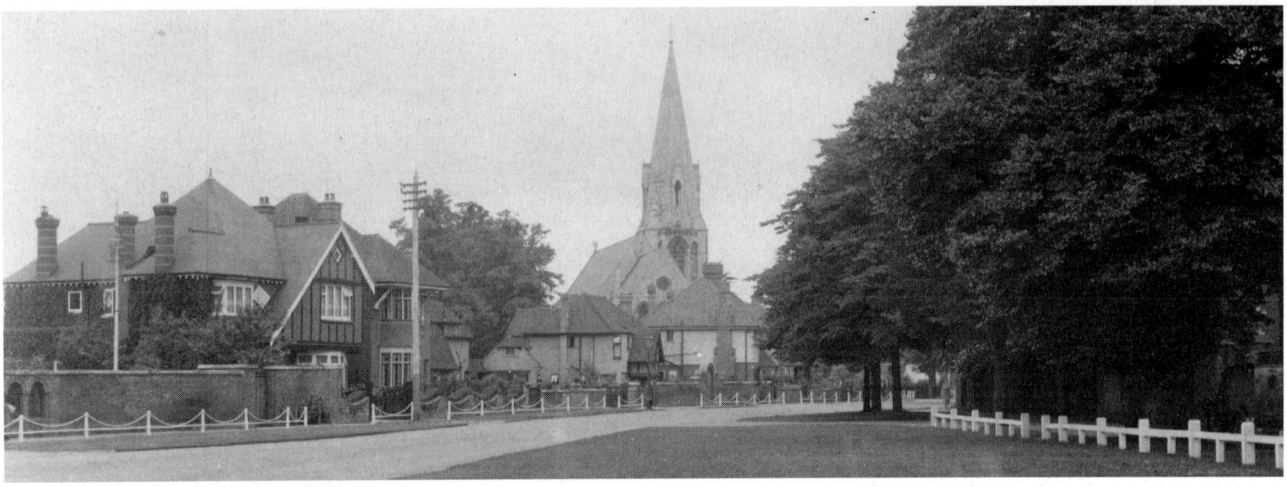

Returning from Minchenden Crescent to the Green, we turn left at the start of Waterfall Road and almost immediately come to Christ Church, which is a product of the Walker family's generosity.

Isaac Walker inherited Arnos Grove shortly before his death in 1853 and, when Southgate became a parish in its own right separate from Edmonton, in 1859, Isaac's widow (who was John Donnithorne Taylor's sister) gave land to build the church. She and her eldest son, John, were its two largest financial supporters.

The houses in the picture are named, from left to right, Endsleigh, Fontainebleau (behind the telegraph pole), the Homestead (set further back from the road) and Tudor House (with the porch). The next house is semi-detached, the nearer half being unnamed and the further one being named Oaklands.

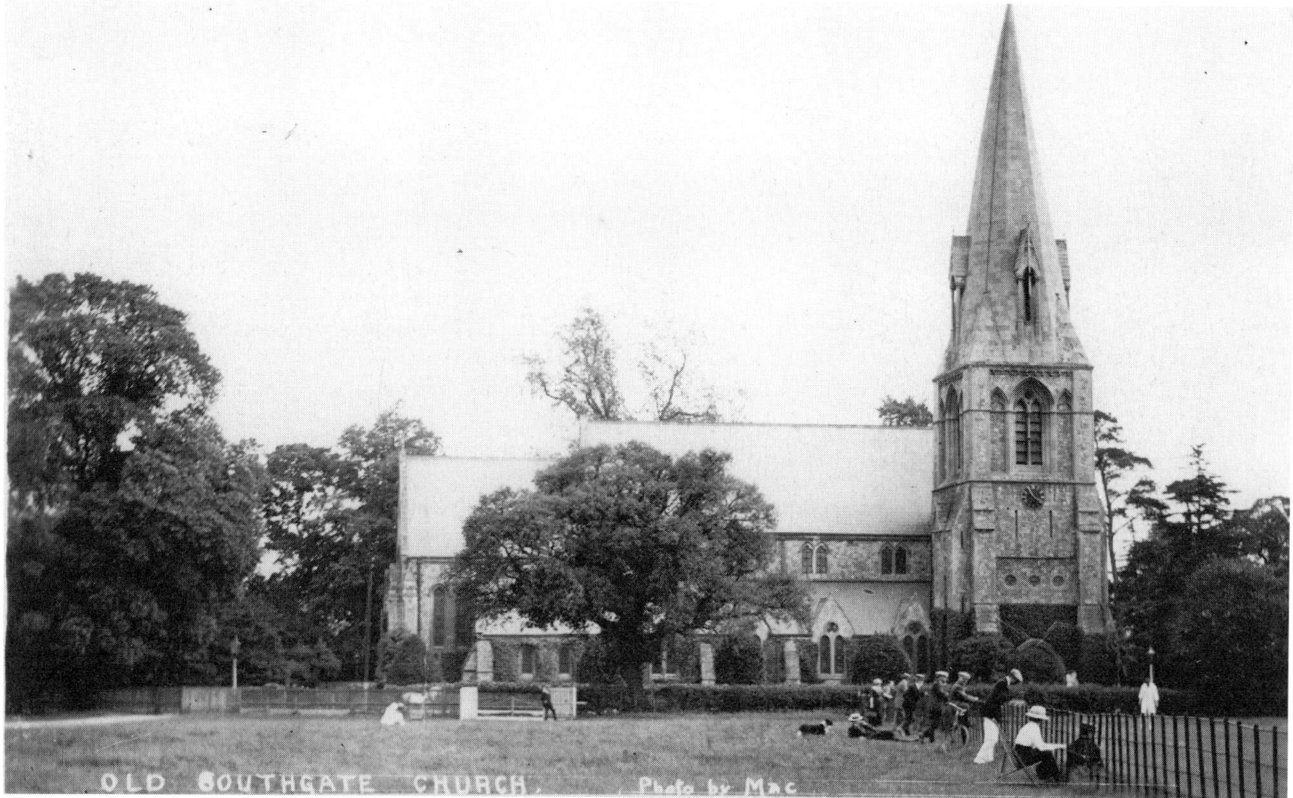

Christ Church stands on Waterfall Road just beyond the Green. It was designed by Sir George Gilbert Scott and was built in 1863 alongside the old Weld chapel, which was then demolished. William Morris & Co. supplied the fine stained glass for the windows to designs by Edward Burne-Jones and Dante Gabriel Rossetti. The clock was a later addition to commemorate Queen Victoria's Golden Jubilee in 1887.

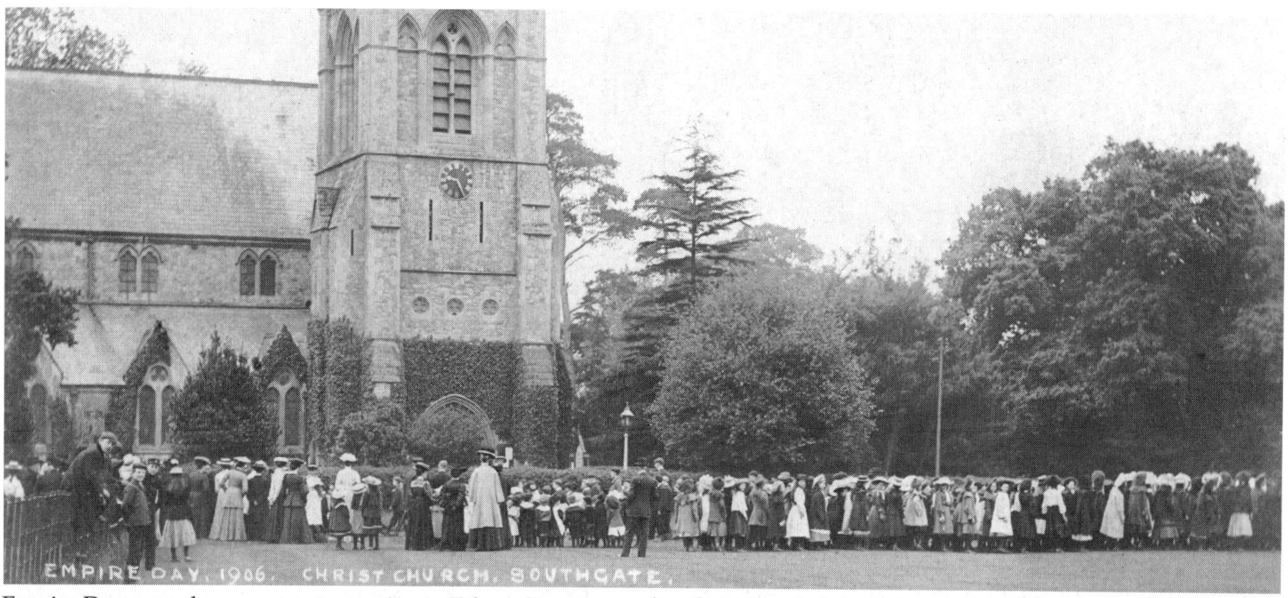

Empire Day was always a great occasion in Edwardian times when Britain ruled the largest empire the world had ever seen. The first Empire Day celebrations were held on 24 May 1902, which would have been Queen Victoria's birthday had she not died the previous year. In this 1906 photograph the scholars are dressed in their Sunday best and lined up outside Christ Church, probably to attend a service of thanksgiving and sing patriotic songs before spending the rest of the day at leisure on the playing fields just across the road.

Empire Day was not officially recognised as an annual event until 1916, although many schools celebrated it before then by allowing their pupils a day's holiday from school to attend its parades. Its significance waned in the 1950s as the empire broke up; in 1958 it was renamed British Commonwealth Day and, when that failed to inspire the public, the occasion was renamed 'Commonwealth Day' and the date was moved to the Queen's official birthday of 10 June.

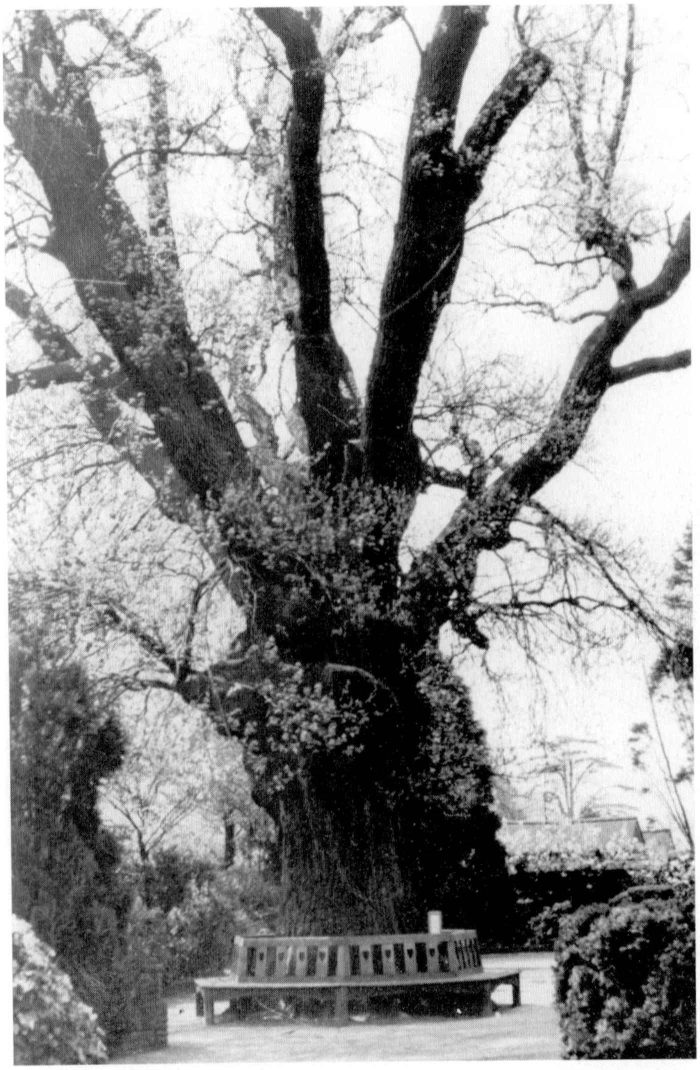

A little further down Waterfall Road, set in a small enclosure which was opened by the Mayor of Southgate in May 1934, stands an old oak tree known as the 'Minchenden Oak'. In days gone by this site was in the grounds of Minchenden House and the tree is the oldest living object in the area, as well as being the only tangible survivor of the Chandos era.

In 1825 it was measured at 15 feet, 9 inches in girth with a spread of 118 feet. By 1900, when it was estimated to be 800 years old, the measurements were 21 feet, 3 inches, a spread of 136 feet, and a height to 60 feet. It lost two major limbs in a gale in 1899 and has since suffered other damage and pruning, but it lives on.

The picture below was taken during a match between Southgate Cricket Club and the MCC on 16 June 1910. The ground, which used to be known as Chapel Fields and is just across the road from Christ Church, is the home of Southgate Cricket Club and for many years has been the centre of the villagers' sporting activities and celebrations. John, the eldest of the Walker brothers, spent large sums on returfing the ground and he founded Southgate CC in 1855.

The seven Walker brothers were all fine county players and the annual matches between the village and an All England XI on what now became called the Walker Ground have passed into folklore. All the great cricketers in England would gather here to play the men of Southgate. Crowds of 10,000 would flock to watch these great social and sporting occasions, spread over three days in August. There was always a great carnival atmosphere with flags and bunting in profusion and the band of the 2nd Life Guards providing the musical entertainment. The hosts and organisers of these events were the Walker brothers themselves. Their generosity was renowned and their home, Arnos Grove, would be thrown open for their guests to use. Between 1858 and 1863 inclusive, there were six three-day matches between an All England XI and the 16 of Southgate, of which Southgate won five and lost one. The brothers were also very involved with the administration of the game and the establishment of the Middlesex County headquarters at Lords in 1877.

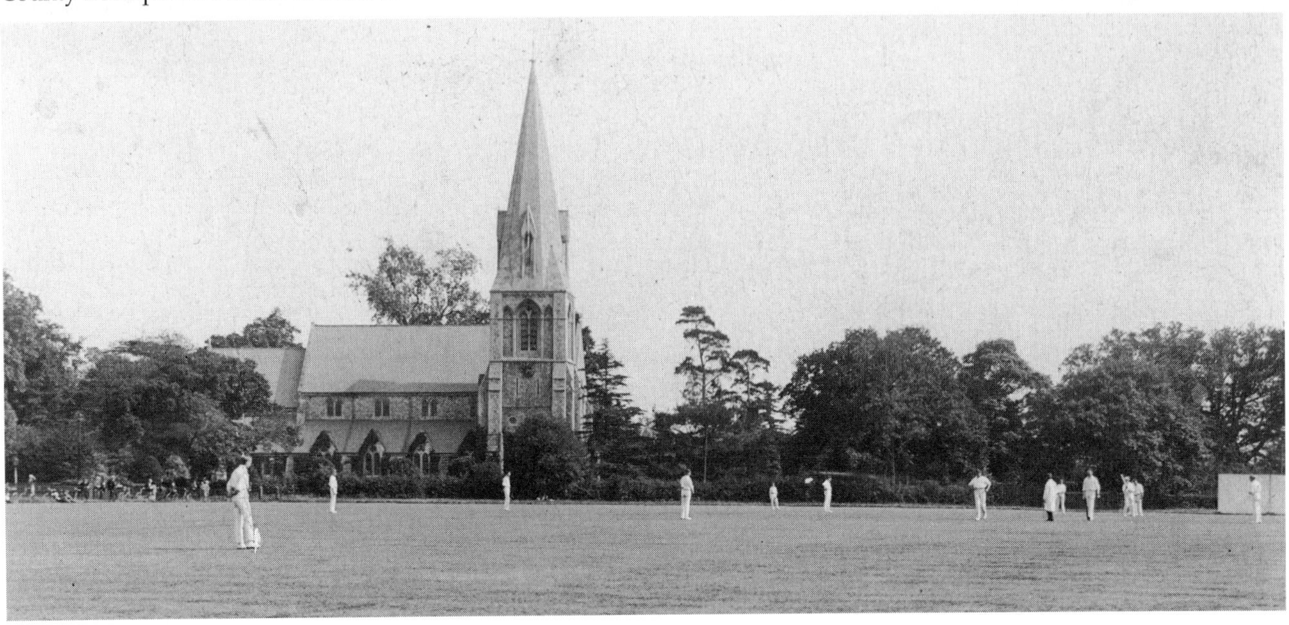

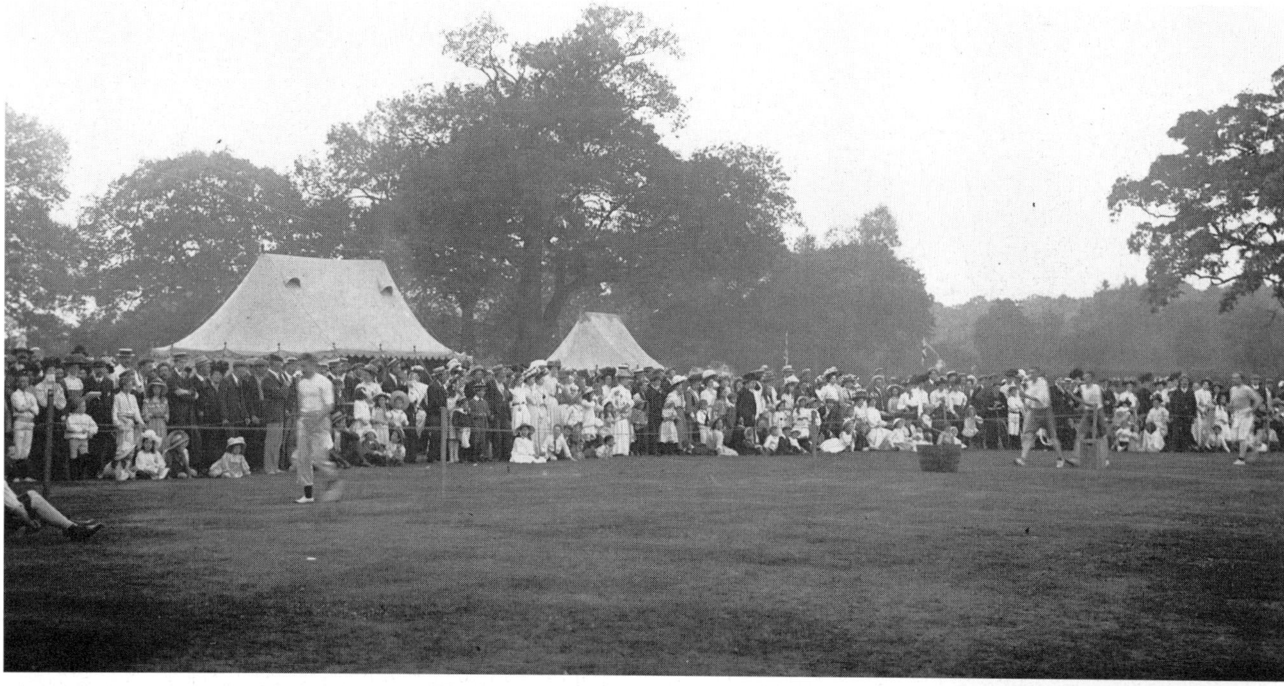

The village sports days began around 1888 with annual cricket matches being played between the police and local tradesmen in the Chapel Field. In 1900 a few more sports were added to the programme and the following year 'Southgate Village Sports' were officially established and flourished for the next 10 or 12 years. Collections were held to raise money to cover expenses, which included a band and, in 1906, a firework display. That year Mrs George Edell distributed the prizes; Mr and Mrs Edell were well known and liked in the village.

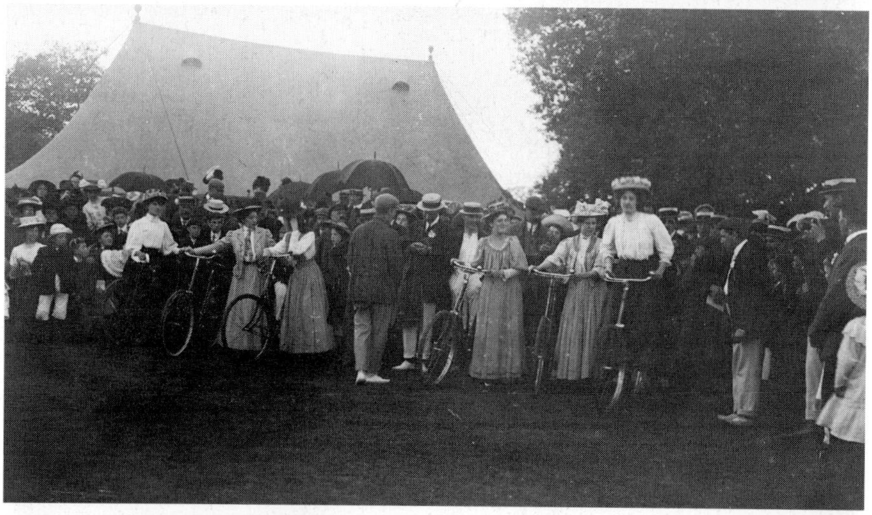

The 1906 sports, pictured on these pages, were held on 16 August; they included the cricket match and lunch in a marquee with the band and pipers of Y Division of the Metropolitan Police in attendance. The other sports began after lunch and the day ended with dancing from 8 to 10 p.m.

The pictures show (from top) a walking race, what appear to be preparations for a ladies cycle race, a Band of Hope drill display. On the opposite page (from top) the Veteran's Race (after lunch too!), a tug of war between children, a girls' demonstration with Indian Clubs (*femmes formidables* indeed), and the Tradesmen's Race. The weather wasn't at its best but there seems to have been a good turnout of spectators who look to have thoroughly enjoyed themselves.

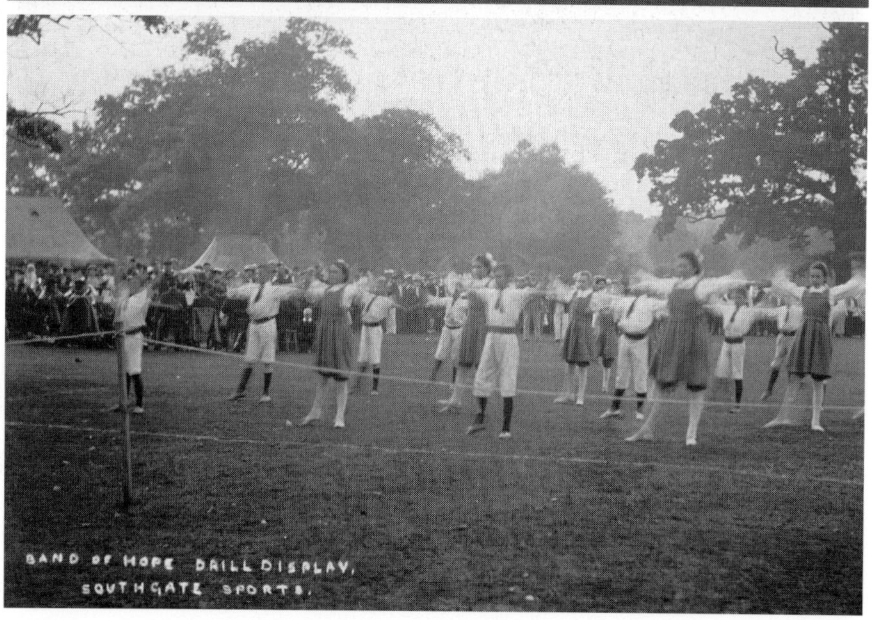

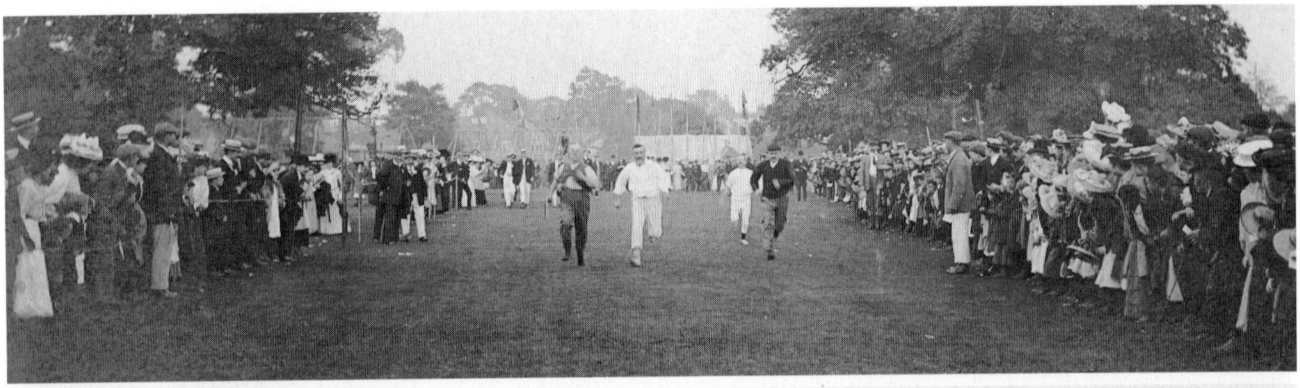

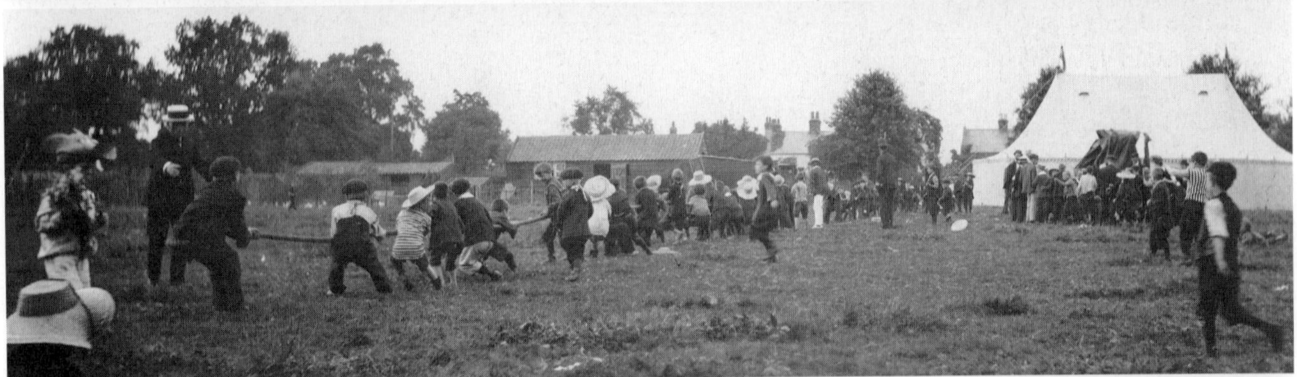

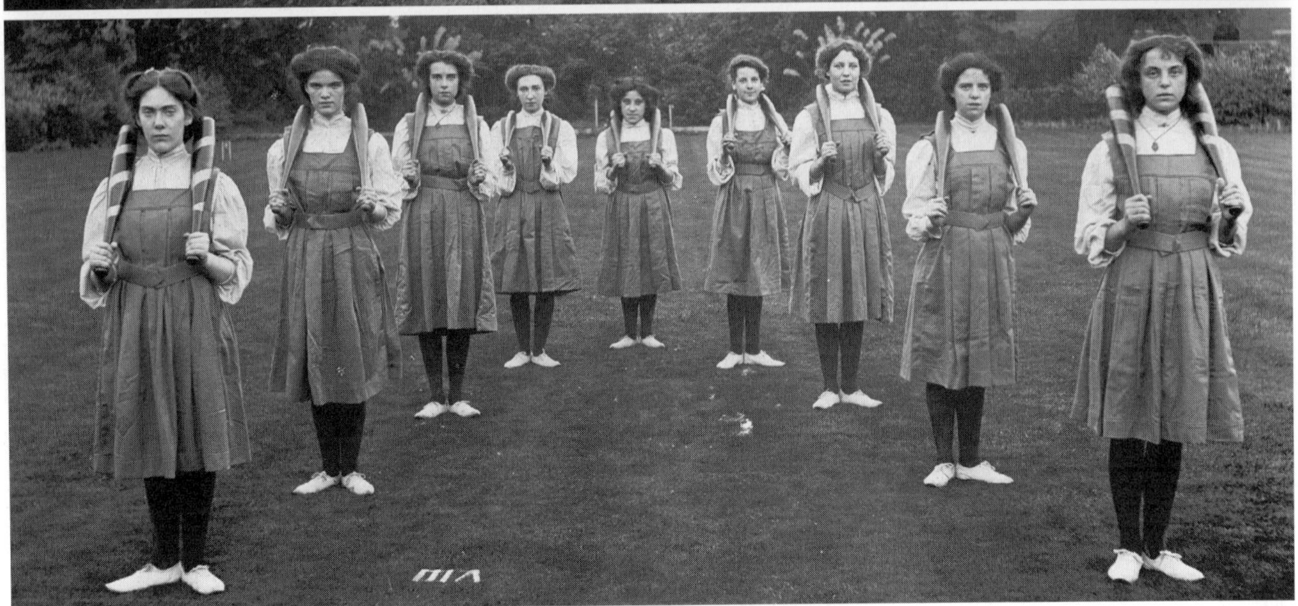

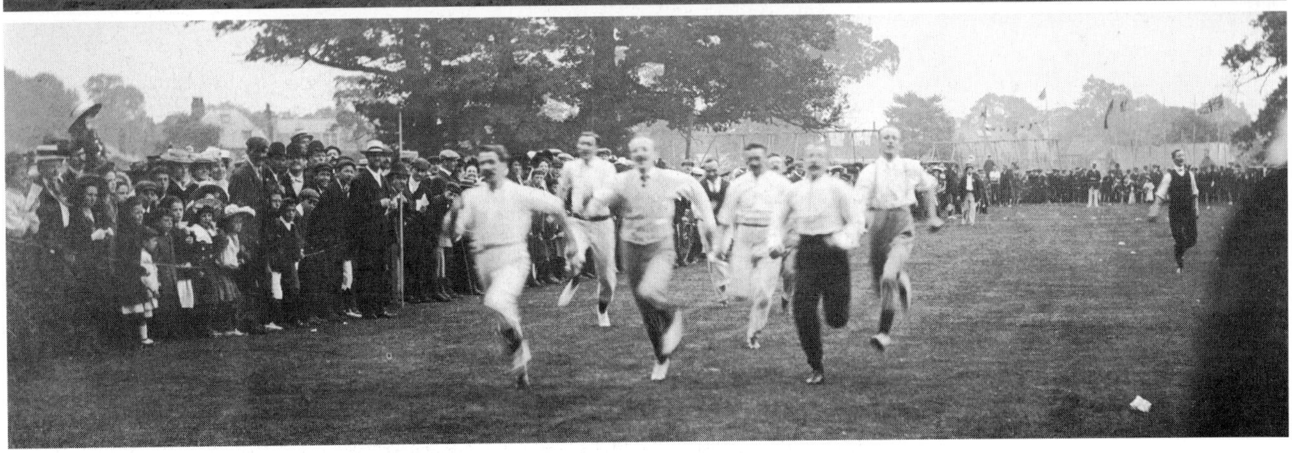

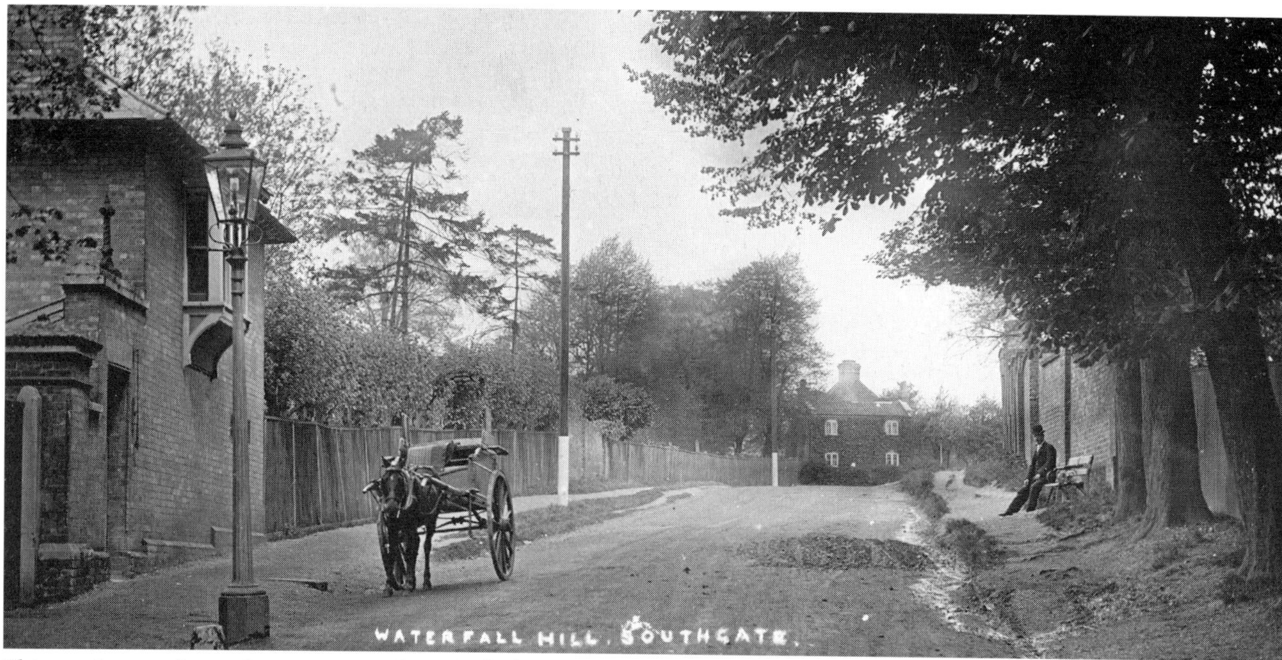

This road was shown but not named on both the 1801 Enclosure map and the 1867 Ordnance Survey map. By 1871 it was known as Colney Hatch Road, in 1892 it was partly Church Lane and partly Southgate Road, whilst the 1896 Ordnance Survey calls it Church Hill! It had acquired its present name, Waterfall Road, by 1904, although it is often referred to locally as Waterfall Lane.

The picture above dates from around 1920 and the view is looking up the hill towards Southgate Green. Brook House, the home of Dr Harry Corner, stands on the left with the pony and trap waiting outside. For many years he ran a hospital there for patients considered to be suffering from mental illnesses. In the middle distance the road makes a sharp turn to the right in front of Ivy Cottage, which stood opposite what is nowadays the end of Chandos Avenue. The cottage was a well-known landmark on Waterfall Road for many years but it lay derelict for some years in the 1930s and in 1940 the ARP used it in their mock exercises as a bombed-out building, eventually demolishing it.

The high brick wall on the right once enclosed the Beaver Hall estate, among whose owners was Henry William Schneider, the man who financed the exploration that led to the discovery of huge deposits of haematite just outside Barrow-in-Furness and so led to that town's development as a centre for ironmaking and shipbuilding. He became an Alderman and Mayor of Barrow and his statue stands in the town.

Henry moved out of Beaver Hall in 1869 and the following year John Walker bought the estate, demolished the hall and added the grounds to his Arnos Grove estate. The road was gradually developed after 1928 and is nowadays lined with fine bungalows and houses.

A terrace of four linked houses has been built where Ivy Cottage once stood and Waterfall Close now runs off left to where the adjacent Whitehouse Farm used to stand until it was demolished in 1934.

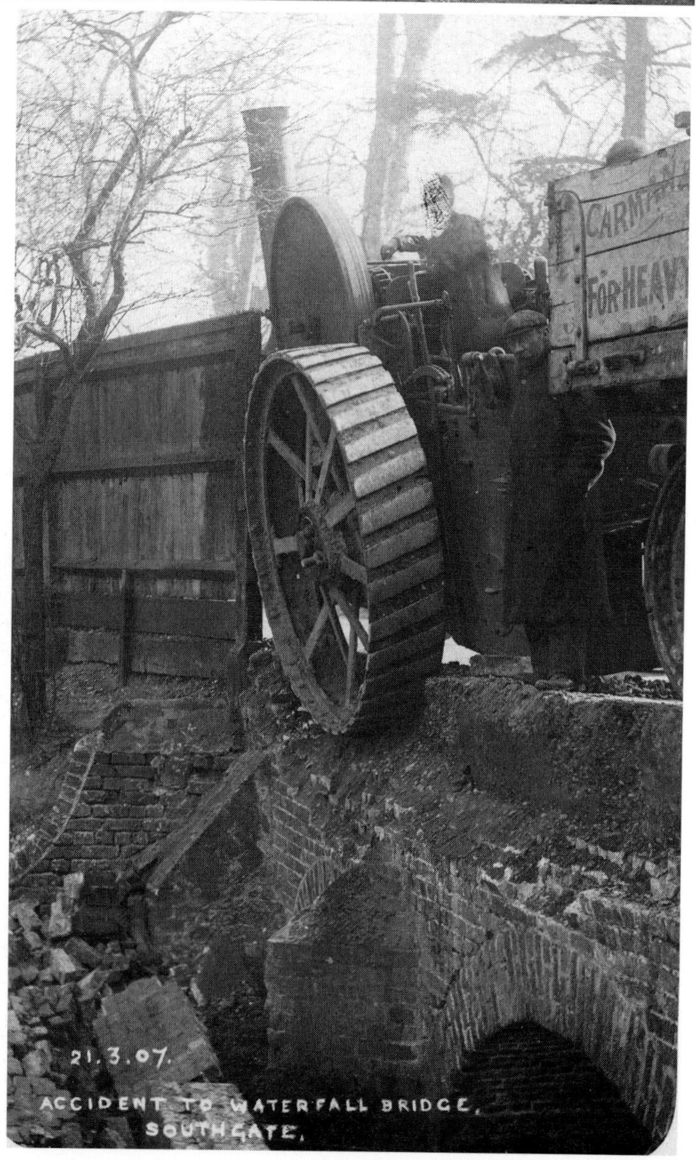

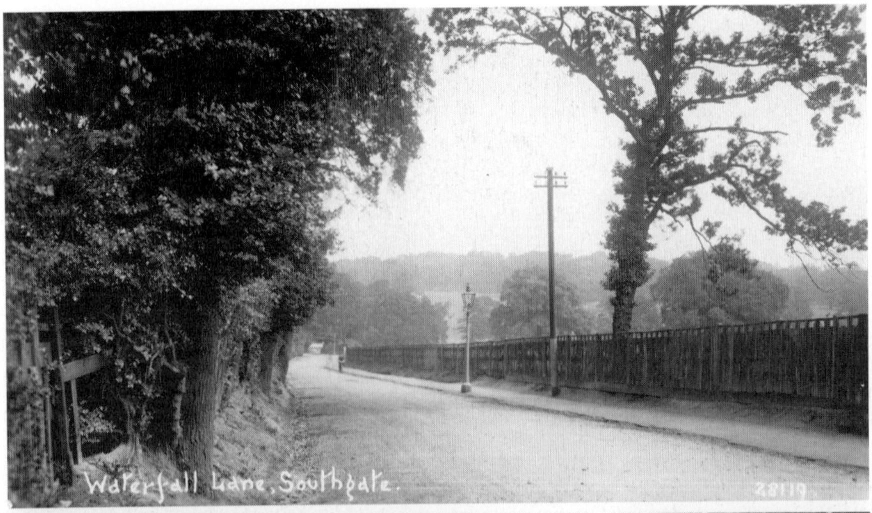

The location of this picture appears to be the same as the photograph opposite, but looking in the other direction down the hill towards Waterfall Bridge where the road crosses Pymmes Brook.

Pymmes Brook rises at Barnet and enters Southgate at Waterfall Road before crossing Arnos Park. It then flows through Palmers Green and Upper Edmonton before veering south to join the River Lee at Tottenham.

Nowadays the road is bisected halfway down the hill by Ashfield Road, which goes off to the right and Abbotshall Avenue which goes off to the left.

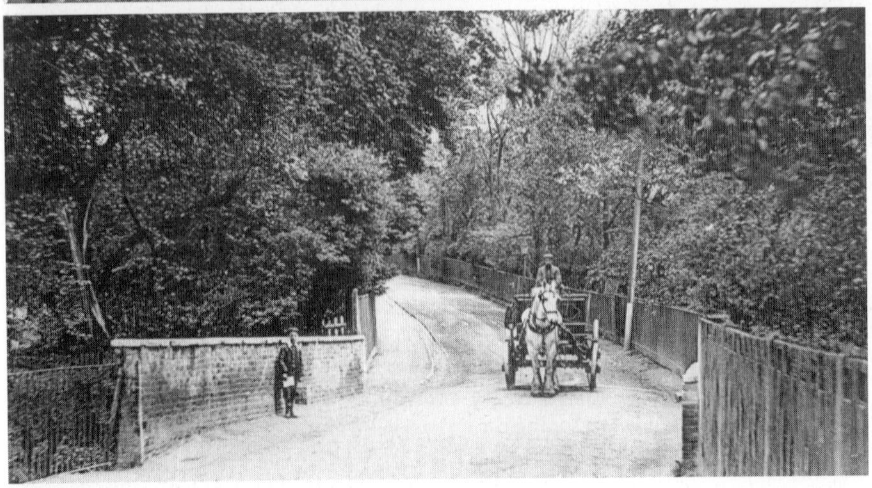

A 1906 scene that is unrecognisable today. The horse and cart have come down Waterfall Hill from Southgate Green and are about to cross the bridge spanning Pymmes Brook.

The bridge is still there but has been rebuilt and considerably widened. A large roundabout has been constructed a few yards away on the Southgate side and the road is nowadays spanned by the huge brick viaduct that carries the Piccadilly Line overground at this point between Southgate and Arnos Grove Stations.

The driver of this traction engine must have lost control of his load as he came down the hill from Southgate on 21 March 1907 and his engine has demolished one side of the bridge. We don't know whether the man standing on the engine in the picture below is the driver but in the left picture the photographer has scratched out his features, possibly to save him further embarrassment. The incident wasn't reported in the local papers so his identity will remain a mystery forever.

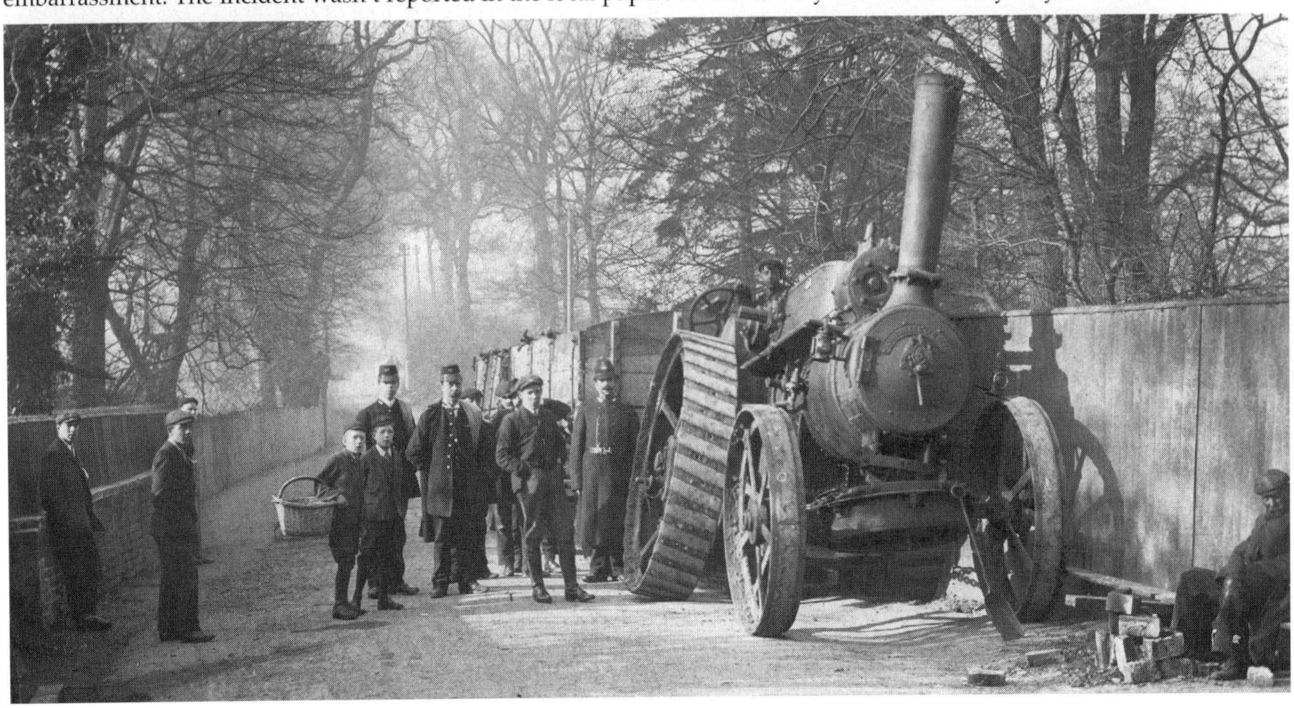

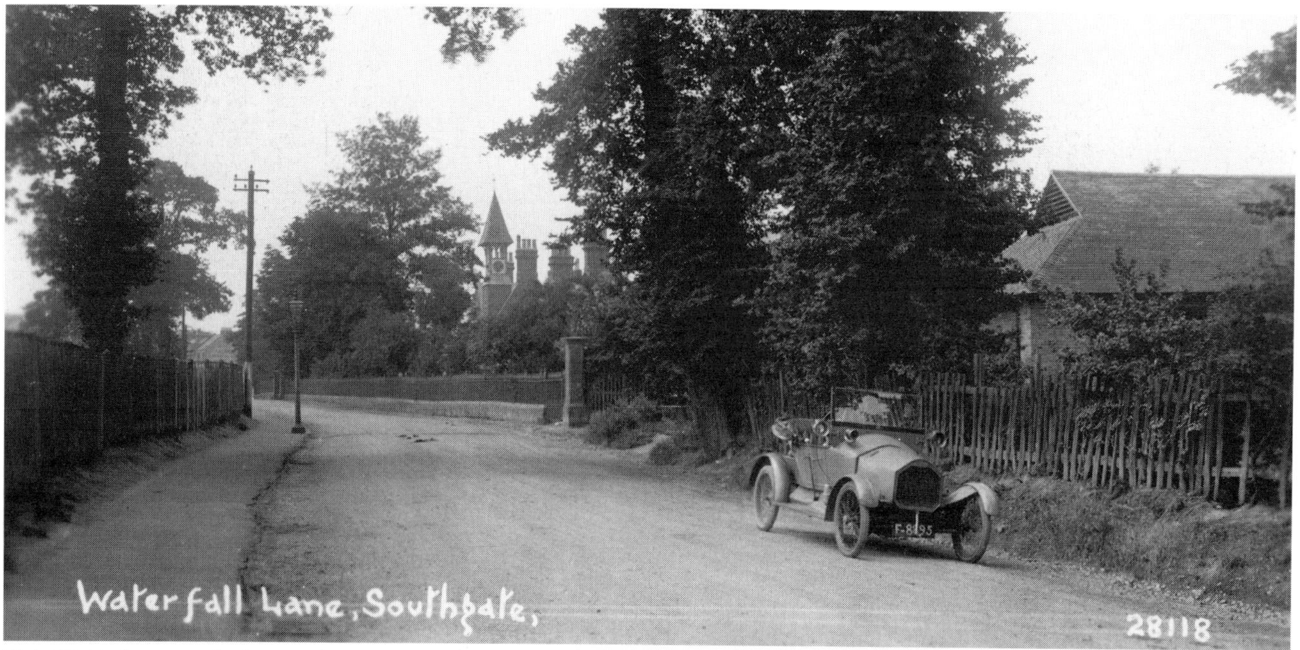

This 1925 photograph shows the area near the far end of Waterfall Road as it approaches the junction with Brunswick Park Road, formerly called Colney Hatch Road. This junction was always known as Lander's Corner after A.K. Lander, the monumental masons who traded there. The building in the centre with the pointed turret is the Clock & Watchmakers' Asylum, which was built on the curve of the junction. The home was supervised by a warden and provided accommodation and sustenance for those retired from the profession. The buildings were demolished in the 1950s to make way for flats.

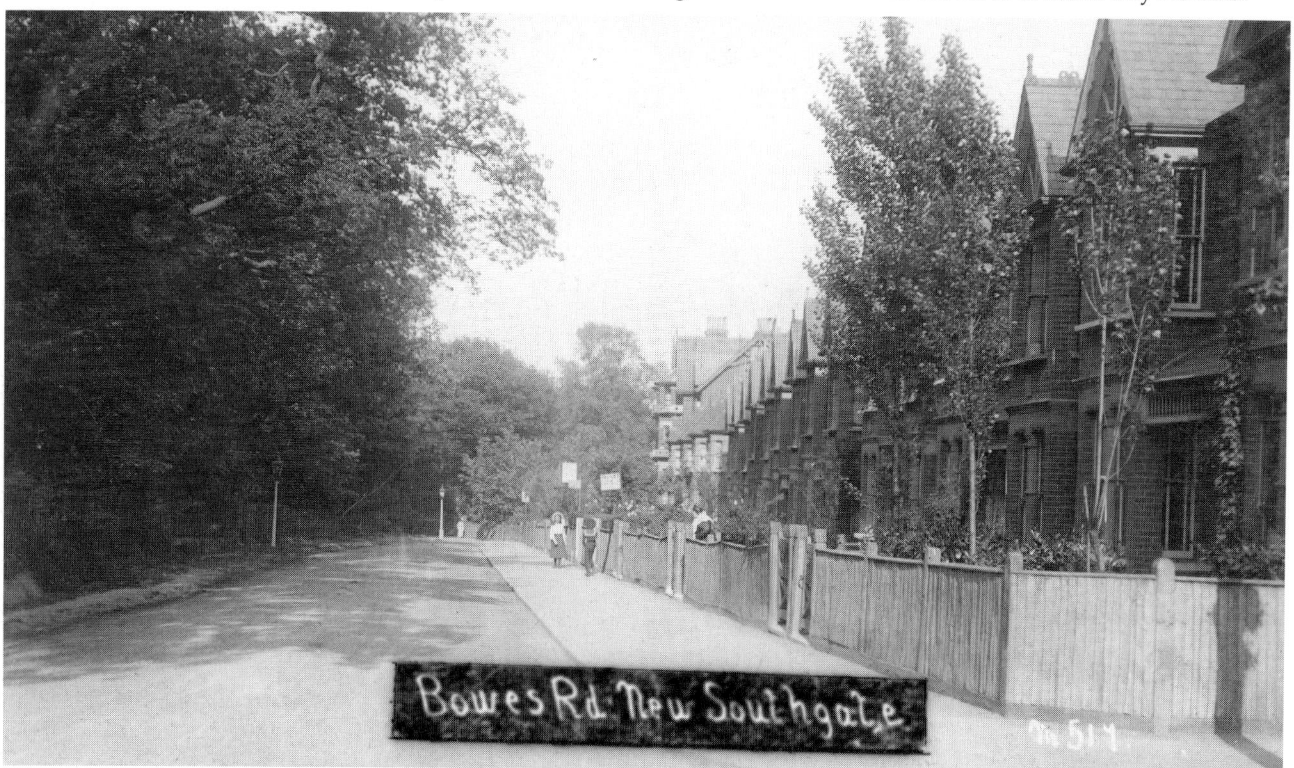

Now that our route has taken us into New Southgate, let's do a short tour of the area before we return to Southgate Green.

This village was originally called Colney Hatch but when its name became closely associated with the huge asylum with the same name just along the road, the villagers had its name officially changed to New Southgate.

Roughly speaking, the village was a triangular shape with its apex to the south. It was bounded on its northern side by Bowes Road, on its north-eastern side by the allotments behind Palmers Green Road and on its north-western side by the Great Northern Railway's line into Kings Cross. Betstyle Road, nowadays the High Street, ran through the middle and joined Waterfall Road and Brunswick Park Road at Lander's Corner.

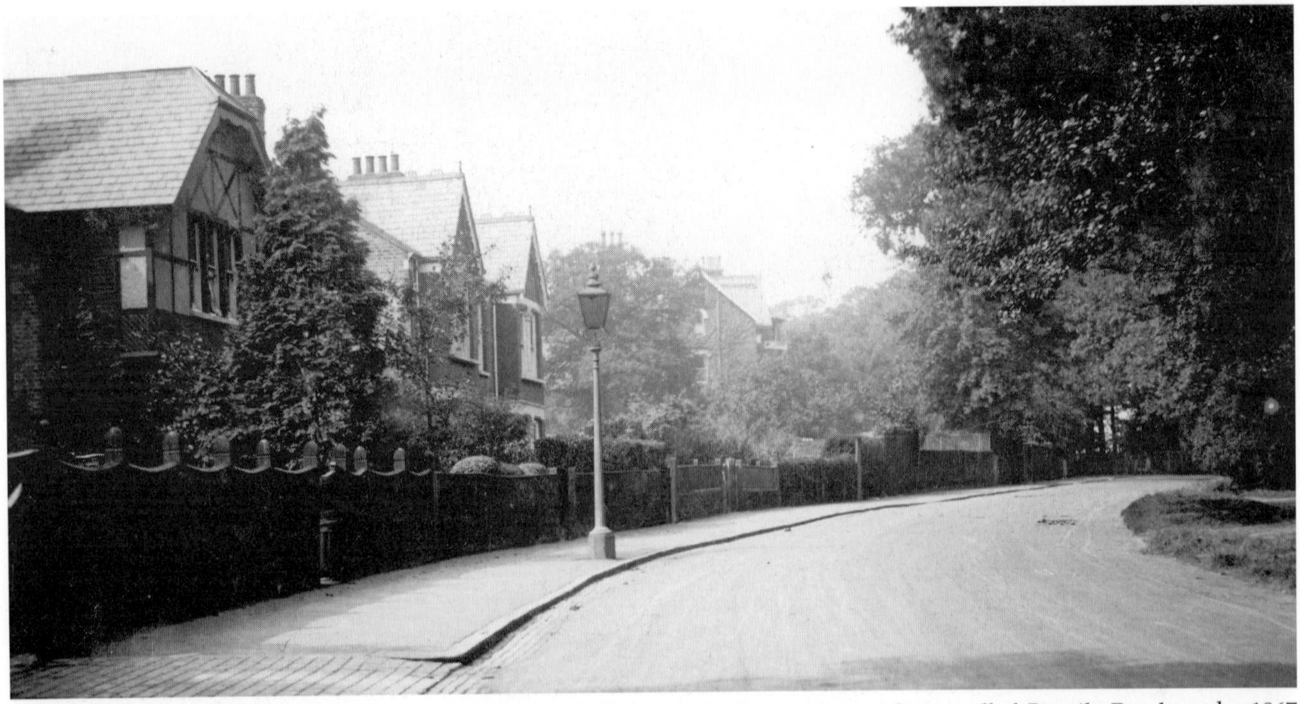

Bowes Road is an old thoroughfare. It was marked on the 1801 Enclosure map and was called Betstile Road on the 1867 Ordnance Survey map, but had acquired its present name by 1881. It is nowadays a busy main road and its eastern section forms part of the North Circular Road. However, these pictures show what a quiet rural road it once was - the lower opposite picture was taken in 1909 while the one above was taken nearby about 10 years later.

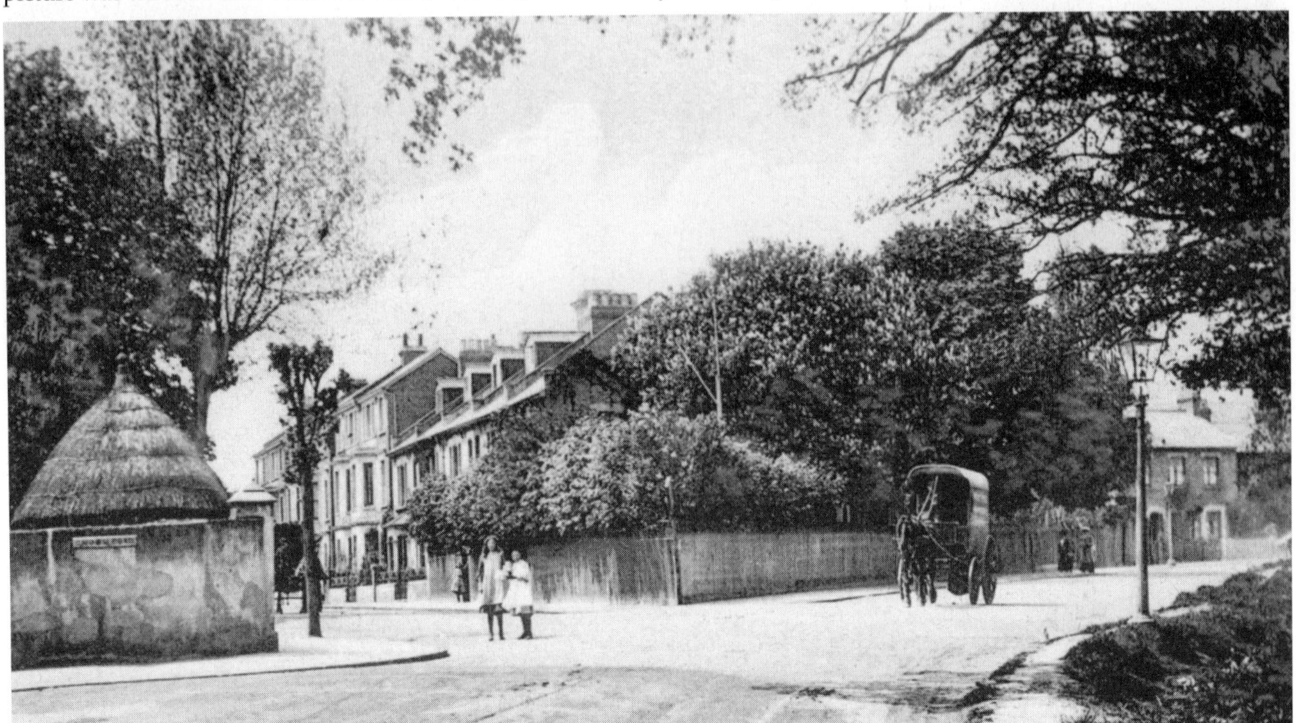

The note on the back of this 1927 postcard reads, 'Just a pretty patch of private roads of Four Ways covered with houses of a good middle-class and within a few minutes walk of Old Southgate and many charming country walks and rides for the pedestrian and cyclist'.

The location appears to be where Cross Road, coming in from the left, and Grove Road, in the centre where the girls are standing, join Bowes Road just a little way east of Lander's Corner, towards which the delivery van is heading. If this location is the right one, the two girls standing in the middle of Grove Road would be quite safe today because that end of the road has been blocked off in the interests of safety on Bowes Road, thus turning it into a cul-de-sac.

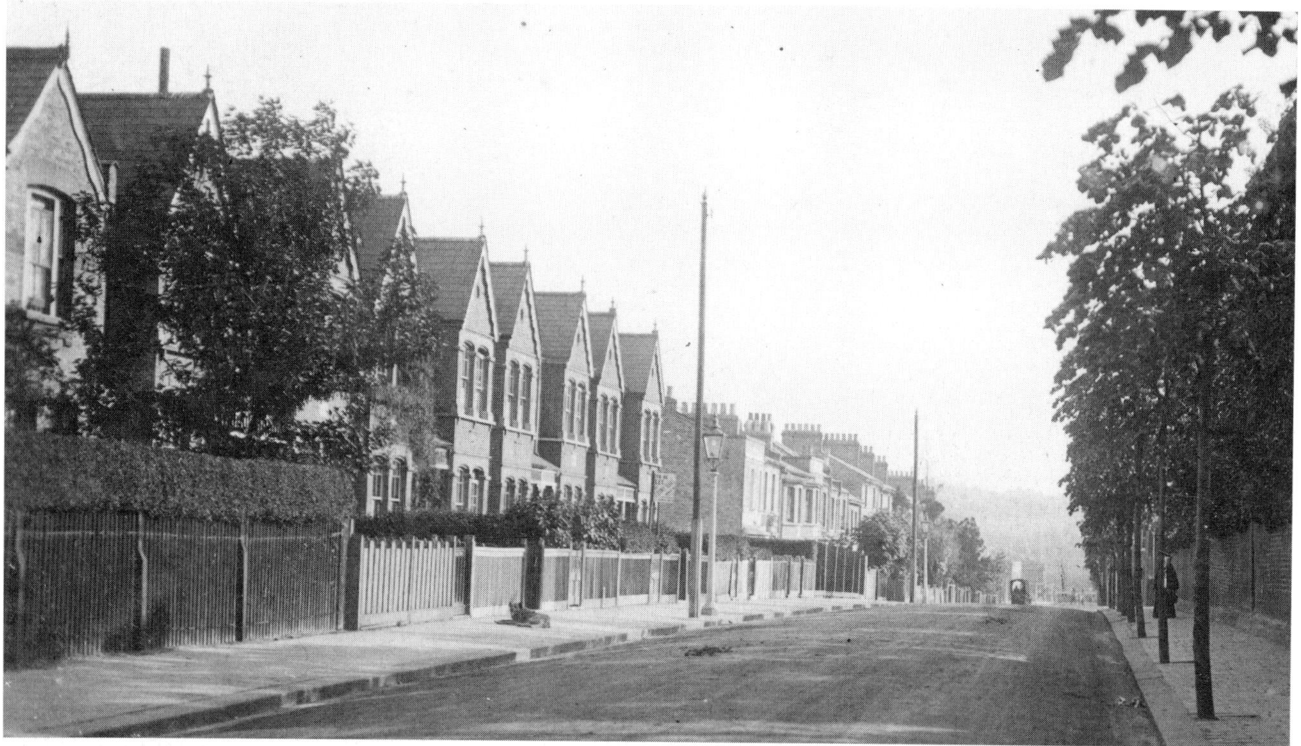

Walking a little further eastward brings us to Palmers Road. This used to be part of the Colney Hatch estate and was formerly known as Palmers Green Road. It formed the north-eastern boundary of the village and had acquired its present name by 1901. The 1867 Ordnance Survey map shows that it had been partly developed by that date but only on the west side. By the end of the century larger houses had been built on the other side of the road, which backed onto allotments running down to the Bounds Green Brook. This picture is dated September 1909.

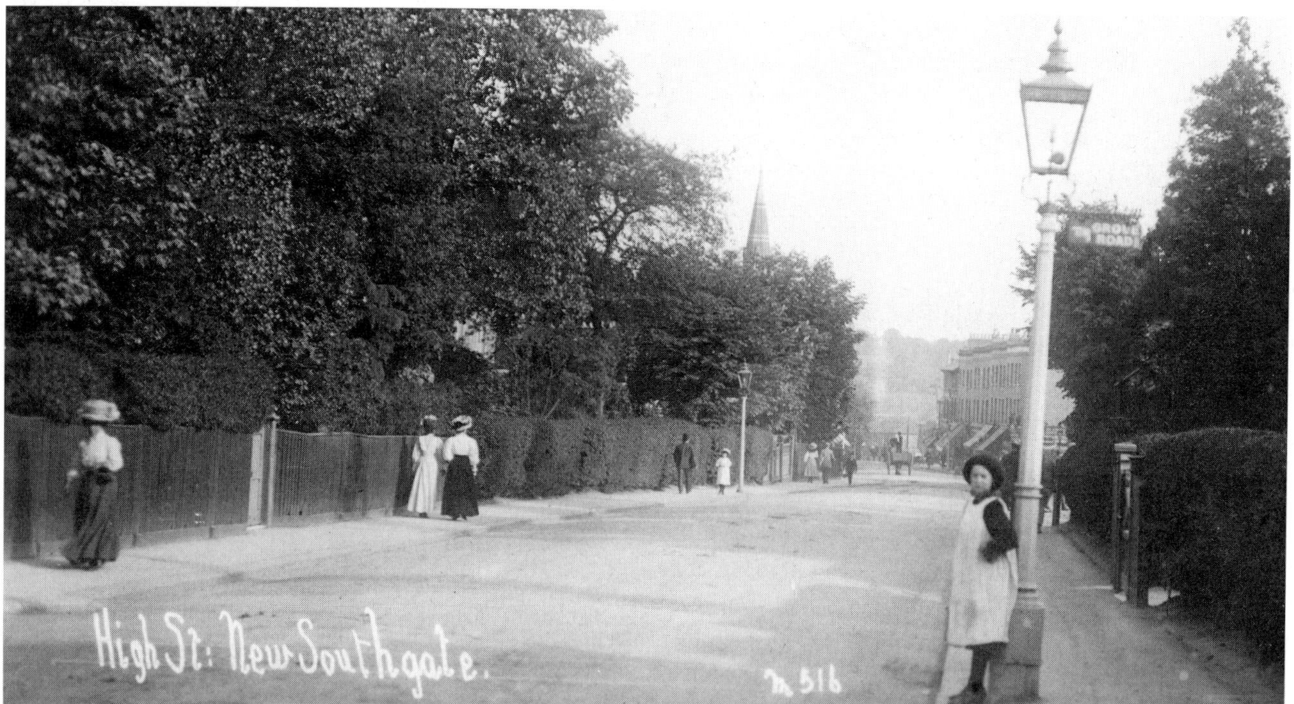

At the bottom of Palmers Road we used to be able to turn right into High Street, formerly called Betstyle Road, which was the main street running north-west through the centre of the village and joining the other roads at Lander's Corner. But not anymore - modern redevelopment has resulted in High Street being truncated to less than half of its former length; its northern end is blocked off so that it no longer makes a junction with the other roads at Lander's Corner, whilst the southern part ends at its junction with Springfield Road. This 1909 photograph shows High Street, looking north towards St Paul's church.

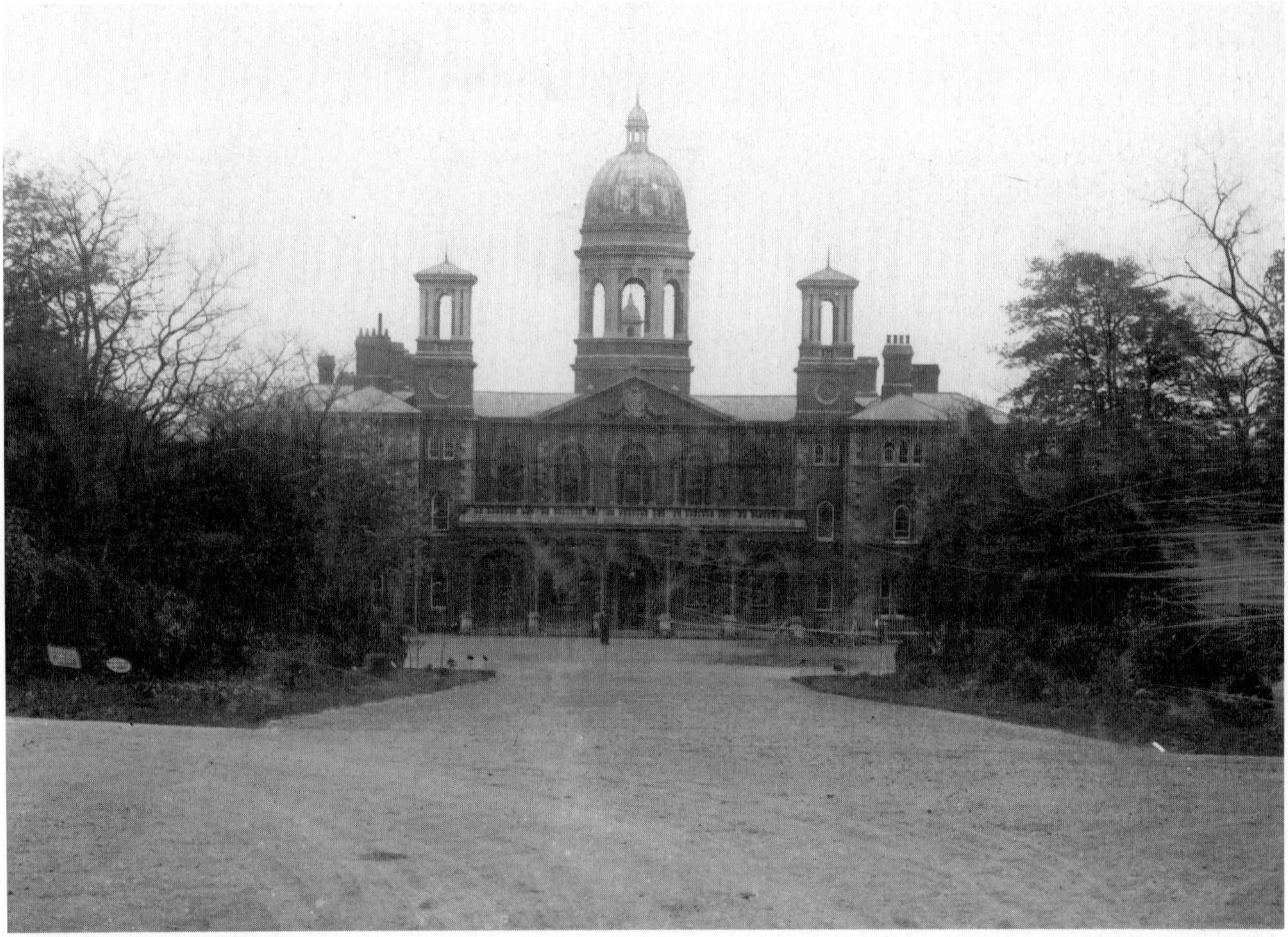

The Middlesex County Pauper Lunatic Asylum at Colney Hatch was opened in 1851. The nearby Colney Hatch Station on the Great Northern main line into Kings Cross was opened primarily to serve it; the station was later renamed New Southgate.

In 1848 a competition had been held to find the best building design for the asylum and the winner was S.W. Daukes with his Italianate style entry. The foundation stone was laid by Prince Albert in May 1849 and the building cost nearly £400,000. When it opened in 1851, Colney Hatch was the largest asylum in Europe. Its frontage was over 1,880 feet long, there were six miles of corridors and the site covered 14 acres of ground. Until that time most asylums had controlled their patients by means of straight jackets and other inhumane restraints but Colney Hatch was designed to be run on the then novel principle of 'no restraint'. There was a large farm on what is nowadays Friern Village, there were workshops for tailoring and other trades, and the patients were also involved in cooking and cleaning in the hospital, the idea being to give the patients work to do so they wouldn't become bored.

Originally intended to house 300 to 400 patients, it was soon housing 1,000 and by 1856 there were nearly 1,500. Extensions were built between 1857 and 1859 so that the asylum could house 2,000 patients. Unfortunately, the increase in patients was not matched by an increase in the number of trained staff; they became unable to cope with the large number of patients and by the 1860s the straight jacket and other outdated methods of restraint were having to be used.

By the 1880s the asylum had become infamous throughout London and the locals had had enough. They managed to disassociate themselves from the hated name of Colney Hatch by getting the name of their village and its railway station changed to New Southgate.

In 1889 control of the asylum was transferred to the London County Council who added more accommodation in the 1890s in the form of wooden huts; by 1898 the asylum was home to 2,500 patients. Unfortunately, in 1903, three of these huts caught fire and 51 patients lost their lives. The huts were replaced by brick buildings in 1908.

In 1918 the asylum became known as the Colney Hatch Mental Hospital, in 1937 as the Friern Mental Hospital and, in 1959, simply as Friern Hospital. After a long period of decline it eventually closed in 1993.

A large part of the asylum's grounds were sold off for high quality building development and the buildings, which once echoed to the cries of its inmates, have now been converted into luxury flats and apartments called Princess Park Manor.

It's now time to leave New Southgate and return to Southgate Green to start the next part of our tour.

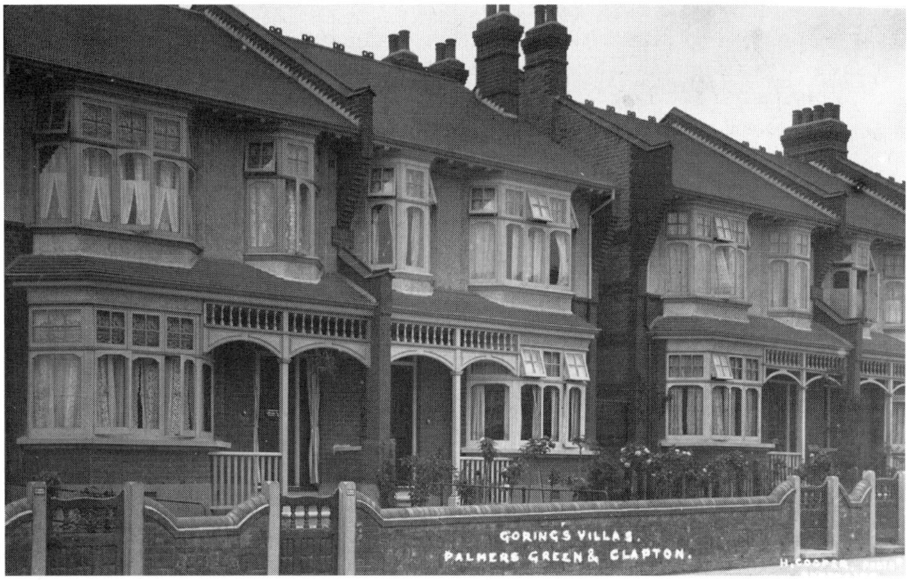

We are now coming to the areas developed by local builders in Edwardian times following the break up of the great landed estates previously owned by families such as the Taylors of Grovelands and the Walkers of Arnos Grove.

One of the best-known local builders was W. Goring whose house and office were situated in Fox Lane. His advertisement in the Southgate Urban District Council Official Guide for 1908 reads as follows:

'Fox Lane Estate – High Class Villa Residences in Fox Lane, The Mall, Selborne and Oakfield Roads. These villas contain large and lofty dining room, drawing room with French casements leading into garden, 4 large bedrooms with fitted wardrobes (some with 5 or 6 bedrooms), bathroom, kitchen, scullery and usual offices, large coal cellar, well ventilated under floors. Perfect sanitation. Latest improvements everywhere. Fine garden front and rear. Tastefully decorated. Inspection invited. Free deeds. Free conveyance. All roads and paving charges included to Fox Lane. Side or back Tradesmen's Entrance. Lease 99 years at moderate Ground Rent. Houses built to order. Prices from £360 to £800, can be bought with small deposit, balance on very easy terms. Freeholds can be bought. Customers can select their site and have houses built to their own plans. Electric bells and gas.'

Villas such as the ones pictured here can be seen in many areas of Southgate and Palmers Green. Although these were mainly semi-detached houses the status of their purchasers can be gauged from the references to them having separate tradesmen's entrances and electric bells which would be used to summon the servants.

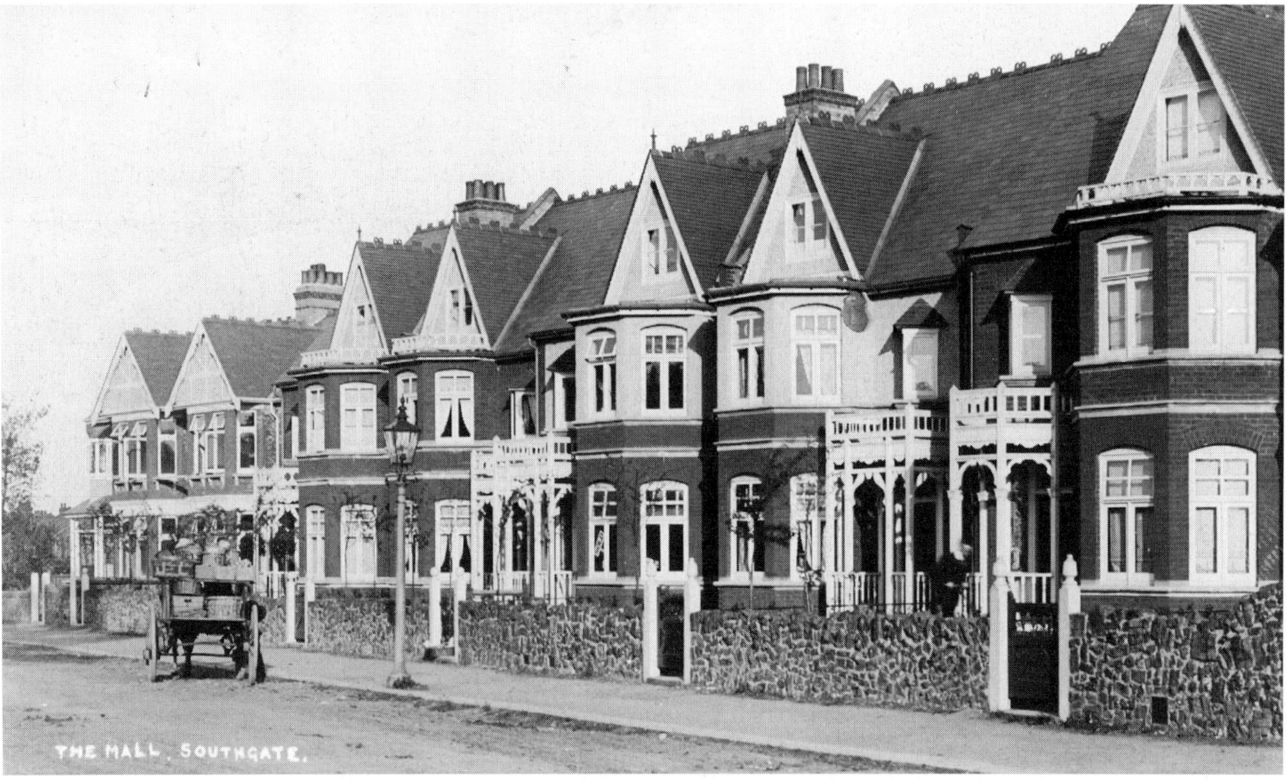

We'll start this section of our journey with a walk down the Mall which runs alongside the Cherry Tree and ends at a junction with Fox Lane. The 1801 Enclosure map shows it as a footpath leading from Southgate Green to Fox Lane and although it had gained its name by 1867, this is what it remained until 1908 when it was upgraded into a road because the area was being developed for housing. The Edwardian houses start beyond Oakfield Road, which is where the road used to become a footpath.

Before that time we would have walked down the footpath, across some open fields, through a clap gate where Oakfield Road now joins, and into the woods. Before long the path forked and we could either continue straight on to the hamlet of Clappers Green or take the left fork, which would take you onto Fox Lane by the Village Pound.

The Mall's most famous resident was Dame Flora Robson who, as a young girl, lived at No. 62, which was named 'The Lawe'.

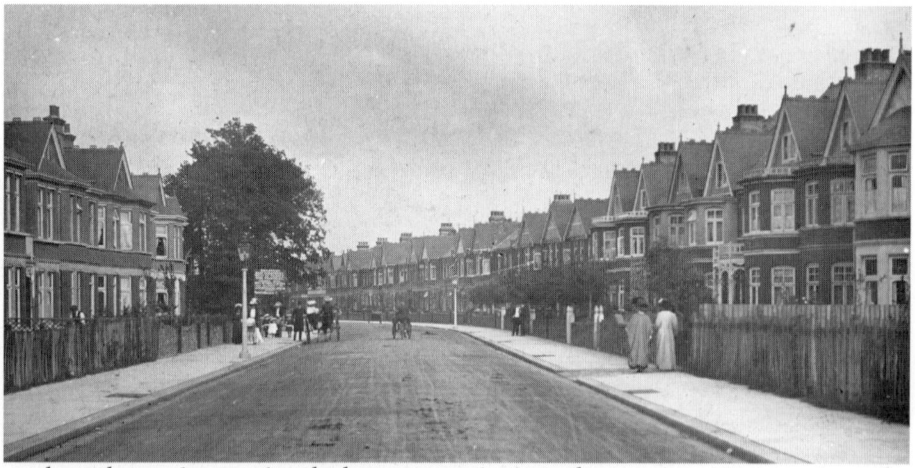

The above and lower opposite pictures show the road soon after the houses were built. In the one above, looking down the road towards Fox Lane, all the ladies are well-dressed and are wearing floral hats. Two ladies in a carriage have stopped to talk to a gentleman in a top hat near to a sign advertising further building plots in the road. The picture at the bottom of the previous page, taken near the Fox Lane end of the road, shows some of the careful detail that was put into these houses, including their unusual garden walls, which were built out of reject bricks! The horse-drawn cart standing at the roadside is loaded with a variety of wicker baskets – might it be collecting the laundry? The road was not 'made up' until around 1910; but walking down The Mall today it is good to see that many houses still have their original features, especially their double doors. A few still have tiled paths but not many. Most gardens have been turned into carports and nowadays there are speed bumps along the road.

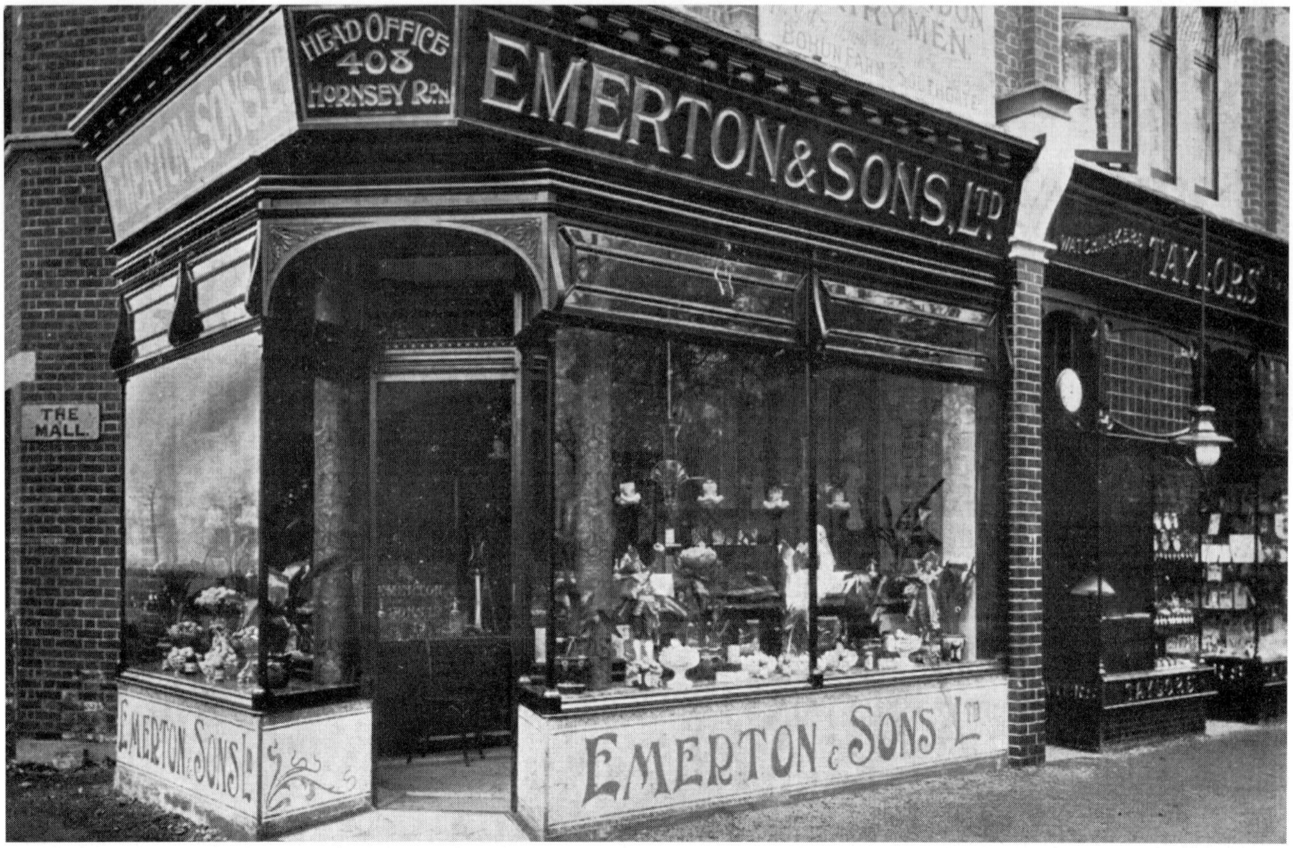

Retracing our steps back down the Mall to the Cherry Tree, we turn left into the start of Cannon Hill. The first four shops here were built in the Victorian era and this picture shows the one situated on the corner of the Mall. Emerton & Sons Ltd had a dairy and ran several shops in north London including another one just down the road in Palmers Green. Strangely, their shop window in this picture doesn't appear to display any dairy products but just look at their beautiful signs, in gold above the door and windows and in mosaics underneath. The premises are now taken by the Chez Gianni French restaurant.

Next door, with a large exterior gas lamp suspended from above, is the shop of Taylor's, the watchmakers, whose gold-leaf sign rivals their neighbour's for style.

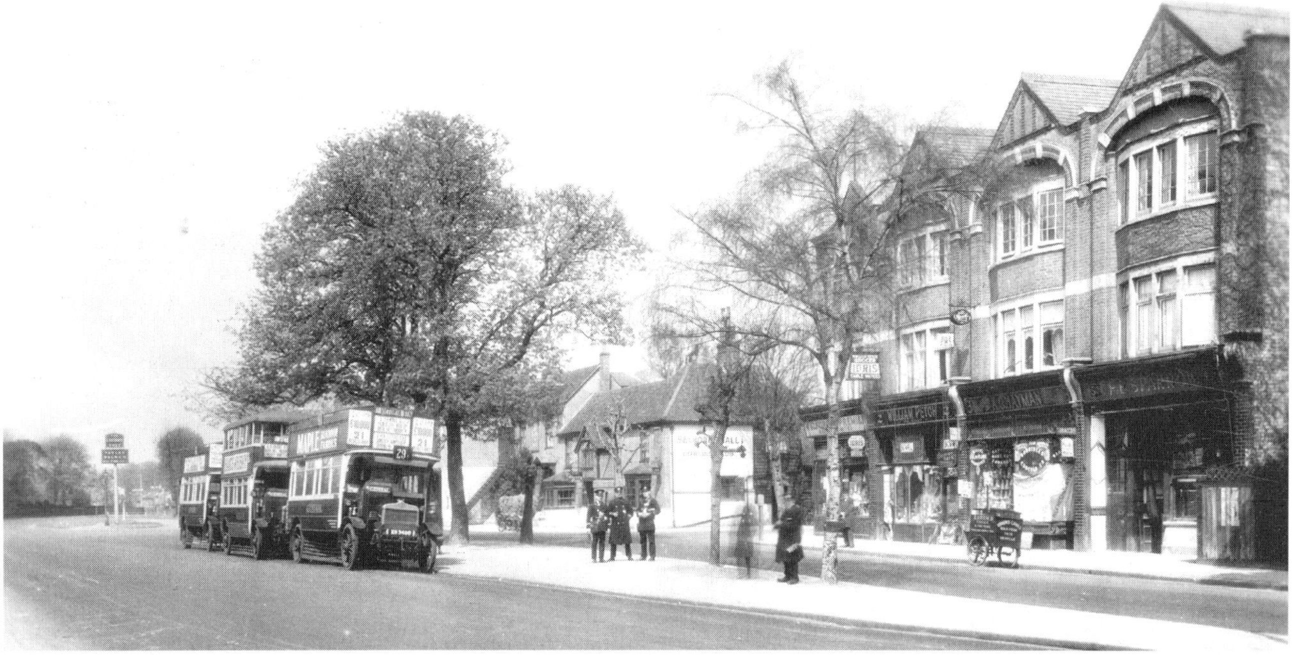

Slightly later views of Cannon Hill, and there have been changes in shop ownership. In the upper picture Emerton's shop is now owned by Welford Premier Dairies whilst Taylor's watchmaker shop is now owned by a grocer, William Petch. The other two shops in the picture are Albert George Hayman, confectioner, and Frederick E. Sparrow's dining rooms.

The little cart standing outside Hayman's shop is a stop-me-and-buy-one tricycle selling Ebben's Cakes. Notice that there is a gap in the row after the four shops – the remainder of the parade was not built onto it until several years later.

Motorbuses of the General Omnibus Company had replaced horse buses in 1912 and began the well-known No. 29 service to London's Victoria Station. Notice that all three buses have solid tyres, which must have given an uncomfortable ride on the roads of the time.

By the time of the lower picture the corner shop had changed hands yet again and was by then owned by United Dairies.

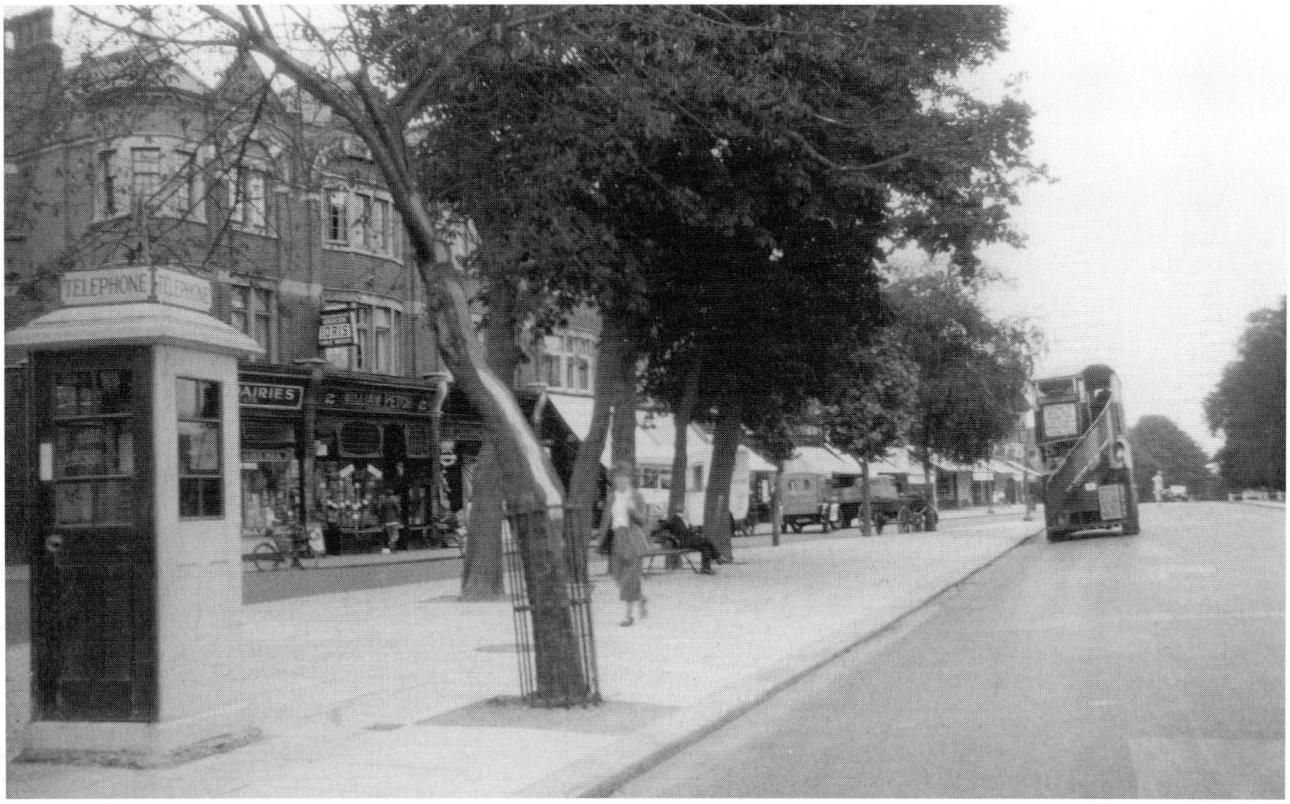

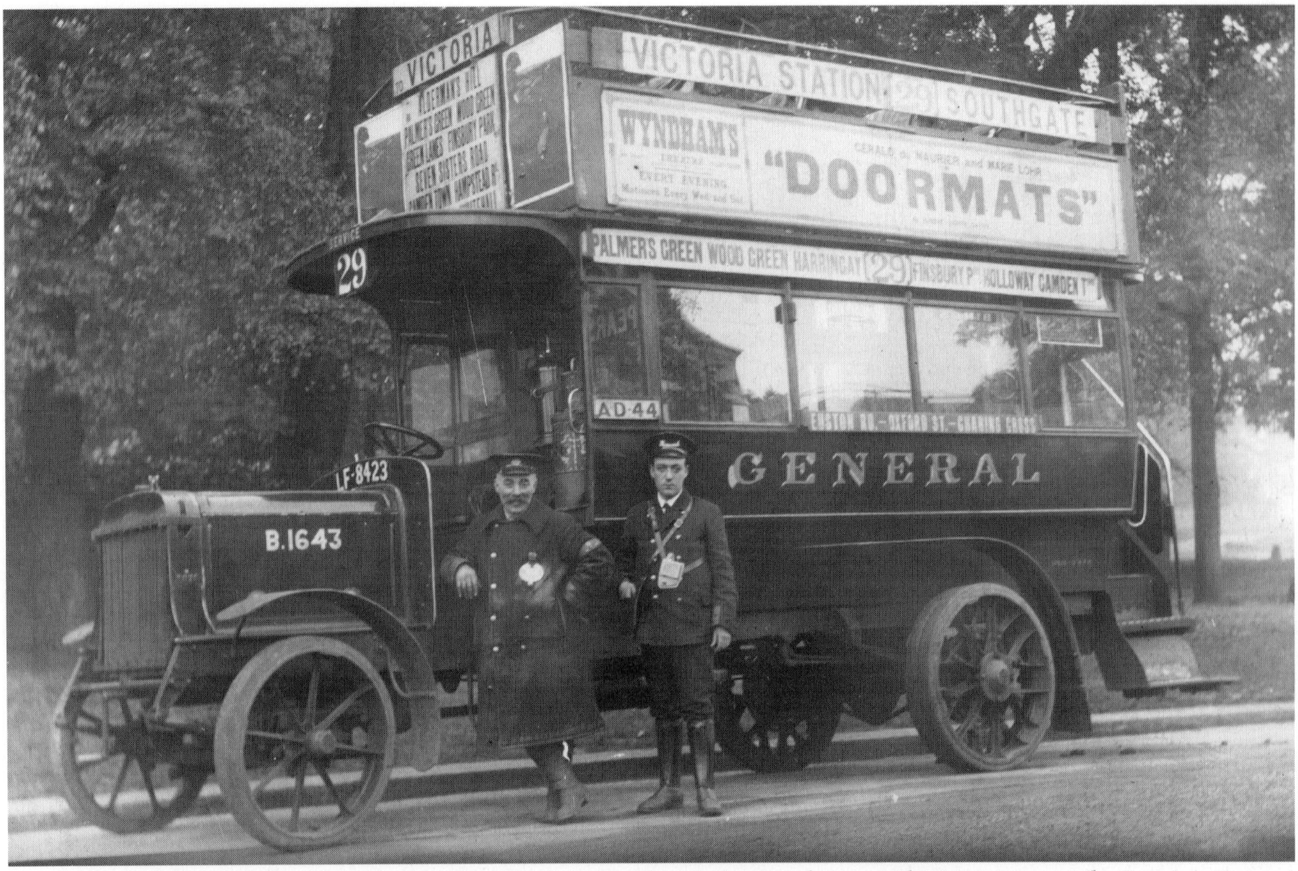

This vehicle with solid tyres is a 'B' Type bus, designed by Frank Searle who was Chief Engineer of the London General Omnibus Company. The bus had a 34-seat capacity and it first entered service in 1911; by 1913 around 2,500 buses of this design had been built at LGOC's premises in Walthamstow. Nine hundred of them were subsequently shipped to France to move troops behind the lines during the First World War. The No. 29 service operated between Southgate and Victoria Station via Palmers Green, Wood Green, Seven Sisters Road, Finsbury Park, Camden Town and Hampstead Road.

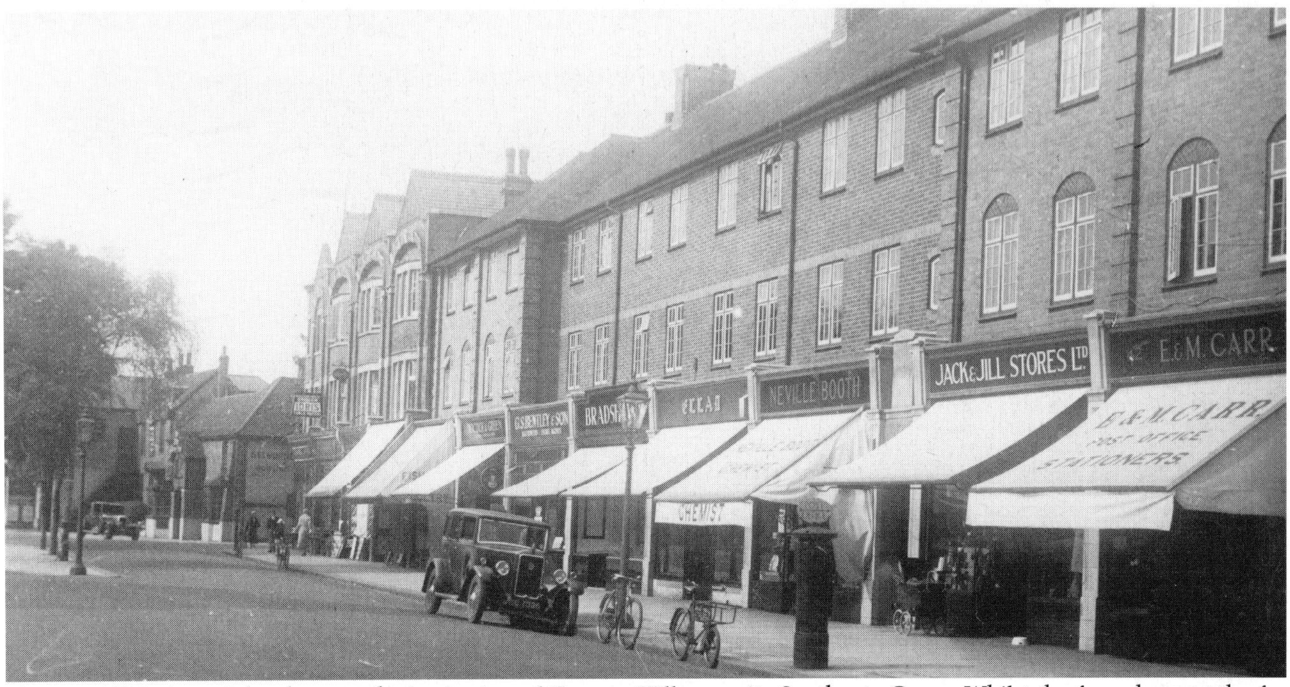

This is a 1934 view of the shops at the beginning of Cannon Hill opposite Southgate Green. Whilst the four shops at the far end were built around the turn of the twentieth century, the eight on the right date from 1933 - almost brand new at the time - and their services ranged from chemists to estate agents.

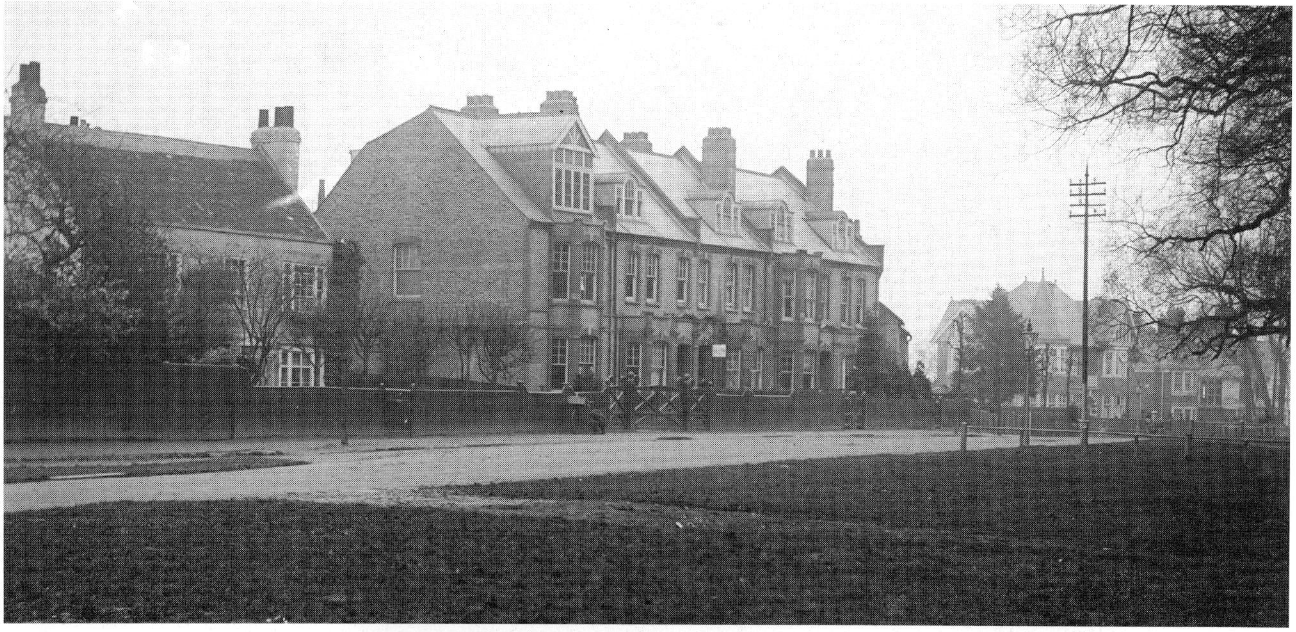

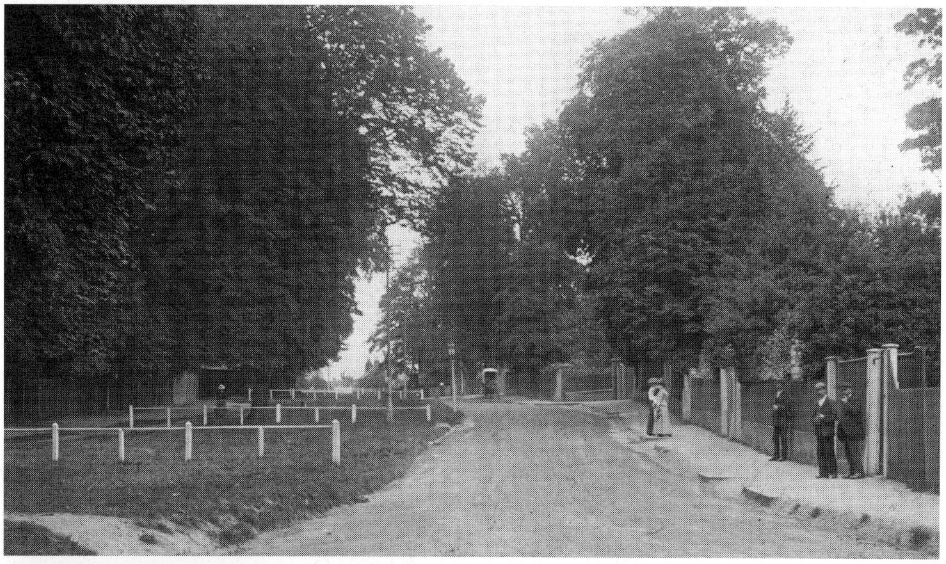

Cannon Hill is an old thoroughfare that was marked on the 1801 Enclosure map. The above picture, dated 1908, shows the stylish houses on the left-hand side, a short distance down the road from Southgate Green, whilst the picture on the right shows the view up Cannon Hill towards Southgate Green. The gates and garden walls of these houses are on the right whilst the trees on the left form the boundary of the Walkers' estate of Arnos Grove.

The lower picture is taken from a little further down Cannon Hill just below its junction with Selborne Road, which joins from the right and whose new houses were occupied by 1906. Possibly the road was named after Selborne in Hampshire, which was the builder's home village. This picture also shows J. Green's bakers shop, which stood at this end of Selborne Road until 1912. It had been built in 1749 and became Green's bakery but it was replaced in 1912 by a stylish new building, which is still there today with the significant dates of 1749 and 1912 carved on the front. It hasn't been a bakery for many years and nowadays it is the premises of the M. & J. Tool Hire Centre.

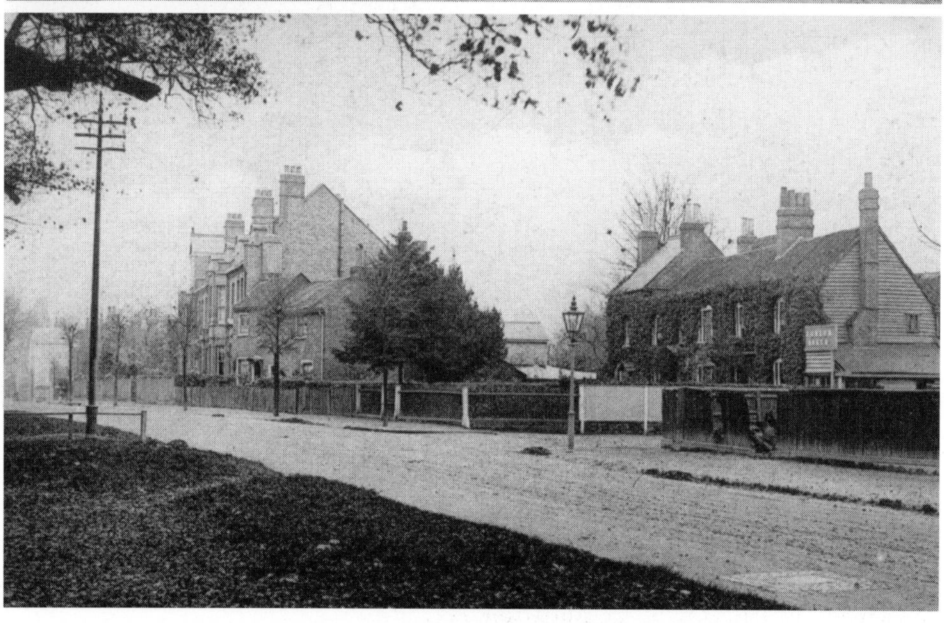

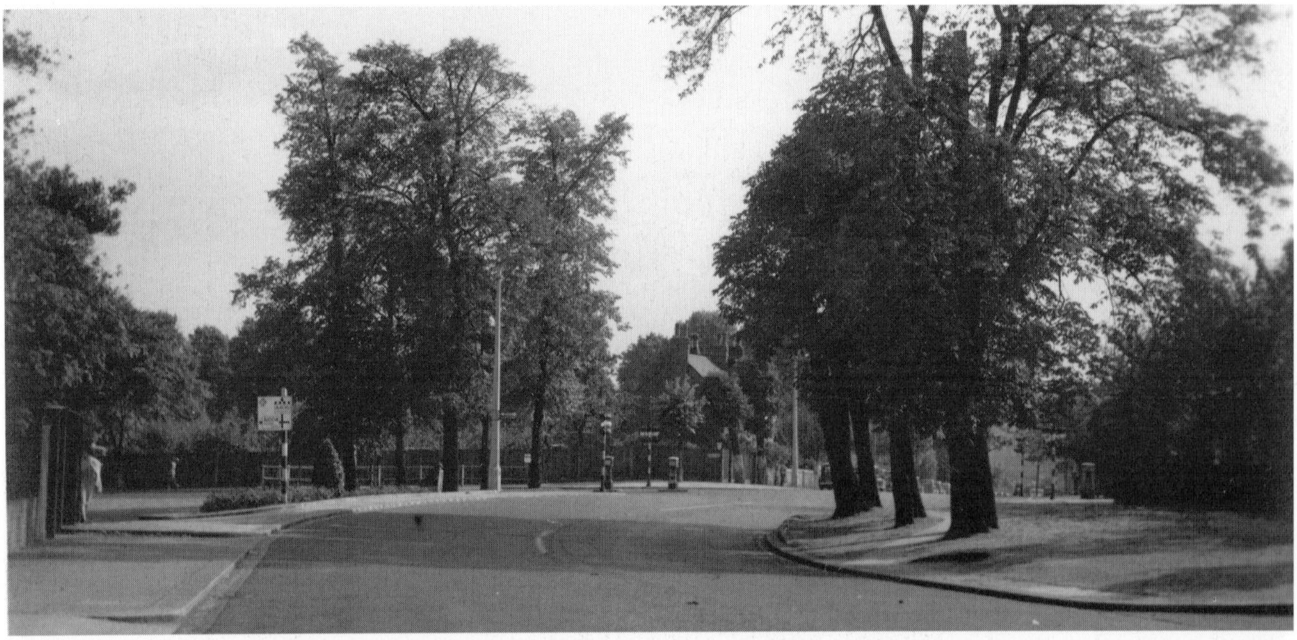

When the sale of the Taylor estates took place in 1902 the gates in Aldermans Hill at the entrance to the driveway up to Grovelands House were purchased by Councillor Corke, who presented them to the council in 1903 to be re-erected at the top of Aldermans Hill as an entrance to Broomfield Park. Here they became known as the Village Gates; they were hung on substantial brick piers and became a popular and familiar sight to the villagers.

The iron gates were removed during the Second World War, presumably because of their scrap value, and replaced with wooden ones. However, one day in January 1953, a number of council workmen appeared on the scene and pulled down the gates and their supporting piers. This destruction appeared to be quite unnecessary and caused a local furore; letters were sent to the local press bitterly condemning the council's action and demanding explanations but none were forthcoming. Instead, the council erected a small token structure on the opposite side of the road at the junction of Aldermans Hill and Cannon Hill, in memory of the lost village gates. It still stands but is almost unnoticeable at this busy junction.

In the picture above Cannon Hill gives way at the road junction to the beginning of Powys Lane which runs on down the hill whilst Aldermans Hill diverges to the left. The old Village Gates were situated almost straight ahead at the corner of Broomfield Park but their replacement on the left of the picture can hardly be seen.

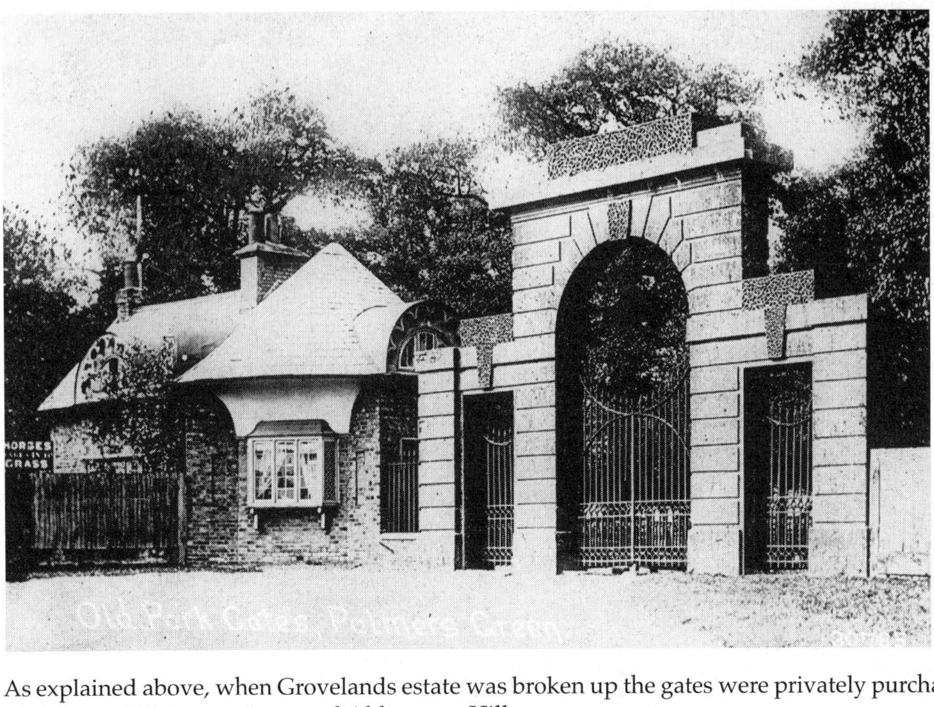

Having reached the Village Gates and with Broomfield Park in front of us, this is a good time to take a look at Broomfield House and its park on our way to Palmers Green.

This picture shows what used to be the main gateway into Grovelands estate and which originally stood in Aldermans Hill near its present junction with Old Park Road. This road continued through the countryside of the Old Park estate between Aldermans Hill and Fox lane, crossing the Mall footpath to emerge briefly at the Pound by the Woodman Inn. From here the drive continued into Grovelands estate, to circle around the lake and lead up to the house.

As explained above, when Grovelands estate was broken up the gates were privately purchased and reinstalled at the junction of Cannon Hill, Powys Lane and Aldermans Hill.

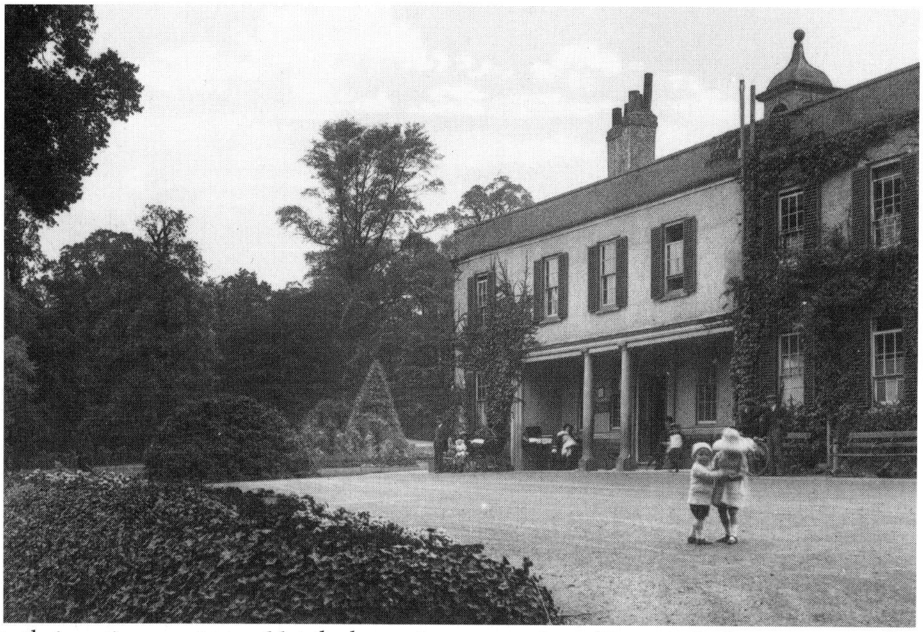

Broomfield House and its surroundings date from the sixteenth century when a hunting lodge was built on the site. It is certain that a large house has been there since 1624 although it has been considerably rebuilt and improved since then; the inner core of the house certainly dates from the sixteenth century but the staircase and hall, with their painted murals, were built in the early eighteenth century. The original façade and roof structure were altered in the 1800s and false half-timbering was added as recently as the 1930s.

After having several early owners the house was purchased in 1816 by the Powys family from Wales who lived in it for a number of years. Eventually they moved back to their native country and let the house to a succession of tenants. Its last tenant was Sir Ralph Littler QC who lived there from 1874 until 1901 when the Powys family decided to put the house and grounds on the market.

In 1903 the house and 54 acres of its grounds were acquired by Southgate Council for £25,000. Since then the property has undergone a variety of uses including a school, maternity centre, dental clinic and a health centre. In 1925 part of the house was opened as Broomfield Museum with a changing series of local exhibitions and permanent collections of stuffed animals and birds. There was also a café on the ground floor. The house was given over to the military during the Second World War and the museum didn't reopen until 1949.

Sad to say, the house was partly destroyed by fire on 25 April 1984 and has stood derelict ever since, swathed in plastic sheeting and scaffolding, whilst various bodies argue over its future. In 1996 it had been hoped that Whitbread's would convert it into a restaurant but nothing came of this. Since then Enfield Preservation Society has played a leading part in preventing Enfield Council from demolishing the house. Another fire in December 1994 caused serious damage, most of the first floor being lost as well as much of the original timber framing of the 1550s. This picture from July 1913 shows the house in happier days.

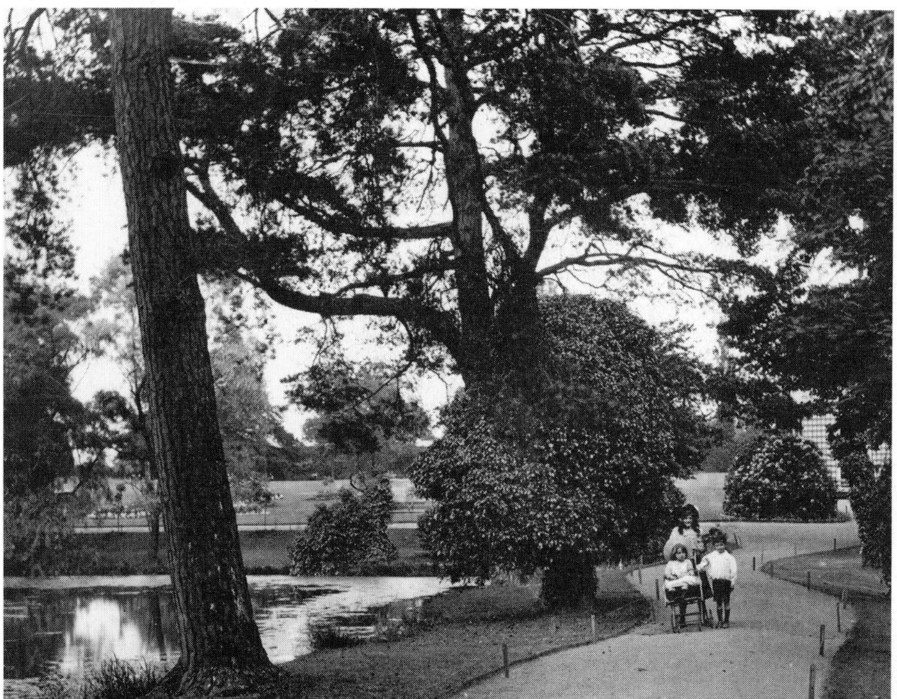

A view of Broomfield Park's gardens in 1927. Much of the original estate was sold for building but 21 hectares survived and were acquired by the borough of Southgate in 1902 as a park, which was opened on 23 April 1903 by W.B. Brown Esq., JP.

In the park's early years one of the lakes was used as a public bathing pond, but bathing was subsequently stopped on the grounds of public health and new indoor baths were built in the borough. The bandstand was built on the lower lake in 1928 and is still in use today. A running track was also built to the east of the house but only its outline remains today.

An avenue of elm trees used to run westwards towards Southgate but these succumbed to Dutch Elm disease in 1978 and have been replaced by young lime trees.

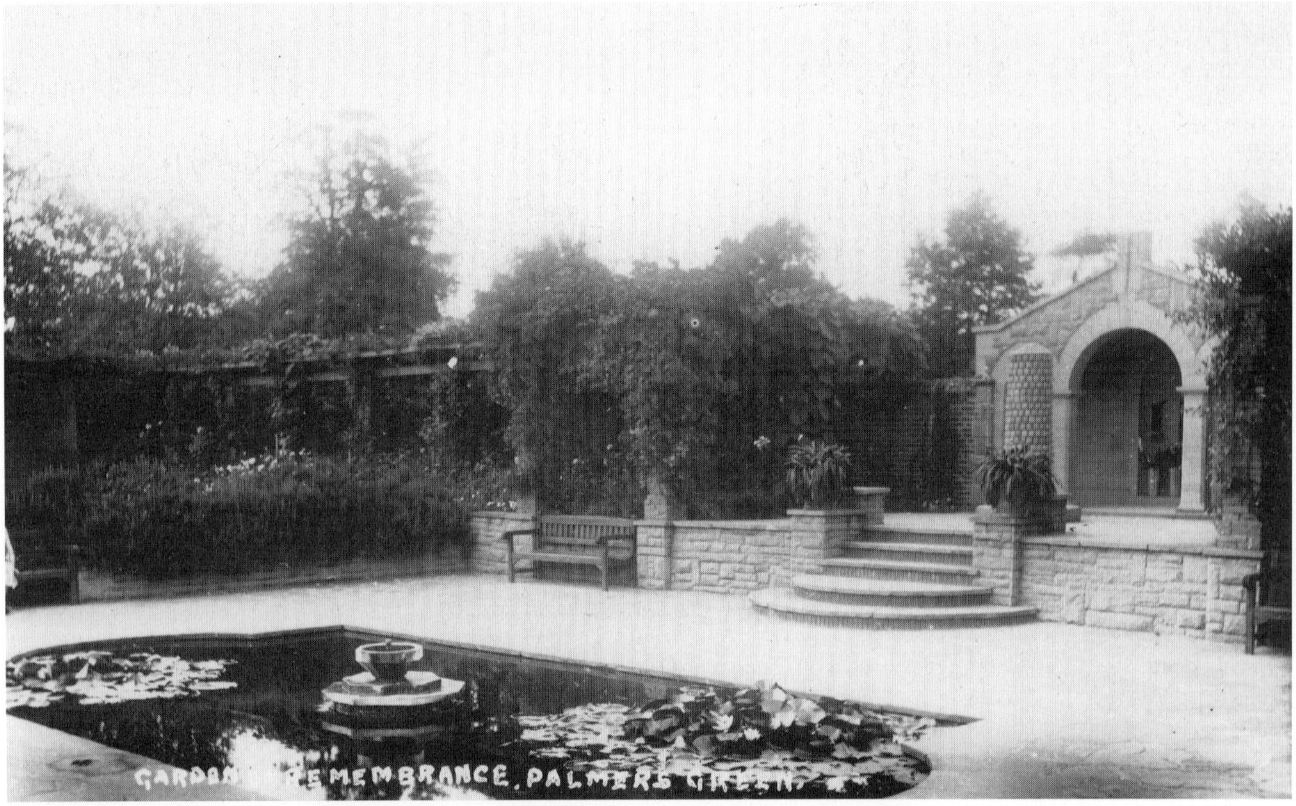

The Garden of Remembrance was built in Broomfield Park as a memorial to the Southgate men who gave up their lives in First World War and was opened on 7 July 1929 by Admiral Lord Jellicoe.

The garden contains a pond and an ornamental pergola, which is known as the Pergola Walk. It also houses the memorial cairn, constructed of stones, which was erected in memory of those men who died. At the base of the cairn are the words, 'Each stone symbolises a life laid down'. The memorial was later extended to include the casualties of the Second World War.

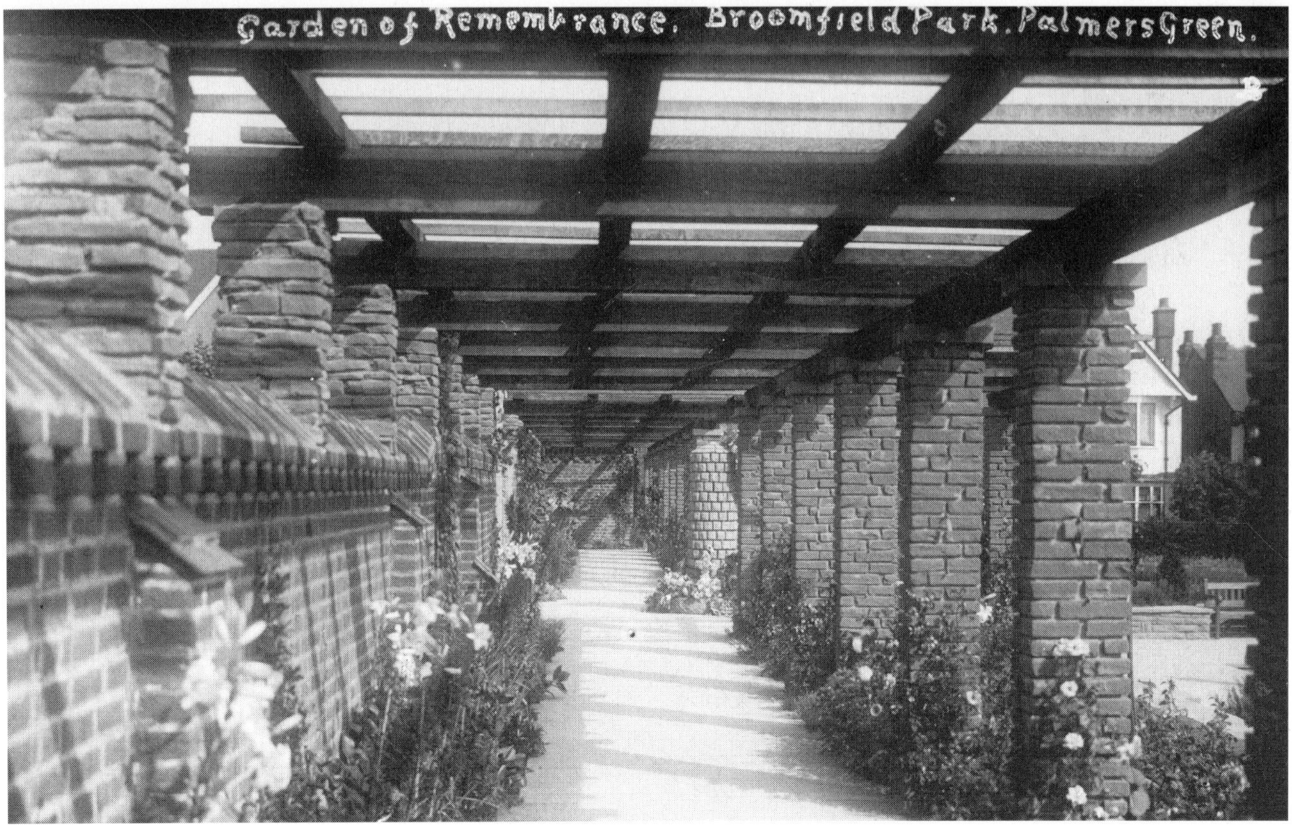

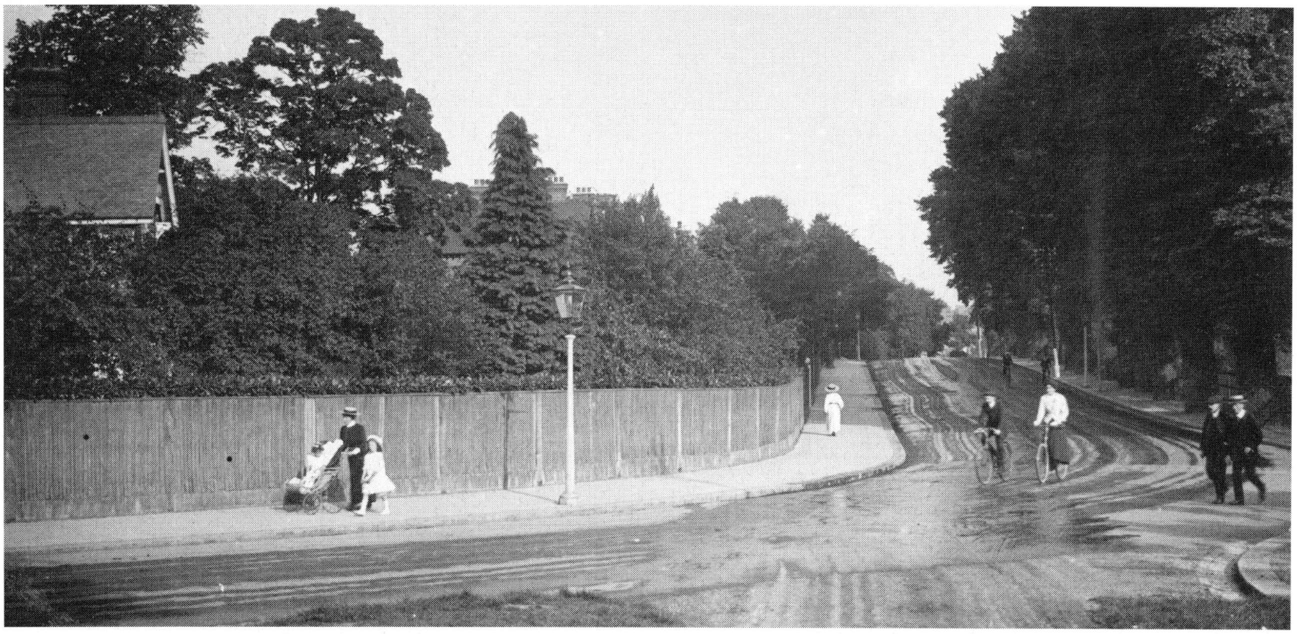

Let's walk back across the park and return to the site of the Village Gates at the top of Aldermans Hill. This is an early road that is marked on the Enclosure map of 1801 and in the picture above we are looking down the road in the direction of Palmers Green with Broomfield Park on the right. The road is named after Alderman Sir William Curtis (1752—1829) who lived at Cullands Grove, which was situated on the left of this picture in the angle between Aldermans Hill and Cannon Hill. He was a great friend of the Prince of Wales and was a fat, jovial and convivial man. He was also a long-serving Alderman of the City of London and a Tory MP. After his death in 1829 his estate was put up for sale and was bought by John Donnithorne Taylor who demolished the mansion house in 1840 because he didn't like to have a fine house on his estate that rivalled his own home at Grovelands.

Going down Aldermans Hill the first road we come to on the left is Ulleswater Road. This road and its neighbouring roads were built on part of the Old Park estate, which had been sold for building in 1902. Their names were probably given to them by Charles Griffiths Lawson who had become Southgate's first surveyor on its separation from Edmonton in 1881 and had previously held an official post at Ullswater in the Lake District; other nearby roads were named Derwent and Lakeside and the area became known as the Lakes estate. 'Ulleswater' is the old spelling of the name on Victorian maps and guide books.

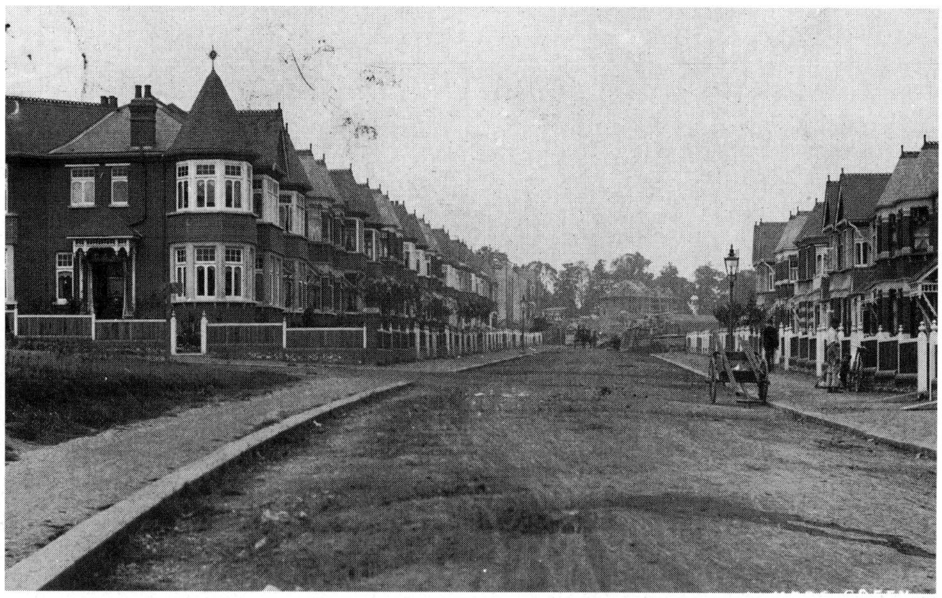

Ulleswater Road was the most affluent part of the Lakes estate. Built by the firm of W.J. Edwards, house prices ranged from £375 to £1,400. The first houses were occupied by the end of 1905 and in 1913 No. 59 was being advertised in the *Recorder* newspaper as a modern substantially built semi-detached residence at £430 leasehold with ground rent of £8. It was described as comprising a dining room, drawing room, kitchen, three bedrooms, kitchen, scullery, WCs, tool house, coal shed etc., and a large garden.

The council was proud of its new estate and houses in this road and in nearby Derwent Road; they featured prominently in the Southgate Urban District Council Official Guide of 1905.

In this picture of Ulleswater Road, Conway Road is on the left and the estate is still under construction. Later residents have generally been kind to the houses, many of them having retained the original doors, windows, porches and other details which go to make them such fine examples of Edwardian housing.

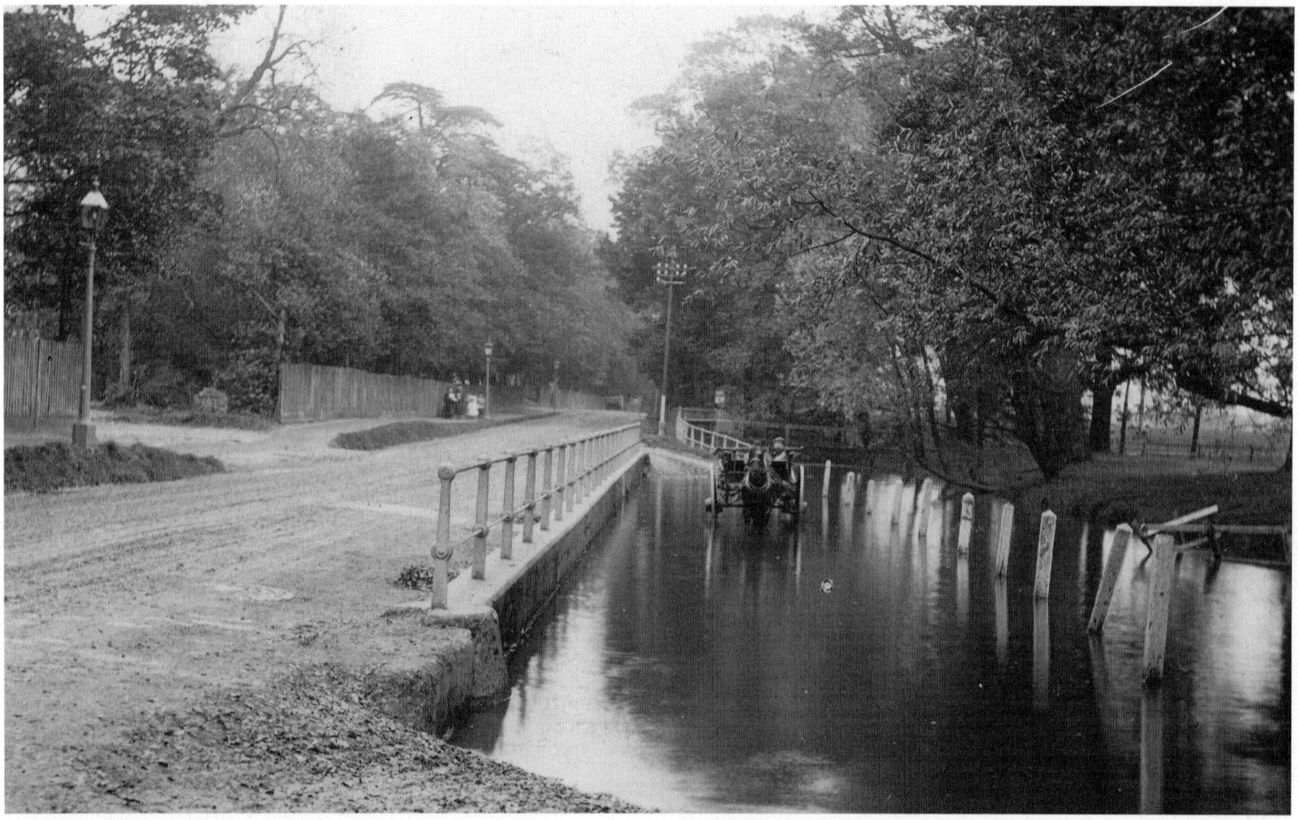

The horse pond alongside Broomfield Park, also known as the 'long water', was situated a little further down Aldermans Hill opposite to where Derwent Road enters it today. The retaining wall and railed barrier protected the pond but the road allowed entry and exit from either end. Horses and carriages would quietly splash their way through to cool off on a hot summer's day. It was filled in during in 1908, probably because of the rebuilding of the roadway and pavement (they certainly appear to need it!) and the extensive building development across the way that by then stretched right across to Fox Lane.

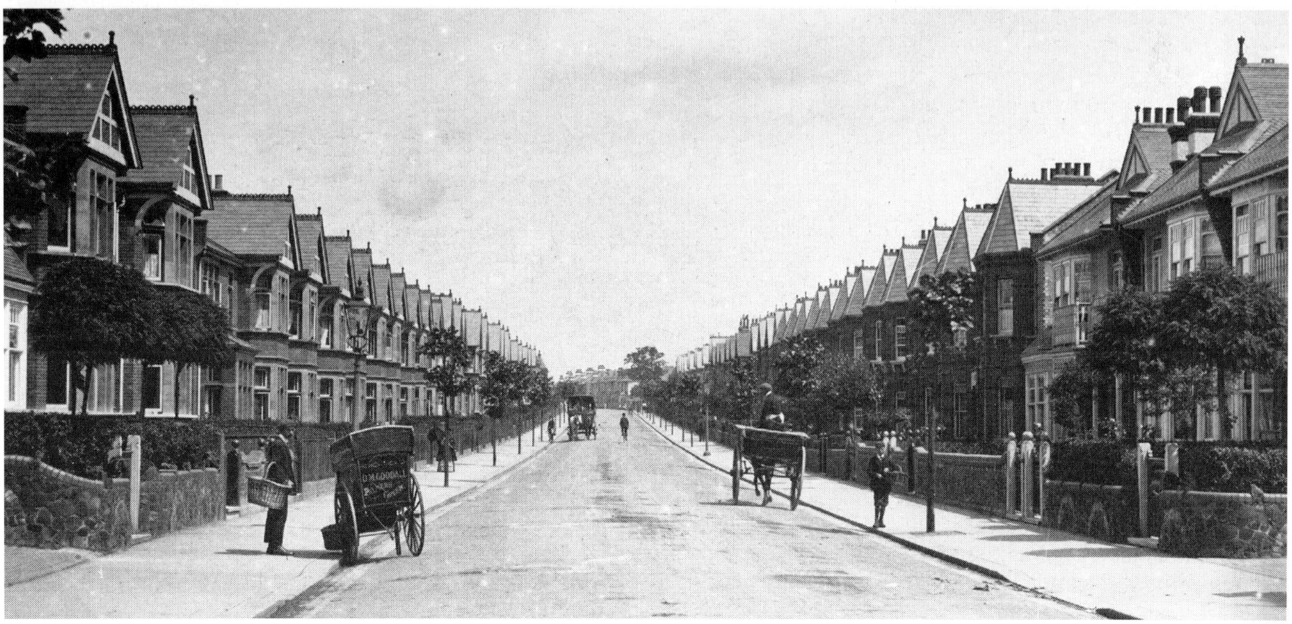

Continuing on our way down Aldermans Hill we come to Grovelands Road on the left. The houses here are very similar to those in Ulleswater Road and the Mall though not as ornately decorated. All the same, nowadays they are still well-kept with plenty of original features remaining.

In the distance the two horses pulling a delivery van are waiting patiently in the road whilst their driver delivers a parcel to one of the houses, passed by a cyclist going in the opposite direction. On the right a young workman is driving a one-horse cart down the road, whilst on the left the baker's deliveryman from D.M. Goodall of Palmers Green is busy on his rounds.

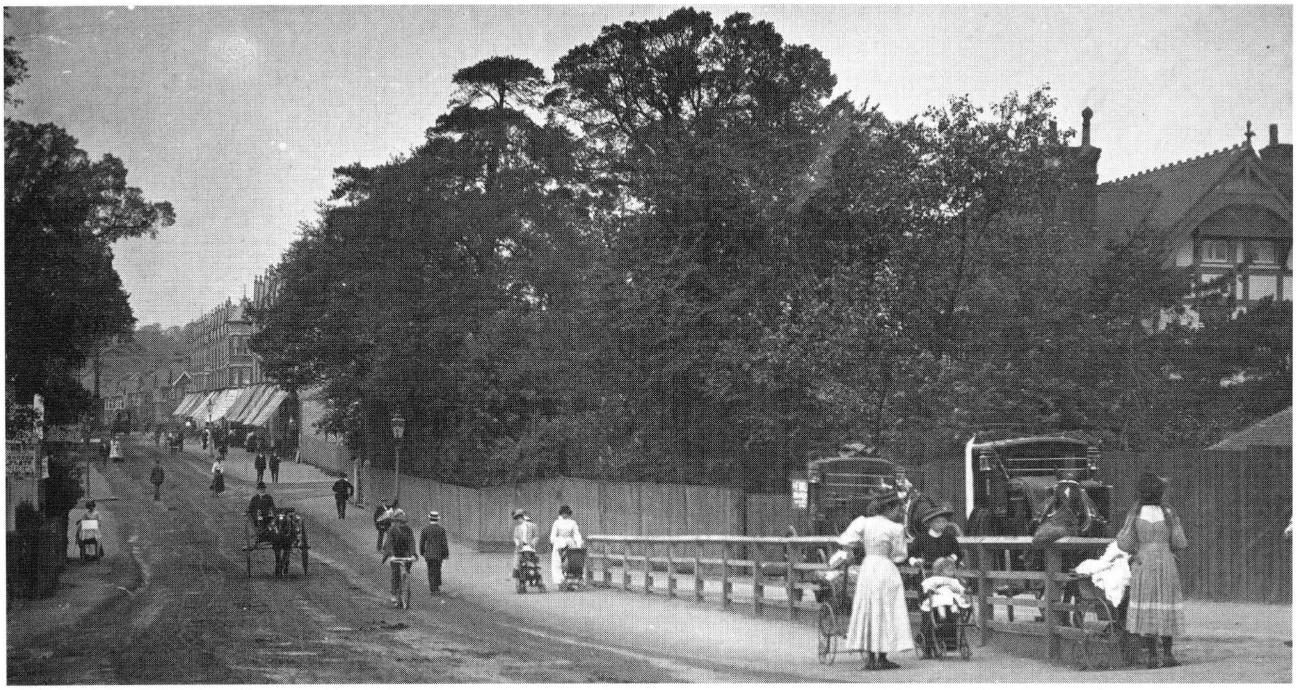

We are now at the Palmers Green end of Aldermans Road, looking back towards Southgate. The row of shops is called Park Parade and the date of the picture is September 1910. Old Park Road is on the right with Grovelands Road beyond it, passing between the two rows of shops. Broomfield Avenue runs off to the left opposite Old Park Road.

The large house on the right behind the fence is Old Park House itself. It had been built for Colin Docwra, the son of Thomas Docwra of Swanage who in 1833 had founded the well-known firm of public works contractors. The house was demolished just before the outbreak of the Second World War in order to build flats in its place.

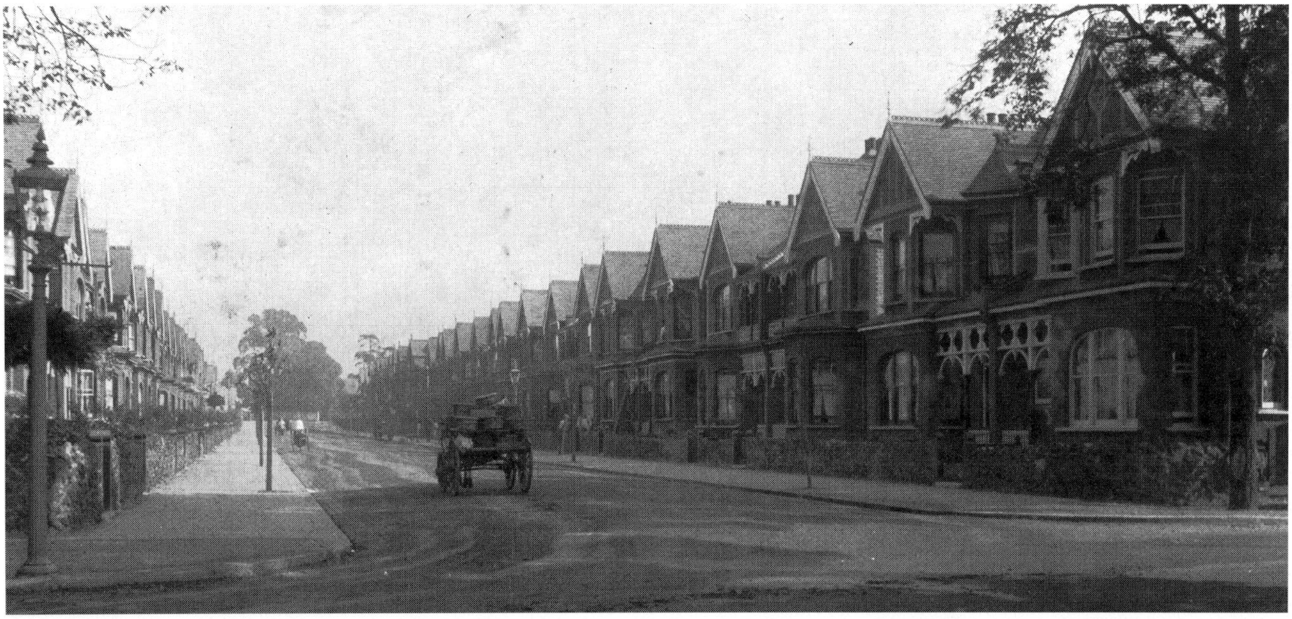

Broomfield Avenue, off Aldermans Hill, was built on part of the Broomfield Park estate. In bygone years what later became the avenue was known as Warren Lane and led to Warren Field, so named because of the abundance of rabbits.

In 1902/03 a little row of houses in the lane called Warren Cottages was demolished to make way for the new Broomfield Avenue's houses. The cottages were sold to the contractor for £10 in total.

The first houses were built in the section of the lane between Aldermans Hill and Broomfield Lane. They were all occupied by 1905 and the first picture shows them in as they were in 1910, looking up the avenue towards Aldermans Hill. The houses were advertised as being semi-detached containing five bedrooms, bathroom, two toilets, large dining room, drawing room, large hall with fireplace, kitchen, scullery, servants' side entrance, paved yard, good gardens, and they were tastefully decorated and fitted with electric bells and gas. These houses could be purchased at prices starting at £450.

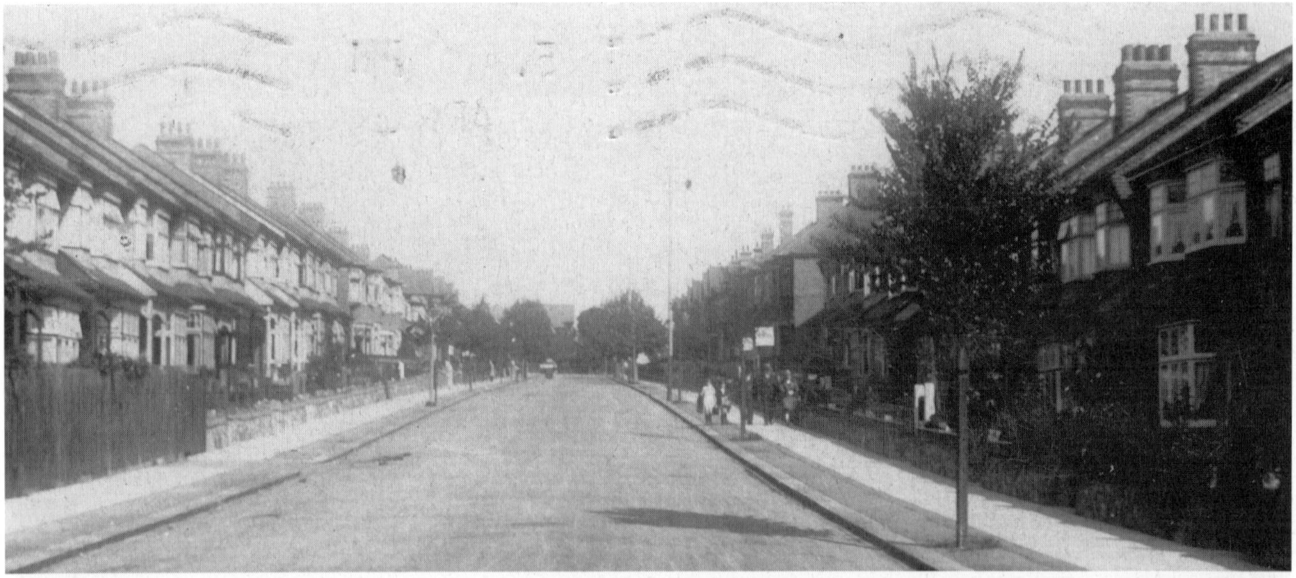

The 1914 Ordnance Survey map shows the section north of Broomfield Lane to be fully developed but the section to the south was still under construction. This was interrupted by the First World War and was not completed until the 1920s. The above picture shows this southern section in 1931, looking up towards Broomfield Lane.

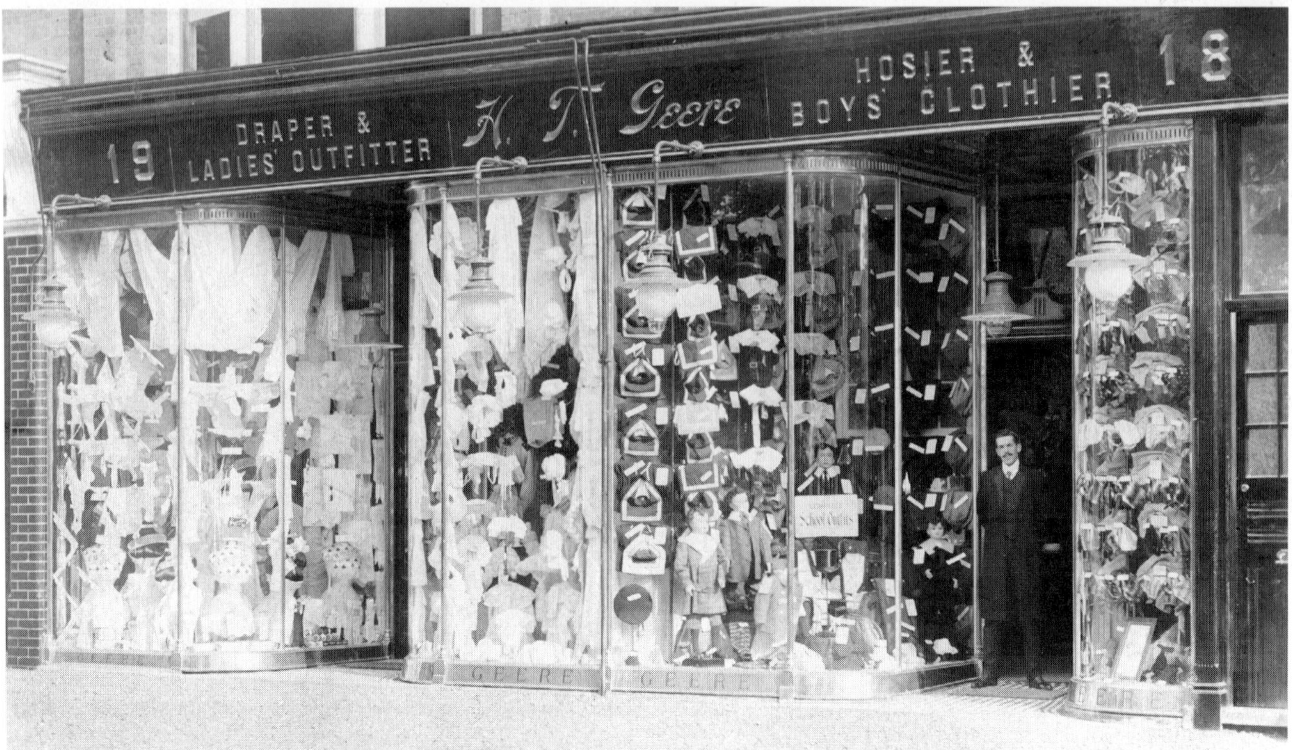

This is Harry Geere's well-stocked drapers shop in Aldermans Hill's Park Parade in 1907 with Mr Geere himself standing proudly in the doorway. One of his advertisements in the local directory said, 'Suits made to order from 35/-. Cut, fit and style guaranteed. Gentlemen waited on at their private residences'. Another of his advertisements reads, 'Complete Juvenile Outfitter, Hosier, Hatter, Bespoke Tailor, Fancy Draper. My blouse stock is the smartest in the district and most up-to-date. West End styles at moderate prices. A splendid stock of Ladies Underwear. All the newest shapes in corsets'.

The sign in the window to his left is advertising complete school outfits whilst the furthest window is displaying tailor-made corsets designed for the 'wasp' waists that were fashionable at the time.

Unfortunately Mr Geere's business didn't survive the economies of the First World War. Since then the shops in Aldermans Hill have been renumbered and his premises are now Nos. 86 and 88, and occupied respectively by Cathy Jones and Corrine Pascal's Dental Surgery and by Pets Corner. Their shop fronts have been considerably altered but the Park Side Café next door at No. 90 still has the same style of boarding above the shop windows.

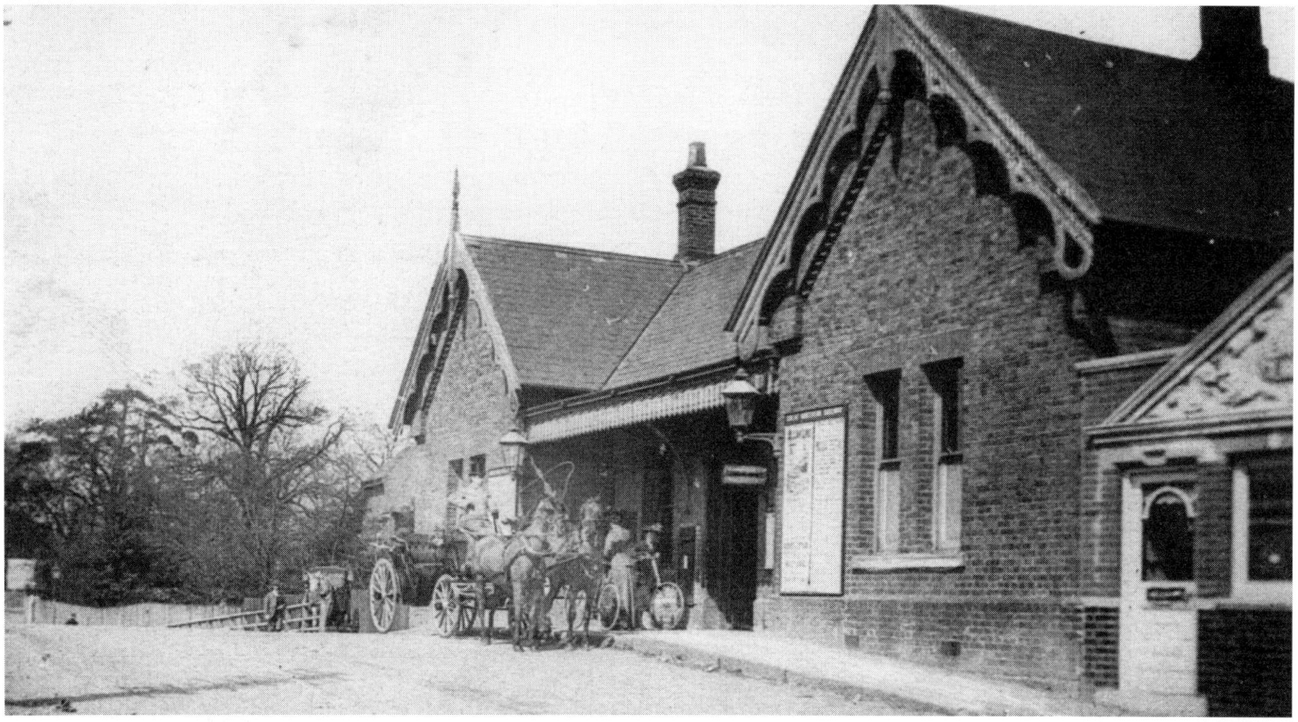

Two interesting views of the Great Northern Railway's Palmers Green & Southgate Station, which opened in 1871 with 16 weekday trains each way to Kings Cross and four on Sundays. The local bus service from Avenue Road in Southgate was rerouted from New Southgate & Colney Hatch Station to Palmers Green. The fare from Palmers Green Station to the Cherry Tree was 2*d*., to Chase Side was 3*d*. and beyond there was 4*d*.

The horse buses were originally run by local publicans. Robert Davey (the Fox), William Pickard (the Crown), Frank Lowe (the Rising Sun) and Henry Bray (the Cherry Tree) were just four of the licensees running services before the arrival of the motorbus in 1912. The horse buses would stop and wait in the little cobbled yard at the Southgate side of the station to allow those early day commuters on or off the bus. That cobbled yard altered very little in over 100 years until a new entrance to the car park was formed in recent years.

The first picture shows the station in Victorian days, looking towards Southgate. One of the horse buses can be seen in the background, standing in the cobbled yard, but the vehicle standing at the front of the station appears to be a luxurious two-horse landau with a top-hatted coachman sitting on the box. Two ladies wearing full skirts are standing with their bicycles by the station entrance and on the wall beside them is the post box inscribed 'VR' that is still there today.

Herbert Gales was stationmaster for many years and Wharncliffe Silkstone Colliery Co. Ltd. occupied the station yard.

The lower picture shows the station from the opposite direction in 1905, looking down towards the Triangle. More advertisements have appeared on its walls; the 'Where to Live?' poster on the left and the white poster on the right are both extolling the virtues of the Northern Heights as being 'London's Healthiest Suburb'. The two smaller posters are advertising the sale of building land in the area whilst the last poster shows a lady golfer recommending the golf courses that could be reached by the Great Northern Railway and its allied companies at Skegness, Woodhall Spa, Knaresborough and Cromer. Next door is the office belonging to Herbert Clarke Ltd, coal merchants, and then comes the row of shops known as Station Parade.

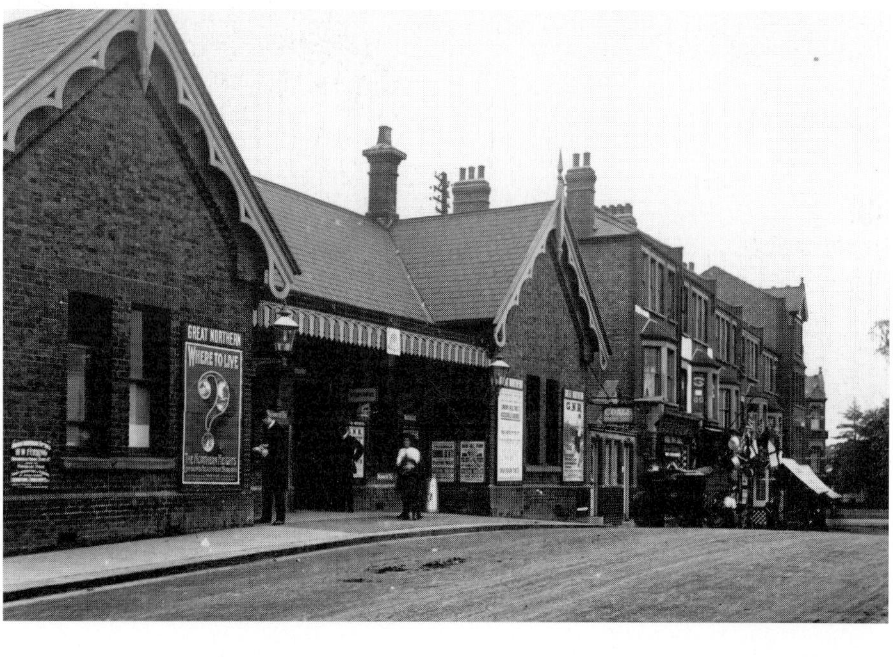

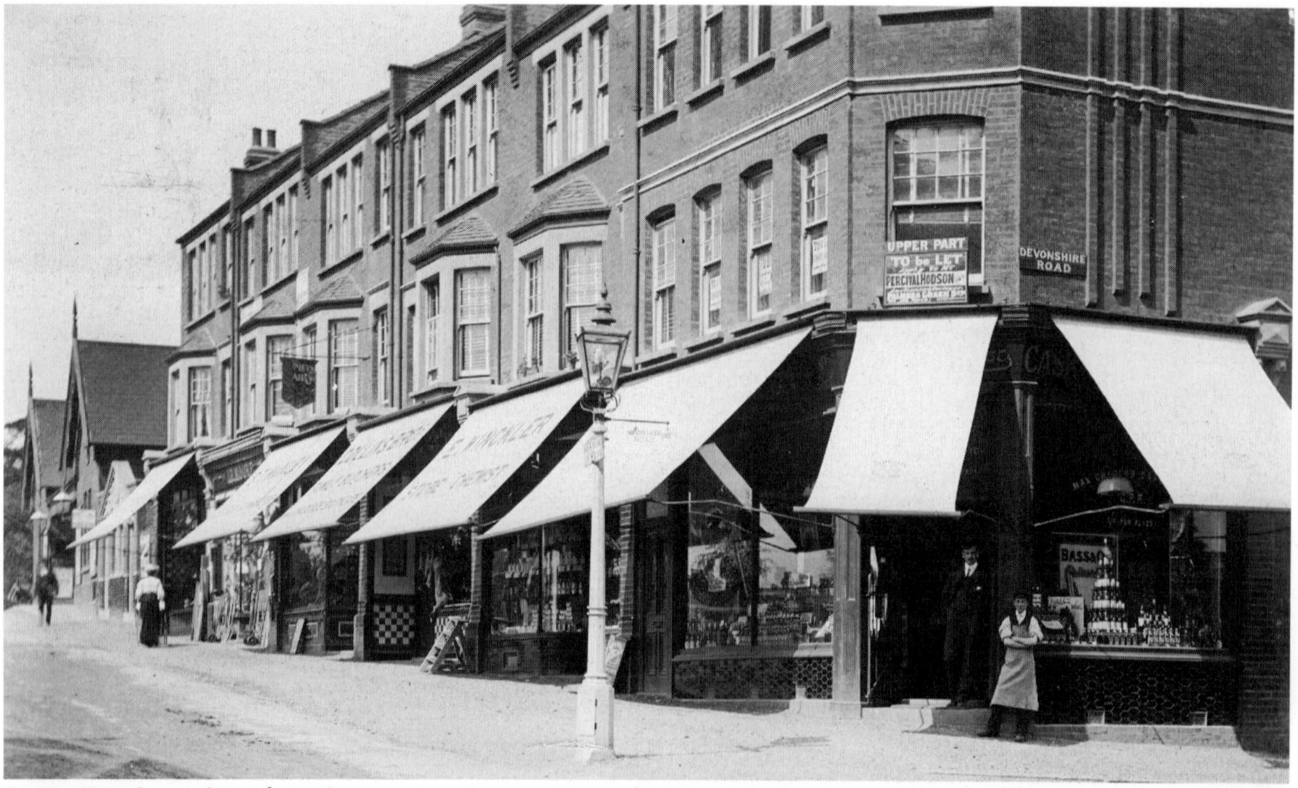

Station Parade ran from the railway station down to Devonshire Road. In the above picture, which dates from around 1903, the shops - from right to left - are Harry Green, wine and spirit merchant, E. Winckler, chemist, Collins Bros., butchers, Edwin T. Manley, dairy, J.R. Moore, ironmongers, and an unidentified shop.

The lower picture dates from only a year or two later but already there have been several changes in the ownership of the shops but no changes in their businesses. The line-up from right to left is now Thomas Philip Marshall, wines and spirits merchant, Ernest A. Barton, chemist, Collins Bros., butchers, Emerton & Sons Ltd, dairy, John Knowles & Co. Ltd, ironmongers, and Rupert Brown, laundry. In both pictures Herbert Clarke Ltd, coal merchants, are next, followed by the railway station.

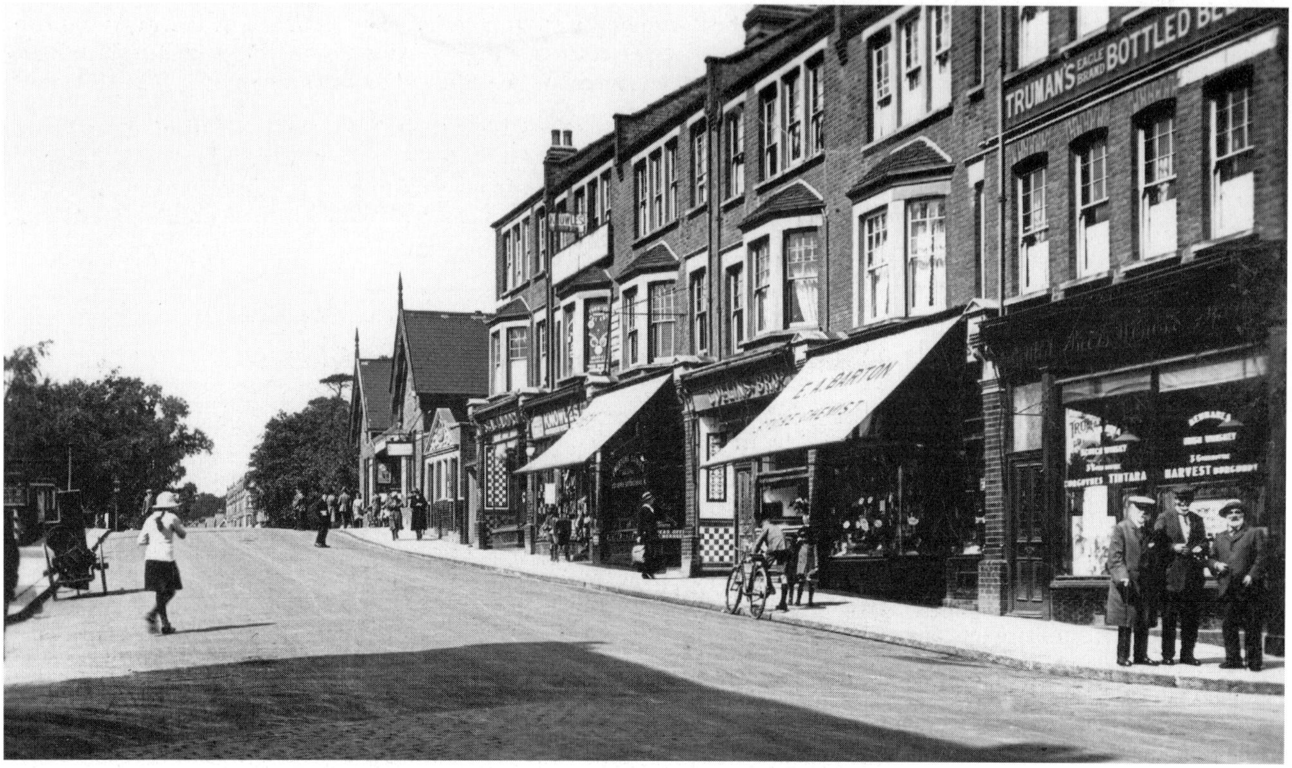

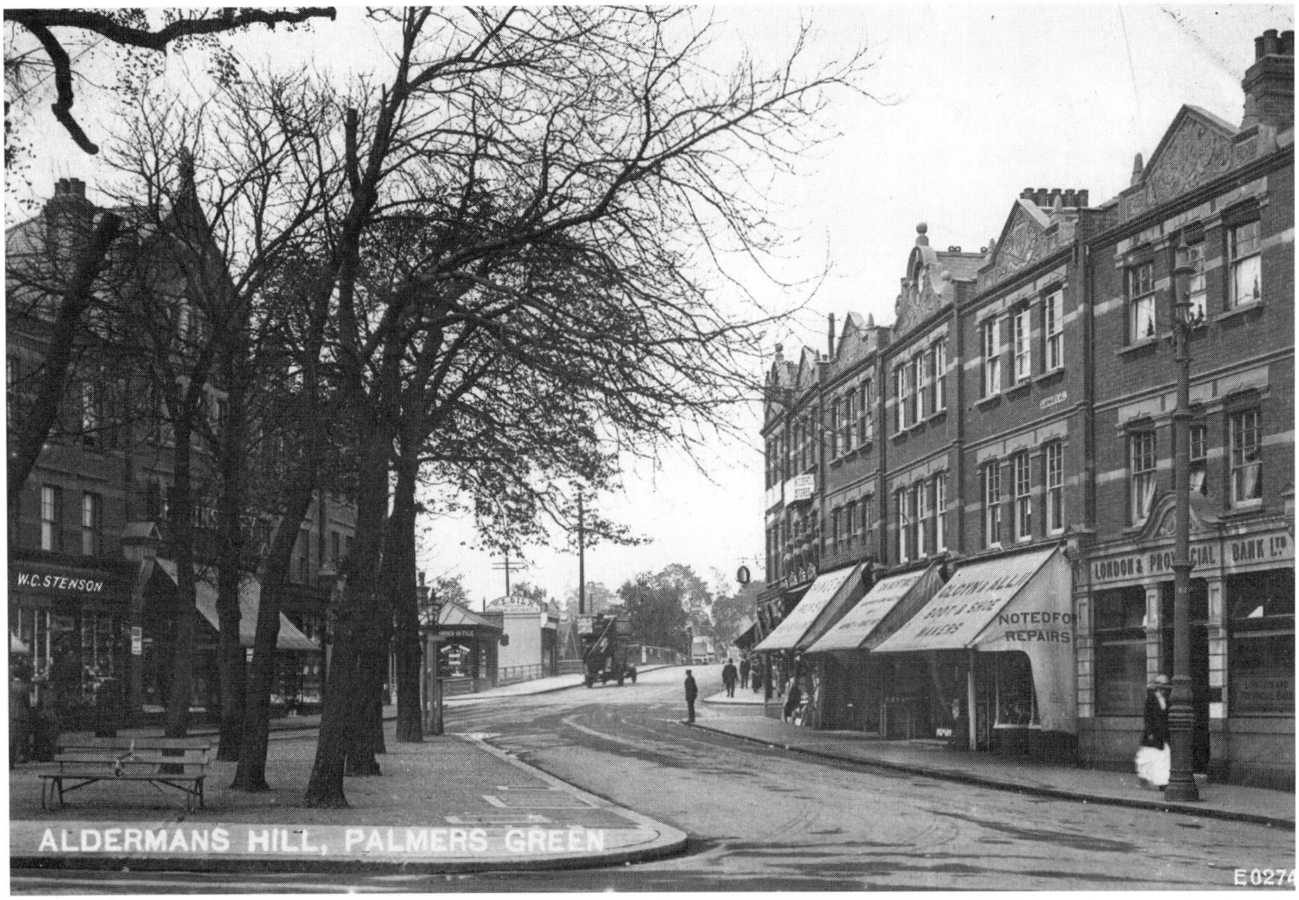
W.C. STENSON
NOTED FOR REPAIRS
BOOT & SHOE MAKERS
LONDON & PROVINCIAL BANK LTD
ALDERMANS HILL, PALMERS GREEN
E 0274

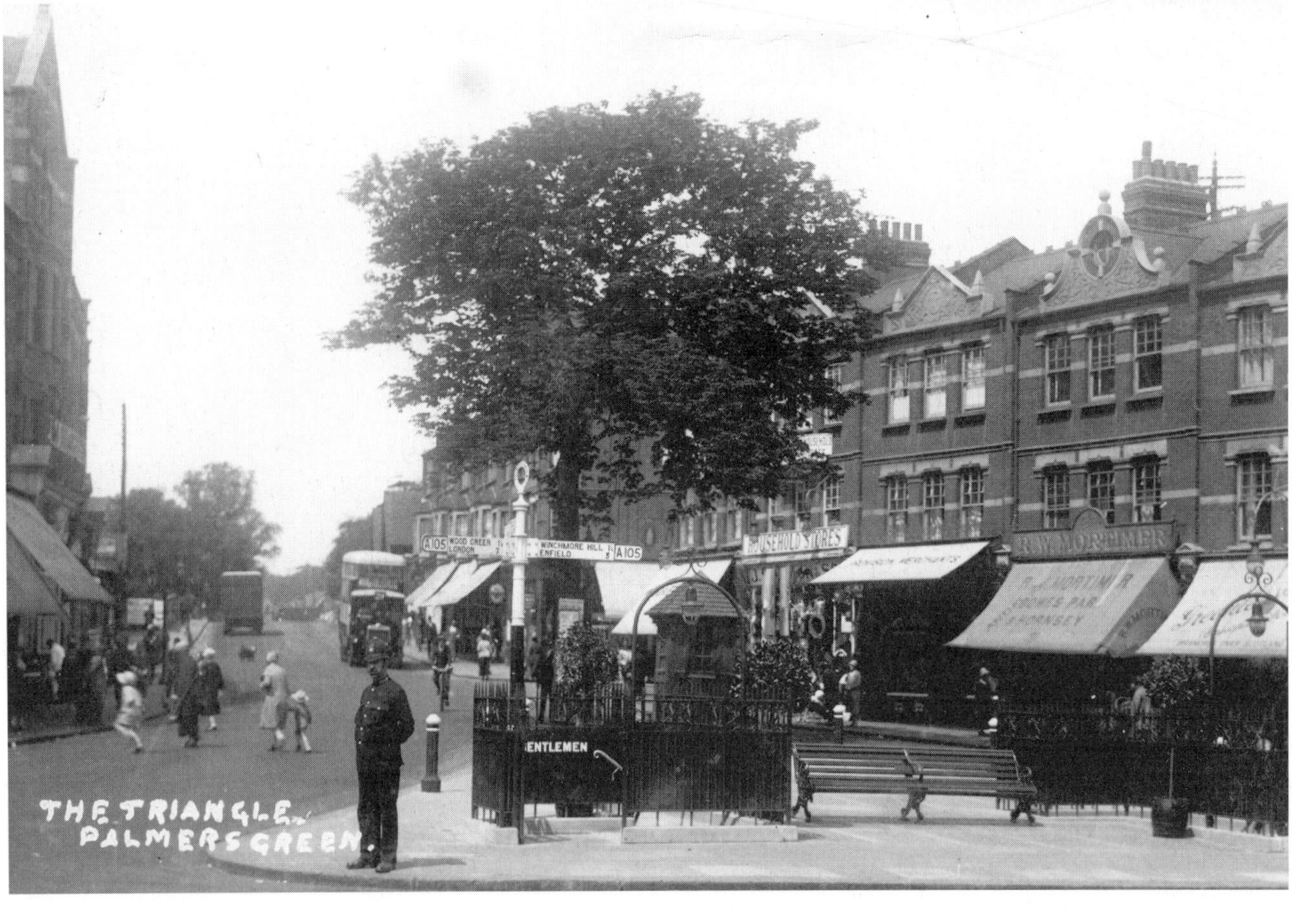
A105 WOOD GREEN LONDON
WINCHMORE HILL ENFIELD A105
HOUSEHOLD STORES
R.W. MORTIMER
GENTLEMEN
THE TRIANGLE, PALMERS GREEN

Reaching the bottom of Aldermans Hill, we are at the point where it makes a triangular junction with Green Lanes. Not surprisingly, the area itself is known as the Triangle.

In the two opposite pictures we are looking back up Aldermans Hill with Devonshire Road entering from the right beyond the shops. Both were taken from a similar position, the upper picture sometime shortly after 1912 and the lower in the late 1920s, but just look at the differences between them on the Triangle itself. All the trees in the upper picture have been chopped down apart from one at the apex of the Triangle and have been replaced with public conveniences and a police call box. The surface of the Triangle looks to have been newly paved and the roadway now appears to have a proper tarmacadam surface.

In the earlier picture the businesses on the right begin with the London & Provincial Bank (taken over by Barclays Bank in 1918), followed by Gloyn & Allin, bootmakers, R.W. Mortimer, butchers, Prince Bros., provision merchants, J. Salmon & Son, grocers, and end at Devonshire Road with Manor Farm Dairy Ltd. The gabled building on the left across the road was a Sainsbury's shop.

Despite the gap of around 15 years the only change in shopowners in the later picture is that the bootmaker's shop by then belonged to Greenlees & Son.

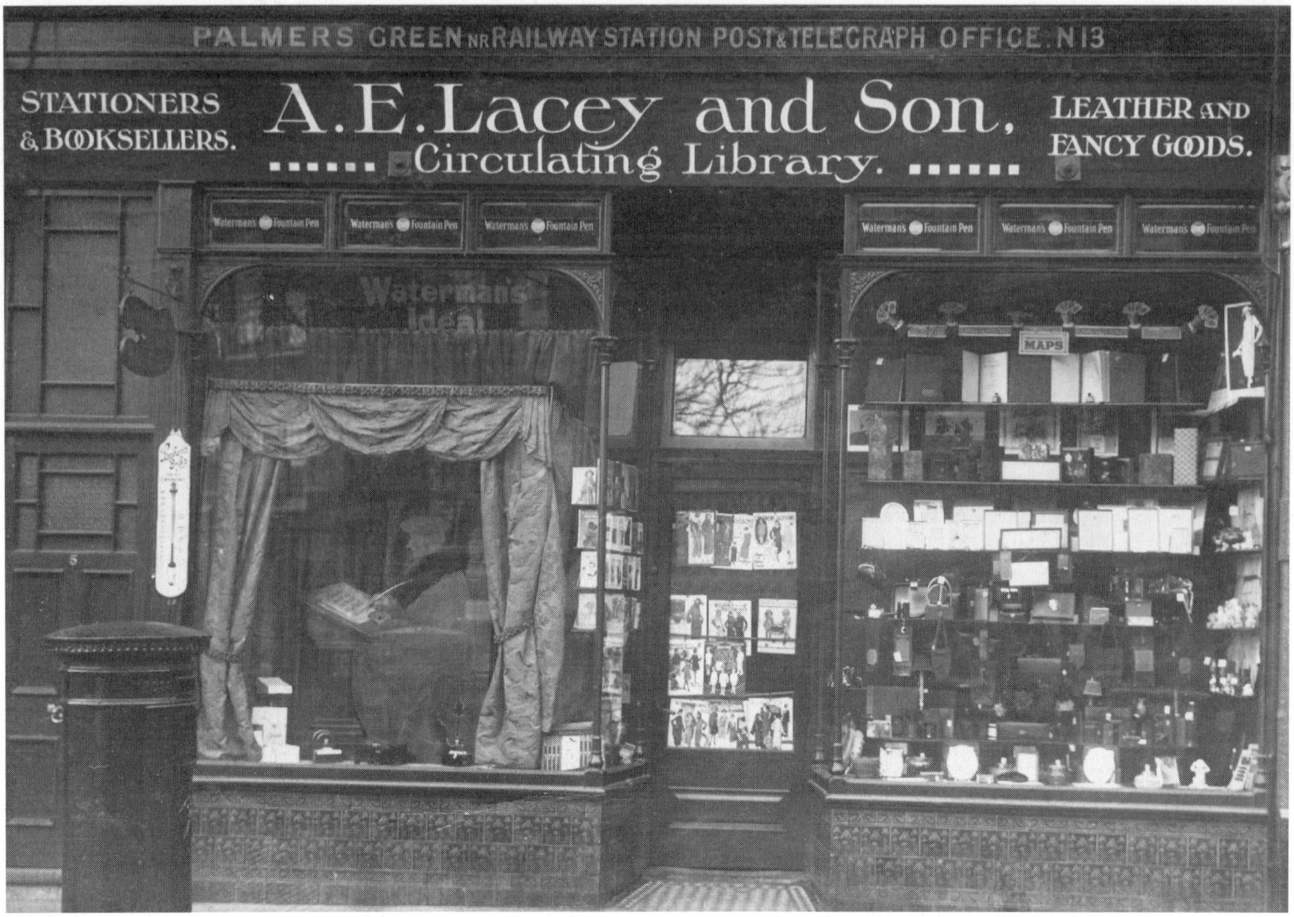

A.E. Lacey & Son's shop at No. 5 was located on the western side of the Triangle. This picture shows it in 1923 when it sold a wide range of goods as well as being the local post office and circulating library. It is now a branch of W.H. Smith.

The items in the right-hand window are mainly leather and fancy goods whilst the door is covered with lots of magazines, mainly about dressmaking; but who is that sitting in the window on the left? He appears to be a life-size model of a medieval scholar wrapped in a cloak and writing with a quill pen onto parchment.

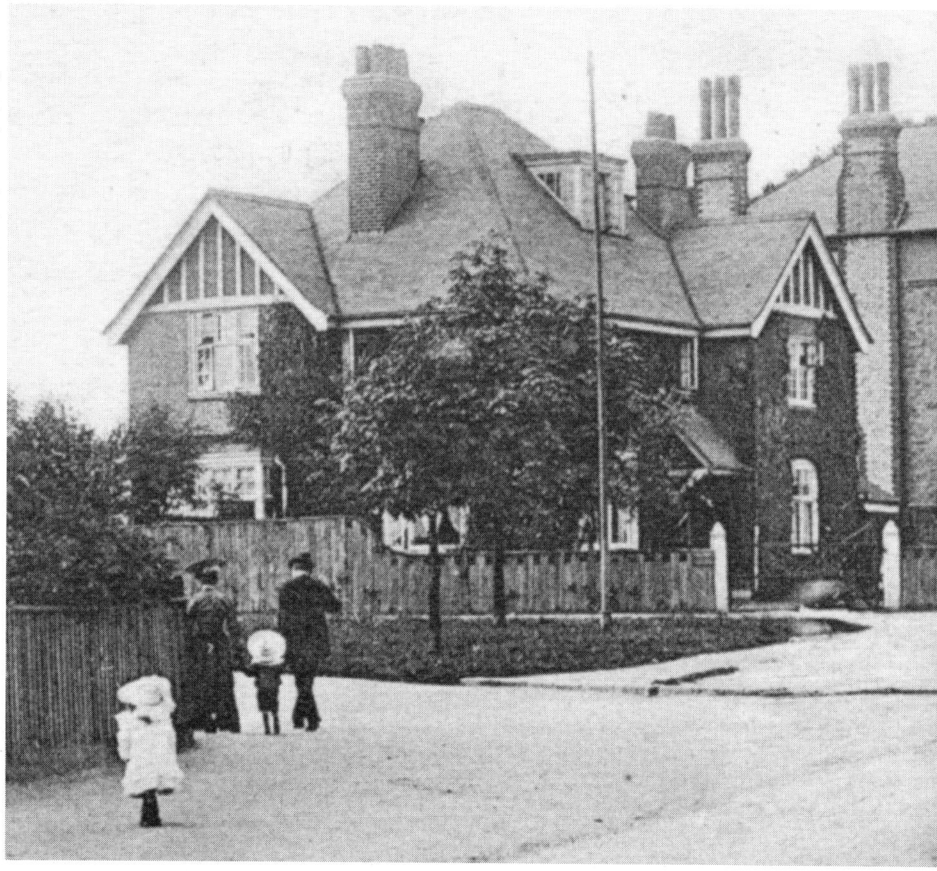

Continuing on our way from the Triangle, we take the right-hand fork onto Green Lanes and immediately come to Old Park Villas on the right. In this picture, which shows the houses in 1904, we are standing by the corner of Broomfield Lane on the left and Oakthorpe Road on the right, looking back towards the Triangle.

These magnificent Edwardian villas, which still look impressive today, are nowadays mainly used as professional offices except that the Triangle Motor Company occupies the middle portion. One thing that has changed over the years is the junction itself. No more leisurely horse-drawn traffic ambling along or the horses taking refreshment at the cattle trough at the corner of Broomfield Lane; traffic lights stand in its place and the lane itself is continually busy with traffic going to and from the supermarket that has been built nearby.

When the Southgate Local Board of Health was set up in 1881 it originally used a modest office at Ash Lodge close to the Cherry Tree Inn at Southgate Green. These premises soon proved to be too small for the purpose and the new offices shown in the picture below were built in 1893 at the junction of Green Lanes and Broomfield Lane, an old thoroughfare which was marked on the 1801 Enclosure map (its name first appears on the 1896 Ordnance Survey map).

The horse is enjoying refreshment at the same cattle trough as that shown in the upper picture. Hampton's were general contractors and had a yard in Broomfield Lane.

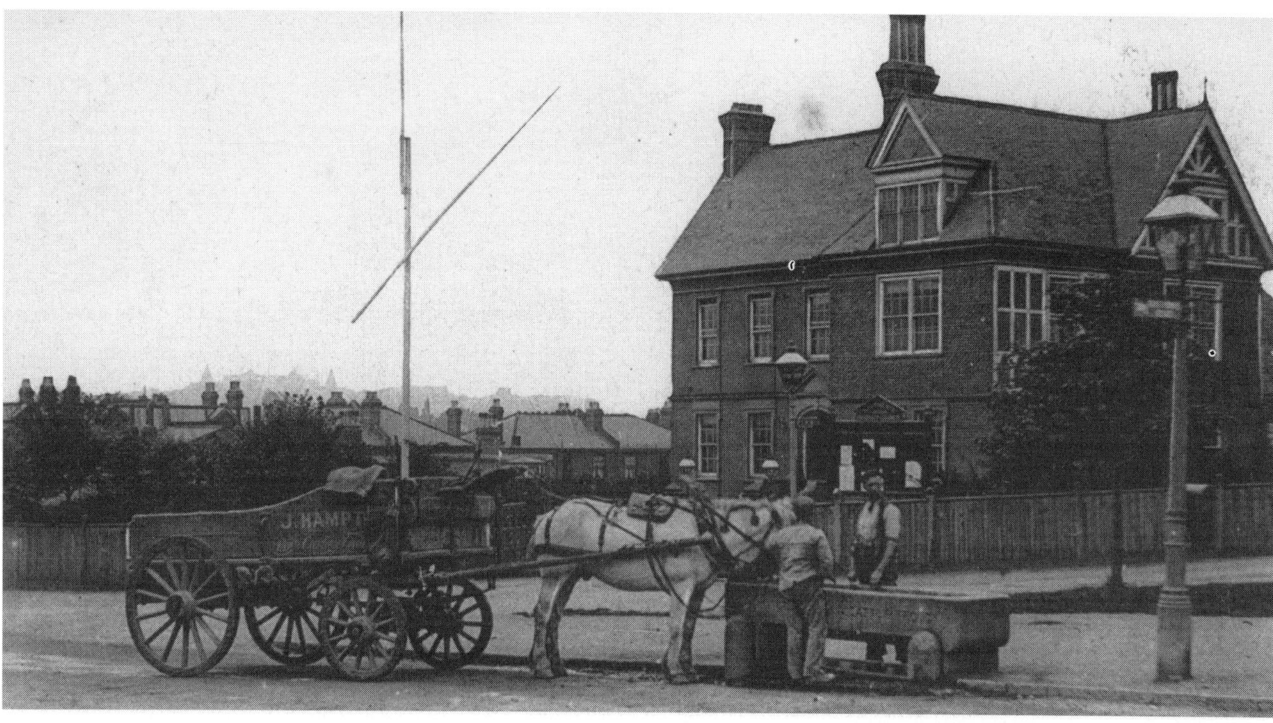

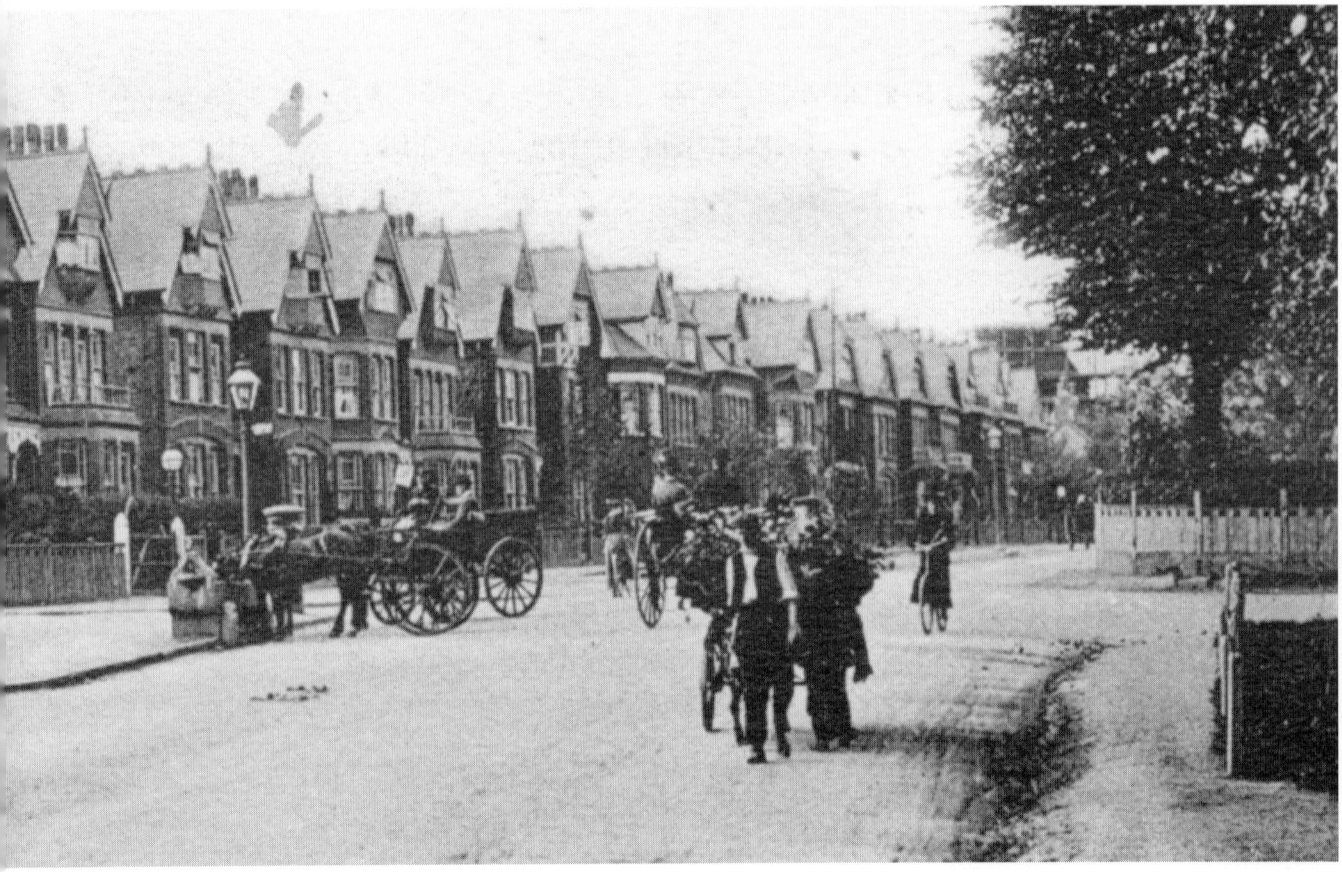

As a result of the 1894 Local Government Act the Southgate Urban District Council superseded the Southgate Local Board of Health. The building was enlarged in 1914 and became Southgate Town Hall, acquiring its clock tower in the process as shown below. The road junction was remodelled and a small triangular traffic island was created, the post box replacing the cattle trough. The tall iron post is supporting the tram wires that by now ran beyond Palmers Green. The building was further extended in 1940 when the library was added with its entrance on Broomfield Lane; this is the form in which it is seen today.

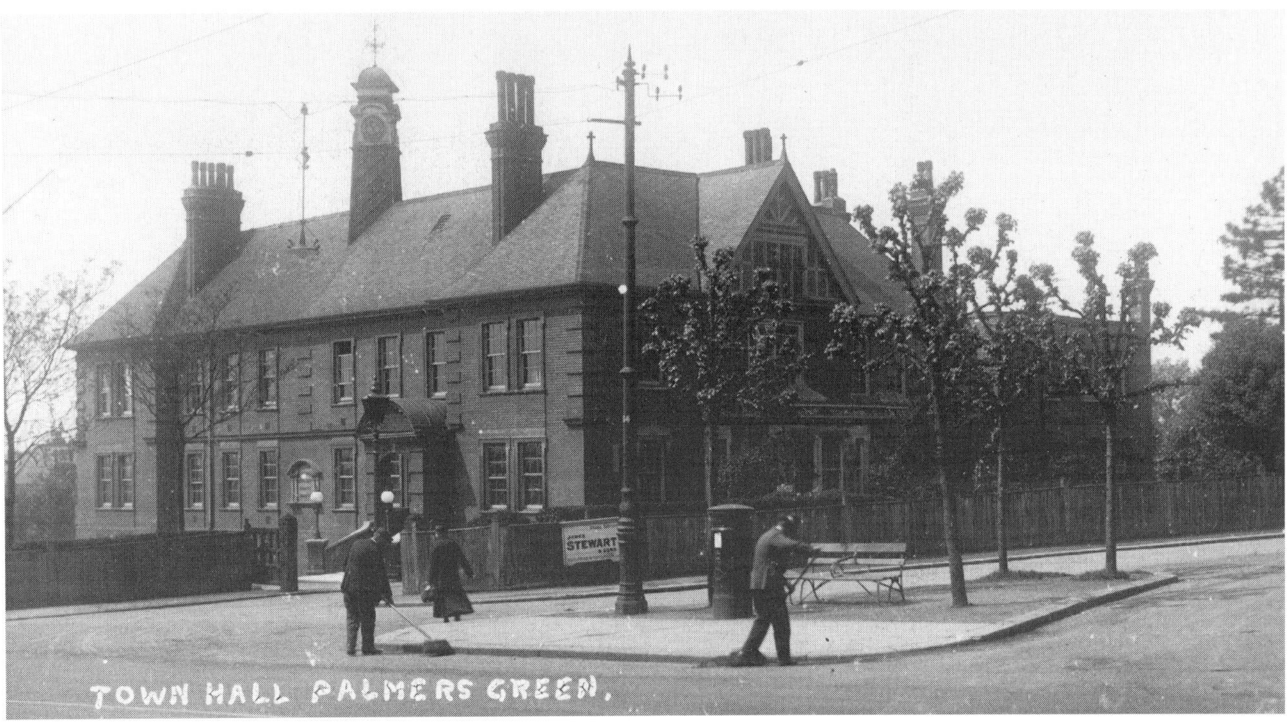

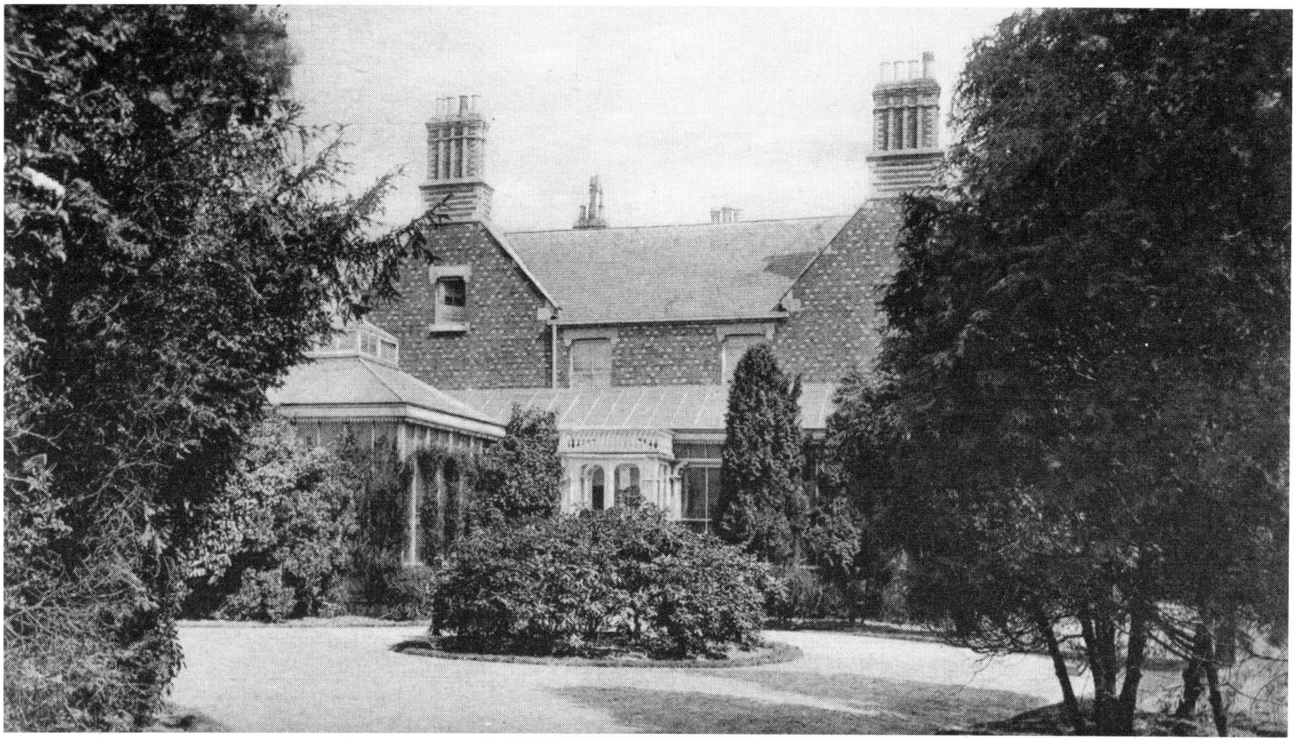

In our next picture we have crossed the road in front of the Town Hall into Oakthorpe Road, which is directly opposite Broomfield Lane. The 1801 Enclosure map calls it Chequers Green Lane and it appears in the 1867 Ordnance Survey map as Kings Arms Lane, named after the pub that formerly stood on the corner. The pub was demolished around 1850 and the sadly derelict Truro House now occupies its site. The road had acquired its present name by 1905.

Oakthorpe was a large house on the north side of the road where St Angela's School now stands. Probably built in the 1870s and standing in beautiful grounds surrounded with fine trees and lawns, for many years it was the home of Dr C.D. Ginsberg. He was the foremost Hebrew scholar of his day and became a local justice of the peace. In 1907 he became the first President of the Palmers Green Liberal Association and died at Oakthorpe in 1914 at the age of 84.

The stables and coach-house led onto a paved courtyard and a separate building, the library, housed the doctor's large collection of bibles and other religious works. In the basement there was a large kitchen, butler's pantry, capacious cupboards and ample cellarage.

In 1916 the property was bought by the Ursulines who transformed it into St Angela's Convent, a boarding and day school. The Ursulines were an order of nuns in the Roman Catholic Church that was founded in 1535 at Brescia, Italy, by St Angela Merici for the education of girls.

For a long time the school was under the direction of Rev. Mother Monica and it was shortly after her death in 1932 that the Ursulines left and the Daughters of Providence took over. They already had a school in Wood Green which continued as a secondary school, with Oakthorpe becoming the junior school. After the Second World War the numbers of pupils continued to increase and a new school building was erected in 1953. In 1971 a new convent was built and the old house demolished. In 1974 a new school in the grounds was opened as St Angela's Roman Catholic School for Girls and Sister Mary Agnes became its first headmistress.

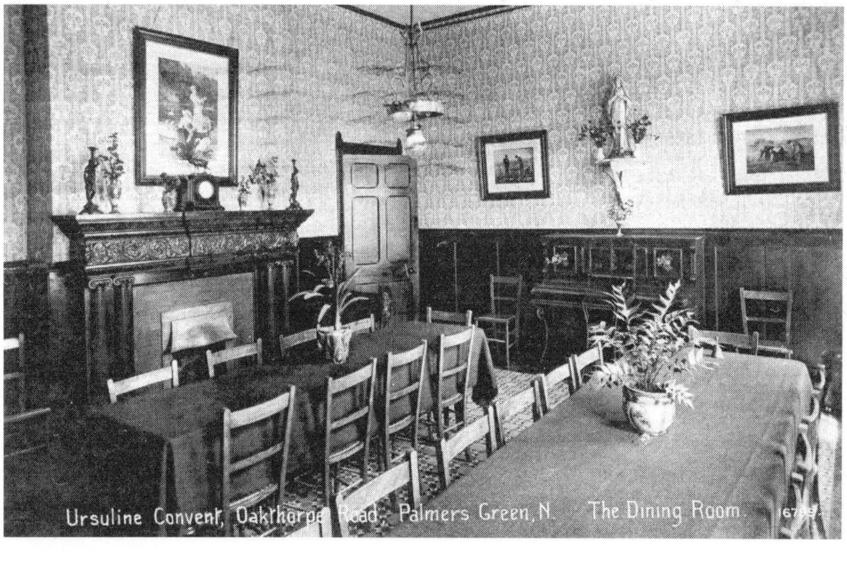

The above picture shows Oakthorpe in 1924 when it had become the Ursuline Convent; the lower one shows its dining room four years later. No trace now remains of the old house but the circular bed of shrubbery in the drive is still *in situ* in front of the new convent.

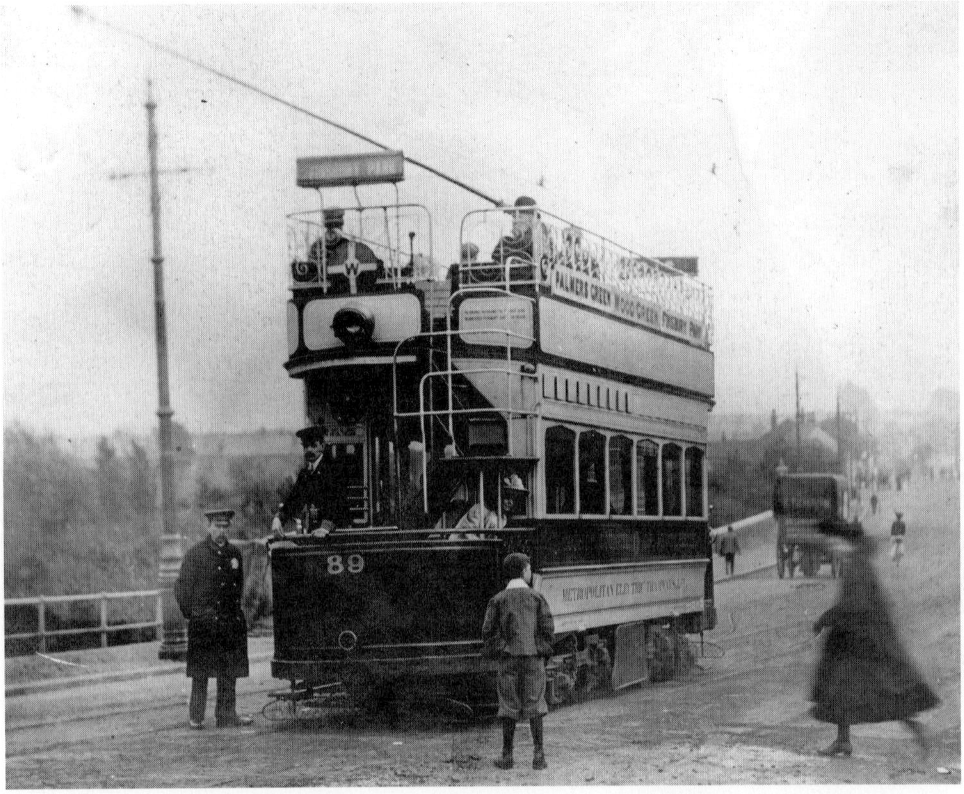

Returning onto Green Lanes, a little further down the road from Broomfield Lane - but before Palmerston Crescent - the road crosses over the New River on Kings Arms Bridge. When the electric tram service was extended northwards from Wood Green in 1907 it couldn't get any nearer to Palmers Green than this bridge until it was rebuilt and strengthened. In this picture we see one of the Metropolitan Electric Tramways trams at the bridge on the opening day of 7 June 1907. The crew are posing at the front of the tram and it's obvious from the direction of the trolley pole and its destination indicator that it is about to return to Finsbury Park.

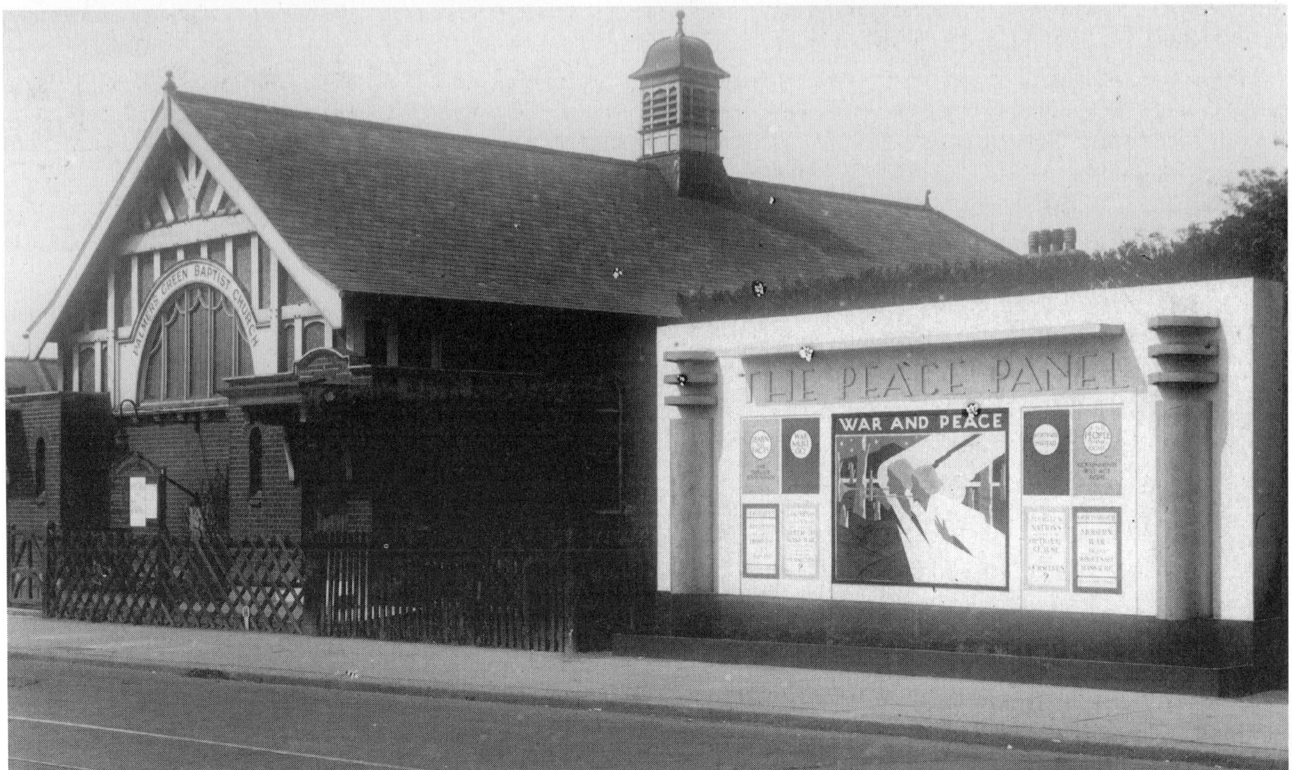

Palmers Green Baptist Church is situated a little further along the west side of Green Lanes. In the 1930s the Peace Panel stood next to it in front of the church's garden. This was the decade that saw the rise of Fascism in Europe, which led to the increasing threat of another world war. Having suffered the loss of so many young lives in the First World War, there was a strong feeling in many quarters that everything possible should be done to prevent another war. The exhortations on the posters on this roadside panel propose 'War Must Go', 'Learn the Facts and Inform Your Friends', 'Modern War means Wholesale Massacre' and 'If the People Think Right, Governments Will Act'. The panel was still there in the late 1930s but by that time its sentiments were about to be overtaken by events.

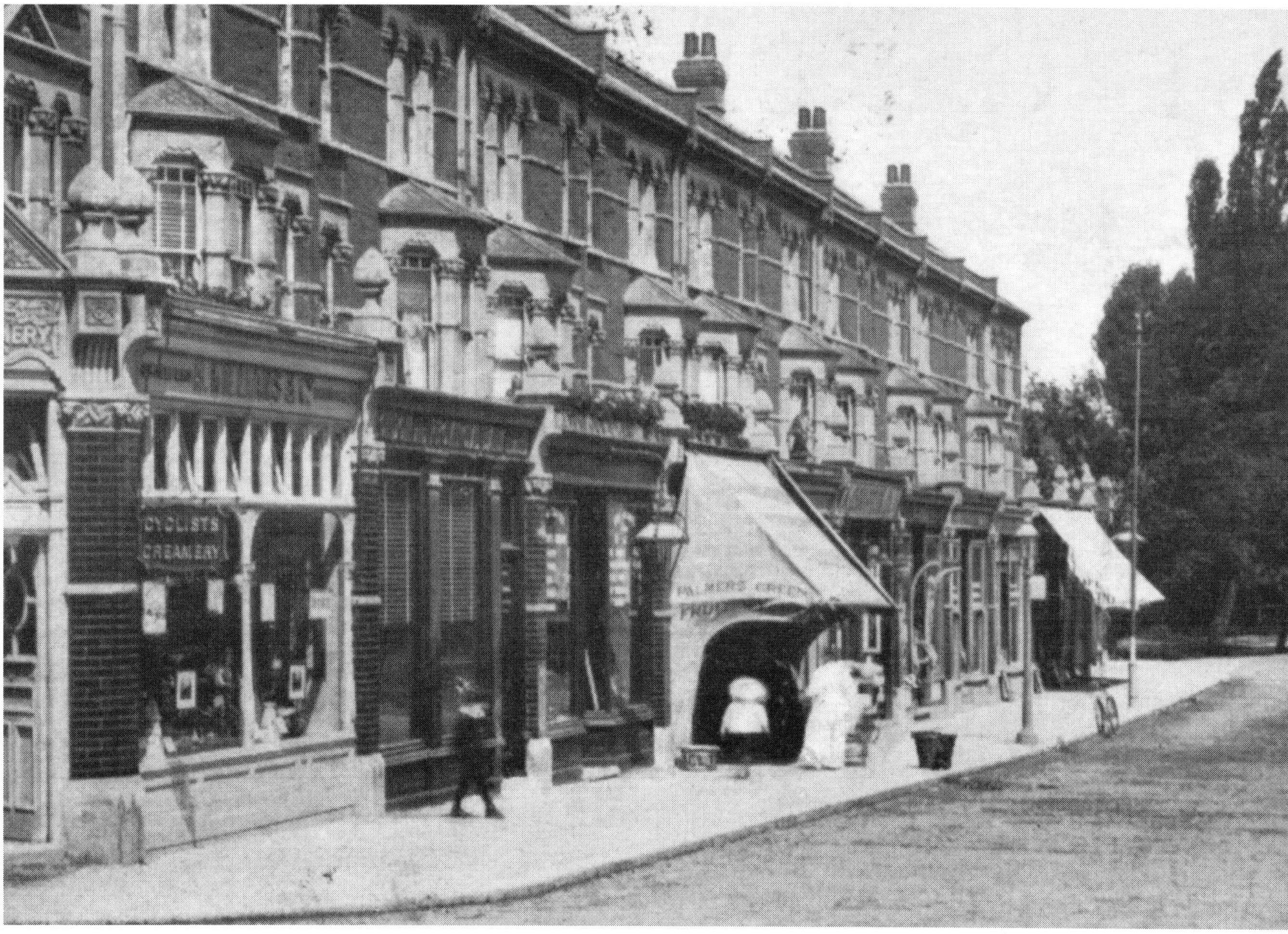

Below: Just beyond the location of the last picture and on the other side of the road was Regents Avenue, the location of a spectacularly unsuccessful roller skating rink. This had become a very popular pastime in the early 1900s and the rink at Palmers Green was built by a speculative builder named John C. Hill. It was opened on 1 October 1910 to great acclaim with 700 skaters in attendance to enjoy its fantastic maple floor. The entrance fee was 6*d*. and hire of skates cost another 1/-. Three sessions were held daily, from 11 a.m. to 1 p.m., 2.30 to 5.30 p.m. and 7.30 to 10.30 p.m. Several steel trusses supported its huge roof span, and the dormer windows built into the ridge and windowed upstands that ran the full length of the hall made it light and airy. A full military band played suitable music during the afternoon and evening sessions.

Unfortunately for Mr Hill he had entered the business just as the craze for roller-skating had begun to wane. Attendances soon dwindled dramatically and the venture had lasted barely 15 months when he closed the hall and sold it early in 1912 to the London General Omnibus Company for £4,000. The bus company converted it into a bus garage ready for the extension of the No. 29 bus route to Southgate. At that time there was intense competition on this route and the LGOC was in competition with the Uneedus and Admiral bus companies.

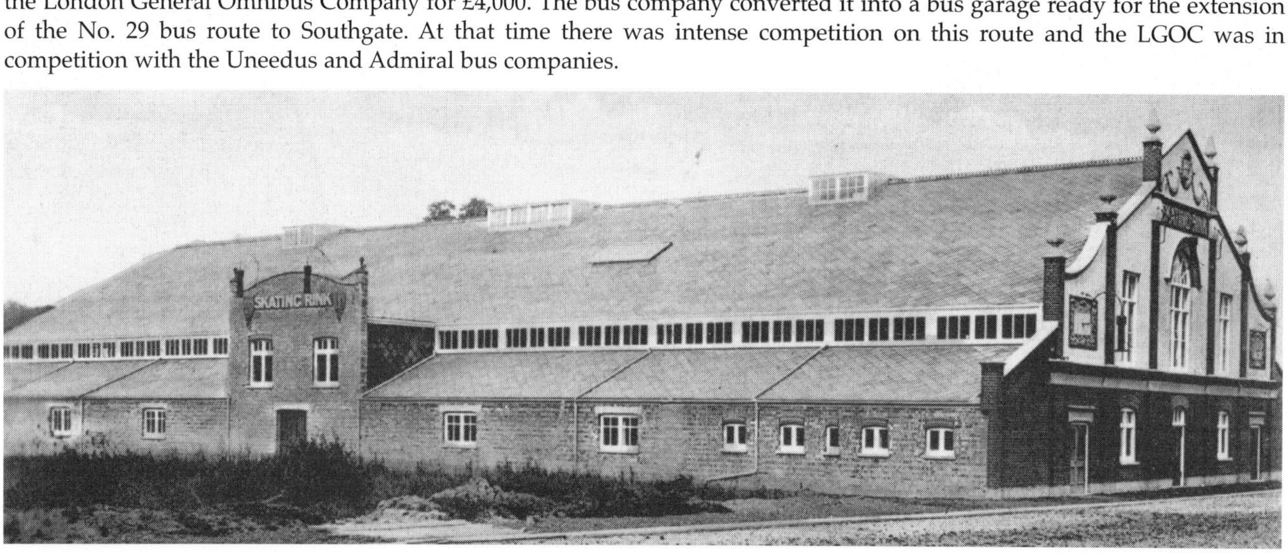

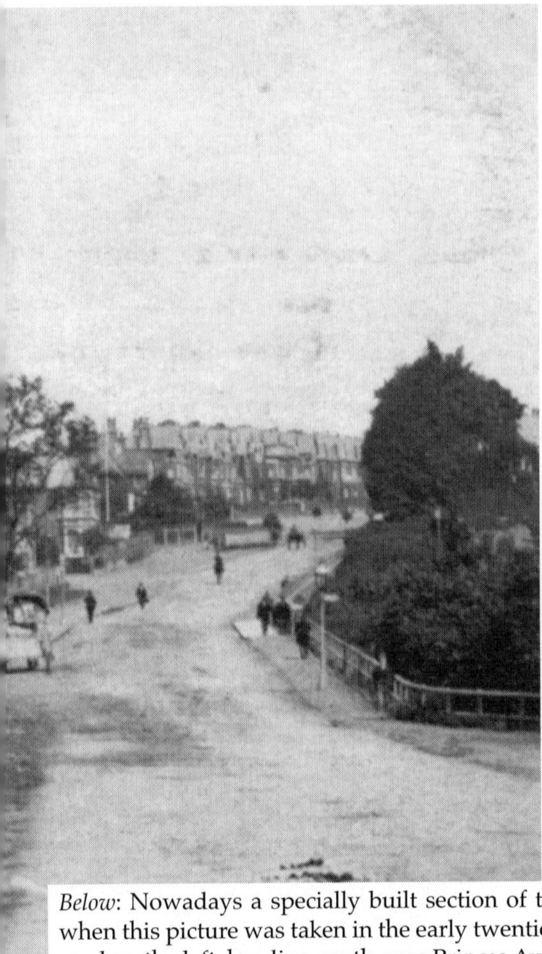

Left: We are still on Green Lanes, which the 1801 Enclosure map calls the Green Lanes Turnpike Road. It was the principal north—south road through Palmers Green and Winchmore Hill to Enfield.

This view of 1903 is looking north from the Lanes' junction with Bowes Road, which joins on the immediate left. Some of the parade of shops is still there but what remains is nowadays in an extremely down-at-heel condition. Only five of the shops are still there today, the nearest ones on the left having been demolished in order to widen Bowes Road to form a section of the North Circular Road.

The North and South Circular Roads were cobbled together in the 1920s from existing streets to form a semblance of a ring road around London. Even before the Second World War the North Circular Road had seen significant realignments of existing junctions and these were continued after the war, culminating in the present-day road which is largely four-lane and dual carriageway. By contrast the South Circular Road still wends its way through several former village high streets in south London and is a nightmare to drive along. In the 1960s the Greater London Council (GLC) drew up plans to upgrade the North Circular Road to motorway standard, the new motorway to be called the M15, but these plans were cancelled in 1973 and the road has since been upgraded piecemeal to its present standard.

The road junction is nowadays known as Clockhouse Junction but at the time of the picture Bowes Road, formerly known simply as Cock Lane, still makes a 'T' Junction with Green Lanes.

The indentation on the right is the forecourt of the Cock Inn, which was very spacious to accommodate horse-drawn carriages. Known to have been there in 1730 and having gone through several transformations and alterations over the years, the pub is nowadays a sports-oriented venue named the Faltering Fullback.

Below: Nowadays a specially built section of the North Circular Road continues eastwards from Clockhouse Junction, but when this picture was taken in the early twentieth century Green Lanes continued southwards without interruption. The next road on the left, heading south, was Princes Avenue; this photograph, taken part-way down it, is looking west with the shops on Green Lanes visible at the end of the road. This is another area of solid Edwardian houses; unlike several other streets, their gardens are too small to accommodate cars in so they are mainly still intact.

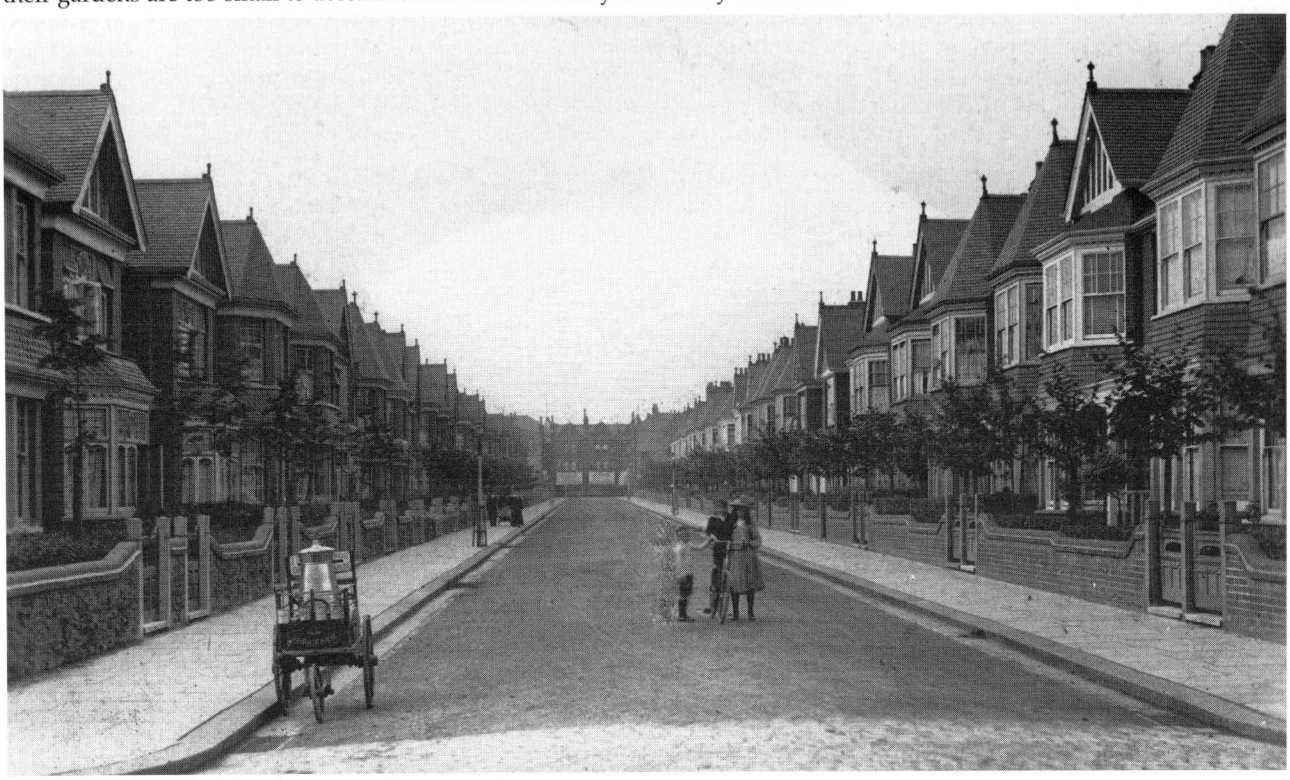

We are now straying just beyond the boundary of Palmers Green into Bowes Park to look at the remaining fragments of Old Bowes Manor.

The Bowes Manor estate was bounded by Bowes Road to the north, Lascotts Road to the south, Green Lanes to the east and the New River to the west. It covered about 33 acres and the lands were thought originally to have been owned by Asgar, the Master of the Horse and Constable of the Army to William the Conqueror. In 1413 the whole estate, together with other lands, were surrendered to King Henry V who immediately granted them to the Church of St Paul.

There used to be a majestic avenue of elms running east to west along the line of what is now Sidney Avenue and the arched gateway into the grounds (probably the archway shown here) stood approximately on the site now occupied in that avenue by No. 15. The mansion itself was a commodious place with many spacious rooms and outside were ample stabling, coach houses, cowsheds and several horticultural and kitchen garden buildings. There were tennis courts on the lawns beside the house and a grand 'Rose Walk' nearly 200 yards long.

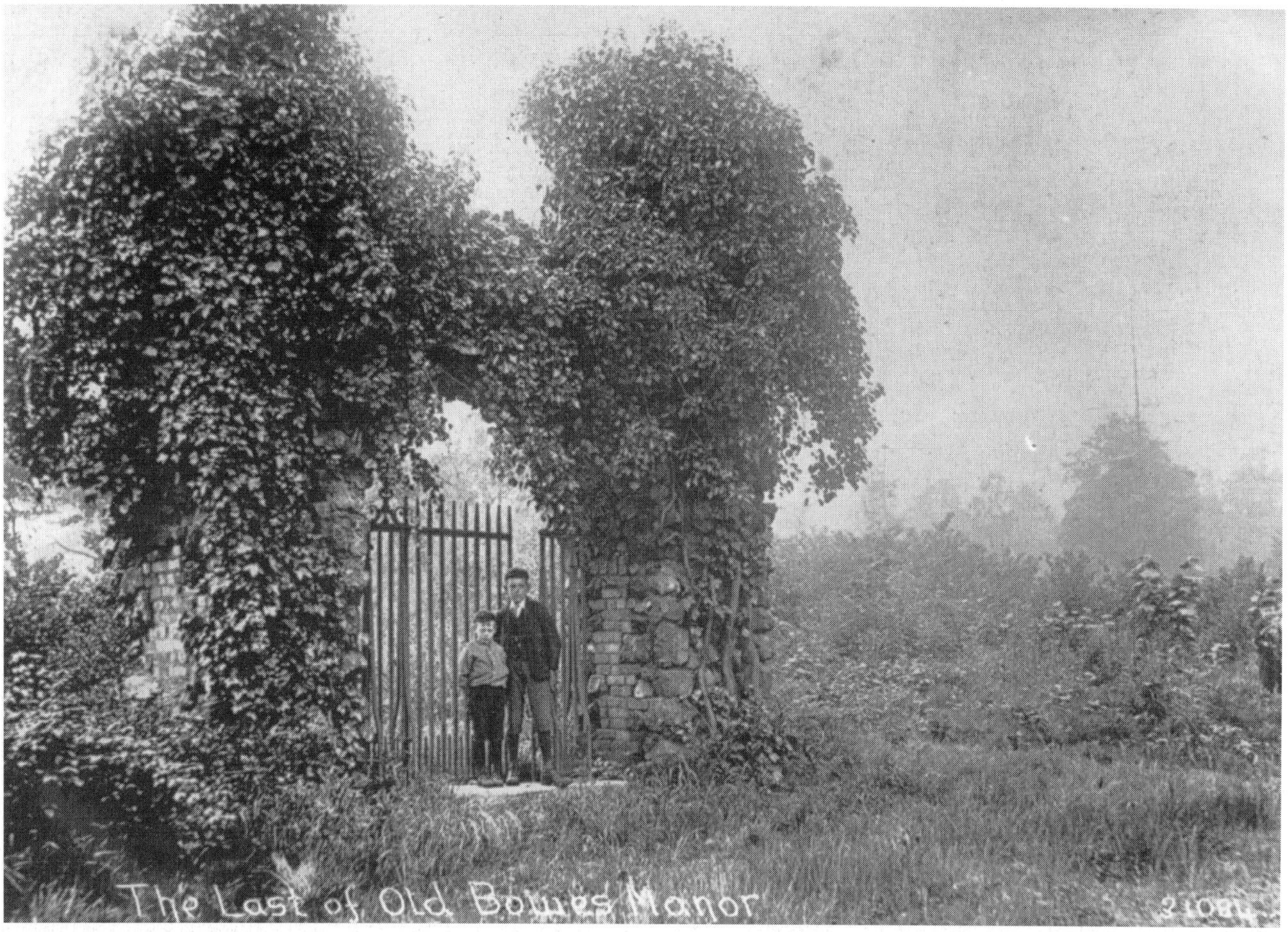

Its most celebrated owner was Thomas Wilde, the son of a city solicitor, who studied law and eventually became Lord Chancellor with title of Baron Truro of Bowes. One of the highlights of his career came in 1843 when he introduced into the House of Commons the postal reform bill designed by Rowland Hill, which resulted in the famous 'Penny Post'.

Lord and Lady Truro used to hold lavish garden parties in the grounds of Bowes Manor, many of them attended by members of the Royal Family.

However, he died in 1855 and the estate was purchased by Thomas Sidney who lived in the manor house until his death in 1889. He was an Alderman of the City of London for 36 years, which encompassed being Lord Mayor in 1853/54, being Sheriff of the City and County of Middlesex, and he was also MP for Stafford for 10 years.

During his time at Bowes Manor, Thomas began to develop the western side of the estate and around 1870 he laid out Palmerston Road and he also gave the site for the building of St Michael-at-Bowes which was consecrated on 21 April 1874. Bowes Park Station opened in 1880 and very soon the area became a high-class residential area.

After Alderman Sidney's death the estate was put up for sale but there were no buyers. It was leased for a few years to the Guardians of the Poor of St Mary's, Islington, and then in 1899 it was sold for development. Five avenues were built east-to-west across the grounds, namely Sidney, Melbourne, Kelvin, Belsize and Spencer. The manor house itself was lost beneath these new avenues, as this sad picture demonstrates.

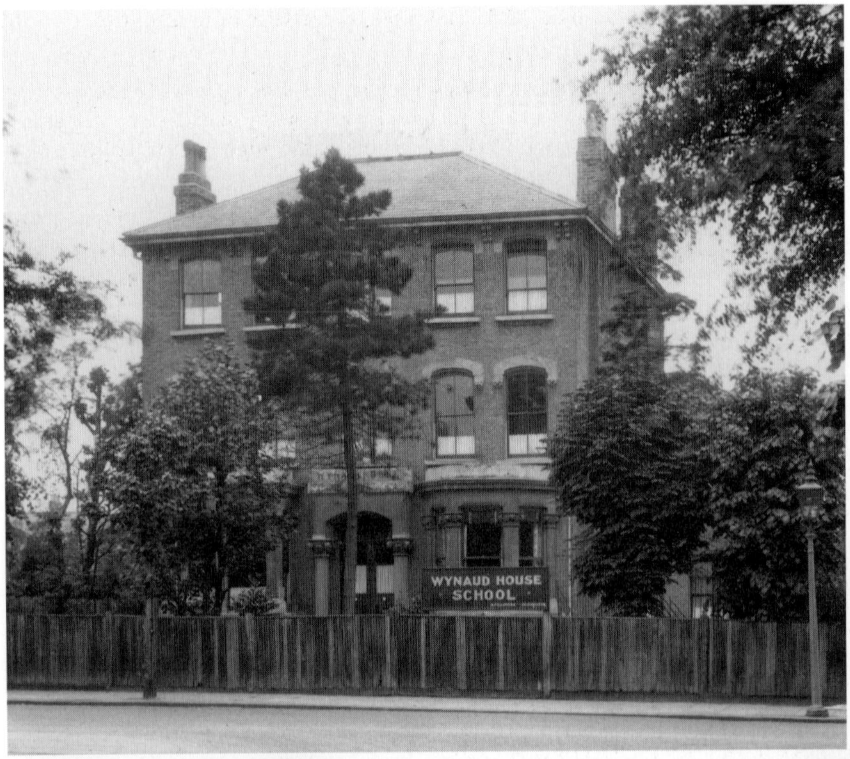

Whilst we are on this area let's have a look at Wynaud House School at No. 79 Palmerston Road. Its proper name was Bowes Park School for Girls and it was a high school for girls above eight years of age and also provided preparatory classes ('kindergarten') for boys and girls. Its advertisement in the 1908 book published for Southgate District Council by the Suburban & Provincial Development Association lists the headmistress as Miss D.E. Barham BSc (Lond.) who held a Cambridge Teachers Training Certificate, and she was assisted by a large staff of 'resident and visiting teachers with university qualifications'. Pupils were prepared for the Oxford & Cambridge Local and Higher Local Examinations, the London Matriculation, the Science & Art Examinations of the Board of Education and the Examinations of the Associated Board of the Royal Academy and the Royal College of Music. Pupils' fees ranged from a guinea and a half to four guineas according to age.

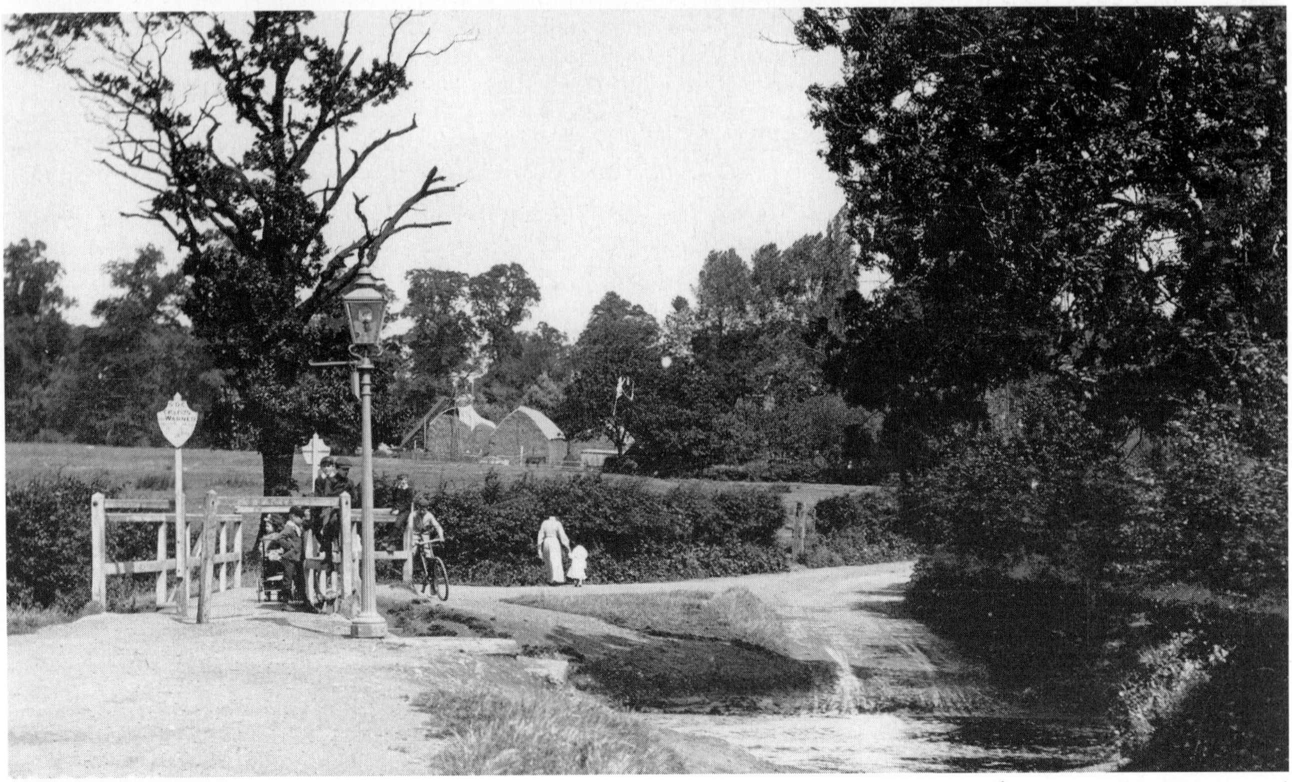

It's now time to turn around and return to Clockhouse Junction, then cross the road and walk what is nowadays a noisy and smelly few hundred yards westwards along Bowes Road (the North Circular Road) until we can turn right into Powys Lane and our next picture.

This shows the crossing of Pymmes Brook that was known as the 'watersplash'. Approaching from Bowes Road, the footbridge for the use of pedestrians and cyclists was on the left whilst horses and carriages would splash through the waters alongside. All around was farmland and the haystacks of Broomfield Farm can be seen in the distance.

When Powys Lane was made up and developed in 1907 the watersplash disappeared and was replaced by the stone road bridge that is there today.

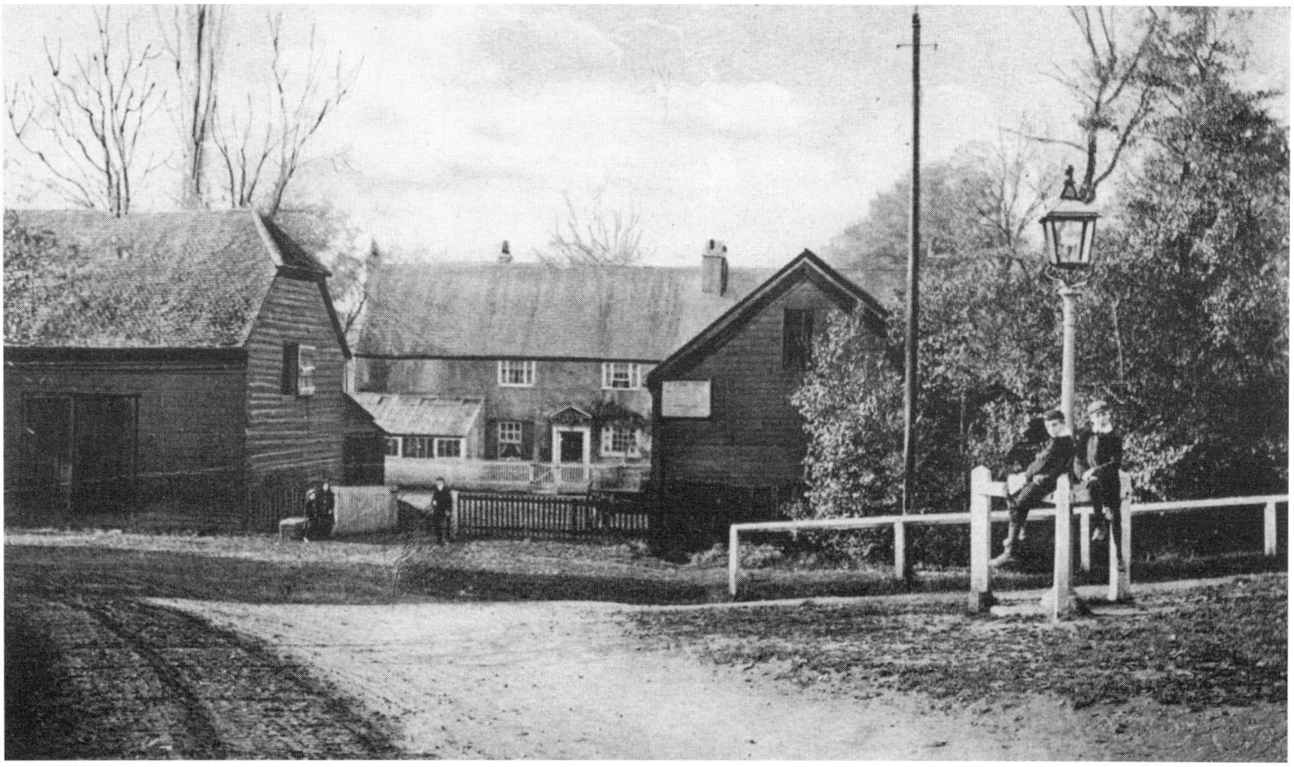

Above: Walking up Powys Lane we come to a fork in the road with Broomfield Lane going off to the right and Broomfield Farm situated on the left-hand side. It was owned by Jabez Hampton, who was also a cartage and public works contractor with as many as 50 horses and carts. We have already seen one of them at the cattle trough outside Southgate Town Hall. The majority of the horses were stabled just to the north of Broomfield Lane, east of the railway tracks, and a blacksmith's and wheelwright's shop were set up amongst the complex of stables. The farm was demolished in 1912 to make way for housing development.

Below: Broomfield Farm is in the background of this picture, which shows the fishpond that used to be situated near the junction of Powys Lane and Broomfield Lane. It became known as Littler's Pond after the last tenant of Broomfield House, but it disappeared around 1906/07.

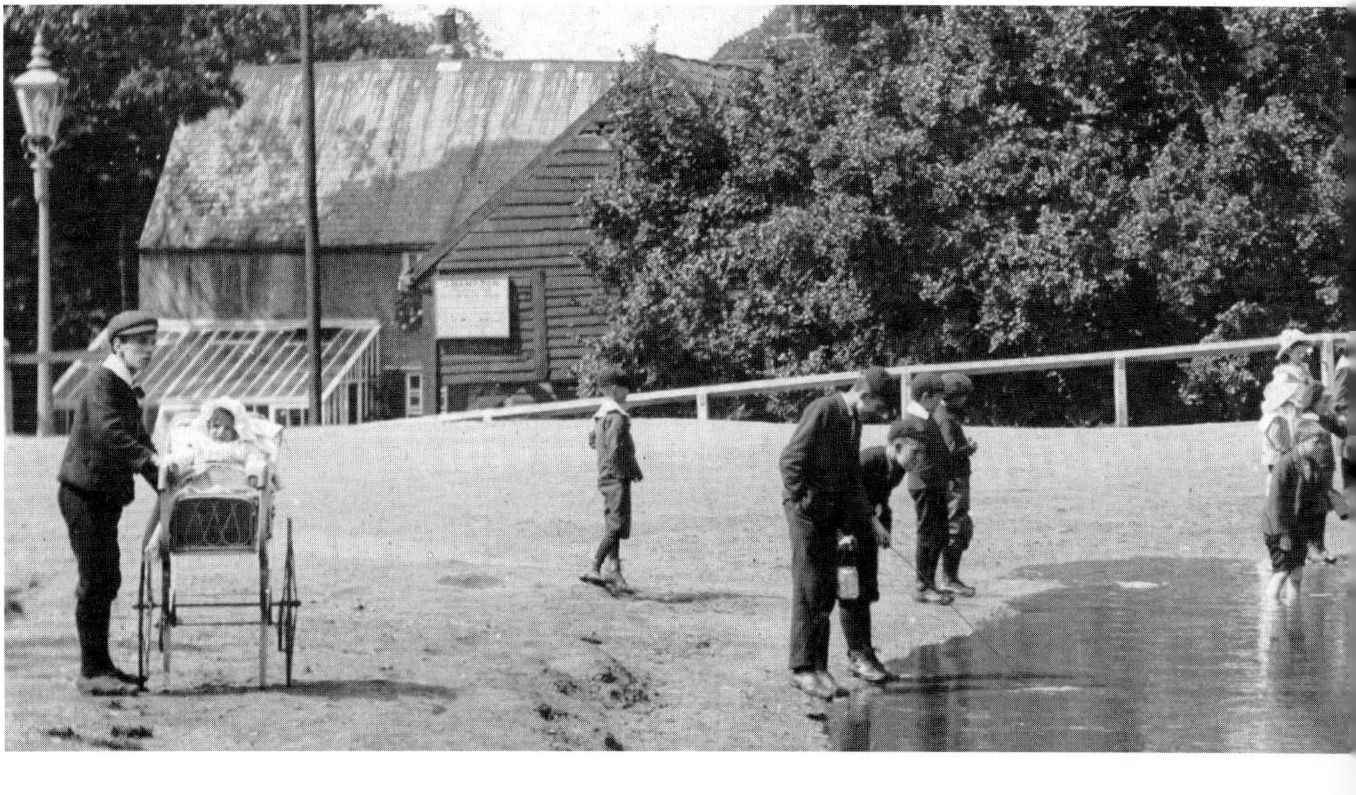

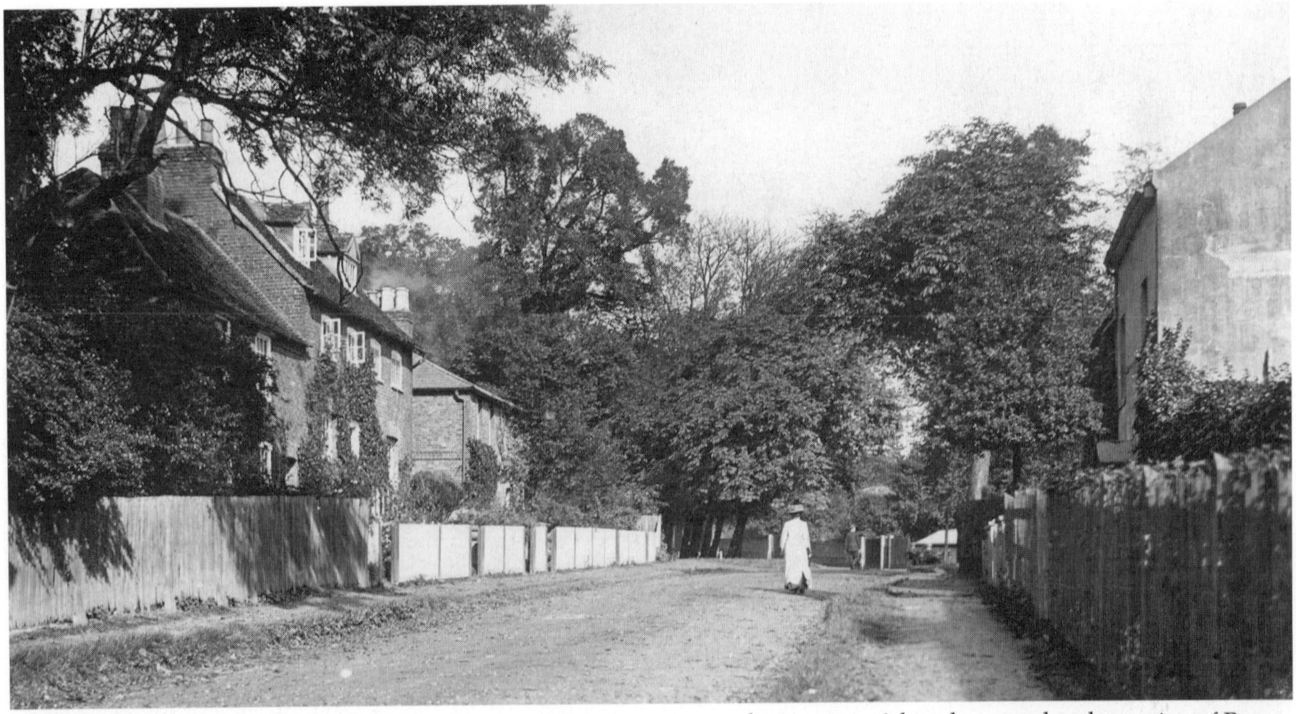

Above: Walking a little way up the left-hand fork in the road, we get to the location of this photograph – the section of Powys Lane leading up towards the Village Gates and the junction with Aldermans Hill.

Powys Lane was marked on both the 1801 Enclosure map and the 1867 Ordnance Survey maps. Philip Powys, a Welshman, purchased the Broomfield estate in 1816 on the death of William Tash; he set about improving the road around the perimeter of the grounds and gave his name to the western section of the road which runs from its junction with Aldermans Hill down to its junction with Bowes Road.

Philip Powys subsequently returned to Wales but he retained ownership of the estate and let it out to a succession of tenants, the last one being Sir Ralph Littler.

This photograph dates from 1934 and was taken near the junction with Aldermans Hill, looking north. Nowadays the road is still lined in parts with mature trees but the buildings in the picture have long since gone, replaced by modern houses.

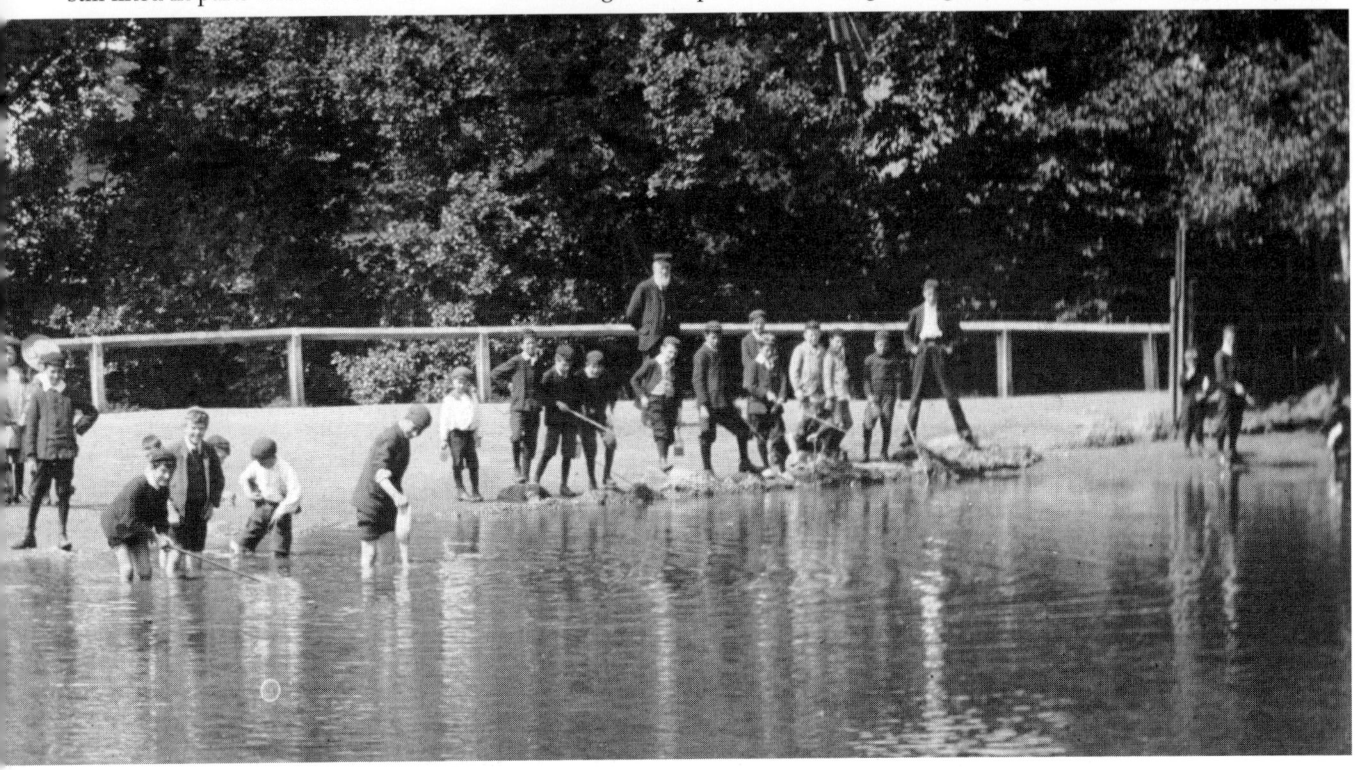

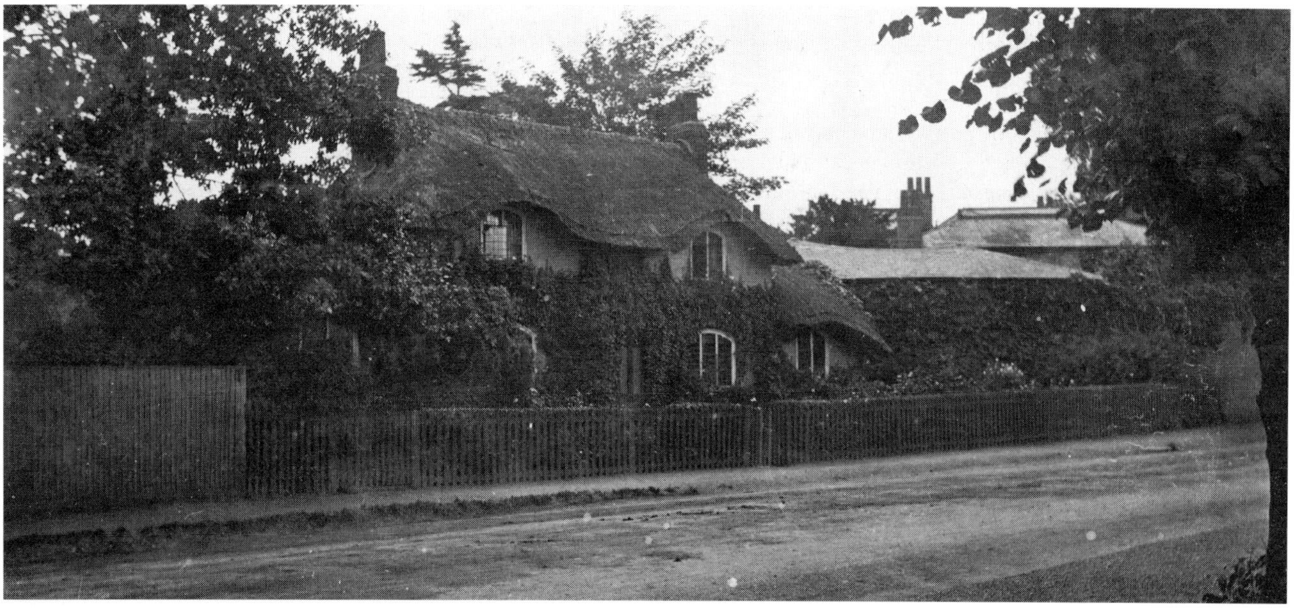

Continuing along Broomfield Lane we come up to the junction with Green Lanes. Here, we turn left past the Old Park Villas we passed earlier in the book and arrive back at the Triangle.

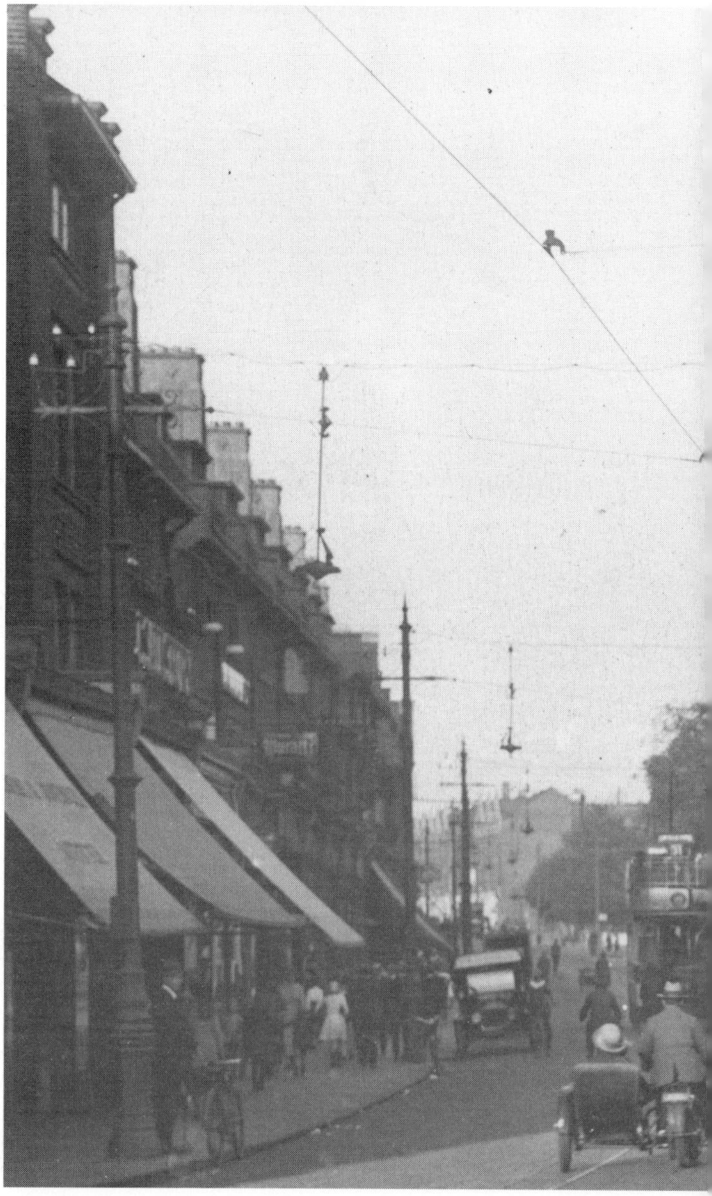

It is difficult to imagine today, amidst the motor traffic going in all directions at the Triangle, that this thatched house named Fern Cottage once stood facing Green Lanes at the base of the Triangle on the site of the present-day Westlake's Shop at No. 262 and opposite what used to be Evans & Davies's department store.

Fern Cottage, or the 'Thatched Cottage' as it became universally known, was built in 1795 by Thomas Lewis, the then Governor of the Bank of England, as the lodge to his eighteenth-century mansion which itself was called simply the Lodge. When the cottage was built, Green Lanes was in the depths of the country and was no more than a rutted track along which cattle would be driven up to market. Originally the estate's gardener and his family occupied the cottage.

The Lodge later came into the hands of John Donnithorne Taylor who let it out to a succession of tenants in return for a handsome rent. The last of these was a Mr Argenti – professionally a wealthy Greek banker and in his spare time the 'Fairy Godfather of Palmers Green', who in the summer threw massive hay parties for the local children and at Easter gave them painted hard-boiled eggs.

In 1906 Fern Cottage's front garden was swallowed up due to the widening of Green Lanes prior to the arrival of the tramways two years later. The cottage continued to be used as a dwelling place until 1911 but by this time it was showing clear signs of decay. It was then that Percy Whellock FRHS bought the lease and converted the cottage into a florist's shop; restoration work was carried out in 1916 to give it a new lease of life and two acres of nursery were developed at the rear of the cottage.

The cottage was eventually demolished in 1938 and was replaced by a branch of Burton's tailors and subsequently by Westlake's. The mansion house itself was demolished in 1911 and the estate was broken up for development.

Now going northeast from the Triangle in the direction of Enfield, this photograph dates from the early 1920s; the fine edifice of the London, County & Westminster bank on the right that was built in 1914 still looks impressive and is nowadays a branch of the NatWest. Beyond it is the Palmadium, which was opened on Christmas Eve 1920 and was described as 'London's most magnificent picture house'. It could seat 2,500 patrons, the interior looked like an opera house, and accommodation included the stalls, a dress circle and an upper circle as well as theatre-style boxes. Originally the entertainment comprised a stage show and a full orchestra as well as the films, the orchestra supplementing the silent films until the talkies arrived in 1927. The 'Palm Court' attached to the cinema was used as a 'British' restaurant during the Second World War. Similar to works canteens, these were set up by the Ministry of Food and run by local authorities; a main course usually cost around 1/*6d*.

The Palmadium became a 'circuit cinema' (i.e. part of a chain) in 1951 and was renamed the Gaumont, but it closed in 1961, being replaced by a shopping parade currently occupied by Store 21 clothing store, Kodak Express, William Hill bookmakers and G. Mantella jewellers.

Beyond the Palmadium are hoardings concealing the undeveloped frontage of the Lodge estate. Nowadays this entire side of the street is taken up by modern shops.

Across the road the parade of shops (the Market, Nos. 316-397) was designed in the new-Tudor style developed by Charles Voysey. By 1914 Palmers Green had the makings of a first-class shopping centre. The earliest business in the parade was Grout & Co., a family run drapery store which began trading at No. 397 Green Lanes in 1914. At one time Palmers Green had its own department store, Evans & Davies at Nos. 305-311 Green Lanes, which opened on that site in 1920 and flourished for many years until it fell on hard times. The business was purchased by the Co-op but declined still further and finally closed sometime around 1980. The premises were refurbished in 1987 and nowadays are occupied by MultiYork Furnishers.

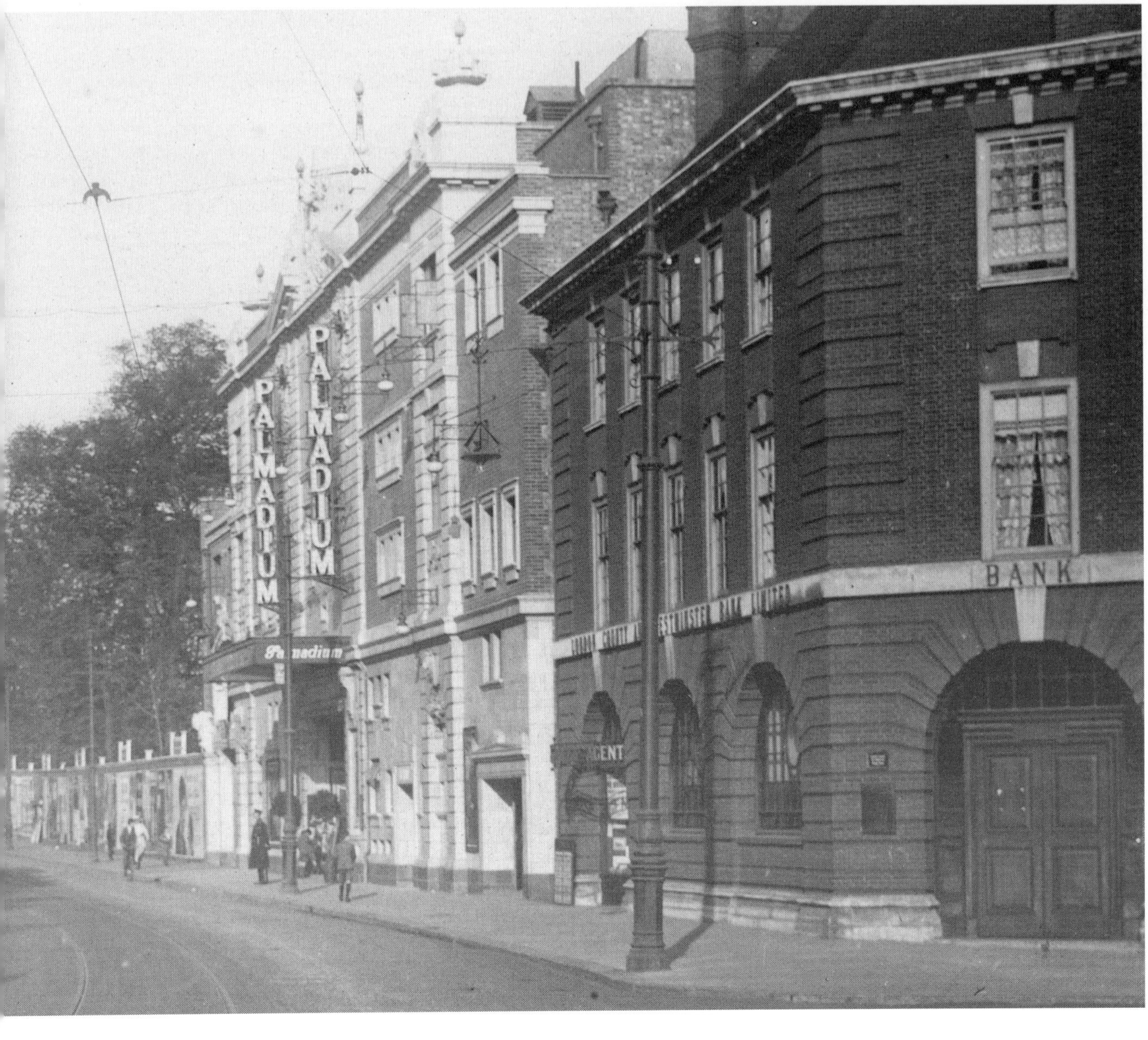

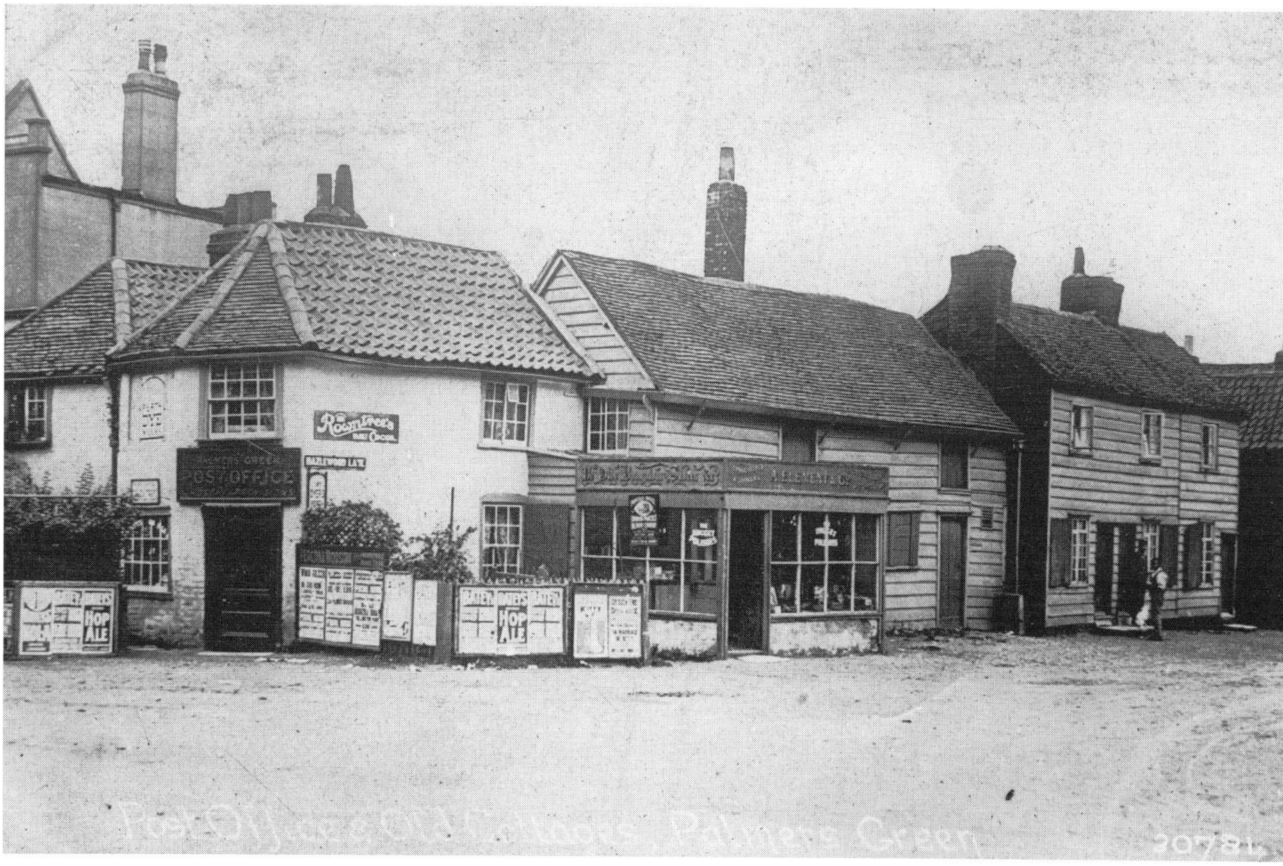

Continuing up Green Lanes, this post office and shop on the corner of Hazelwood Lane and Green Lanes used to be the village centre of Palmers Green. At the time of this late-nineteenth-century photograph the small shop in the centre was owned by A. Clements & Co. and subsequently by Stearn's, bakers and corn chandlers, but around the turn of the twentieth century the premises were taken over by Walter Perrin, bespoke boot makers and repairers.

Around 1924 the buildings were demolished and replaced by the National Provincial Bank on the corner and a block of modern shops leading up to the new post office on Green Lanes. The building on the corner later became a job centre but is now the premises of Anthony Webb estate agents. The modern buildings standing on the site of the old ones on the right of the picture, which are in Hazelwood Road, are now the premises of IKA Solutions Ltd who sell cash registers and EPOS systems.

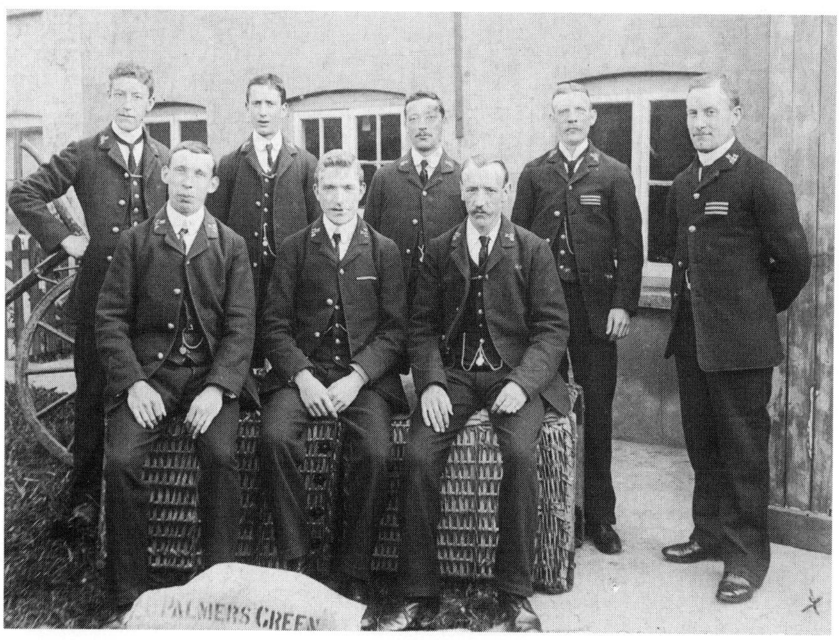

A 1920s photograph of the staff of Palmers Green Post Office. In 1904 the post office was moved from the corner of Hazelwood Lane to Lacey's shop in the Triangle and in 1907 a new sorting office was built in Green Lanes, opposite Fox Lane and close to the site of the old one. This in turn was demolished in 1931 to make way for the new integral post office, which opened on 1 January 1932 on the same site.

Whilst we are on the site of the old post office, it will be interesting to take a look down Hazelwood Lane. This was marked on the 1801 Enclosure map when it was the approach road to Hazelwood Farm. The 1867 Ordnance Survey map shows it crossing the New River by a footbridge and the road continuing as a footpath to join Kings Arms Lane (now Oakthorpe Road and Connaught Gardens). It was known by its present name by 1861.

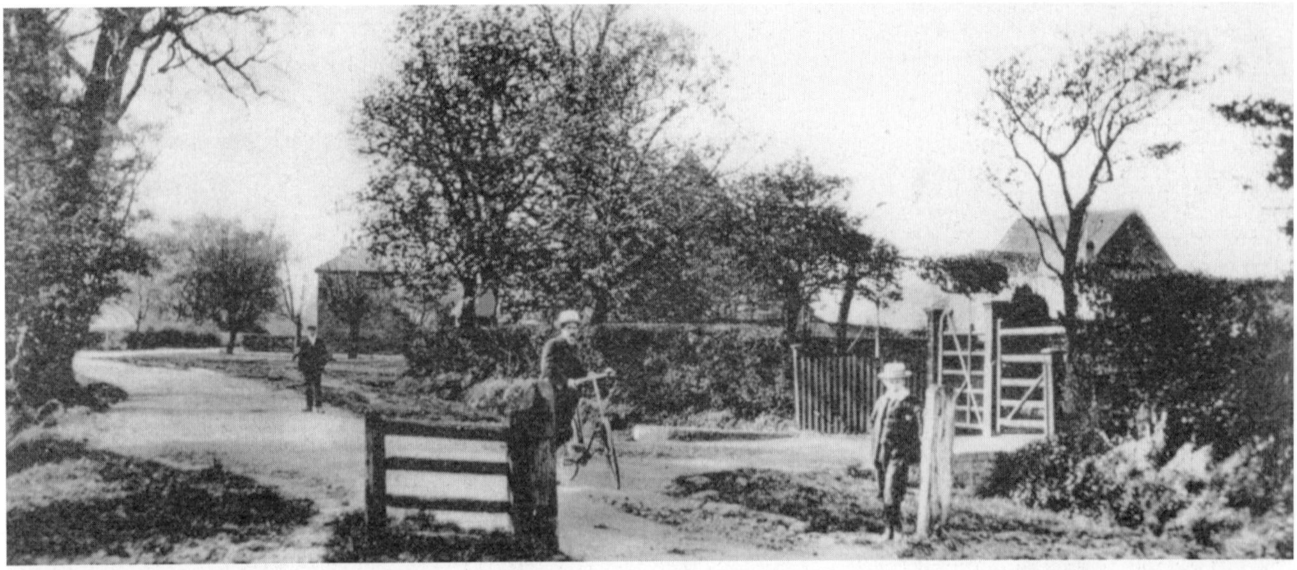

The Hazelwood Park estate, which lay between Hazelwood Lane and Hedge Lane west of the New River, was developed between 1902 and 1910. The eastern end of the lane was mainly developed in the 1920s and a new road bridge was built over the New River in 1927 to replace an old one. Hazelwood School, built in 1906, is now on the site of the old farm buildings in the picture above.

At the time of this picture Hazelwood Lane was still a quiet country lane that stretched eastwards as far as Hazelwood Farm, which is pictured here and lay beyond a pond on the north side of the lane near the junction with New River Crescent. Beyond that, there was the New River itself, and a network of footpaths on its eastern side leading across the fields to Kings Arms Lane and from there onto the Silver Street side of Edmonton.

The Hazelwood Park estate was purchased for development by Albert F. Simmons in 1902. House prices ranged from £525 freehold and £365 leasehold with ground rents at £6.10s. per annum. Easy terms of purchase could be arranged; alternatively you could arrange to rent a house from £32 per annum.

The row of houses in the photograph below, taken in 1924 at their junction with Lightcliffe Road, is called Hazelwood Villas. The plaques on which the name is inscribed are still on the front of the houses at each end of the terrace. The sign in the window of the nearest house is offering the freehold of the house for sale for £525.

Nowadays cut off from the North Circular Road, which passes to the south, the Edwardian houses in Hazelwood Road start north of Callard Avenue and most still have original features such as their porches, beautiful front doors with stained glass, black and white mosaic tiles in their driveways, and walls built of reject bricks similar to those in the Mall.

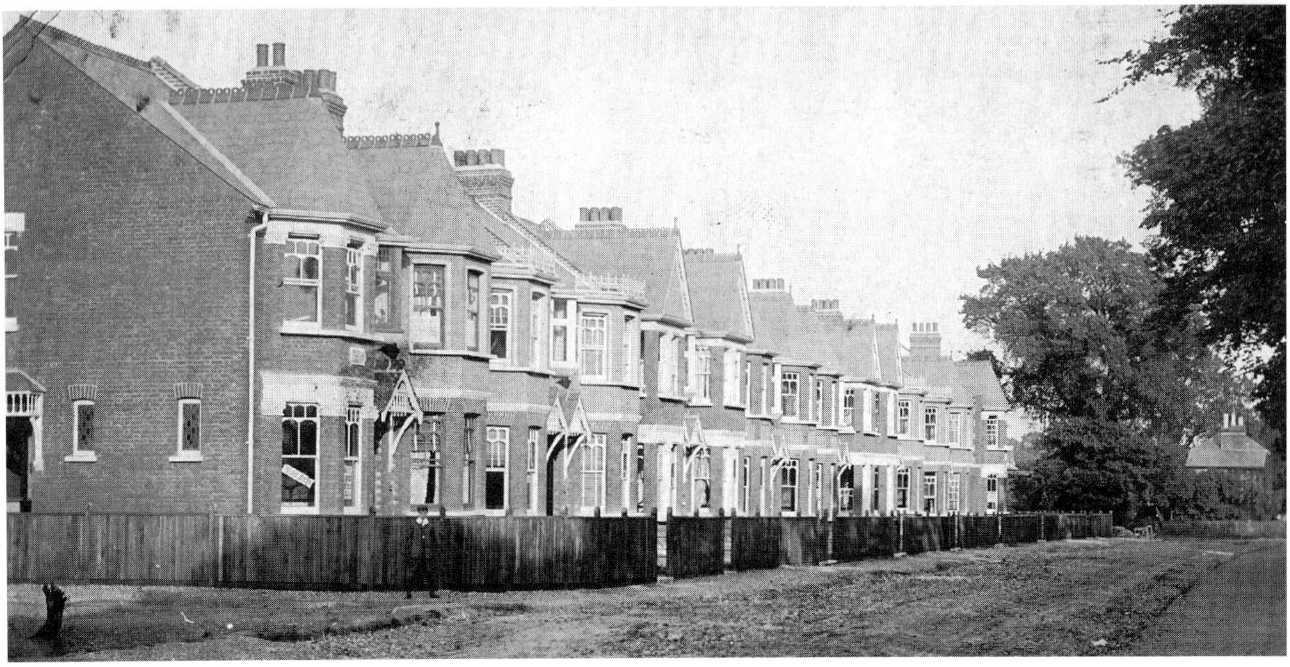

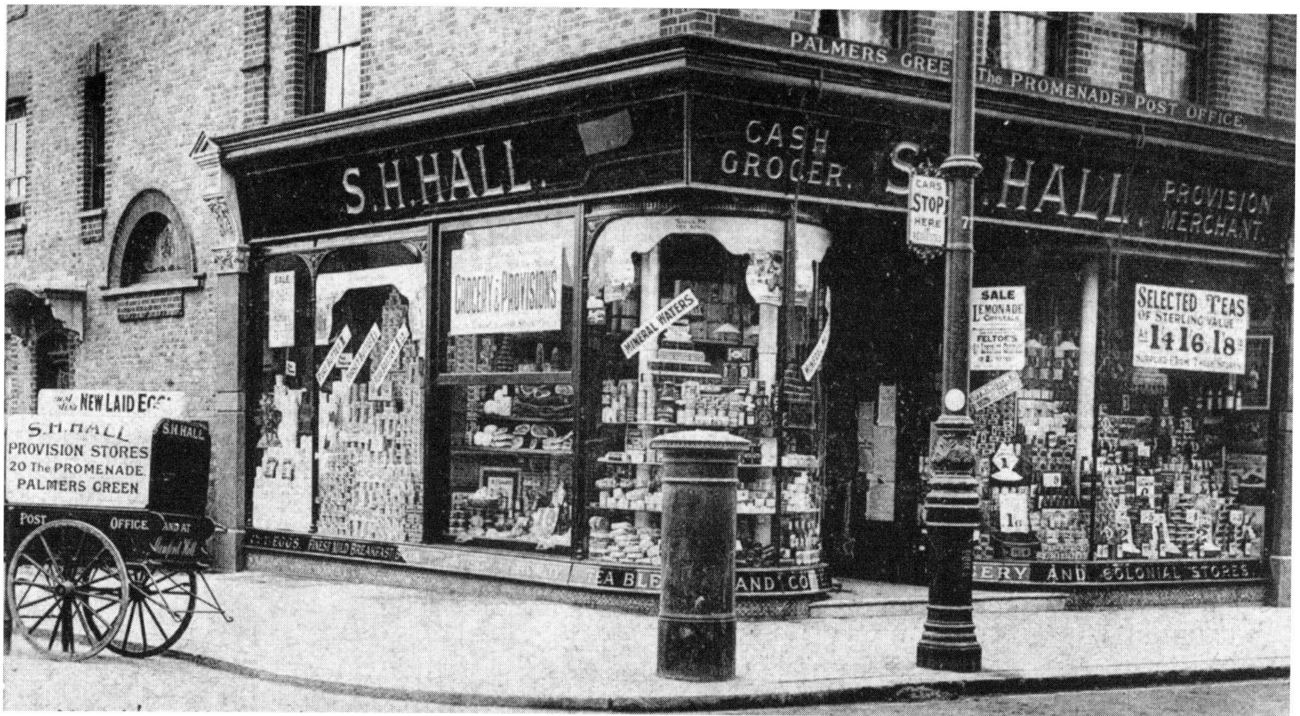

Returning from Hazelwood Lane onto Green Lanes, and walking further along it beyond another two side roads, on the right, at the corner of Windsor Road, we come to the former premises of S.H. Hall, a cash grocer and provision merchant who also ran the post office in the area after the main office at the corner of Hazelwood Lane had been transferred to Lacey's shop in the Triangle.

The physical outlines of his shop are still there, instantly recognisable even to the rounded corners of the doorway, but the premises are now occupied by Ladbroke's bookmakers. The date carved on the wall above the shop is 1908.

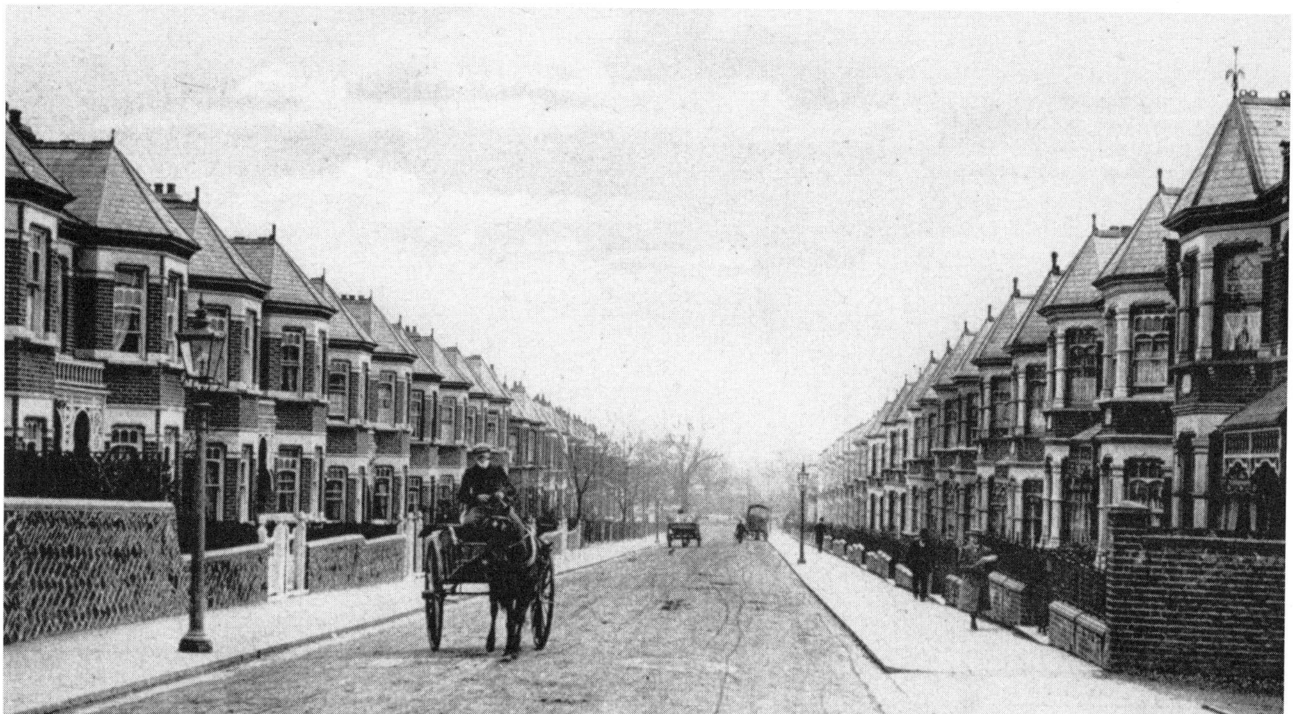

The next road on the right is Osborne Road, which was part of the Hazelwood Park estate. The first houses were occupied by 1903 and it's thought that the road may have been named after Osborne House on the Isle of Wight.

This picture dates from 1909. Going down nowadays from Green Lanes most of the houses look very smart and ornate; many have their original porches and tiled paths, along with original doors featuring stained glass and coloured tiles in the vestibules.

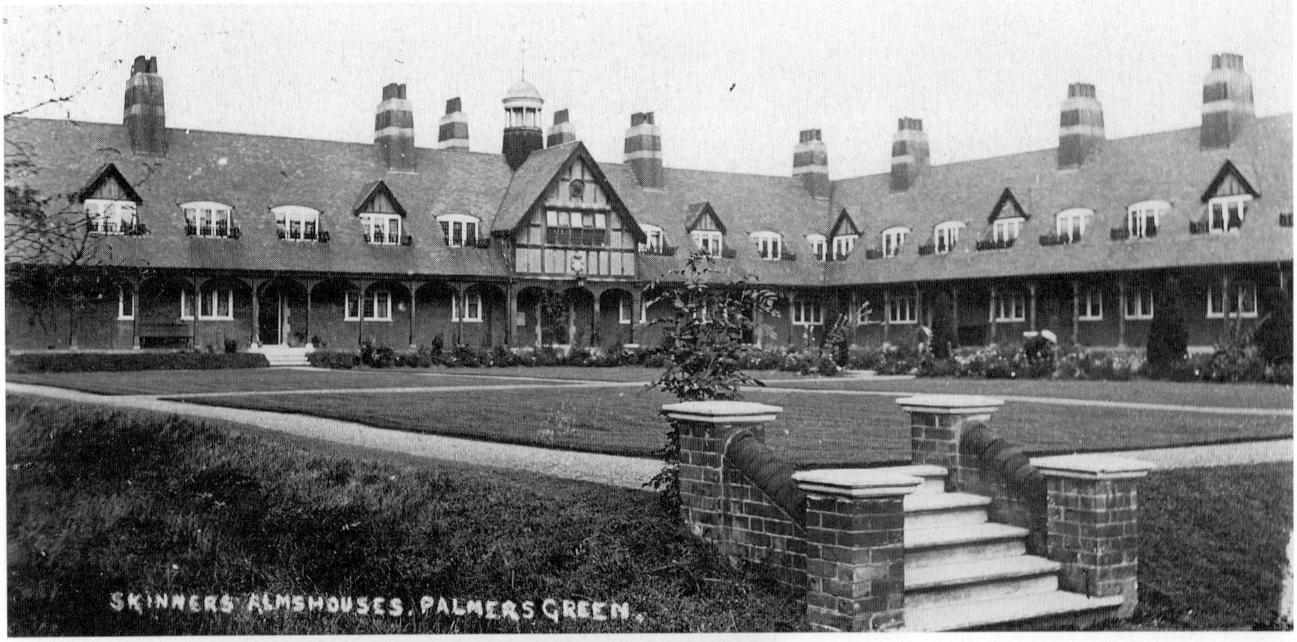

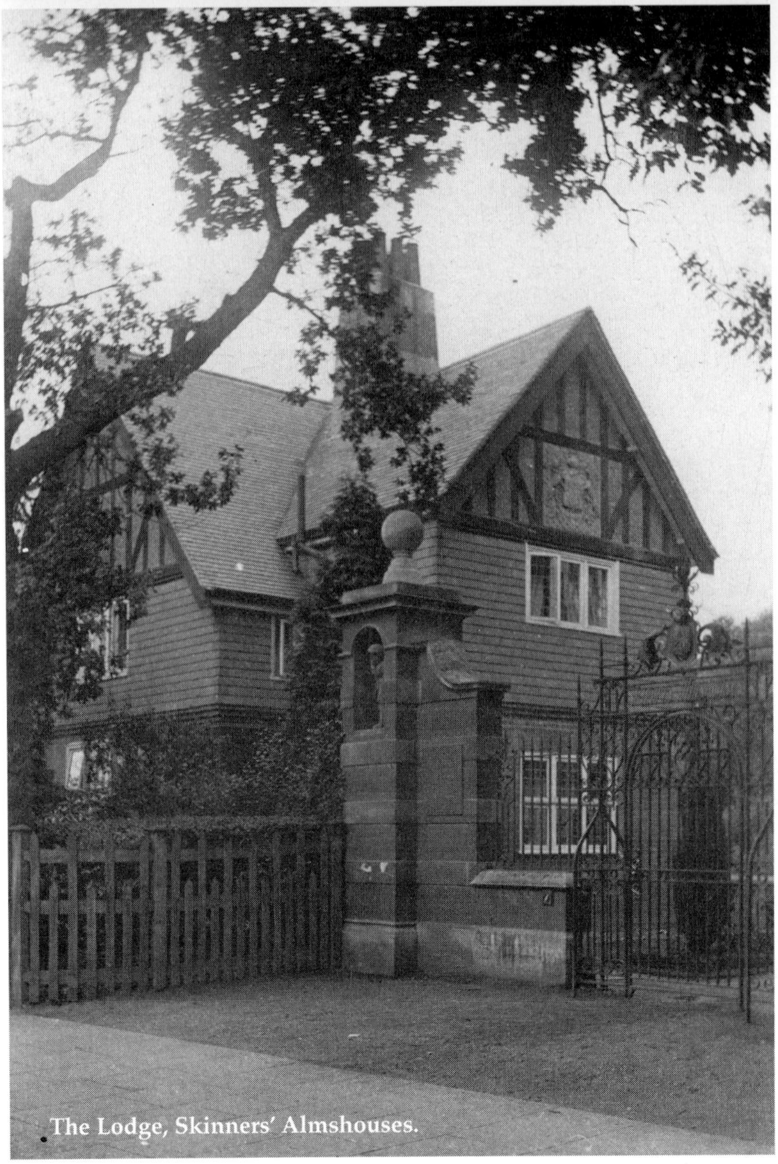
The Lodge, Skinners' Almshouses.

Crossing the road towards the Fox Inn, at the corner is the site of the Skinners' Almshouses. The history of the Worshipful Company of Skinners, which is one of the Great Twelve City Livery Companies of the City of London and known for short as the Skinners Company, goes back to the thirteenth century. They were incorporated by charter by Edward III in 1327 and were once an important force in the land as fur traders. Whilst the company has long since ceased to exercise its right to control the use, manufacture and sale of furs, it continues to administer its schools, almshouses and charitable trusts.

The almshouses were built in 1894 on what had been Mr Graves's farm. They extended around three sides of a spacious lawn and garden facing Fox Lane and were designed to provide homes for the aged, poor and needy members of this ancient trade. There were wrought iron gates at the entrance with ornamental stone piers either side. The left-hand pier at the entrance stated that in 1551 Sir Andrew Judd, citizen and skinner, founded almshouses for six poor men at Great St Helens in the City of London. The right-hand pier was inscribed that in 1688 Lewis Newbury Esq., citizen and skinner, founded almshouses to house 12 poor women at Mile End.

Unfortunately the almshouses were accidentally destroyed by fire in 1966. In 1969 the site was redeveloped and nowadays offers 48 state-of-the-art sheltered apartments with one and two bedrooms for frailer older people.

Access is now from Fox Lane via Pellipar Close and the new building is named Skinners' Court. The Coat of Arms of the Skinners Company is displayed on its glass frontage together with its motto, 'To God only be all Glory'.

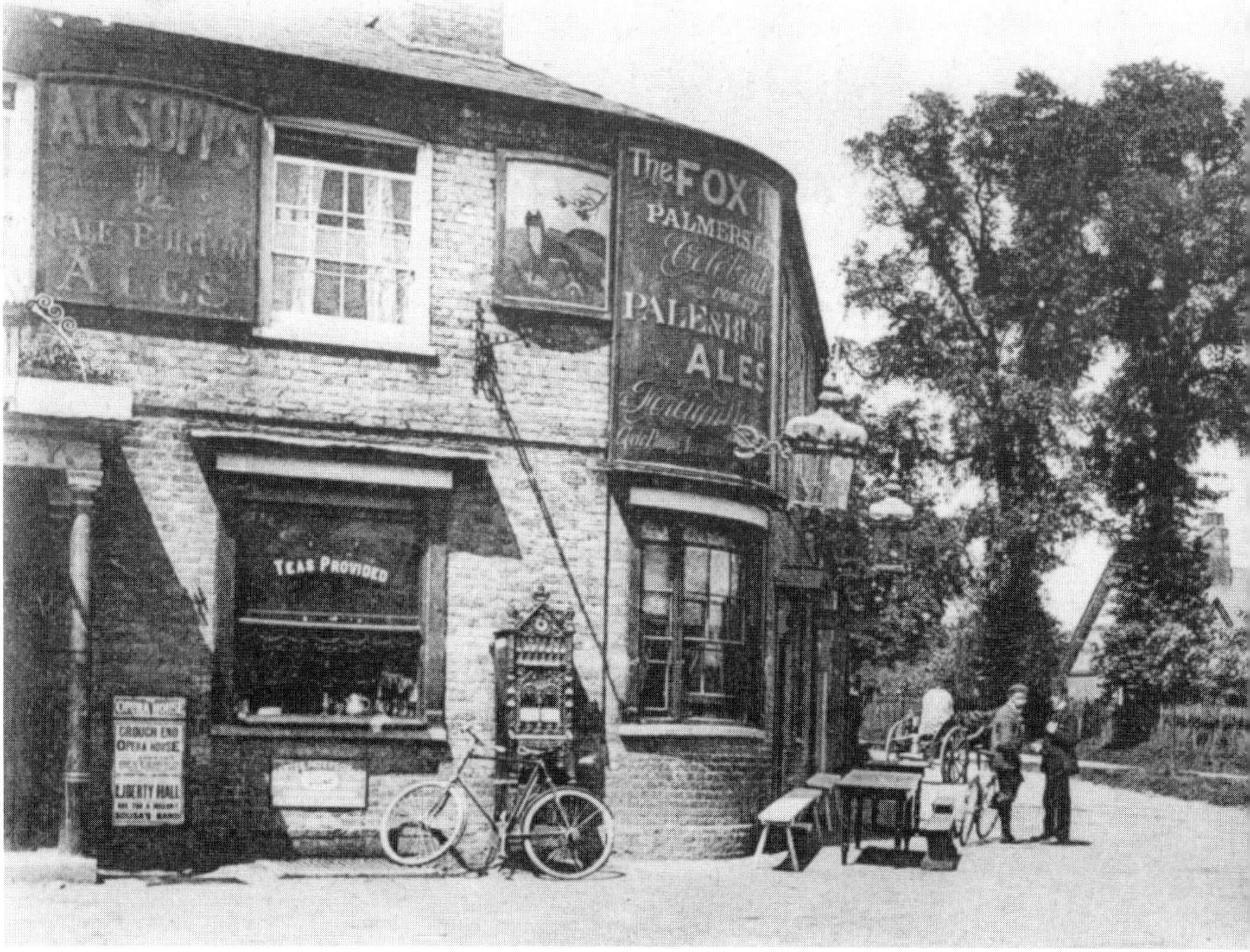

Facing the Skinners' Almshouses on the corner of Fox Lane was the Fox Inn itself. The name of Fox is shown on the 1801 Enclosure map and it is known that in the fourteenth century a family called Fox owned some land near the top of the lane. By 1841 a part of the western side near the footpath from the side of the Cherry Tree was known as Clappers Green. The lane remained nothing more than a track right up until the turn of the twentieth century; there were no pavements, no kerbstones and no lighting and once across the railway bridge there was open countryside on both sides with the vast Old Park estate stretching southwards as far as Aldermans Hill. It was the sale of the Taylor estates in 1902 and the subsequent sale of the Clappers Green Farm (bounded by Dog and Duck Lane) to the north in 1908 that brought about the changes we see today.

By 1860 the landlord, Robert Davey, was running a two-horse bus to Holborn, Oxford Street, Bank, Bayswater and Paddington. The bus was housed in one of the large wooden sheds at the rear of the inn. He was the first operator to order and run a bus designed with a spiral staircase for access to the upper deck. This gradually replaced the old method, a straight iron ladder up the back of the vehicle.

This picture shows the Fox Hotel before it was rebuilt in 1904 into the elaborate Edwardian pub that still stands today. On warm summer days drinks would be served through the open windows to the customers sitting on the forms and tables provided outside. At this time the old pub was around 200 years old and its landlord was Arthur Davey (Robert's son) who had been born there in 1867.

It is said that John Donnithorne Taylor was passing the Fox Inn one day with his hunters when the landlady came out and shook some carpets which startled the hunters. When he remonstrated with her she is said to have replied that she would shake her carpets when she liked. 'Yes', said JDT, 'but not where you like.' According to local legend he promptly bought the inn and gave the landlady notice to quit. This may be an apocryphal story but he certainly did buy the inn in 1864. The Society of Tradesmen and Labourers met there from 1794 until 1825.

By the time the inn was sold in 1902, as part of the sale of the Taylor estates, there was stabling for 11 horses and a skittles alley. It was bought for £11,020 by the brewers Huggins & Co., who rebuilt it in 1904 into the pub we see today.

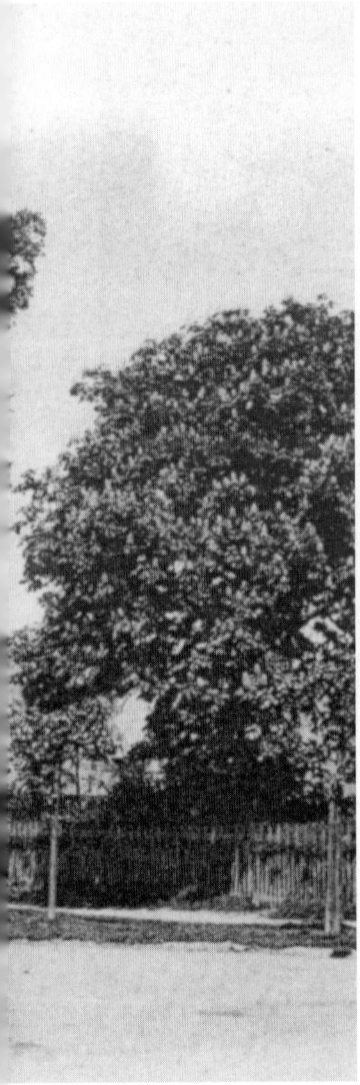

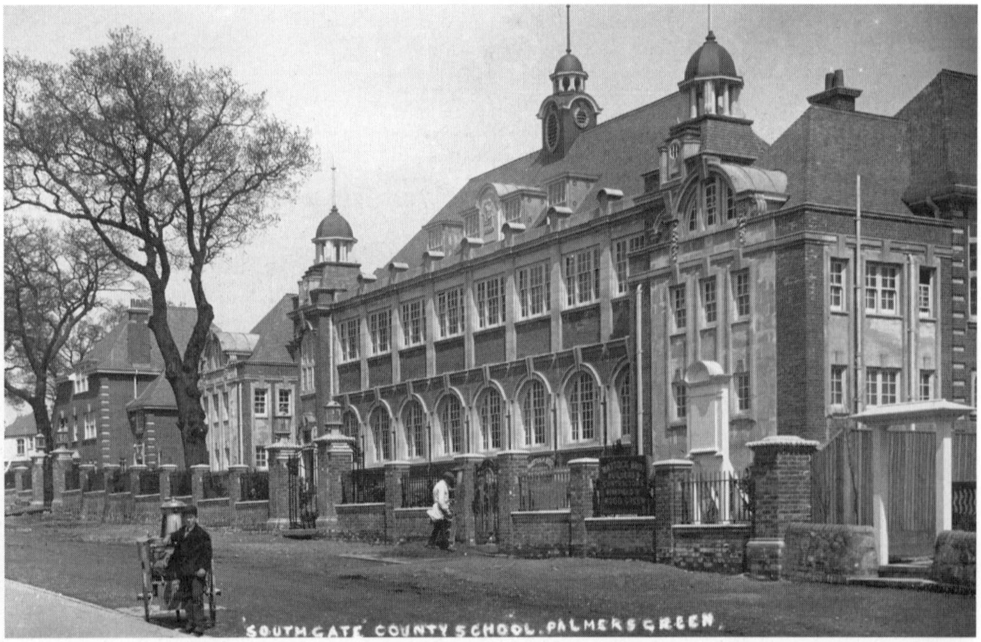

On our way up Fox Lane we come to the former Southgate County School. This was founded in 1907 at Broomfield House under the headship of Mr A.T. (Bunny) Warren. At that time it was a boys' school and by 1909 it had 163 pupils. Meanwhile a temporary school for girls had already opened at Avondale Hall in Hoppers Road where about half that number attended under a headmistress and four teachers.

The impressive new school in Fox Lane, for both sexes over the age of 11, was opened on 17 February 1910 by Alderman Col. H.F. Bowles (later Sir Henry Bowles). It had been built by Messrs Mattock Bros. of Wood Green at a cost of £13,493.

In 1960 the school transferred to new buildings in Sussex Way and the building was taken over by Minchenden Lower School. However, when they subsequently merged with Arnos School in Wilmer Way under the name of Broomfield, the school in Fox Lane closed in 1987 and was converted into apartments, whilst 39 houses were built on its playing fields. The former school building is now named Corrib Court.

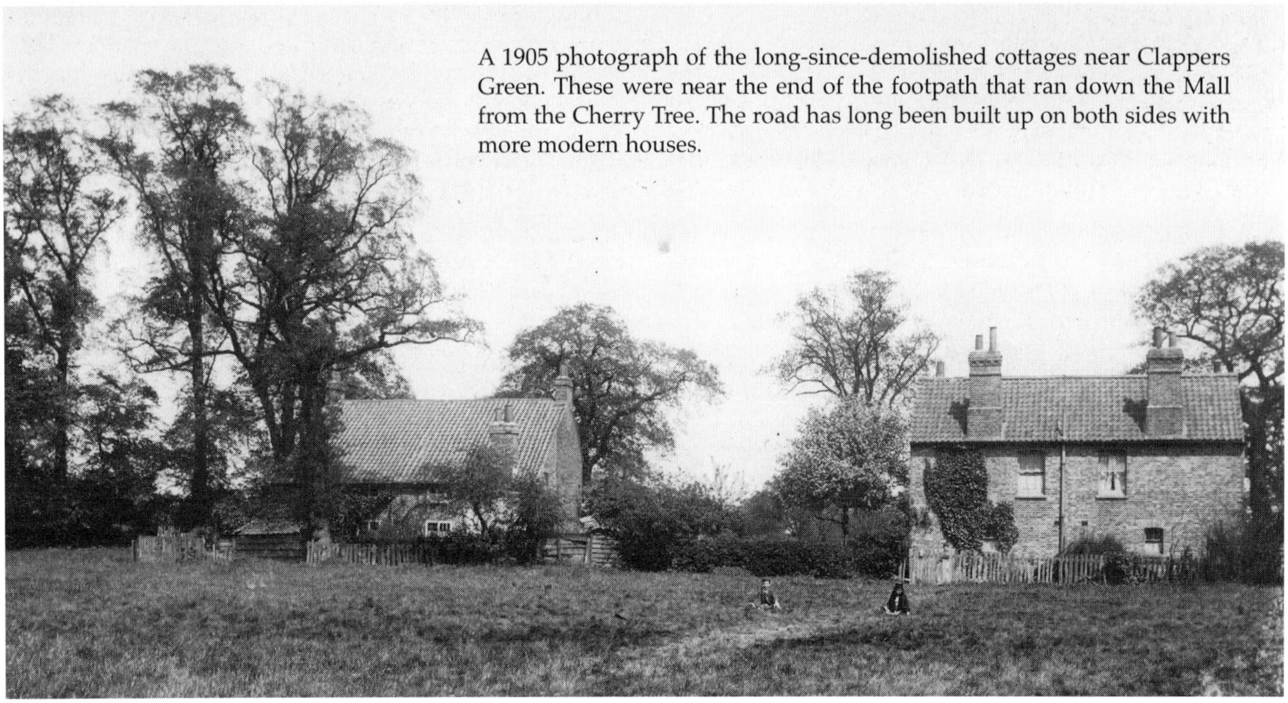

A 1905 photograph of the long-since-demolished cottages near Clappers Green. These were near the end of the footpath that ran down the Mall from the Cherry Tree. The road has long been built up on both sides with more modern houses.

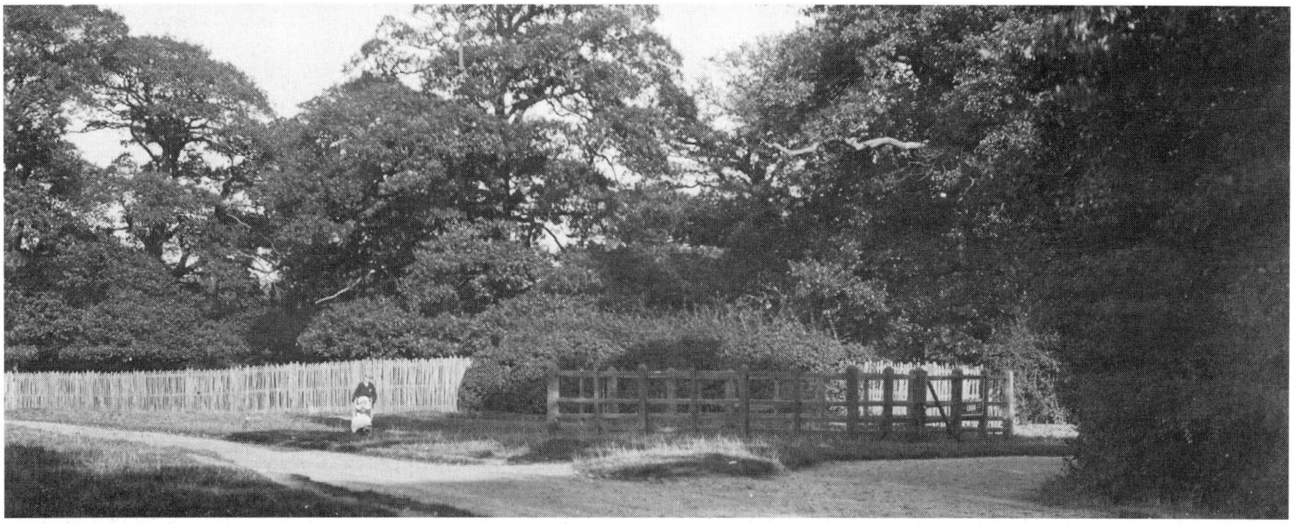

A little way further along Fox Lane the road made a junction with Bourne Hill, which joined it from the right by the village pound.

The pound, which still stands in a truncated form at the junction of Bourne Hill and Fox Lane, was an enclosure in which stray animals would be impounded until their owners claimed them and paid a fee to the keeper of the pound or 'pinder', as he was called, to secure their release.

There was a scale of charges laid down. If the animal remained impounded for eight hours it had to be fed and the cost would be subsequently charged. A pail of water and a feed of hay would cost the owner eightpence. In addition there were sometimes charges for a claim from one of the villagers regarding damage caused by the animal whilst straying. If the pinder was satisfied that the claim was fair he would insist on the payment for damages before releasing the animal back to its rightful owner. There was no appeal: the pinder's decision was final.

For many years the pinder was Miss Carter who lived in the nearest of the four cottages in Dog and Duck Lane (renamed Bourne Hill in 1901) opposite the entrance to the old footpath through Winchmore Hill Woods. In 1897 Henry Reed, landlord of the Woodman from 1893 to 1924, became the pinder until the pound's closure in December 1904. The last official entry was for a pig kept in the summer of 1904 although, later that year, nine gipsy horses were impounded but released unlawfully by their owners who refused to pay their dues. After the pound was closed, the council took it over and retained a token enclosure as a historical monument.

Both pictures show the southern end of the pound looking northwards with Fox Lane entering on the left and Bourne Hill entering from the right on the far side of the pound. Nowadays, both roads are lined with houses.

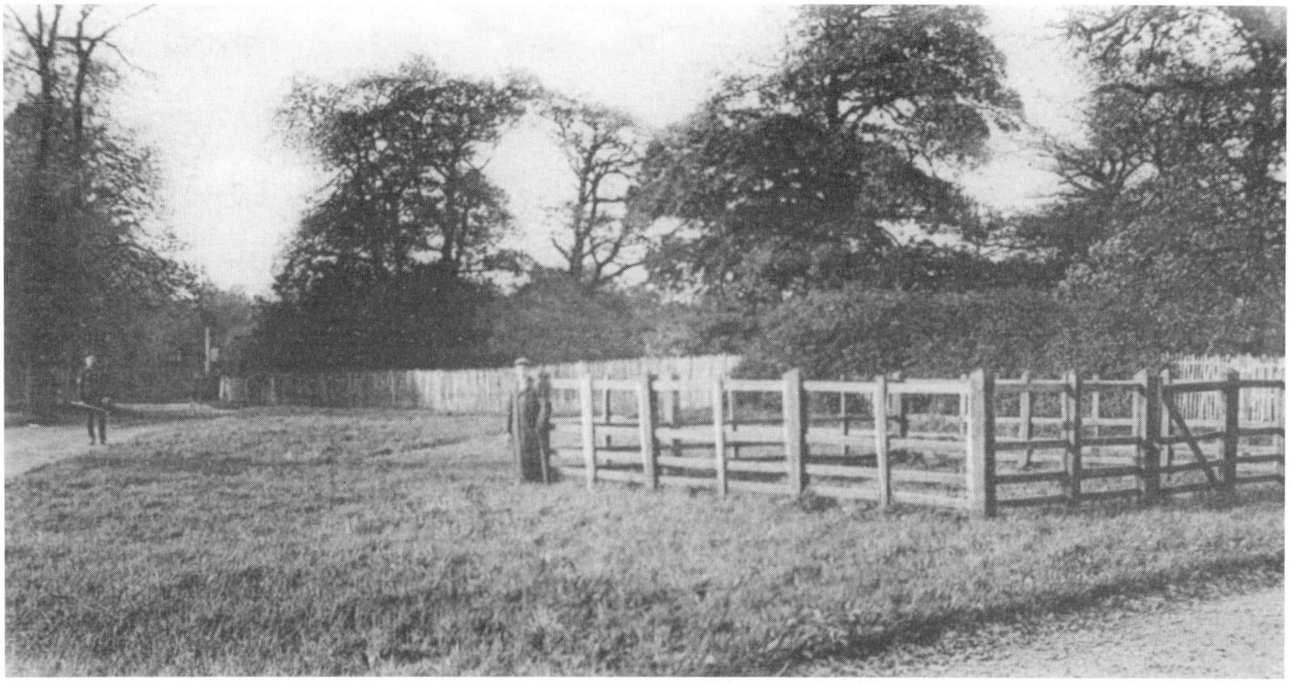

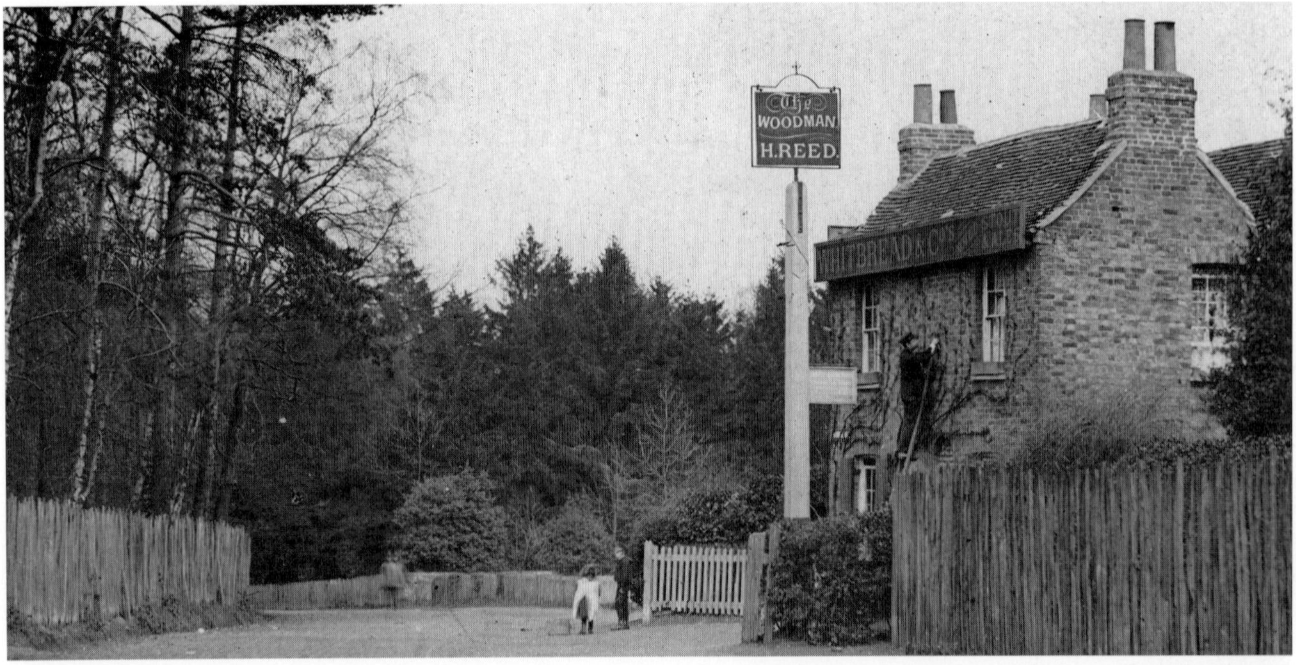

Just beyond the pound we come to the Woodman pub standing on the right at the top of Bourne Hill. It started life in 1727 as two country cottages but in 1868 Henry Wale, a retired police sergeant, was granted a license to serve ale from his front sitting room and the building has been a pub ever since.

It was refurbished and enlarged in 1996 when Whitbread sold the freehold to Discovery Inns, the most noticeable additions being the rear bar and conservatory restaurant.

Although Henry Reed was the licensee during the period when both these photographs were taken, it is the upper one that appears to be the oldest. The Whitbread signboard running the length of the pub looks rather worn and there are neither advertisements on the wall nor a porch at the front door. Could that be Henry himself up the ladder, fixing the creeper?

The lower picture was probably taken only a few years later in the height of summer. The faded Whitbread sign has been replaced by a more substantial one, advertisements for Idris mineral water have been placed on the gable end and on the post to which the pub's sign is fixed, a drainpipe runs the full height of the gable and the front entrance is now protected by a rustic porch. In the first picture the road looks dry and dusty and in good condition, but look at the state of it in the second! The well-dressed family standing at the side of the road with a pram wouldn't have stayed clean for long if they ventured across it.

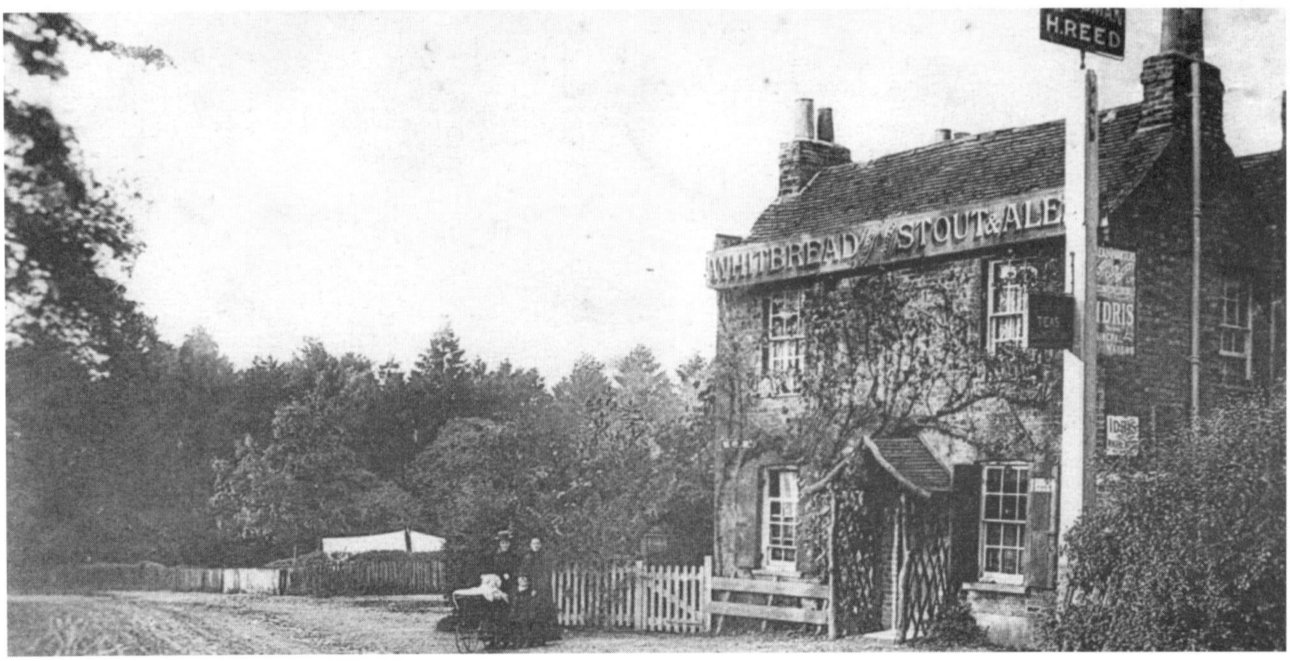

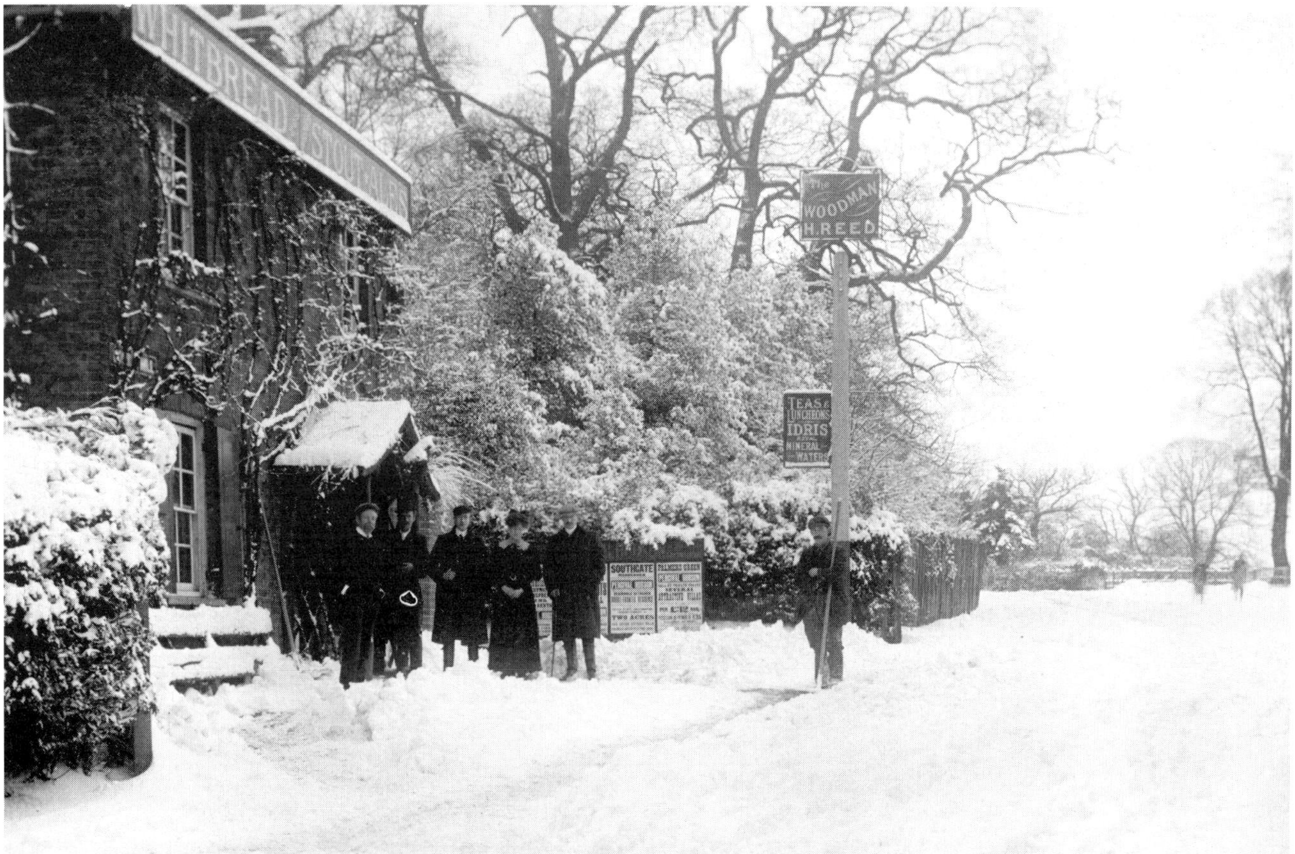

This picture shows the Woodman after a heavy snowfall on Boxing Day 1906 . The man on the right leaning against the post is holding a large sweeping brush, which he has just used to clear a narrow path through the snow for the guests. Most interesting here are estate agent Percival Hodson's advertisements standing against the fence. The right-hand one is offering to lease out several attractive villas in Palmers Green at an annual rent of £32, with a down payment of £25 and the remaining £7 paid as rent. The advertisement next to it is offering a desirable detached double-fronted residence in Southgate; unfortunately the price isn't mentioned.

The picture below was probably taken at the same time as the one above and is a little further down Bourne Hill. Perhaps the family were on their way to the Woodman for their Boxing Day lunch.

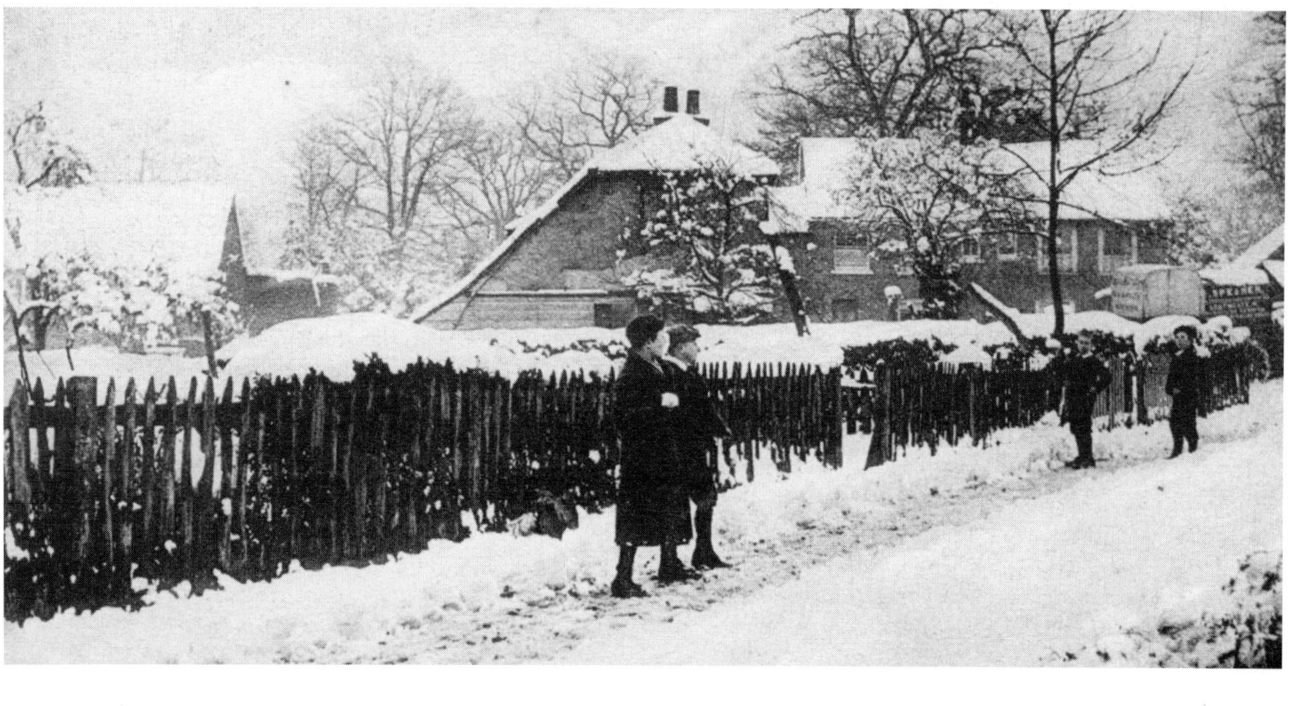

Suitably refreshed we must now leave the Woodman and walk back down the road for a little way. This time we take the left fork in the road, leaving the pound to our right, and very soon we come to a stile on our left, pictured here. Climbing over the stile we find ourselves on a narrow footpath that leads through the beautiful Winchmore Hill woods all the way up to Winchmore Green.

At least, that is what we would have done in 1903 when this picture was taken of the old man leaving the woods after collecting kindling wood. It is hard to imagine nowadays that this is the entrance to Broad Walk.

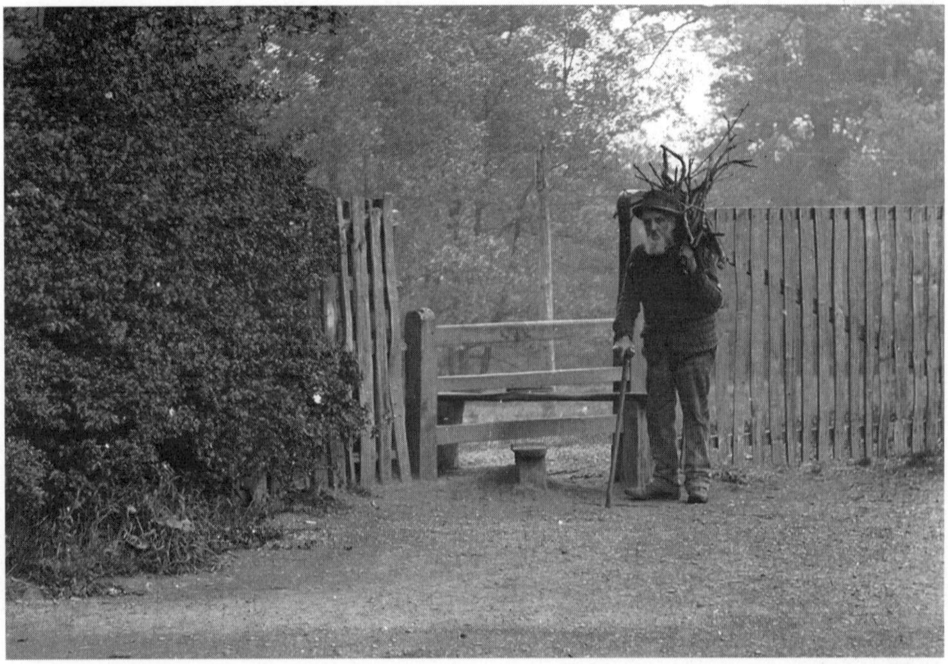

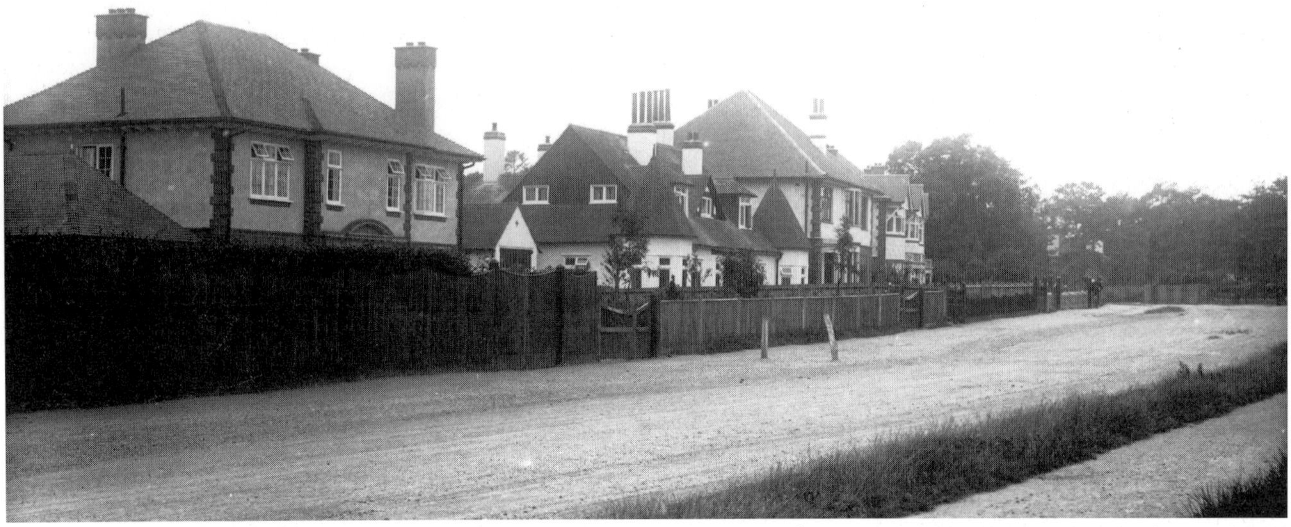

When the Grovelands estate was sold its trustees divided this part of Winchmore Hill woods into spacious plots and sold them separately to individual purchasers who wished to have their own unique, architect-designed houses built. The road was named Broad Walk and was laid out in 1919 but no houses were built until the 1920s. Its development was a very slow process; building work on the prestigious plots went ahead through the late twenties and into the thirties.

This picture shows Broad Walk in the 1920s near its Winchmore Hill end. It was generally recognised as being the 'posh' road in the district and became known locally as 'Millionaires' Row'. At one time the road was lined with oak trees but the hurricane of 1987 took its toll and several of the mature trees were lost or disfigured.

The houses may have been prestigious but look at the roadway. This remained little more than a muddy track until 1936/37 because of a lawsuit between the residents of Broad Walk and Southgate Borough Council who denied responsibility for making up the road. In the end a compromise was reached whereby each party paid half of the cost; this gave the residents the opportunity to spend an extra bit of money themselves and the result was the distinctive redbrick herringbone-patterned pavements that we see today.

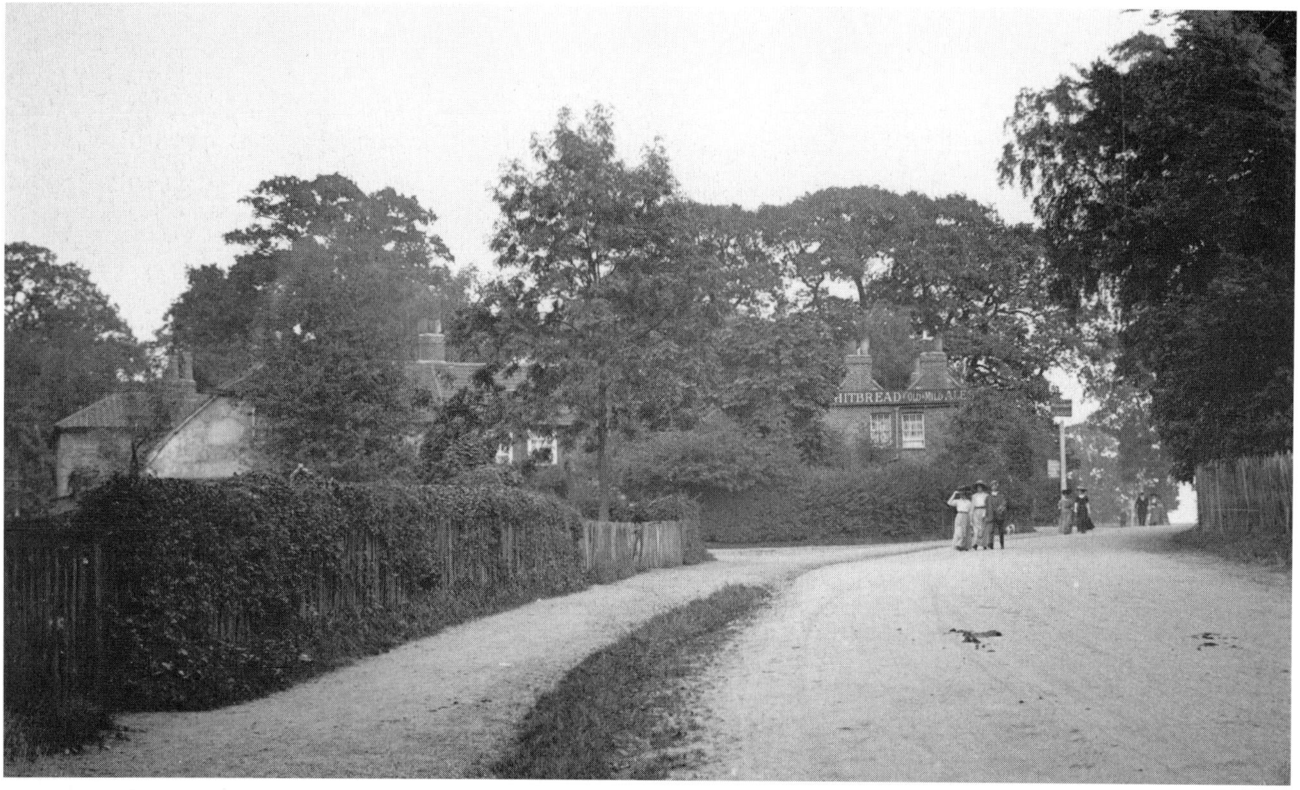

Returning to Bourne Hill, it's summertime and this group of elegant people are strolling past the Woodman and down the Bourne in the direction of Southgate. From their smartly dressed appearance they may have been on their way to or from church.

In 1851 this area was known as Bourneside because of the small stream at the bottom of the road that feeds the lake in Grovelands Park over on the right.

At the time these photographs were taken, the Bourne was a leafy and tranquil country road. By the late twentieth century it had become the A111 major road and provides motorists with a useful link between the North Circular Road and the M25 motorway near Potters Bar. The hedge-lined road has been widened and straightened out of all recognition; it carries a heavy volume of traffic and loitering in the roadway, as below, is not to be recommended nowadays!

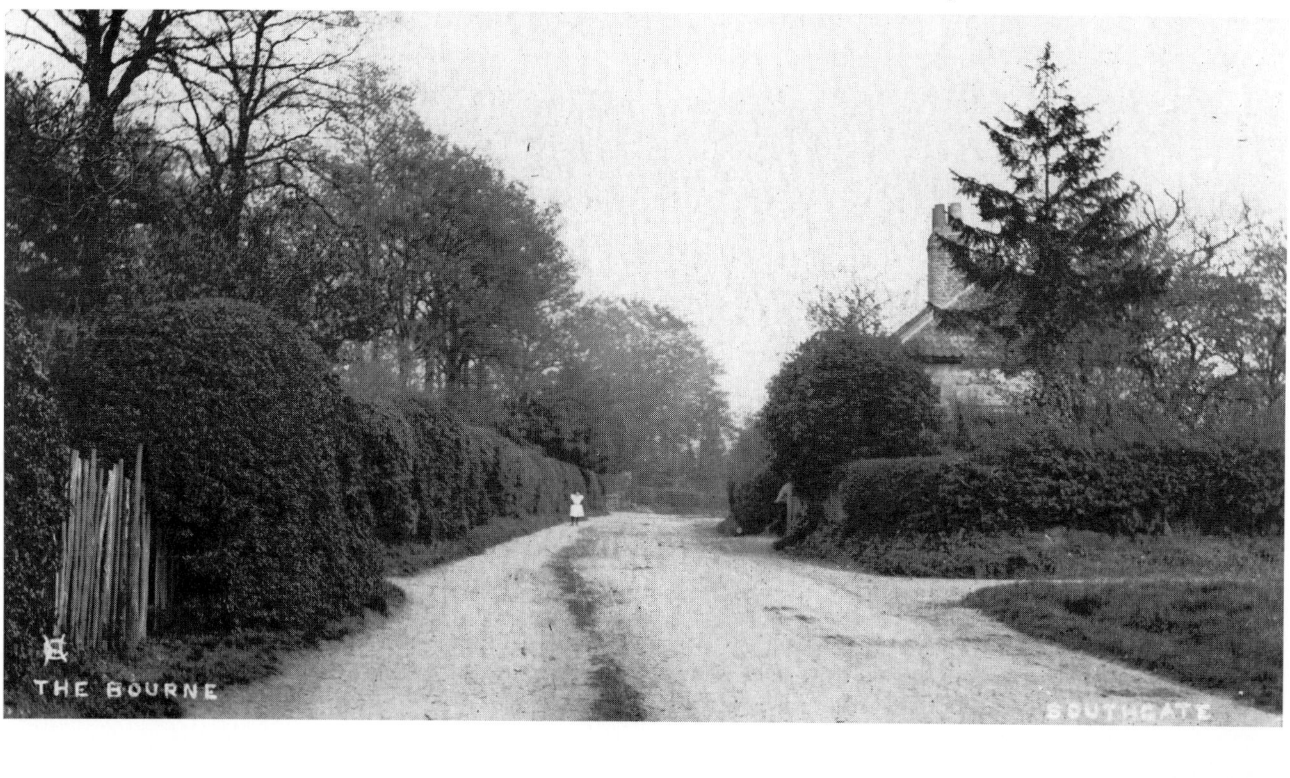

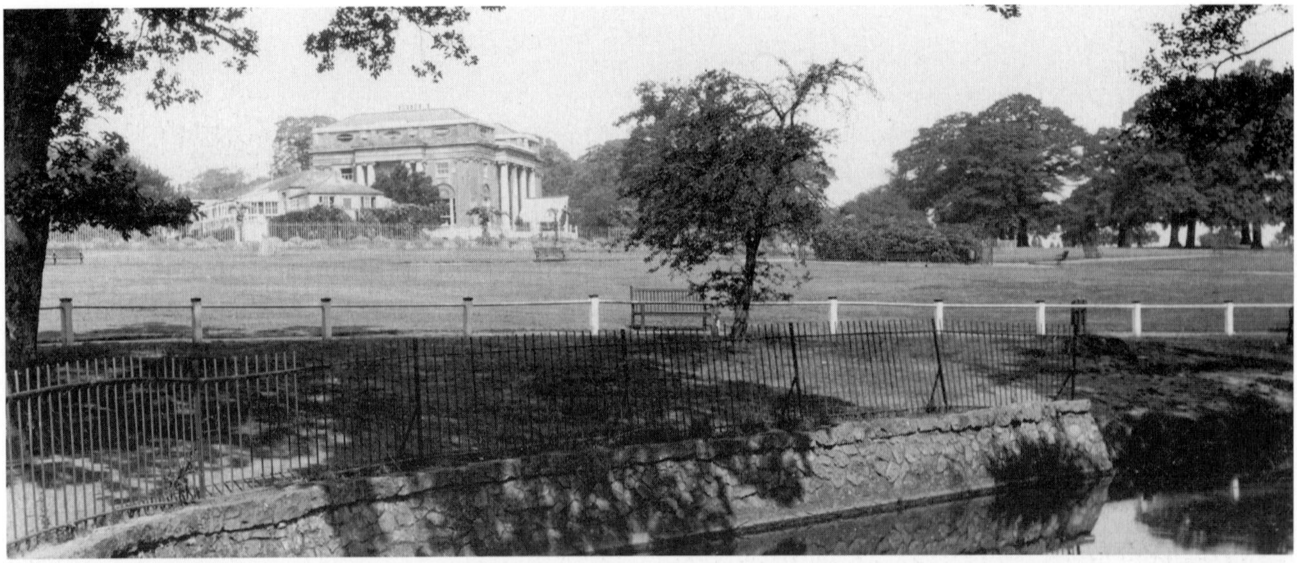

A little further along the Bourne and over to the right amidst parkland is Grovelands Hospital. This began life as the mansion house that was built in 1797/98 for Mr Walker Gray and he called it Southgate Grove. John Nash was the architect and Humphry Repton landscaped the gardens. In 1835, after the death of Walker Gray, the house and estate were bought by his nephew, John Donnithorne Taylor, who renamed it Grovelands. The eventual sale of his estate in 1902, as explained in the introduction, triggered the start of development in the area.

Following the outbreak of the First World War Captain Taylor agreed to let the house and its immediate grounds rent-free to the Southgate branch of the Middlesex Voluntary Aid Organisation for use as a hospital for wounded soldiers. In a short time they had equipped the house to take up to 70 patients and it opened as a hospital on 17 June 1916. After the war Captain Taylor decided to sell and in 1921 the Southgate VAO purchased the house and gardens. They handed it over to the Great (later the Royal) Northern Group of Voluntary Hospitals who continued its good work throughout the Second World War. After the war ended it was taken over by the state in 1948 when the National Health Service was established and then, under reorganisation in 1974, by the Enfield & Haringey Area Health Authority. Economies had to be made and the hospital closed in 1977. The house then stood empty and decaying until 1985 when the Community Psychiatric Centres company purchased the building and eight acres of ground to run as Grovelands Priory Hospital, providing 65 beds for patients suffering short-term mental illnesses. Annexes were built to the rear to house the patients' bedrooms. The house itself, which is used mainly for administrative services and consulting rooms, has been restored to its former glory and was formally opened on 19 October 1986. In recent years probably its most high-profile patient was ex-President Pinochet of Chile although his presence at the hospital was kept quiet at the time.

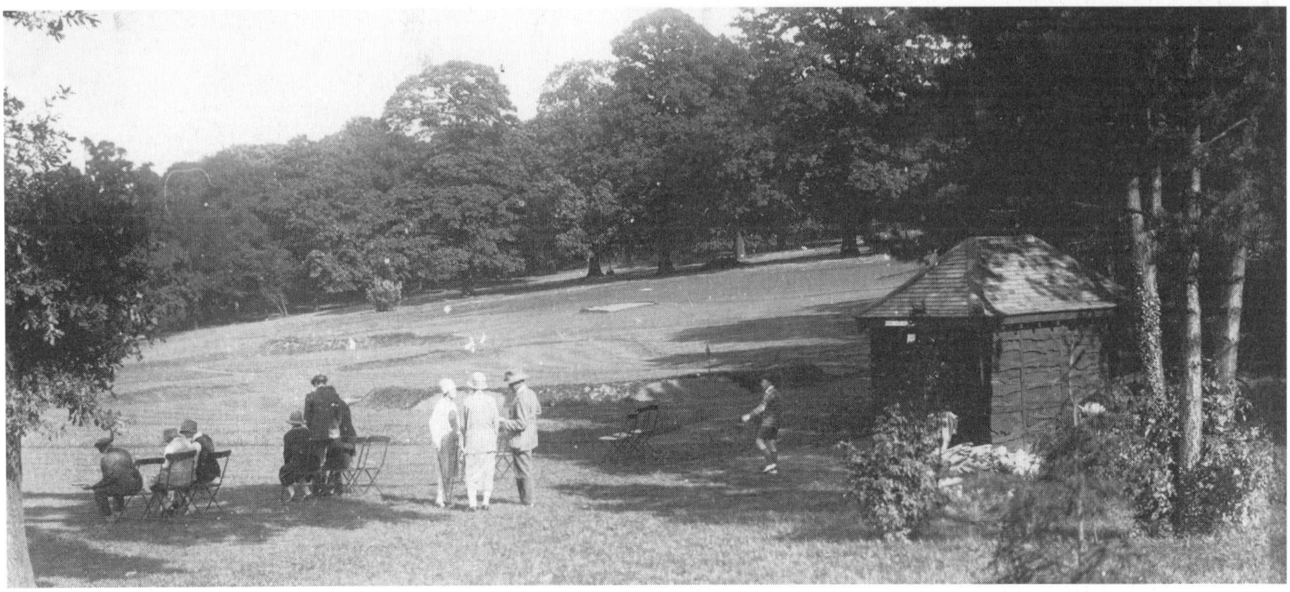

Among the public amenities provided by Southgate UDC after they purchased the area that became known as Grovelands Park was a nine-hole pitch and putt golf course, seen here in 1932. The course is still open today and offers visitors the facility to play a round of nine par-three holes with hired clubs and balls at very reasonable prices.

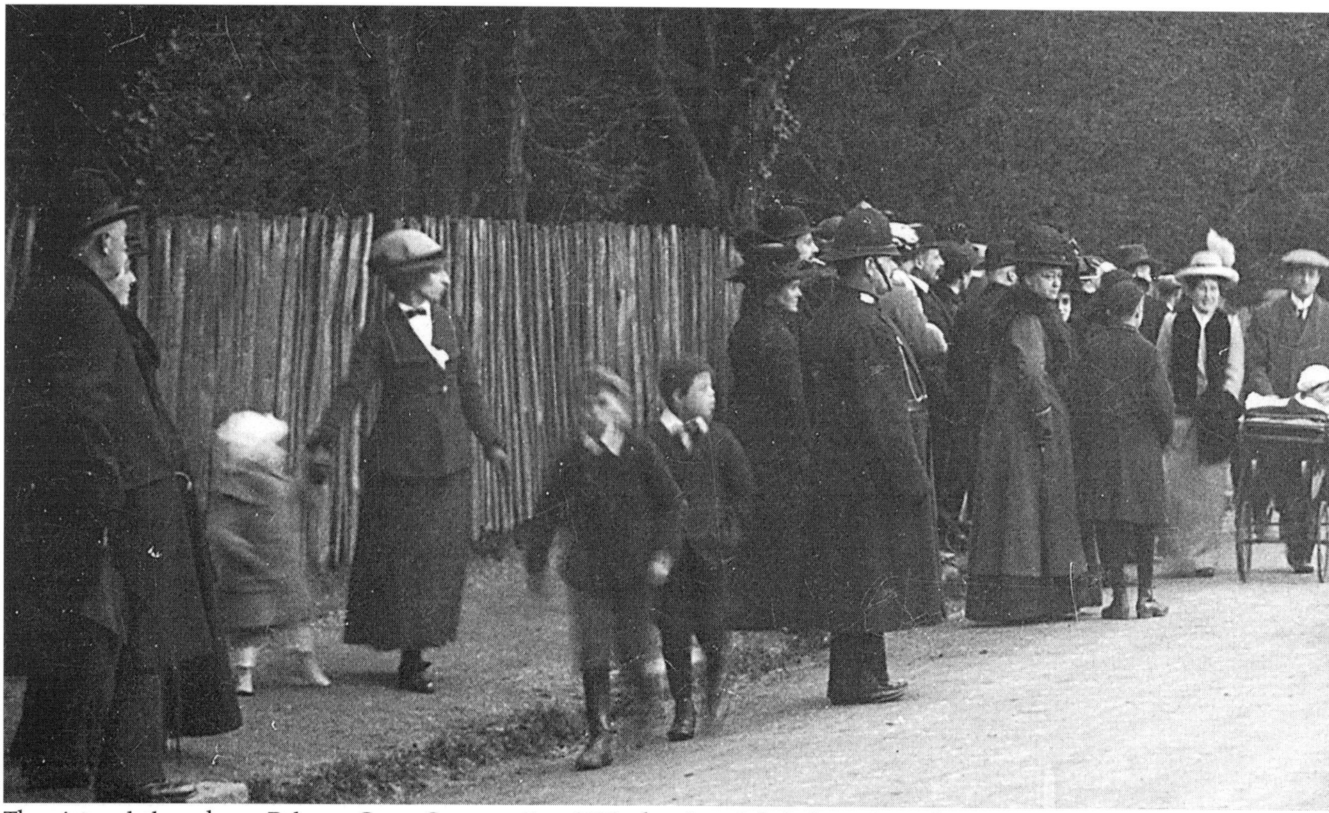

The picture below shows Palmers Green Congregational FC who played their 'home' matches in Grovelands Park. This team photograph was taken at the end of their 1925/26 season, probably in Grovelands Park. Their church is now the United Reformed Church in Fox Lane.

Southgate FC was founded around 1883 and they used to play their matches on the field behind the Cherry Tree. The opposite photograph shows Southgate & Wood Green FC during their 1921/22 season. It has a note on the back saying 'Some of the boys of Clackson's'. The local trades directory lists the firm of W.H. Clackson as being vulcanite workers with premises in Wood Green at Douglas Road and White Hart Lane.

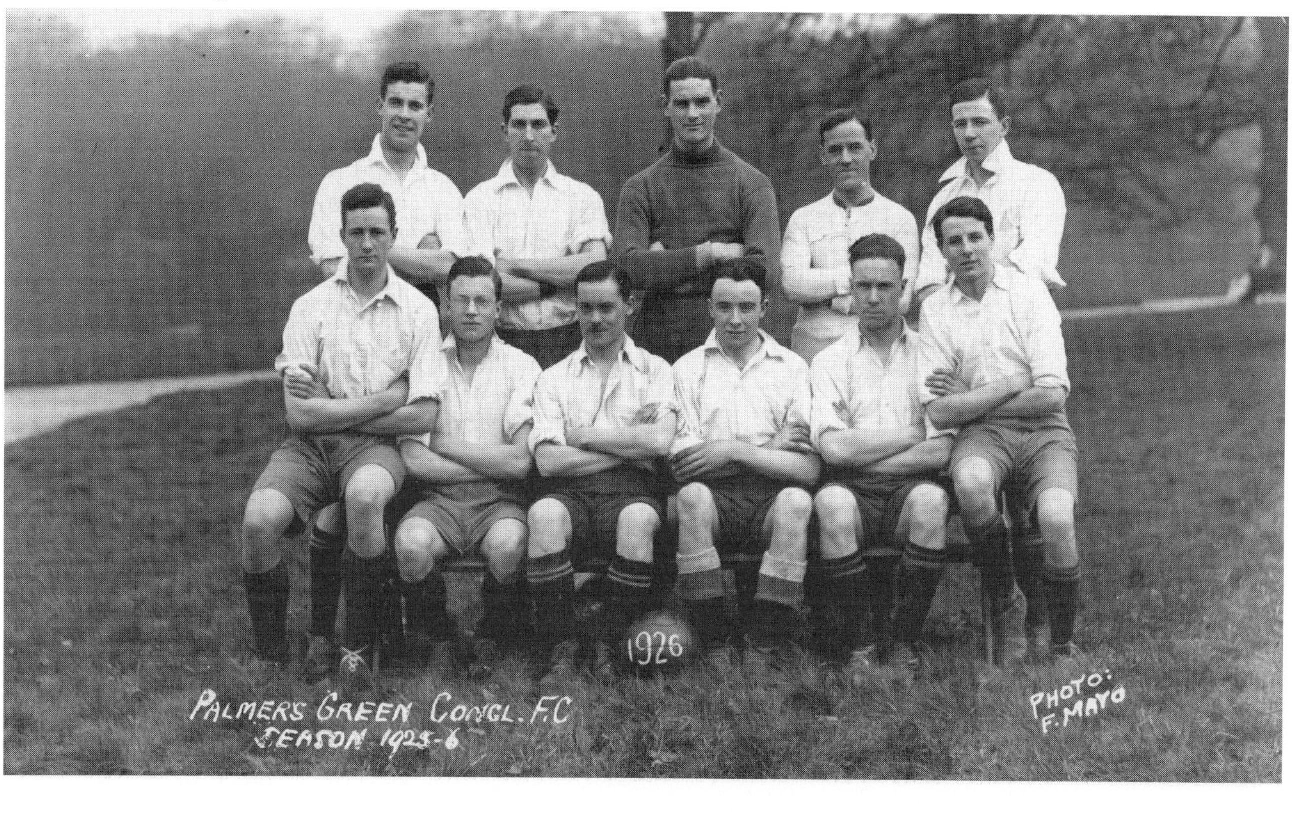

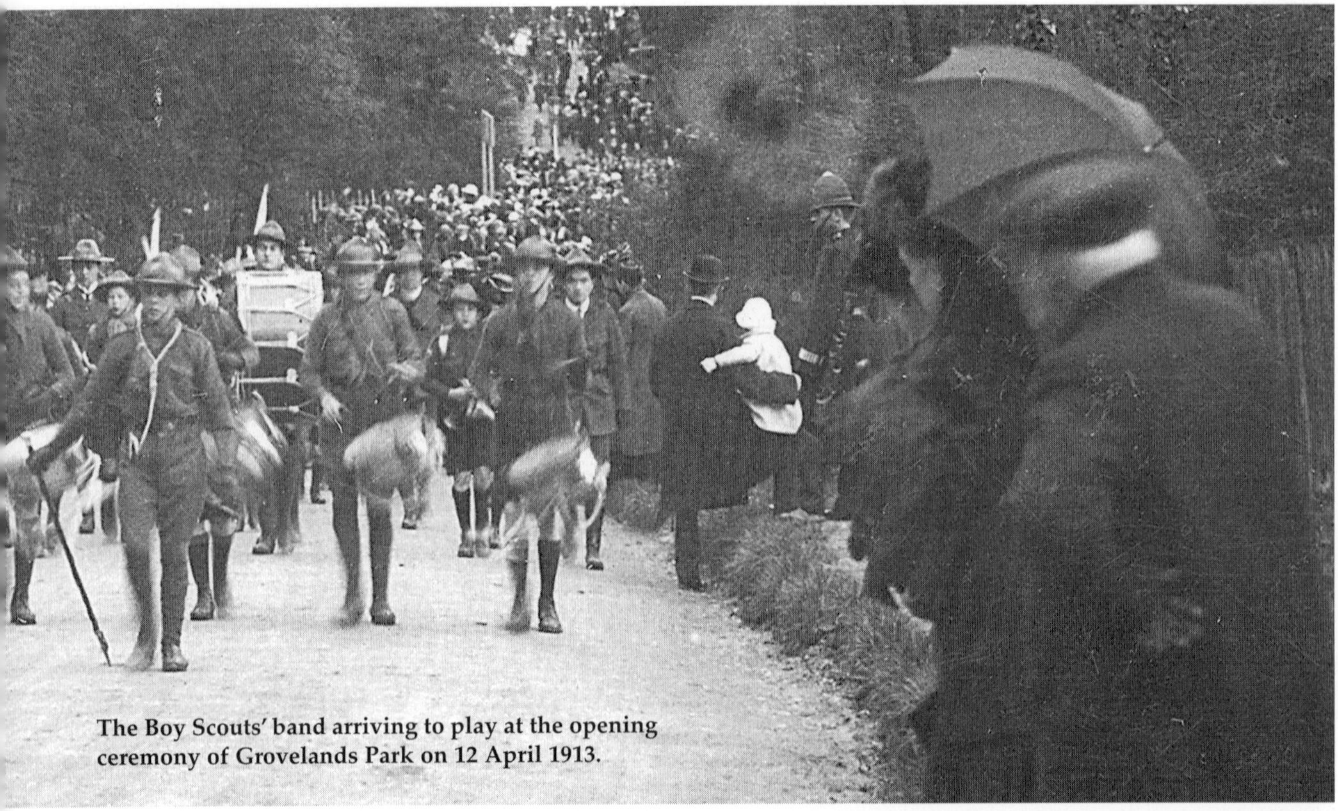

The Boy Scouts' band arriving to play at the opening ceremony of Grovelands Park on 12 April 1913.

When the Grovelands estate was put up for sale in 1902, Lot 9 comprised the mansion house and its grounds extending to 314 acres. They failed to reach their reserve price and were withdrawn from the sale. Over next few years several schemes were proposed, coming to nothing, although in 1911 Southgate UDC purchased 64 acres of the grounds (which they subsequently increased to 91 acres) and Grovelands Park was officially opened on 12 April 1913 by the Lord Mayor of London, Sir David Burnett.

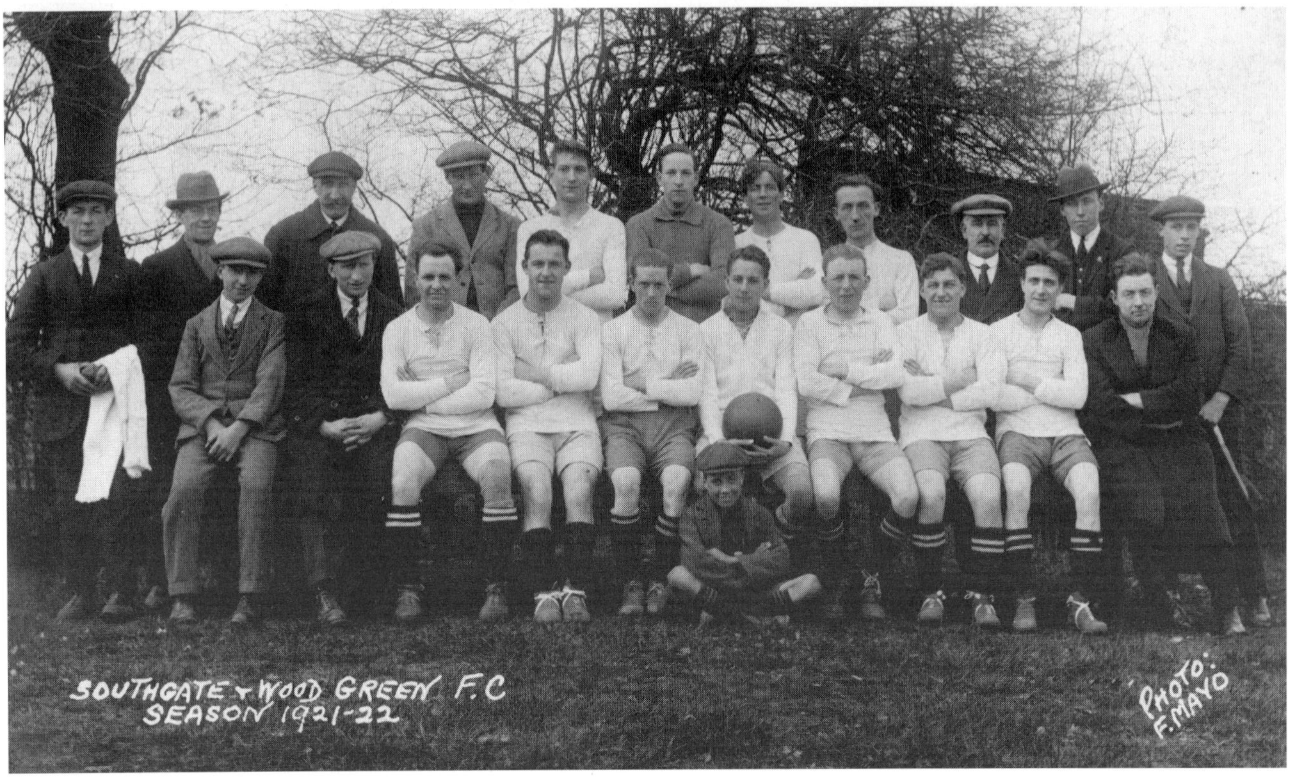

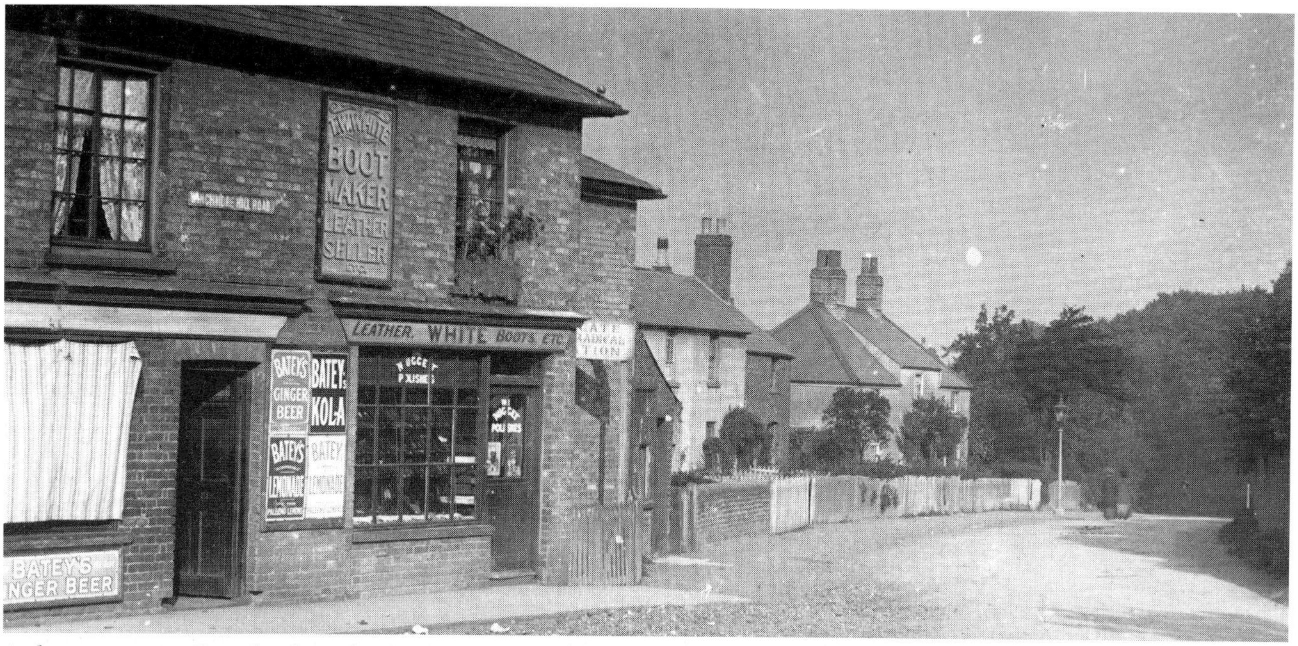

A short way past Grovelands and we are back in Southgate Circus and ready to start the last part of our exploration of the area. We turn right into Winchmore Hill Road, which originally was simply a continuation of Chase Side. It was known in 1834 as Chase Side Road and in 1851 as Chase Side, but had acquired its present name by 1871.

This picture was taken from the present-day Southgate Circus and is looking up the road towards Winchmore Hill. Well into the twentieth century Winchmore Hill Road remained a country lane with not a single house on the south side except for Hope House, which was said to be the dower house of the Taylors of Grovelands. This was a late eighteenth-century farmhouse with its own gardens and land; it is believed to pre-date the 1797 Grovelands mansion itself.

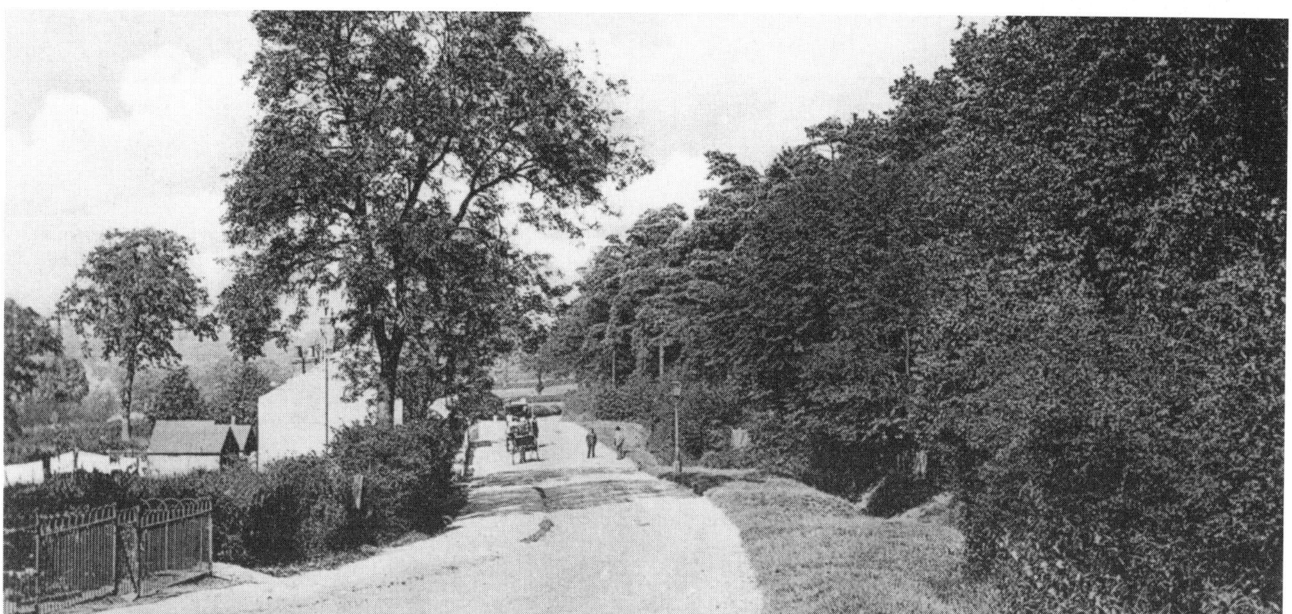

Another view of Winchmore Hill Road and its beautiful surroundings around a century ago. We are again looking up towards Winchmore Hill with the Grovelands estate at the roadside on our right. A short distance beyond Hope House, when it reached the far end of the estate, the road used to make a right-angled turn to the right and run along the estate's northern perimeter before becoming Church Hill and entering the village of Winchmore Hill. Nowadays the road no longer runs directly alongside the estate because Wynchgate and Park View Roads have been built parallel to it on what used to be part of the estate's parkland.

Well into the 1920s and 1930s – as long as the gentry remained – farm labourers, nurserymen, village shopkeepers, tradesmen and other such cogs of the area's rural economy remained in place. They shared Winchmore Hill with an ever-increasing number of new suburbanites, and their old cottages remained standing in the midst of the new suburban developments. Some of the old village shopkeepers continued to trade on the Green until the 1960s.

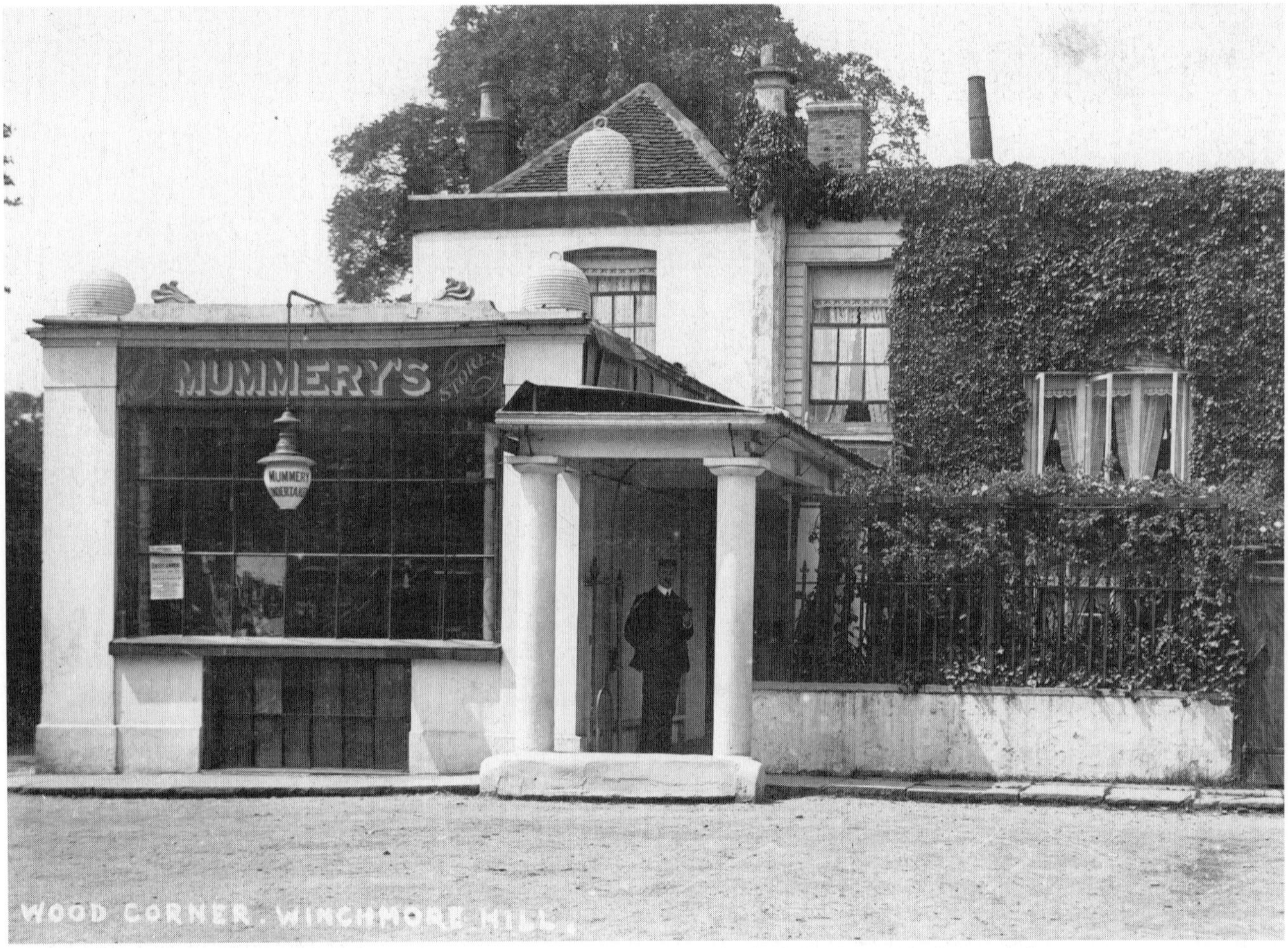

We've now reached the centre of Winchmore Hill village and are standing at the corner of the Green where there was a small gathering of cottages that was known as Wood Corner; it was situated where the path through Winchmore Hill woods that is nowadays Broad Walk joined Winchmore Green.

Until the early years of the twentieth century Winchmore Hill was a secluded little village that was always resolutely opposed to the idea of becoming part of metropolitan suburbia. The old village centre has survived at the top of the hill as the Green and extends into some of the surrounding roads. The Green is the focal point where five major roads (Hoppers Road, Broad Walk, Church Hill, Wades Hill and Station Road) converge. It was originally much larger but the widening of the many roads that surround it and the creation of pavements and other encroachments have gradually whittled the area away to less than half its original size. Around 1900 the village pond was situated on the eastern section of the Green with ducks and geese swimming contentedly on its waters but it became polluted; in 1908 the council filled it in and replaced it with a much smaller artificially enclosed pond, complete with a fountain and situated nearer to Hoppers Road.

The real Edwardian Winchmore Hill is situated between Hoppers Road and Green Lanes; in other parts the farms, fields and most of the country estates have disappeared beneath suburban housing developments and by 1939 no-one could argue that the area was in any way rural.

This picture dates from 1905 when Mummery's shop fronted Wood Corner and looked out onto the Green. They ran a varied business from this shop, ranging in scope from being undertakers to offering a service of movers, storers, packers and shippers. Their predecessors in the building throughout most of the nineteenth century were a notoriously shifty retail outlet named Udall & Child. This family ran the shop as a grocery-cum-drapery business and specialised in selling smuggled goods brought across the Essex and Hackney marshes by packhorse. French lace, brandy, schnapps, silks, tea and tobacco were among the contraband sold openly over the counter. The shop was well known throughout Middlesex and it's said that the Green was often filled with carriages whose owners were inside the shop, selecting the goods they wanted. Amazingly this openly illicit trading never seems to have attracted the attention of the revenue officers – possibly they were amongst its customers!

The path leading from Bourne Hill through Winchmore Hill woods terminated at the left side (facing the camera) of the shop. The building was demolished around 1912 to make way for Broad Walk and the business moved to No. 63 Station Road, just downhill from the station on the opposite side of the road, where they established a good reputation as good quality house furnishers.

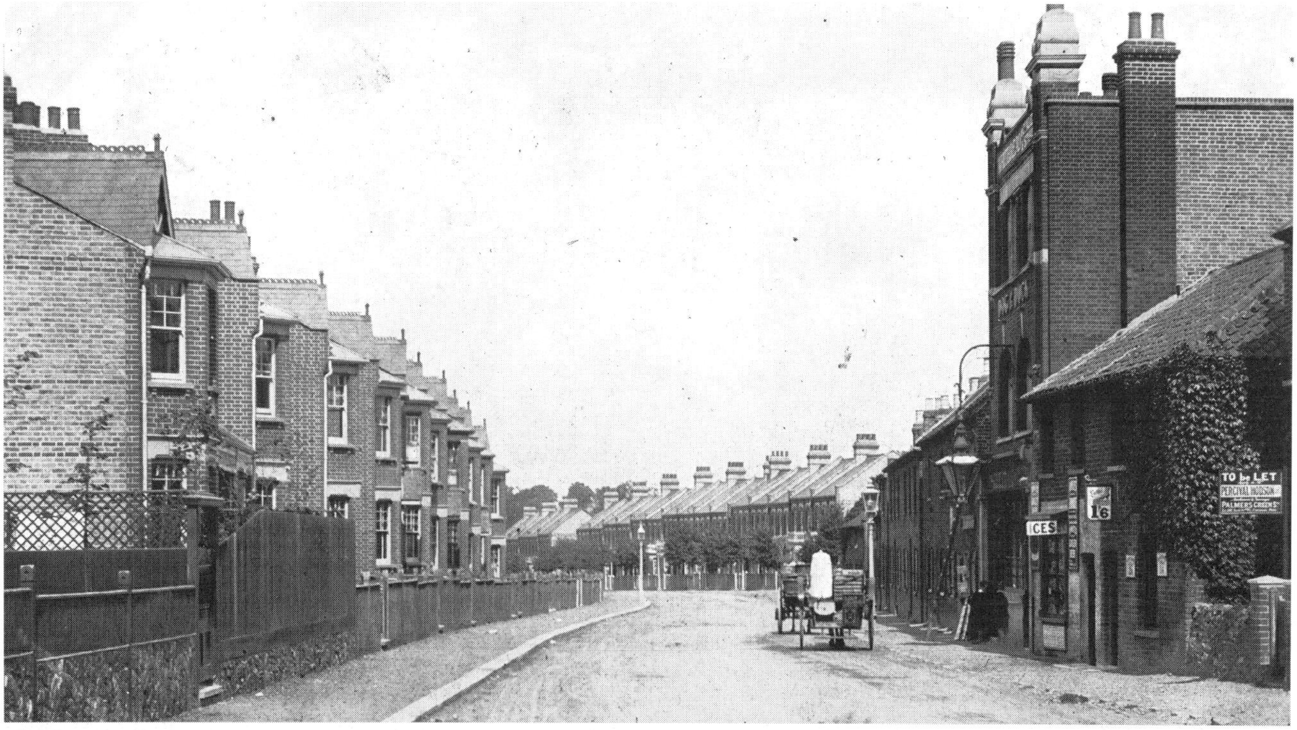

The final part of our journey takes us down Hoppers Road back towards Palmers Green. This is another old thoroughfare; it is called Hoppers Lane in the 1801 Enclosure map. It runs from Winchmore Hill down to a junction with Bourne Hill and onwards to join Green Lanes a short distance further on.

This picture shows the road with its then recently built houses in 1905, looking north from its junction with Bourne Hill towards Winchmore Hill. The Dog & Duck pub on the right is still there; it was rebuilt as a proper pub in 1900 having previously simply consisted of two of the cottages in the road where the owner had been granted a licence to sell ale.

The road layout in this area was radically altered in the early 1970s. Prior to then traffic coming down Bourne Hill crossed the railway bridge in a straight line and met Hoppers Road opposite Stonard Road almost at right angles. By this time Bourne Hill was the major road and the junction necessitated its traffic making an abrupt turn to the right to continue their route towards Green Lanes. Because of increasingly heavy traffic, in 1971 it was decided to build a skew bridge across the railway at this point to reduce the hazard. Nowadays Hoppers Road no longer forms the junction with Green Lanes as it used to, as this end section has now become the continuation of Bourne Hill. The old bridge is now used as a public walkway on the north side of the new bridge.

Below is Avondale Hall, a former public hall that stood at the Green Lanes end of Hoppers Road and which is now the central part of Palmers Green Girls' High School.

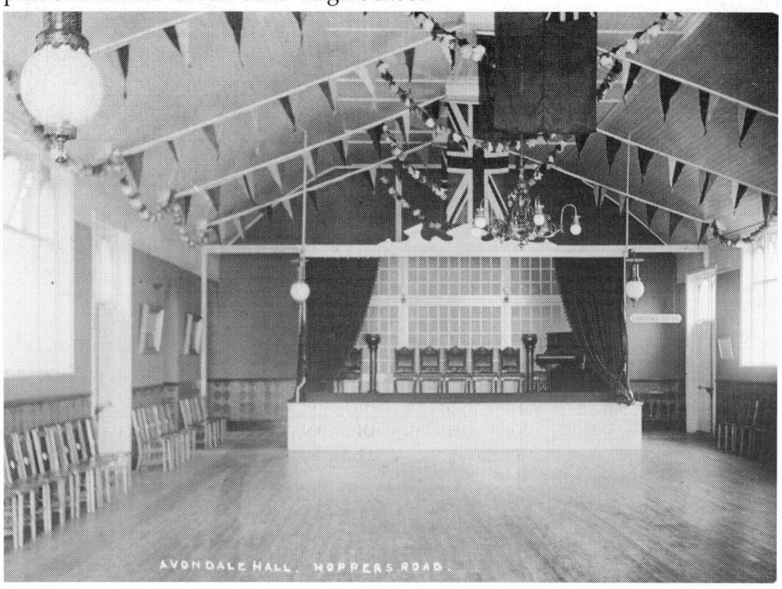

The school was started by Miss Alice Hum at No. 1 Osborne Road, the house on the corner with Green Lanes, but around 1907 it moved into the hall, which Miss Hum had purchased. Later additions were made to the school; these were built around the hall, which thereby became its central section.

In earlier times the hall had served as a temporary home for the Presbyterians and Congregationalists and in 1909/10 as a girls' school, then as the boys' school section of Miss Hum's school. This was phased out and in 1918 the entire girls' school was transferred there.

Former pupils include the poet and novelist Stevie Smith (1902—71) and the distinguished actress Dame Flora Robson (1902—84). Both attended Miss Hum's original school and transferred to Avondale Hall in 1918.

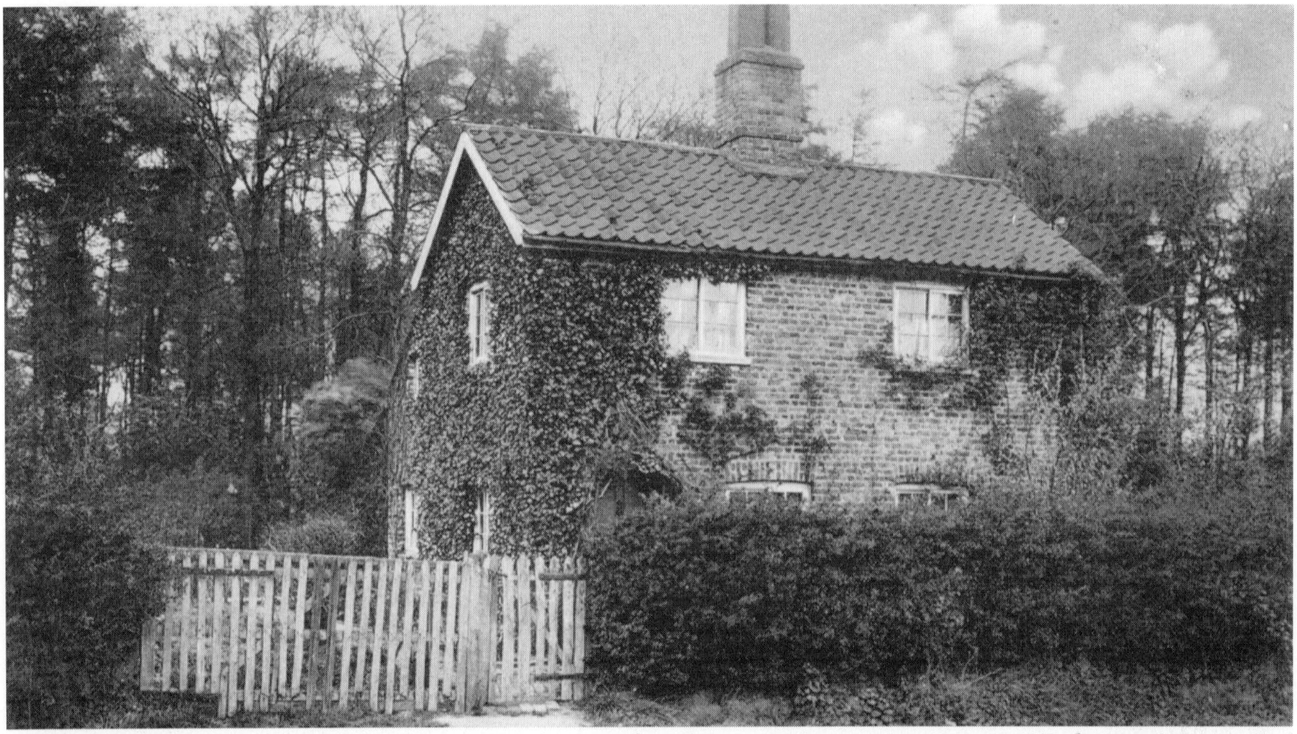

Although the Dog & Duck pub is in Hoppers Road it was the adjacent road, nowadays Bourne Hill, that used to be called Dog and Duck Lane. It is shown by that name on the Enclosure map of 1801 but had acquired its present name by 1901. This rustic cottage stood at the bottom of the hill near its junction with Hoppers Road; the modern telephone exchange now stands on its site.

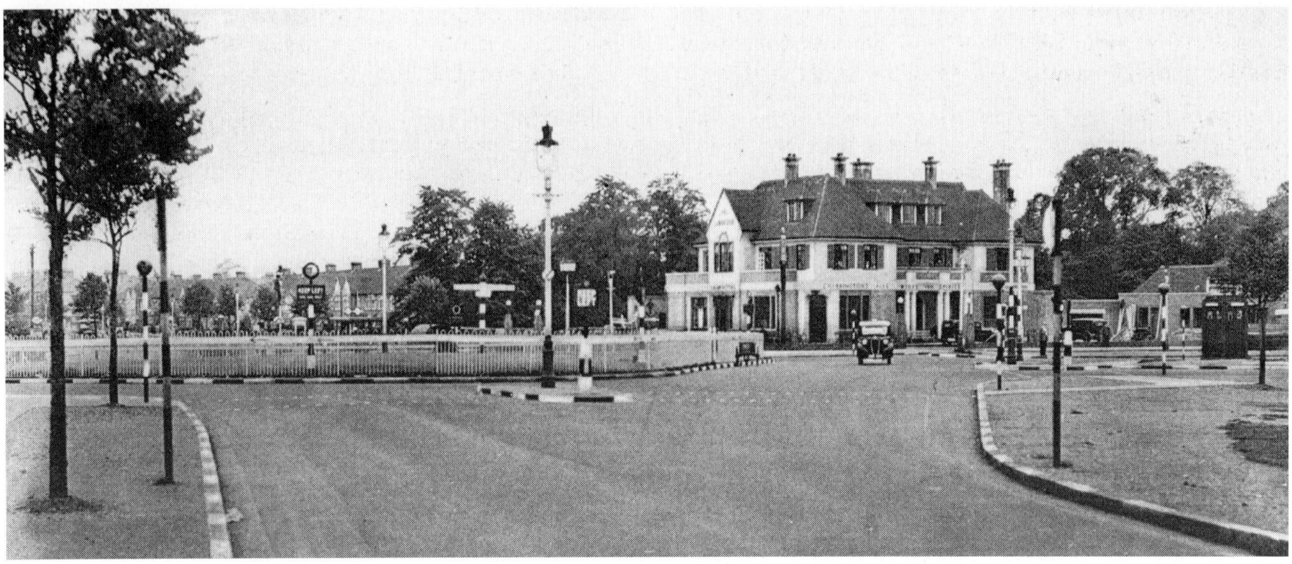

The final stage of our journey is to cross Green Lanes and go down Hedge Lane to see how one of the North Circular Road's busiest junctions used to look in the 1930s. In the picture overleaf the photographer is standing in Great Cambridge Road with the westbound North Circular Road running across the picture and off to the left. The Cambridge public house is just out of sight on the left but its sign is prominent by the roadside.

In the picture above the view is from Hedge Lane with the North Circular Road running east and the Cambridge pub across the road. This lane was marked on the 1801 Enclosure map and had acquired its present name by 1861. It has also been known as Wyerhall Road. Photographs taken in the 1920s show it to have been a rutted track lined on both sides with dense hedges and passing through open countryside and farmland. It was originally a continuation of Silver Street but the two sections have been severed by the construction of Great Cambridge Road and the North Circular Road.

The Cambridge Arterial Road was built in the 1920s from Tottenham to Wormley to relieve traffic on Fore Street and Hertford Road. By 1939 there was dual carriageway from Tottenham to this roundabout, which in those days was called a gyratory system. The Cambridge pub on the roundabout was demolished in the 1980s for road widening improvements.

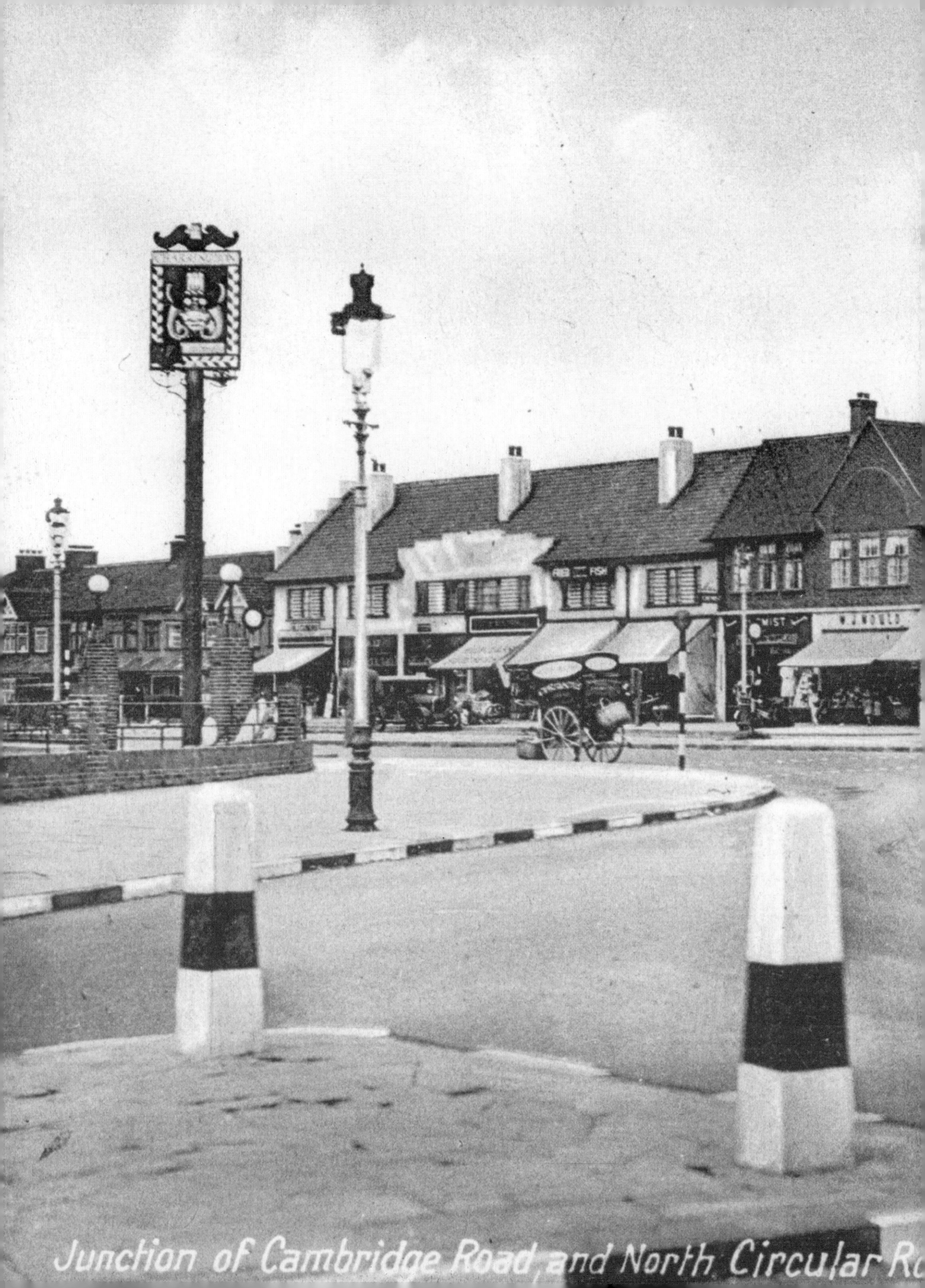

Junction of Cambridge Road, and North Circular Ro